THE FLETCHER JONES FOUNDATION
HUMANITIES IMPRINT

The Fletcher Jones Foundation has endowed this imprint to foster innovative and enduring scholarship in the humanities.

The publisher and the University of California Press Foundation gratefully acknowledge the generous support of the Fletcher Jones Foundation Imprint in Humanities.

Revival from Below

Revival from Below

*The Deoband Movement
and Global Islam*

Brannon D. Ingram

UNIVERSITY OF CALIFORNIA PRESS

University of California Press, one of the most
distinguished university presses in the United States,
enriches lives around the world by advancing scholarship
in the humanities, social sciences, and natural sciences. Its
activities are supported by the UC Press Foundation and
by philanthropic contributions from individuals and
institutions. For more information, visit www.ucpress.edu.

University of California Press
Oakland, California

Library of Congress Cataloging-in-Publication Data

Names: Ingram, Brannon D., author.
Title: Revival from below : the Deoband movement and
    global Islam / Brannon D. Ingram.
Description: Oakland, California : University of
    California Press, [2018] | Includes bibliographical
    references and index. |
Identifiers: LCCN 2018014045 (print) | LCCN 2018016956
    (ebook) | ISBN 9780520970137 | ISBN 9780520297999
    (cloth : alk. paper) | ISBN 9780520298002 (pbk. : alk.
    paper)
Subjects: LCSH: Deoband School (Islam)—History.
Classification: LCC BP166.14.D4 (ebook) | LCC BP166.14.
    D4 154 2018 (print) | DDC 297.6/5--dc23
LC record available at https://lccn.loc.gov/2018014045

Manufactured in the United States of America

25 24 23 22 21 20 19 18
10 9 8 7 6 5 4 3 2 1

Contents

Preface   *vii*

Introduction   *1*

1. A Modern Madrasa   *31*
2. The Normative Order   *55*
3. Remaking the Public   *92*
4. Remaking the Self   *116*
5. What Does a Tradition Feel Like?   *138*
6. How a Tradition Travels   *160*
7. A Tradition Contested   *179*

Conclusion   *207*

Notes   *219*
Bibliography   *275*
Index   *303*

Preface

In a way, I began working on this book as an undergraduate, long before I had even heard of the Deobandis. I think I can even pinpoint a specific moment: reading Bruce Lawrence's *Defenders of God* for a seminar paper on fundamentalism and modernity. Even more precisely, I remember being captivated by a single idea from that book: that "fundamentalists are moderns but they are not modernists." Since then, the social-scientific category of "fundamentalism" has lost much of its cachet, giving way to newer and more dynamic approaches to understanding religion and politics. But the idea that movements that define themselves against the modern are irrevocably (though never monolithically) shaped by modernity has continued to fascinate me. This idea is, by no means, some sort of skeleton key that unlocks the "truth" about movements like the one I describe in this book. On the contrary, this book argues that modernity, as an analytical lens, has certain limitations. Regardless, for me, the idea has been a generative one.

To the extent that my thinking about this topic began in college, it seems appropriate to start there in marking the profound intellectual debts I have built up over the years. At Reed College, R. Michael Feener introduced me to the study of Islam, and Kambiz GhaneaBassiri and Steven Wasserstrom cemented that interest. The formidable theory and method in religious studies courses I took with Arthur McCalla have stuck with me. Even today, I still think majoring in religion at Reed was probably the single most intellectually consequential decision I ever made.

At the University of North Carolina, the (literally) once-in-a-lifetime opportunity to study with a cluster of scholars in the Triangle—Carl W. Ernst, Bruce Lawrence, Ebrahim Moosa, Omid Safi—shaped my interest in Sufism, Islamic law, and South Asia. I thank Ebrahim for sharing with me his intimate knowledge of madrasa culture and South Africa, and for being a consistently reliable resource as this project has developed. Above all, I thank Carl for supervising the dissertation on which this book is based. He did far more than supervise a dissertation, of course. Carl modeled (and continues to model) what ethically engaged, public-facing scholarship looks like. If I can identify a specific moment when my interest in the Deobandis began, it would be when Carl lent me his personal copy of Rashid Ahmad Gangohi's fatwas (which, I will note for my colleagues who were at the October 2017 conference in honor of Carl, I *have* returned, at long last).

I did research for this book on three continents (Asia, Africa, and Europe). It would not have been possible without the help and assistance of numerous people. Waris Mazhari opened doors for me in Deoband and Delhi. Ashraf Dockrat and Ismail Mangera opened them in Johannesburg. Akmed Mukaddam and Abdulkader Tayob put me in touch with key interlocutors in Cape Town. Throughout my stay in South Africa, Abdulkader and the Centre for Contemporary Islam at the University of Cape Town gave me invaluable institutional support. The archival work on which the final two chapters rely could not have been done without the help of the librarians of the National Library of South Africa branches in Pretoria and Cape Town, the Documentation Centre at the University of Durban-Westville, and the University of Cape Town's African Studies Library. I would also like to extend my gratitude to McGill University's librarians for indulging my incessant digitization requests for materials from their Islamic Studies Library.

Revising the dissertation was nurtured in the supportive community I have been so fortunate to have at Northwestern University. I want to thank my colleagues in the Department of Religious Studies who have read, patiently listened to, and commented on bits and pieces of the book over the years. A number of my colleagues, in Religious Studies and beyond, read the book in its entirety: Elizabeth Shakman Hurd, Sylvester Johnson, Richard Kieckhefer, and Rajeev Kinra. I thank them all for their generosity. But I want to single out Beth Hurd, with whom I codirect a Buffett Institute research group, Global Politics and Religion. This book has benefitted in countless ways from my conversations with her and with the scholars we have hosted.

Beyond Northwestern, two scholars deserve extra special thanks. First, Muzaffar Alam read a draft of the book and then devoted almost an entire day to sitting with me in his office, giving me copious notes in a way that only he can: orally, quite nearly from memory, and with reference to relatively obscure late-colonial texts that most Mughal historians have probably not heard of, let alone read. Second, Muhammad Qasim Zaman also read a draft and was exceptionally generous with his criticisms and suggestions, drawing on his peerless knowledge of the *'ulama*. It's no exaggeration to say that every conversation I've been lucky to have had with Qasim over the years yielded new epiphanies. I am in his debt.

Along the way, I have benefited from presenting chapters in progress at a variety of workshops and conferences. I presented chapter 1 at the University of Leipzig workshop "Muslim Secularities: Explorations into Concepts of Distinction and Practices of Differentiation," a version of which is forthcoming in a special issue of *Historical-Social Research*. I thank the two anonymous readers for their valuable comments. I presented chapter 3 at the Max Planck Institute for Human Development in Berlin, and parts of chapter 4 at the University of Chicago workshop "Inhabiting Pasts in Twentieth Century South Asia." I thank the conveners of these workshops, respectively: Markus Dressler, Armando Salvatore, and Monika Wohlrab-Sahr; Margrit Pernau; and Daniel Morgan and Fareeha Zaman. I also presented bits of the book at multiple American Academy of Religion and Annual Conference on South Asia meetings, too many to list, and my gratitude goes out to all my colleagues who have heard my papers over the years and given me feedback, many of whom I name below.

A first book accumulates all manner of debts. In addition to those I have already named, I thank the following individuals for various roles they have had in this process, from the very early stages of planning the dissertation and applying for funding, from comments on conference papers to the final months of editing and revising the book, and everything in between: Kecia Ali, Khalil Ali, Mira Balberg, Anna Bigelow, David Boyk, Laura Brueck, Farid Esack, Katherine Ewing, Muneer Fareed, Kathleen Foody, Simon Fuchs, Nile Green, Juliane Hammer, Sana Haroon, Marcia Hermansen, Owais Jaffrey, Scott Kugle, Henri Lauzière, Christopher Lee, Lauren Leve, Maria Magdalena-Fuchs, Daniel Majchrowicz, William Mazzarella, Mark McClish, Barbara Metcalf, Ali Altaf Mian, Muhammad Alie Moosagie, Austin O'Malley, Robert Orsi, Matthew Palombo, Scott Reese, Dietrich Reetz, Waqas Sajjad, Zekeria Ahmed Salem,

Noah Salomon, Muhammad Khaled Sayed, J. Barton Scott, Max Stille, Randall Styers, SherAli Tareen, Alexander Thurston, Cristina Traina, Goolam Vahed, Brett Wilson, and Maheen Zaman.

The initial research for this book was supported by an International Dissertation Research Fellowship from the Social Science Research Council, with funding from the Andrew W. Mellon Foundation. Finishing the dissertation was funded by a fellowship from the University of North Carolina at Chapel Hill. Finally, at Northwestern, a Faculty Fellowship from the Kaplan Institute for the Humanities gave me the time to complete the revision into a book. My editors at the University of California Press, Cindy Fulton, Archna Patel, and Eric Schmidt, have been helpful and patient from the beginning. I also want to thank my two anonymous readers for their immensely helpful feedback. Finally, a number of people helped me get the book over the finish line. My copyeditor Carl Walesa went through the book with lapidary precision. Jeffrey Wheatley read the page proofs cover to cover. PJ Heim put together the wonderful index.

All translations are my own, unless otherwise noted. I have chosen to keep diacritics to a bare minimum, using only (') for 'ayn, and (') for hamza. (One exception, for simplicity's sake and because I use the word so often, is the word 'ulama, for which I omit writing the hamza: 'ulama instead of 'ulama'.) I have generally opted to spell names and transliterate words in ways that best reflect how they are pronounced in Urdu: "Thanvi" instead of "Thanawi," "qazi" instead of "qadi," and so on. There are two prominent exceptions: I write "Hadith" (as opposed to "Hadis"), and "Shari'a" (as opposed to "Shari'at"). For English-language South African materials, I write Muslim names and other words as they are written by the authors, even though these diverge widely from standard spellings: "'Ali" often becomes "Alie," "'Abd al-Qadir" is written "Abdulkader," "masjid" is spelled "masjied," and so on. Similarly, I write the names of South African Deobandi organizations the way they are written in South Africa—for example, "Majlisul Ulama" (as opposed to "Majlis al-'Ulama").

I finish this book amid the near daily assaults on women, Muslims, people of color, the poor, the environment, truth, civility, decency, kindness, and common sense that have defined our current politics. In such dark times, I feel so grateful for the love, joy, levity, and laughter that my wife, Lindsay, and my daughter, Charlotte, bring into my life. I dedicate this book to them.

Introduction

O Faithful, save yourself and your family from the
torments of Hell.

—Ashraf 'Ali Thanvi, sermon in Kanpur, 13 March 1923

On a chilly evening in early 2009, I was wandering around the spartan
guest house of the Dar al-'Ulum Deoband, the renowned Islamic seminary named after the city, Deoband, where it was founded in 1866. I had
just arrived from the United States to begin the research for this book.
The Dar al-'Ulum Deoband is now the central node in a network of
Deobandi seminaries that span the globe. Despite its modest size, the city
of Deoband is a bustling place, its markets teeming with life late into the
night. The circuitous paths leading through the bazaar toward the seminary are lined with scores of shops selling Arabic and Urdu books, prayer
rugs, Qur'ans, and other assorted Islamic paraphernalia. At the juncture
of several of these lanes stood a dormitory for the Dar al-'Ulum's alumni
and guests, where I was staying during my sojourn in Deoband.

The rooms had multiple beds, and this night I shared my room with
some Sri Lankan Muslims undertaking preaching tours for the Tablighi
Jama'at, now the world's largest Muslim revivalist organization, one
that grew directly out of Deobandi teachings. The Sri Lankans retired
early, and so I wandered into the courtyard, where a group of young
men—alumni, it turned out—were sitting in a circle chatting in Bengali.
Curious about my presence, they summoned me toward their circle and
made a place for me to sit. In the conversation that followed, as with
many to come, I had to give an account of myself. What was I doing
there? Why had I traveled seven thousand miles from home for the sole
reason of researching the Deoband movement? As with so many

conversations I would have over the course of researching and writing this book, politics came up immediately.

Students and graduates of the Dar al-'Ulum Deoband are all too aware of the accusations against their institution in the media. They know the extent to which the global War on Terror has brought the Dar al-'Ulum Deoband and other Islamic seminaries under critical scrutiny. They know that journalists and policy makers have taken aim at the Dar al-'Ulum Deoband in particular because the Taliban emerged from Deobandi seminaries in northwestern Pakistan. As I sat with these alumni from West Bengal, one of them asked me, "Do you think we are part of the Taliban? People come here and do not want to know about us because of the scholars that come from here. No, they want to know about what the Taliban does, so many miles away. Look, let me show you." He proceeded to draw a large circle on the floor with his finger. "This space here is everything this school has done. Now take just the smallest point in this circle," he said, pointing to an imaginary, arbitrarily chosen dot in the circle. "There is the Taliban." So it is part of the Deoband movement, I asked, not just an aberration? "Sure, fine," he replied. "But you must look at the whole circle."

This book is about the whole circle. Though the book will briefly address the Deoband movement's relation to the Taliban, that relationship is only a thread of the larger fabric that makes up Deoband. The scholars, students, ideas, and texts emanating from the seminary at Deoband and from its affiliated institutions around the world, taken as a whole, constitute arguably the most influential Muslim reform and revival movement outside of the Middle East in the last two centuries. Indeed, the great scholar of Islam and comparative religions Wilfred Cantwell Smith long ago declared: "Next to the Azhar of Cairo, [Deoband] is the most important and respected theological academy of the Muslim world."[1] Thus, readers hoping for a simple diagnosis of Deoband as an "Islamist" or "fundamentalist" movement will be disappointed. However, I trust that even these readers—or *especially* these readers—will find something of value here.

Long before the Taliban, the Dar al-'Ulum Deoband and affiliated institutions were known for a number of things: their scholarly prestige, their role in the struggle for Indian independence, and—the focus of this book—their controversial stance on Sufism, the complex of beliefs and practices that is usually glossed as Islamic "mysticism." Deobandis were, and remain, critical of a range of practices—pilgrimage to Sufi saints' tombs, celebration of the saints' death anniversaries, celebration of the

Prophet Muhammad's birthday—that have been central to Sufi practice in India and elsewhere. From a Deobandi perspective, these beliefs and practices border dangerously on "worship" of the Prophet Muhammad and the Sufi saints. To counter them, Deobandi scholars have issued countless treatises, tracts, and fatwas (legal opinions) on these practices from Deoband's inception to the present day. But Deobandis were never opposed to Sufism. On the contrary, they have seen Sufism as an *essential* part of a Muslim's moral life. They sought to reorient Sufi practice around an ethics of pious self-transformation *and* to reorient veneration of the saints around their virtues, not their miracles. Nevertheless, many of Deoband's detractors have branded Deobandis as positively *anti*-Sufi.

Like many Sufis before them, the Deobandis have seen Sufism as inseparable from Islamic legal norms. These, in turn, are inseparable from Islamic ethics and politics, broadly conceived. This book, therefore, treats Deoband's interrogation of Sufism and Sufi devotions as part of several broader ways in which the movement has shaped major debates within global Islam in the modern era. By orienting the history of the Deoband movement around its understanding of Sufism, other dimensions of the movement come into focus: law (to the extent that Islamic law and Sufism were deemed inseparable, despite the fact that Deoband's critique of Sufism was made through law), ethics (to the extent that Deobandis understood Sufism as, in essence, ethical cultivation), and politics (to the extent that Sufism informed an affective attitude toward the very conditions for politics). Thus, to say that this is a book about Sufism—which in no small way it is—misses an important point: it is also about Sufism *through* law, Sufism *as* ethics, Sufism *in* politics.

The Dar al-'Ulum Deoband emerged in 1866 in the wake of a precipitous end to Muslim political power in India. Although Muslim sultans and emperors had dominated much of the Indian subcontinent since the thirteenth century, their power had steadily declined beginning in the middle of the eighteenth. But many Muslims saw the ruthlessness with which the British quashed the uprising of 1857 and the subsequent exile of the last Mughal emperor, Bahadur Shah Zafar, as the very nadir of their political fortunes. Like others, Deoband's founders wondered how India's Muslims could move on from such a catastrophe. They responded with a relatively simple program: they would revive India's Muslims, and perhaps even the global Muslim community (the Ummah) at large, through a renewed engagement with the canons of religious knowledge that had guided Muslims for centuries. They would do so, moreover, by way of a new kind of seminary—dependent not on courtly largesse but on individual

Muslims' donations—with a central administration, a salaried faculty, and a slate of exams to gauge students' progress. This model would be easily replicated by other institutions. The graduates of these seminaries would, in time, be known as "Deobandis": students of the Qur'an, the Hadith (reports of the words and deeds of the Prophet Muhammad), and Islamic jurisprudence, many of them Sufis initiated into one or more of the four major Sufi orders of India (Chishti, Naqshbandi, Qadiri, Suhrawardi), and committed to the task of reform (*islah*). These graduates would typically go on to work as teachers, preachers, imams, writers, and publishers. Today there are Deobandi seminaries around the world, with the Dar al-'Ulum Deoband as the central node in an intricate network bound by people, texts, institutions, and ideas.

A core argument of this book is that we cannot fully understand Deoband without understanding the modalities through which it became global. As this network has become increasingly complex, it has raised questions as to what exactly constitutes "Deoband" as a tradition. What happens when the Deobandi contestation of Sufism travels into new social and political contexts beyond South Asia? To what extent is it mobile? Is mobility tantamount to portability? In other words, what forms of contestation does it meet? What accommodations does it make? If the first part of this book establishes how Deobandis articulated their reformist agenda in colonial India, the latter part explores how this agenda played out in South Africa, home to the largest and most prominent Deobandi seminaries outside of South Asia as well as to wide support for the very Sufi practices that Deobandis have most fiercely contested.[2] South Africa is by no means the only country outside of South Asia where Deobandis have settled, but it has by far the most significant Deobandi presence.[3]

Besides being the most important site of Deobandi thought outside of the Indian subcontinent, what makes South Africa crucial to understanding the Deoband movement is that Deobandi texts, scholars, and ideas became the object of extended public debate there by non-Indian Muslims who brought vastly different perspectives to them—a debate informed by the richness and depth of the Muslim presence in South Africa, where Muslims have had a continuous history for nearly three and a half centuries. It is partly through this South Asia–South Africa connection that this book also attempts to grasp how "Deoband" coheres, or occasionally fails to cohere, as a tradition.

This book proceeds, then, under the premise that traditions do not fall like manna from the sky, fully intact, fully theorized; rather, they are created, debated, maintained, challenged, resuscitated—often retroactively. On one level, "tradition" for the Deobandis is simply the Sunna, the model for human behavior exemplified by the Prophet Muhammad and transmitted through his words and deeds. On another, "tradition" is an imagined, affective bond between scholars and students, Sufi masters and disciples— one traversing borders and boundaries, linking books and bodies. Through these very human forms of mediation, Deobandis believe, the Sunna is continuously revived and renewed. But these forms also foster and maintain a sense of what makes Deoband itself stand out as a movement—a tradition *within* Tradition, perhaps. The founders of Deoband certainly understood themselves to be doing something extraordinary, but it is only in retrospect that the full extent of what they did became clear to their successors and followers. Often these later generations reimagined their collective origins through the politics of the present. This book will regard Deoband as an Islamic tradition in its own right, one positioned at the nexus of centripetal and centrifugal forces: on the one hand, shared identities that bind this movement *as* a movement; and on the other, the inevitable fissures that emerge in a movement of such global reach.

What I explore here is not just a contestation centered on Sufism, though Sufism will be the lens through which many of these debates transpire; it is also a clash of divergent political and ethical imaginaries and the forms of authority that undergird them. One of the contentions of this book will be that religious authority cannot be defined or conceptualized apart from the spaces in, through, and upon which it is projected. In his reflections on the relationship between space and forms of rhetoric, Carl Schmitt distinguished between the "dialectics of the public square, the *agora*," and the "dialectics of the lyceum and academy."[4] This distinction bears on the entire Deobandi project of public reform and the difference between how Deobandis addressed the public on the one hand, and how they addressed fellow classically trained scholars of Islam, known as the *'ulama*, on the other. For within the broader ambivalence of this book—Sufis critiquing Sufism—there is another, more subtle ambivalence regarding how to help the public understand the spiritual dangers of certain beliefs or practices without undermining the authority of the *'ulama* in the process. This very project entailed conveying complex legal hermeneutics in a language that the public could understand, while disabusing them of the notion that they could comprehend these issues without the *'ulama*'s help. But once Deobandis opened up the possibility of empowering the public to reform *themselves,* managing the tension between just enough knowledge but not too much became impractical. Many readers will be intuitively familiar with the rest of the story, for in some (admittedly limited) ways, this particular story within modern Islam has parallels in the history of Protestant Christianity. To a great extent, the story of modern Islam is one in which "everyday" Muslims now debate legal, ethical, political, and theological issues that had historically been the (never exclusive) purview of *ulama*, rulers, courtesans, and litterateurs. It is also one in which these "everyday" debates transpire in books, pamphlets, and tracts written by lay Muslims, and, more recently, in chat rooms and on online message boards and social media.

Why does any of this matter? Given Deoband's impact on global Islam, its purview encompasses tens, if not hundreds, of millions of Muslims. The debates Deobandis have initiated are a matter of utmost importance for some Muslims—a matter of choosing between salvation and damnation—and one of utter triviality for other Muslims—a fruitless theological cavil at best, and at worst, a stifling distraction from more pressing matters. At the heart of the debate is defining what Sufism *is*, how it is practiced, who gets to define it, and under what authority. A contestation over Sufism is a contestation over Islam itself, by virtue of Sufism's paramount importance in the lives of countless Muslims. It is also a debate *within Deoband* about Sufism, as well as a debate among other Muslims *about Deoband*—its ideologies, its origins, the authority of its scholars, and the legitimacy of its claims to represent Sunni Islam.

This book is the first extended study of Deoband outside of South Asia, of Deoband's complicated and often vexed relationship to Sufism, and of Deobandi scholars' attempts to remake Muslim public life. It engages a veritable efflorescence of work on the Deobandis and the South Asian *ulama* in recent years. Above all, it builds especially on the pioneering work of Barbara Daly Metcalf and Muhammad Qasim Zaman.[5] Though Metcalf ably reconstructed the social milieu of Deoband's origins, she spent little time looking at the actual texts composed by its scholars. And whereas Metcalf limited her scope to South Asia in the nineteenth century, this book explores Deoband as a global phenomenon in the twentieth. Likewise, whereas Zaman masterfully positioned Deoband within the normative Islamic textual tradition, this book pivots away from those intra-*ulama* debates and toward the Deoband movement's attempt to remake the public itself.

Let me also outline some of what, for reasons of space, this book will not do. Insofar as the book focuses on what I call Deoband's "public texts"—texts composed mostly in Urdu and primarily for lay Muslims—

it does not look in depth at Deobandis' Qur'an and Hadith commentaries, though it refers to them as needed to flesh out various arguments. And while it occasionally positions Deoband within classical Sufi discourses in the subcontinent and beyond, we begin in the late nineteenth century and narrate forward. It will leave to other scholars the project of situating Deoband vis-à-vis the (mostly) precolonial scholarship its adherents inherited, especially the endlessly fecund legacy of Shah Wali Allah (d. 1762), whom many Deobandis see as their most important progenitor.

Second, although the last two chapters discuss the Barelvi movement, the Deobandis' historic archrivals, as essential to understanding the Deoband movement's trajectory in South Africa, the bulk of the book does not focus on the Barelvis. This is not because I deem Barelvi arguments as somehow unimportant or irrelevant for understanding this history (indeed, they are vitally important). Rather, it is because there are already major studies of Barelvi thought,[6] and, more importantly, prevailing assumptions already treat Barelvis as the "true" Sufis.[7] Deobandis and Barelvis are, for all intents and purposes, identical to one another: Sunni Muslims, Hanafi in law, Ash'ari or Maturidi in theology, adhering to multiple Sufi orders, and sustained institutionally through madrasa networks. Deobandi and Barelvi seminaries, too, have common features, including fixed curricula, annual examinations, and salaried teachers and staff.[8] In truth, the real fault lines between Deobandis and Barelvis have mostly to do with their divergent views on three theological concepts advanced by some Deobandis and which the Barelvis saw as a profound slight toward the dignity of the Prophet Muhammad: the possibility of God creating another Prophet, or many prophets, on par with the Prophet Muhammad (known as *imkan-i nazir,* "possibility of an equal"); the possibility of God telling a lie (known as *imkan-i kizb,* "possibility of lying"); and the question of whether the Prophet has suprahuman knowledge (known as *'ilm-i ghayb,* "knowledge of the unseen"). Though it refers to these debates, too, they are not the focus of this book, partly because they are somewhat peripheral to Deoband's contestation of Sufi devotions and its remaking of Sufi ethics, and partly because they have been explored in depth elsewhere. Where this book *does* discuss these debates, it does so with reference to their bearing on Muslim publics, for as we will see, some Deobandis castigated Barelvis for inserting into public life what they saw as arcane theological puzzles that should be debated only by trained scholars. (Barelvis insisted, in turn, that the reformist firebrand Muhammad Isma'il (d. 1831), discussed in chapter 2, who inspired the first generation of Deobandis, was the real culprit for initiating these debates in the first place.) In recent decades, both sides have taken defensive postures, attempting to push back against their respective stereotypes. Thus, Deobandis have penned treatises detailing how much love they have for the Prophet,[9] while Barelvis have catalogued all the ways that Ahmad Raza Khan (d. 1921), founder of the Barelvi movement, despised illicit innovation in religious matters (*bid'a*).[10]

One of the myths this book hopes to dispel is a persistent stereotype that Deobandis represent the stern, inflexible Islam of the urban middle classes while the Barelvis represent the popular "folk" Sufism—the "real" Sufism—of rural South Asia. Even a cursory look at the sources for both the Deobandis and Barelvis shows this dichotomy to be utterly untenable, yet it persists within the academy and beyond it. Surely, for instance, the contrast that Marc Gaborieau draws between "reformed" (*réformés*) Deobandis and "unreformed" (*non-réformés*) Barelvis is too neat.[11] The discursive overlap between the Deobandis and Barelvis—legal, juristic, theological, and otherwise—belies facile categorizations of Deobandis as law-centered "reformists" and Barelvis as mystical "counterreformists." Ahmad Raza Khan, to take just one example, shared the Deobandis' revulsion toward popular practices surrounding Sufi saints' tombs. He forbade the lighting of incense, leaving food, taking vows in the saints' honor if they grant some specific request, circumambulating and prostrating before saints' shrines, and a host of other practices that are typically associated with Deobandis. The notion that Barelvis are somehow less concerned than Deobandis with the Shari'a is another common misconception. One of Ahmad Raza Khan's fatwas, issued in 1910, insisted on the mutual imbrication of the Shari'a and Sufism, on the *'ulama* as custodians of Sufi tradition, and on the fact that the overwhelming number of Sufis in Islamic history have meticulously followed Islamic law.[12]

Finally, although this book does not focus on the geopolitics of the Deoband movement, it aims, nevertheless, to contribute to a more nuanced conversation about madrasas—those much-maligned and poorly understood institutions of traditional Islamic learning.[13] This book sees Deobandi madrasas not as radical "terrorist factories,"[14] but as pious institutions that combine scholarship on Qur'an, Hadith, and Islamic jurisprudence (*fiqh*) with a dynamic mobility that has propelled Muslim scholars across the globe. Historically, far from facilitating militancy, madrasa networks were engines behind Islam's global cosmopolitanism, compelling students to travel across continents long before the era of "globalization."[15]

When discussions of Deoband appear in popular media, it is usually in reference to Deobandis' alleged antagonism to Sufism and Sufi shrines. Recent attacks on Sufi saints' shrines in Pakistan have exacerbated this tendency, with reporters labeling the attackers "Deobandi" and reasoning that the attacks stem not from local politics but from Deobandis' primordial, unflinching hatred of Sufism. After one such attack, the British newspaper *The Guardian* concluded, "Sufism is offensive to Muslims from the more ascetic Wahabbi [*sic*] and Deobandi sects, who consider worship of any saint to be heretical, and that the only access to God is through direct prayer."[16] It is worth pausing a moment to unpack this claim. Deobandis would proudly challenge the notion that Sufism is "offensive" to their religious sensibilities; most are, in fact, Sufis. They would also push back against lumping the Deobandis in with Wahhabis, followers of the archconservative reformer Muhammad ibn 'Abd al-Wahhab (d. 1791). This is doubly ironic, since Wahhabis have criticized Sufism *as such* and Deobandis have explicitly denied being Wahhabis. Even the muftis of the Deobandi seminary that nurtured the Taliban have said there is no basis for calling Deobandis "Wahhabis" and have rejected that label.[17] I return to this point in the second chapter and, again, in the conclusion.

Yet there is a much older, more resilient concept that informs *The Guardian*'s analysis: that "mystical" Islam is perpetually in conflict with the "law"—a notion now thoroughly embedded in views of Sufism as "moderate" Islam, one rooted in a much older Orientalist dichotomy between scholar and Sufi. This dichotomy fueled ideas that Sufism could not have possibly come out of Islam, as Orientalists celebrated the "spirituality" of the great Sufi poets as diametrically opposed to what they deemed as the dry legalism of the Qur'an.[18] These tropes are nothing if not persistent. Many still see Sufism as intrinsically tolerant and promote it as an antidote to Islamic militancy. At the same time, Orientalists largely ignored the *'ulama*—and especially, as in this study, *'ulama* who were also Sufis—considering them outmoded relics of Islam's medieval past. This approach to the *'ulama* ignores how they are "custodians" of a tradition that has been "constantly imagined, reconstructed, argued over, defended and modified."[19]

What *is* Deoband? And who is a Deobandi? Deoband is, first and foremost, a *place*: a town of some one hundred thousand residents approximately one hundred miles northeast of Delhi. A "Deobandi" can be a graduate of the Dar al-'Ulum Deoband, or a graduate of one of the hundreds of seminaries formed on its model, or simply someone who adheres to the set of ideologies and dispositions that Deobandis call their *maslak* (literally, "path" or "way")—in other words, someone within what Barbara Metcalf has called Deoband's "concentric circles of influence."[20] On the other hand, graduating from a Deobandi madrasa does not automatically make one a "Deobandi." Some eschew this label outright, either because they do not adhere to the *maslak,* or simply because they insist their worldview cannot be limited to a single ideological mantra. As one madrasa official in Cape Town told me, "I am not a 'Deobandi.' I have not seen Deoband with my own eyes. I am a student of the *din* [religion]."[21]

This rhetorical slippage is ubiquitous in how Deobandi scholars understand themselves. They acknowledge the unique contributions the movement has made to contemporary Islam, yet often decline to recognize it as a "movement" at all, believing it to be nothing more than Sunni Islam per se—a tacking back and forth between identifying Deoband's profound importance and assimilating it to Sunni Islam as such. Yet although Deobandis consider themselves Sunnis par excellence, they would not assert that non-Deobandis are therefore non-Sunnis. They do not claim a monopoly on Sunnism; they simply believe that they best represent it. In the words of the authoritative history of the Dar al-'Ulum Deoband, Deoband "is neither a legal school [*mazhab*] nor a sect [*firqa*], though its opponents attempt to present it as a school or sect to the public. Rather, it is a comprehensive 'edition' of the way [*maslak*] of the People of the Prophetic Model and the Community [*Ahl-i Sunnat wa-l Jama'at*]"—in other words, of Sunni Islam.[22] Yet the very fact that this history presents Deoband as an "ism" (*Deobandiyat*) foregrounds the tension in how to talk about it as a phenomenon without reifying it. Defining "Deoband" too rigidly, then, denies it its elasticity, yet defining it too loosely recapitulates how these terms are bent and stretched in a Procrustean manner within anti-Deobandi polemics, where Deobandis are conflated with groups with whom they share very little.[23] Amid such slippery discourse, we must be wary of reifying the very terms that we seek to analyze.

This task is complicated further when we seek to understand groups and organizations that have spun out of the Deoband movement, whether the Taliban, the Tablighi Jama'at, or political organizations like Jami'at 'Ulama-yi Hind or the Jami'at 'Ulama-yi Islam. These groups grew directly out of Deobandi teachings, were founded by Deobandi scholars, but cannot be reduced to those connections. The Tablighi Jama'at, for instance, has tens of millions of followers. While the Tablighi Jama'at may not be a "Deobandi" organization in the strictest sense of the word, its founder, Muhammad Ilyas, was a graduate of the Dar al-'Ulum Deoband and studied with three of the most prominent early Deobandi scholars: Rashid Ahmad Gangohi, Mahmud Hasan, and Khalil Ahmad Saharanpuri. The Tablighi Jama'at is indisputably linked at every level with Deobandi madrasas, in South Asia, South Africa, and elsewhere. Yet not all those involved in the Tablighi Jama'at have a formal relation to a Deobandi madrasa or other institution, even as they participate, knowingly or unknowingly, in Deoband's reformist project.

If Deoband's influence fans out into an array of ancillary organizations and movements—the "edges" of Deobandi tradition, as it were—this book focuses on the center of that tradition and how it has engaged with and impacted three major aspects of modern Islam: the place of Sufism in the modern world, the position of the 'ulama in Muslim public life, and the very notion of Islamic tradition.

THE PLACE OF SUFISM IN THE MODERN WORLD

In a foreword to one of many books on Sufism written by his father, Mufti Muhammad Shafi' (d. 1976), Muhammad Taqi 'Usmani, a prominent Deobandi scholar of contemporary Pakistan, succinctly posed the "problem" of Sufism in the modern world as many Deobandis see it: "Some believe [Sufism] to be an innovation [bid'a], something apart from the teachings of the Qur'an and the Sunna. Others believe Sufism to be a source of salvation in its own right, a rival to the Shari'a itself."[24] The Deobandis have positioned themselves as treading a middle way between those who would unmoor Sufism from its grounding in Islamic law and those who would reject Sufism altogether. Although this positioning has roots in early Deobandi thought, it has become especially salient in recent history, and above all in Pakistan, where Deobandis have been on the defensive because of their perceived antipathy to Sufism.

Indeed, one *can* argue that contemporary Deobandis' engagement with Sufism is not as robust as it once was. I return to this idea in the final chapter and conclusion. But for now, I stress only that the politics of Sufism have become so vexed that, in some circles, what Deobandis advocate scarcely registers as "Sufism" at all, insofar as the Sufi saints, which some of their critics believe Deobandis have maligned, have become a metonym for Sufism as a whole. Several factors aligned to create this defensive posture. For one, Deobandis' subcontinental rivalry with the Barelvi school has made the celebration of the saints' death anniversaries ('urs) and the Prophet Muhammad's birthday (mawlud, but also spelled mawlid or milad) litmus tests for Sufi authenticity.

Another is that the War on Terror has repeatedly valorized certain *forms* of Sufism as truer or more authentic than others, especially representations of Sufism as inherently peaceful, as the quintessence of "moderate" Islam.[25] Eleanor Abdella Doumato and Gregory Starrett memorably summarized this attitude as one that assumes that "if fundamentalism is the heroin of the Muslim street, Sufism is to be its methadone," even though there is no evidence that Sufis are less violent than non-Sufis or non-Sufis more violent.[26] The politics of who is a "good" Sufi is closely related to, and partly overlaps with, the politics of who is a "good" Muslim. Western governments and policy makers have a long history of shaping and intervening in these debates.[27]

This book contends that debates about which is the "real" Sufism tell us more about the politics of defining Sufism than they do about actual Sufis, let alone Deobandis' relationship to Sufism. Much of what is vaunted as true Sufism is highly "visible": the pomp of the *'urs,* the infectious energy of the *qawwali* performance, saintly relics that exude spiritual power (*baraka*). Conversely, Deobandi Sufism is largely "invisible," subsiding in the disciplinary training that a Sufi undertakes with his or her master, or in commentaries on classical Sufi texts that few read outside of highly elite scholarly circles. It may surprise some readers, therefore, that Deobandis have penned lengthy commentaries on the likes of Jalal al-Din Rumi, Abu Hamid al-Ghazali, and Ibn 'Arabi. But the fact is that the reputations of the Deobandi *'ulama* were forged through the circulation of widely read and highly public polemics. Their detractors have largely ignored what is contained in the biographies and treatises Deobandis have written for their Sufi disciples. In other words, there is a correlation between Deoband's public face and its widespread reputation for extremism.

So how *do* we know who is a Sufi? The scholar of Sufism Arthur Buehler recently argued that "if persons call themselves sufis, academics have no other choice but to take their word for it," even as he proposed a "litmus test" for recognizing Sufis: "the existence of a transformative practice that facilitates ethical development and/or furthers taming of the ego."[28] It is worth noting that, by this account at least, almost all Deobandis would qualify as Sufis. But there is another, more important, point to be made here. Buehler hints at an arguably irresolvable tension in the study of Sufism (or for that matter, Islam): scholars can attempt to avoid making normative interventions in the politics of defining Sufism, but to some degree, any attempt to conceptualize Sufism inevitably does so. That being said, this book conceptualizes Sufism as a tripartite entity, consisting of three intersecting, mutually constitutive dimensions: *literary, interpersonal/institutional,* and *ritual/devotional.* The literary dimension is familiar to most, encompassing the great Sufi poets, but equally, the innumerable treatises on traversing the Sufi path. The interpersonal and institutional dimension concerns relations between Sufi masters and disciples, initiations into Sufi orders, and the inculcation of Sufi ethical virtues through study with, and sitting in the presence of, Sufi masters. Finally, the ritual and devotional dimension concerns the multiple forms of devotional piety that have formed around the veneration of Sufi saints, especially but not exclusively at their tombs. What will become clear is that Deobandis embraced the first two dimensions of Sufism but maintained a complicated, ambivalent relationship with the third. To say that Deobandis are not Sufis is, quite literally, to define Sufism only in terms of ritual and devotion. Their interrogation of Sufism was, in other words, an internal critique of Sufism *by Sufis.*

This "sober" Sufism has an ancient pedigree.[29] A few brief examples will suffice to suggest the scope of Deobandis' premodern Sufi antecedents—Sufis whom, we will see, the Deobandis themselves read and cite. Deobandi vocabularies of spiritual purification, especially techniques of disciplining the ego-self (*tazkiyat al-nafs*), go back to the very origins of Sufism in ninth-century Baghdad with the writings of Harith al-Muhasibi (d. 857) and others.[30] Deobandis' view that Sufism emerged from, and is contained within, Qur'anic ethics recalls Abu Nasr al-Sarraj (d. 988), who was among the first to ground Sufism firmly in the Qur'an; who regarded Sufis, alongside Hadith scholars and legal scholars (*fuqaha'*), as among the *'ulama;* and who argued that Sufis distinguished themselves from *mere* jurists through their rigorous self-interrogation— a theme we will see again and again among the Deobandis.[31] When Sufis began to narrate their history, many looked back to Junayd Baghdadi (d. 910) as a founding figure.[32] Junayd's "sobriety" (*sahw*) would become perhaps the unifying feature of Deobandi Sufism centuries later, as it was for a cofounder of the Deoband movement, Rashid Ahmad Gangohi.[33] The biographer Abu Nu'aym al-Isfahani (d. 1038) wrote Sufi history from the vantage of a legal traditionalist, including two of the eponymous founders of Sunni Islam's legal schools, Ahmad ibn Hanbal and Muhammad ibn Idris al-Shafi'i, among the Sufi saints.[34] Isfahani was not so much a Sufi who wanted to make Sufism palatable to Islamic legal scholars as he was a legal scholar who simply saw no contradiction between Sufism and Islamic law. The work of Abul Qasim al-Qushayri (d. 1072) and 'Ali al-Hujwiri (d. 1073), whom the Deobandis read and cite widely, reinforced the ethical and legal credentials of Sufism.[35] One final example may be the most important of all: many Deobandis looked to Abu Hamid al-Ghazali (d. 1111) as the preeminent theorist of Islam at the intersection of law, ethics, and Sufi piety. For Ashraf 'Ali Thanvi (d. 1943)—the most influential Deobandi scholar in the history of the movement, and to a great extent the central personality of this book—no self-respecting Islamic scholar (*'alim*) was worthy of the name without having studied al-Ghazali's *Ihya' 'ulum al-din,* while he also urges lay Muslims to study the Urdu translation of the condensed version of the *Ihya',* which he personally commissioned.[36]

At the same time that discourses articulating Sufism in Islamic legal language began to emerge, popular Sufi devotions were also emerging—practices that Deobandis would critique in British India centuries later—such as the first organized mass pilgrimages (*ziyarat*) to Sufi saints' tombs in the early thirteenth century.[37] Just as Deobandis were by no means the first Sufis to align Sufism with Islamic legal discourses, nor the first to cast Sufism in the language of Islamic ethics, they were also not the first to critique certain Sufi devotional practices. It is important not to portray these simply as critiques of "Sufism." While Ibn al-Jawzi (d. 1200) was long considered among the first all-out critics of Sufism, George Makdisi long ago noted that, for al-Jawzi and other Hanbalis, "Sufism itself was not being brought into question."[38] If al-Jawzi was primarily concerned with "licentious" Sufi practices, his Hanbali acolyte Ibn Taymiyya (d. 1328)—still considered the ultimate bête noire of the Sufis—was primarily concerned with the Sufi metaphysics of Ibn 'Arabi and certain saintly devotions, and not "Sufism" as a whole.[39]

Yet, beginning in the late eighteenth and early nineteenth centuries, one can discern a crescendo in both the scope and number of accusations against Sufi practices across the Muslim world, as well as the distinctly modern phenomenon of opposing Sufism *tout court*.[40] Up to this point, as Nile Green has put it, "Sufism was inseparable from many aspects of Islam as such," to the extent that "an immediate and wholesale rejection of everything said and done by the Sufis was hardly possible."[41] Until the colonial period Sufism was largely taken for granted as part of the fabric of daily life across Muslim societies from the Maghrib to Java.

Not only is the very notion of critiquing Sufism as a whole a modern idea, but in the modern era, anti-Sufi polemics and Sufi counterpolemics became both more frequent and more intense. Technologies of print and mass media aided Sufis' detractors, who have cast Sufis as partly responsible for the loss of Muslim political power and prestige. In the wake of colonialism, Sufism was criticized from three angles, which we may call, broadly speaking, modernist, Islamist, and Salafi.[42] Modernist critics, like Muhammad Iqbal (d. 1938), often celebrated early Sufi mystics but saw "modern" Sufism as partly responsible for the decline of Islamic civilization. For Iqbal, Sufism had become mired in a world-denying pantheism that sapped the collective élan of Muslim societies. He called for reconstructing a revitalized Sufism around the affirmation, rather than the denial, of selfhood (khudi), as he expressed in a poem titled "Sufism":

> This angelic wisdom, this celestial knowledge
> Are useless in curing the Haram's pain.
> This midnight litany [zikr], these meditations, this intoxication:
> They will not protect the Self [khudi].
> They, too, are of no avail.[43]

Islamist critics, too, blamed Sufism for a host of ills, often seeing Sufis as standing in the way of the Islamization of the state. One of the twentieth century's most influential Islamists, Sayyid Abul A'la Maududi (d. 1979), the Pakistani founder of Jama'at-i Islami, once wrote that "if someone wishes and plans to revive Islam, he must shun the language and the terminology of the Sufis, their mystic allusions and metaphoric references, their dress and etiquette, the saint–disciple institution and all other things associated with it." He called for Muslims to abstain from "these abuses as a diabetic is warned to abstain from sugar."[44] Salafis, who claim to adhere only to the belief and practice of the first three generations of Muslims—al-salaf al-salih ("the pious predecessors")— have also been major critics of Sufism and Sufis.[45] The wide-ranging career of the Salafi activist Taqi al-Din al-Hilali (d. 1987) began with a 1921 "conversion" from Sufism to Salafism after he asked the Prophet Muhammad in a dream whether he should study "exoteric or esoteric knowledge." The Prophet replied: "exoteric knowledge."[46]

It must be noted, however, that these tropes, while influential, typically obscure a far more complex engagement with, and ambivalence toward, Sufism than they suggest at first glance. Maududi tempered his opposition to Sufism over the course of his career, taking up a newfound interest in his family's own Chishti background in the 1970s.[47] Meanwhile, scholars have tracked how Islamist political parties have aligned themselves with Sufi orders in particular contexts, such as contemporary Sudan, and how Islamist icons ranging from Ayatollah Khomeini to Sayyid Qutb adopted and adapted Sufi vocabularies.[48] Even Salafis have not been uniform critics of Sufism. The Syrian Salafi Jamal al-Din Qasimi

(d. 1914) leapt to the defense of Ibn 'Arabi, the bane of many Salafis, against the proto-Salafi hero and icon Ibn Taymiyya.[49] Nevertheless, this outline of dominant tropes in the critique of Sufism helps illuminate how Deobandis differed from these trends in their own critiques. Like Islamists, for example, they believed that Sufism had become burdened with centuries of cultural accretions; unlike them, they believed that the solution was a bottom-up revivification of Muslim subjectivities rather than the top-down reform of a Muslim state.[50] Like the Salafis, they, too, regarded the era of the Prophet's Companions as the paragon of a proper Muslim society, but unlike the Salafis, they saw that era as the very *fount* of Sufism, rather than its antithesis.

THE 'ULAMA IN MUSLIM PUBLIC LIFE

The scholars of the Deoband movement are *'ulama*, traditionally educated Muslim scholars. The contested status of Sufism in the modern world closely parallels, and intersects with, the contested status of the *'ulama* in Muslim public life—the second major theme of modern Islam that this book explores. Like the Sufis, the *'ulama* have been the object of scorn and ridicule in the last two centuries, indeed often from some of the same quarters. Modernists, Islamists, and Salafis blamed the *'ulama*, too, for a plethora of intellectual and social ills (even as many *'ulama* populated their ranks). Jamal al-Din al-Afghani famously castigated the Indian *'ulama* for their alleged failure to solve "worldly" problems, asking, "Why do you not raise your eyes from those defective books and . . . cast your glance on this wide world?"[51] This was in part an indictment of the *'ulama* for allegedly failing to adapt to modernity, and in part a conscientious effort to appropriate the spaces of authority that *'ulama* had traditionally claimed.

As a range of scholars have noted, modernists and Islamists challenged the so-called monopoly that *'ulama* are said to have claimed over the interpretation of the Qur'an, Hadith, and the Islamic legal tradition. Two immediate qualifications of this claim are in order. First, it is essential to note that many modernist and Islamist critics of the *'ulama* were also *'ulama*; there was never a neat demarcation between these groups. Second, scholars have challenged the presumption that the *'ulama* ever had such a monopoly on interpreting the normative textual tradition.[52] Notwithstanding these caveats, it is generally true that before the modern era, the *'ulama* did play a central role not only in interpreting that tradition but also in advising rulers on the basis of those interpretations—a mutually interdependent and often vexed relationship. In the process, they variously legitimated and undermined political powers, sometimes coopting them, sometimes coopted by them.[53]

. As Muslim political hegemony declined globally under the yoke of colonialism, the *'ulama* were increasingly cast as medieval relics holed up in fortress-like madrasas, writing commentaries on obsolete tomes of pre-Copernican astronomy. For their critics, the Deobandis are doubly medieval: as Sufis *and* as *'ulama*. As Fuad Naeem expressed, "A preference for originality over 'tradition' led to an overemphasis on modernist figures on the one hand, and Islamist or 'fundamentalist' figures and movements on the other, often combined with a tacit supposition that the *'ulama* and Sufis represented 'medieval' discourses that would not long survive the triumph of modernity."[54] Deobandis felt this shift acutely. Lay Muslims' cavalier dismissal of the *'ulama* is a motif throughout Deobandi texts. As Khalil Ahmad Saharanpuri (d. 1927) lamented: "In the past, the masses were in need, and the Deputies of the Message [the *'ulama*] were the ones needed. No matter how severe they were, they had an effect. The masses would become worried, repent, and turn back. But nowadays, the *'ulama* have to go begging to the masses to do the work of reform."[55] Still, they held on closely to the idea that they remained vital. Ashraf 'Ali Thanvi put it more bluntly: "It is absurd to think Muslims can dispense with the *'ulama*."[56]

One of the central discourses through which the Deobandi *'ulama* have sought to articulate and maintain that vitality is reform (*islah*), a concept crucial for understanding their role in shaping Muslim public life. The semantics of *islah* (from the Arabic root *s-l-h*) resonate with the most positive and cherished values in the Qur'an, connoting peace and reconciliation (*sulh*), what is right and proper (*salah*), and what is sound, virtuous, or devout (*salih*). The Qur'an aligns *islah* closely with prophets' missions through history. The Prophet Shuayb, for instance, tells those to whom he was sent that he has come to implement *islah* on behalf of God.[57] It is best understood not in the colloquial English sense of "reform," but in the sense of *re-form*. In many contexts, reform is understood in opposition to "tradition." For the Deobandis, the point of *islah* was not to vanquish tradition, but to *reaffirm* it.

The irony of the *'ulama* doing reform is simple: most self-styled reformers took the *'ulama* as an *object* of reform, rather than its agent. Yet *islah* is a ubiquitous term in Deobandi texts. A collection of Ashraf 'Ali Thanvi's reformist treatises is titled *Islahi nisab* (The reformist program).[58] The contemporary Deobandi scholar Mufti Taqi 'Usmani has published a sixteen-volume collection titled *Islahi khutbat* (Reformist sermons).[59] The scope of reform includes not just the social, as in Thanvi's call to reform customs, but subjectivities, as in frequent calls to reform the heart (*islah-i qalb*) and reform the self (*islah-i nafs*). Indeed, Deobandis believed that the moral health of the individual is inseparable from the social health of the body politic, a connection that chapters 3 and 4 explore in depth.

For a range of reasons, these social and subjective iterations of *islah* have been largely ignored by scholars. Geographically, *islah* has been associated with trends in the Middle East, and thematically, with political Islam, independent reasoning (*ijtihad*) in Islamic law, and the Salafi movement.[60] Deobandis, by contrast, have advanced a revival from below, a bottom-up reform largely invisible relative to the top-down reform of Islamist political projects. Above all, the Deobandi effort to remake individual subjectivities has been part of a broader effort to carve out a role for the *'ulama* in Muslim public life.

A term closely linked to, even "used interchangeably" with *islah*,[61] is *tajdid*, "renewal." *Tajdid* is in turn bound up with the concept of the *mujaddid*, the "renewer," who would arrive, according to an oft-cited Hadith, at the beginning of every Islamic century to renew the global community of Muslims.[62] The idea was an important feature of Indian Islamic history. Ahmad Sirhindi (d. 1624) presented himself as the *mujaddid* of the second Islamic millennium, while Shah Wali Allah (d. 1762) was deemed the renewer of the twelfth Islamic century.[63]

Deobandis' invocation of "renewal" (*tajdid*) must be distinguished from Islamists' use of the term. Sayyid Abu A'la Maududi mobilized the language of *tajdid* toward the view that, in his words, "the Islamic system of law . . . needs for its enforcement in all its details the coercive power and authority of the state."[64] As Seyyed Vali Reza Nasr elaborated, "In Maududi's formula, although individual piety featured prominently, in the final analysis, it was the society and the political order that guaranteed the piety of the individual."[65] Deobandis inverted this approach: one had to reform the individual to reform society. And in Deobandi discussions of reform and renewal, the individual and the social are often intertwined. For the founding Deobandi scholar Rashid Ahmad Gangohi (d. 1905), the centennial renewer (*mujaddid*) may not be just one individual at all. While there is no doubt that the imperative of renewal is clear—"repelling illicit innovations [*bid'at*], propagating the Sunna, and reviving long-forgotten prophetic traditions [*sunan*]"—he added that "the reviver of the century may not be a single scholar ['*alim*], but may be, *at any time,* two, four, ten, twenty, fifty, a group of a hundred, or just one. In every century, there will be a *different group of scholars* who will exert themselves in the reformation [*islah*] of religion. *All of them have a share in renewal* [*tajdid*] according to their knowledge [*'ilm*] and rank."[66] This is a remarkable passage. Gangohi decenters the process of renewal, making it dependent not on a single person but a collection of *scholars,* who are distinguished by their *knowledge,* and for whom the act of *tajdid* is, in fact, *islah.* Ashraf 'Ali Thanvi, too, believed that centennial renewal was a process by which the various illicit innovations that emerge each century would be vanquished; but he, too, believed the *'ulama* were instrumental, individually and collectively, in carrying the task of renewal.[67] That being said, there were some who certainly believed that Thanvi himself deserved to be called one of the great "renewers" of the age. 'Abd al-Bari Nadvi (d. 1976)—a Sufi disciple of Thanvi's as well as a prolific writer and translator and a professor at Osmania University in Hyderabad—believed that Thanvi had undoubtedly "reached the highest level of the station of renewal [*mansab-i tajdid*]."[68]

The role of the *'ulama* in reform (*islah*) and renewal (*tajdid*) encapsulates Deobandis' view of the centrality of the *'ulama* in Muslim public life. But their ultimate aim was not simply reasserting the importance of the *'ulama.* Their ultimate aim was saving souls. The epigraph of this introduction is a line from one of the sermons of Ashraf 'Ali Thanvi, delivered in Kanpur in March 1923: "O Faithful, save yourself and your family from the torments of hell."[69] This is his translation, he tells his Urdu-speaking audience, of a phrase from Qur'an 66:6: "O believers, protect yourselves and your families from the fire."[70] In the sermon, and in his more extensive comments on this verse in his Qur'an commentary, *Bayan al-Qur'an,* Thanvi draws on the Sunna to amplify the verse: when even the Prophet was compelled by God to advise his family in belief and practice, "it is all the more obligatory for *you* to reform [*islah*] your family and household."[71] In this deceptively simple declaration, multiple facets of Deoband's reformist project are embedded. Saving souls from eternal punishment is the most important, but two others are noteworthy: "protect *yourselves*" is a call to the individual, an interpellation of a subject in need of reform; "and your *family*" is a call to the social, to replicate the act of self-reform in others. We will see this complementary, indeed reciprocal, relationship between self and society again and again throughout this book.

As we will see in chapter 4, Deobandis believed that an essential corpus of religious knowledge was the prerequisite for guiding others to guide *themselves*, and that Sufism provided the ethical resources to turn that knowledge into practice. And *embodied* knowledge, they would add, is more easily transmitted than merely discursive knowledge, because of its affective power. All of this was intended to bring Muslims closer to God and, thereby, save them from perdition. It is a sentiment shared by Muhammad Shafi', perhaps Thanvi's most prominent disciple in postpartition Pakistan. Shafi' followed al-Ghazali in making an explicit connection between Sufi ethics and salvation. "What the Sufis call 'virtues' [*faza'il*], Imam Ghazali called '*munjiat*,' meaning 'that which grants salvation' [*najat*]," said Shafi'. "Opposite to these, those things that are forbidden and impermissible the Sufis call 'vices' [*raza'il*], which Imam Ghazali calls '*muhlikat*,' meaning 'that which destroys.'"[72]

DEBATING ISLAMIC "TRADITION"

The third major debate within modern Islam that this book explores is how to define and conceptualize tradition. "Tradition" has been a watchword in Islamic studies in the last three decades. The word has become so ubiquitous, in fact, that one may wonder whether its analytical purchase has exhausted itself. Why revisit it here? Simply put, it is impossible to understand the Deoband movement—and, I would argue, modern Islam—without it.

There is no single word in the main languages of the Deoband movement—above all Urdu, followed by Arabic and Persian—that neatly conforms to the English word "tradition," though a constellation of words falls within its semantic range.[73] For the Deobandis, there are multiple, overlapping phenomena that the word connotes. There is, first and foremost, Islam itself, configured through divine revelation and the transmission of the prophetic Sunna. Sufism, too, is a tradition in its own right—so much so that Nile Green has argued persuasively that Sufism is best understood through the lens of "tradition" rather "mysticism."[74] And, finally, there is the tradition of Deoband itself.

Perhaps the most influential definition of tradition in Islamic studies comes from philosopher Alasdair MacIntyre. MacIntyre famously defined tradition as "an argument extended through time in which certain fundamental agreements are defined and redefined in terms of two kinds of conflict: those with critics and enemies external to the tradition, and those internal, interpretive debates through which the meaning and rationale of fundamental agreements comes to be expressed and by whose progress a tradition is constituted."[75] Although MacIntyre may help us understand how traditions defend themselves from external challenges and constitute themselves through the pursuit of internal coherence, I find his definition too cerebral, too centered on ideas and not enough on people—in a word, too discursive. As I argue in chapters 4 and 5, most discussions of tradition in Islamic studies have focused too much on discursivity and not enough on *affect*. I approach affect in terms of ways that emotional valences work in, through, and between bodies—a core theme of affect theory in the last two decades.[76] For my purposes, I am interested in ways that bodily presences authorize particular forms of knowledge. I do not see "knowledge," in the contexts I explore below, as some sort of discrete, cognitive datum—mere *information*—that is passed from one person to the next. For one, Deobandis believe that the reliability of knowledge itself is inseparable from the embodied ethics of the persons who transmit it. (Would you learn Sufi asceticism from someone who isn't an ascetic? Would you study Hadith with a scholar who doesn't live by them?) But in addition, Deobandis—and they are by no means unique in this respect as Sufis, as scholars, or even as Muslims—believe that pious bodies themselves resonate with an energy (*faiz*) that transcends discursive knowledge (*'ilm*) even as it validates it.

While the study of Islam is certainly moving toward a more nuanced understanding of the embodied transmission of knowledge,[77] scholars of Islam have long been predisposed to see tradition transmitted primarily through *texts,* both in the modalities of that transmission and in the content transmitted. This explains, in my view, the resilience of the Asadian formation of Islam as "discursive tradition"—so resilient, in fact, that even Asad's subsequent qualifications of that idea have arguably had less traction than the original essay of 1986 in which he first put it forth.[78] In that essay, Asad argued that "a tradition consists essentially of discourses that seek to instruct practitioners regarding the correct form and purpose of a given practice. . . . A practice is Islamic because it is authorized by the discursive traditions of Islam."[79] This theorization of tradition, indebted to MacIntyre, has been inadequate for developing a language to understand how traditions are transmitted not just through texts but also through bodies.[80] And Asad, to his credit, has attempted to correct the text-centeredness of his earlier formulation, seeing tradition as both discursive and embodied in various, sometimes conflicting, ways.[81] Not only do traditions transmit knowledge; equally, they transmit affective sensibilities, styles of comportment, and demeanors—not *just* knowledge, in other words, but also how to embody knowledge. Asad has also recently explored ways in which traditions are not simply fixated on reproducing the past, but are oriented toward unfolding futures. Traditions are, in a word, "aspirational."[82]

This book poses the question of tradition, for the Deobandis, as part of a host of questions in the study of Islam broadly. Is tradition transmitted through bodies or books? Does tradition convey its own authority? To what degree should individual Muslims have the latitude to engage with tradition directly, and to what extent must that engagement be mediated? Corporeality is embedded in the very etymology of tradition—from the Latin *tradere*, "to hand down." In Adorno's words, *tradere* "expresses physical proximity, immediacy—one hand should receive from another."[83] Books and bodies are, of course, not mutually exclusive; they are mutually constitutive. Books circulate via the bodies that carry them, on the one hand, while corporeal authority is configured through embodiment of scripture and law, on the other. And as Asad suggests, the vitality of a tradition is measured not just by its ability to absorb ruptures but, perhaps even more, by its ability to let internal contradictions subsist. "Tradition accommodates mistakes as well as betrayal; it is not by accident," he observes (to return again to *tradere*), "that *tradition* and *treason* have a common etymology."[84]

As I argue in the fifth chapter, Deobandi tradition falls somewhere between two concepts: Sunna and *maslak*. In Deobandi thought, the *maslak* (literally "way," "path") captures this affective register. This concept connotes the world of shared sensibilities that Deobandi scholars cultivate and pass down through the interplay of books and bodies. I will show how they adapt the Sufi concept of "companionship" (*suhbat*) between master and disciple to argue that books alone are inadequate on their own to transmit tradition. If the transmission of knowledge in premodern Islam—the classic image is one of students sitting in a circle around a scholar, in a mosque or even under a tree, memorizing texts and receiving an *ijaza* (permission) to transmit those texts to others—is the very paragon of an anthropocentric knowledge economy, in which the books are secondary to the *people* who teach them, the "modern" madrasa may be seen as a triumph of bibliocentrism, with its fixed curriculum, salaried faculty, central library, and slate of exams.[85] But it is of course never quite that simple. I argue that Deobandis have attempted to recuperate anthropocentrism in an ever more bibliocentric world in a number of ways: insisting that knowledge cannot come from books alone but requires the guidance of an expert, accentuating the Sufi concept of *suhbat* (companionship) as the sine qua non of moral self-formation, and reasserting the indispensability of the *ulama* as the learned individuals who can help the less learned make sense of difficult and often theologically perilous issues.

The *maslak* is, in a sense, larger and more capacious than what is transmitted through the madrasa. A "common" (*'amm*) Muslim, perhaps someone with a middle-class occupation who reads religious texts in his or her spare time, may participate in the *maslak* without having set foot in a madrasa. In this way, the *maslak* could be usefully compared with what the philosopher of science Ludwik Fleck called a thought collective (*Denkkollektiv*): a "community of persons mutually exchanging ideas or maintaining intellectual interaction."[86] Every thought collective consists of a dynamic interplay between elites and commoners, the esoteric and the exoteric. Barbara Herrnstein Smith described Fleck's thought collective as "a set of nested, mutually interacting circles. . . . At the centre is a small inner ('esoteric') circle of the elite—experts and elders, master builders and laboratory directors. At the periphery is a large ('exoteric') circle—fans, audiences, lay people and the general public. In between is a graduated hierarchy of initiates: students, amateurs, assistants and apprentices."[87] For Fleck, at the center of an esoteric circle is what he called "journal science"—scientists who conduct experiments and publish the results in journals—and at the exoteric edge of that set of concentric circles is what he called "textbook science"—the first stage of initiation into the esoteric circle.[88]

As I show in chapter 3, the Deobandi scholars at the center of their thought collective were clear that lay Muslims (*'awamm*) are no more equipped to opine on legal-theological issues (*masa'il*) than someone who has read a physics textbook is equipped to run a laboratory. This is critical to understanding both the transmission of knowledge across Deobandi tradition and the maintenance of authority within it. This is, of course, an idealized epistemic relationship between center and periphery that, we will see, is never quite as neat and orderly as the scholars at the center imagine it to be. In the final two chapters, we will witness lay Muslims who willfully and conscientiously locate themselves outside these circles altogether and, indeed, reject the authority of the Deobandis and the authoritative structure they have fashioned.

In sum, then, Deobandi tradition arises out of a tension—sometimes productive, sometimes strained—between the anthropocentric and the bibliocentric, between the centrifugal force of a global movement and the centripetal force of intimate encounters, between the dispersal of books and the proximity of bodies, between esoteric centers and exoteric peripheries, and above all, between the "little" tradition of the *maslak,* to which they adhere as Deobandis, and the "great" tradition of the Sunna, to which they adhere as Muslims.

MAIN CHARACTERS AND STRUCTURE OF THE BOOK

A number of main characters associated with the Deoband movement appear again and again in this book. In the first two chapters, we will see how multiple currents of nineteenth-century Islam converge in the founding of the Dar al-'Ulum Deoband, emanating from an array of influential figures: Sayyid Ahmad Barelvi (1786–1831), the jihadi rebel and charismatic leader of a fledgling frontier state; Muhammad Isma'il (1779–1831), Sayyid Ahmad's close associate, whose radical critique of everyday piety electrified Indian Muslims in the early nineteenth century and whose mantle early Deobandis adopted, if not without certain reservations; Hajji Imdad Allah al-Makki (1817–1899), arguably the most important Sufi of late colonial India, who mentored a generation of Deobandis but whose ambivalence about the very devotions the Deobandis critiqued and whose lack of legal training made his legacy a deeply contested one; and Rashid Ahmad Gangohi (1828–1905), patron (*sarparast*) of the Deoband madrasa, whose sober Sufism and law-centered piety shaped the Deoband movement's ethos from its origins to the present day.

But it is Ashraf 'Ali Thanvi (1863–1943), the endlessly prolific visionary of late colonial Deoband, who is by far the central character in this book. It is Thanvi who synthesized law and Sufism in a body of work that is largely responsible for making Deoband a global phenomenon. Thus, while this book is about the Deoband movement, it is also in no small way a book about Thanvi, the pivotal figure around whom the movement formed in the seminally important first three decades of the twentieth century, as well as the teacher and mentor of the generation that began to take the Deoband movement beyond South Asia in the 1940s and '50s. Nevertheless, we must stress that Thanvi does not therefore stand in for the Deoband movement as a whole. On the contrary, his perspectives on some aspects of the movement, especially concerning politics, were sharply rebuked by other Deobandis. But he was arguably the most influential, and undoubtedly the most prolific, Deobandi scholar. In his voluminous work, he simultaneously inherited and processed the legal and mystical influences of his forebears Imdad Allah and Gangohi and popularized those ideas through texts meant for a mass readership in Urdu.

In the process of centering Thanvi, the book inevitably gives less attention to Husain Ahmad Madani (1879–1957), the only figure whose position could legitimately rival Thanvi's as the most important Deobandi of the twentieth century. This is not deliberate. It is the result, rather, of the book's focus on Sufism and Sufi devotions on the one hand, and on Deobandis in South Africa on the other. Thanvi's presence looms over both. By contrast, Madani's stature derives largely from his role in anticolonial politics. The book does discuss Madani in the context of Thanvi's political views in the final chapter.

While the book revolves around Thanvi and his outsize status in the movement, a number of other characters are crucial to the book's narrative arc: Khalil Ahmad Saharanpuri (1852–1927),[89] Gangohi's associate and disciple, whose defense of Deobandis against their critics was instrumental in defining the movement; Muhammad Ilyas Kandhlavi (1865–1944), a graduate of Deoband who founded the Tablighi Jama'at to revive Muslims' commitment to Islam along Deobandi lines; and Muhammad Zakariyya Kandhlavi (1898–1982), arguably the Tablighi Jama'at's most ardent defender, who presided over the global expansion of Deobandi thought in the mid–twentieth century. Finally, the trajectory of the Deoband movement broadly, and Thanvi's predilections especially, take root in South Africa more than any other place outside of South Asia through the work of three figures: Mahmud Hasan Gangohi (1907–1996), a chief mufti of the Dar al-'Ulum Deoband who undertook numerous tours of South Africa to promote the Tablighi Jama'at and initiate Sufi disciples; Muhammad Masihullah Khan (1910–1992), perhaps Thanvi's closest Sufi disciple, who was almost singlehandedly responsible for spreading Thanvi's approach to Sufism, politics, and everything else among scores of South Africans; and, finally, Ahmed Sadiq Desai (1939-), the vituperative student and disciple of Masihullah Khan, whose stringent polemics against fellow South African Muslims shaped how those same Muslims viewed the Deoband movement in the twilight of apartheid.

If these are the main characters,[90] let me conclude the introduction with an outline of the book itself. The first chapter—"A Modern Madrasa"—situates the emergence of the Dar al-'Ulum Deoband in 1866 and the Deoband movement itself within the sense of political and social crisis many Indian Muslims felt in the wake of the failed uprising of 1857. It also provides the social context for Deobandis' belief that a revival of classical learning and the revivification of the Sunna could reverse the perceived decline of Islam. The chapter shows how the decline of first Mughal and then British patronage for Islamic learning, as well as the post-1857 British policy of noninterference in "religious" matters, opened up a space for Deobandi scholars to reconceive the madrasa as a purely "religious" institution rather than one engaged in the production of civil servants, to reimagine the 'ulama as stewards of public morality rather than professionals in the service of the state, and to reframe the knowledge they purveyed as "religious" knowledge distinct from the "useful" secular knowledge promoted by the British. Within this nexus of shifts, in turn, we see also how an Islamic legal discourse was made to function in the absence of a traditional legal apparatus—in other words, without courts or qazis (judges)—a discourse for which mass printed texts in Islamic belief and practice and the publishing of fatwas (Islamic legal opinions), traditionally issued to judges but now issued directly to lay Muslims, were key.

Building on the first, the second chapter—"The Normative Order"—further develops the context for the Deobandis' mission of mass reform. It begins with a brief overview of two formative concepts—illicit innovation in religion (bid'a), and ascribing divine attributes to entities other than God (shirk)—that animate Deobandi thought. It argues that Deobandis appropriated the fecund legacy of the anti-bid'a and anti-shirk campaigner Muhammad Isma'il even as they distanced themselves from his hermeneutical populism—namely, the notion that the Qur'an and the Sunna are "easy" to understand and, therefore, do not require the mediation of the 'ulama. Focusing on the teachings of Hajji Imdad Allah al-Makki and his disciples Rashid Ahmad Gangohi and Ashraf 'Ali Thanvi, the chapter then shows how Deobandis applied the discourse of bid'a and shirk to two forms of devotional piety that were central to Indian Sufism: honoring the Prophet Muhammad's birthday (mawlud), and celebrating the Sufi saints' death anniversaries ('urs).

If the second chapter explains what Deobandis wanted to reform, the third chapter—"Remaking the Public"—explains how, exploring ways that Deobandis conceived the very task of reform, its limitations, and ambivalences. After providing an overview of the rise of the Indian "public" in the latter half of the nineteenth century and its multiple configurations—technological, social, textual—the chapter looks closely at an exchange of letters in 1897 between Rashid Ahmad Gangohi and Ashraf 'Ali Thanvi in which Gangohi chastised his disciple Thanvi for attempting to reform devotees of the mawlud by preaching to them directly. For reasons I show, Thanvi concluded that reforming Muslim publics through the publication of reformist literature was a far more reliable means of implementing reform, second only to the reform that could take place in the confines of the seminary (madrasa) and the Sufi lodge (*khanqah*). In subsequent years, Thanvi would go on to compose a staggering number of reformist texts. But it also shows how he struggled with the ambivalence of reform through books: at every stage, he stressed the irreplaceability of the *'ulama* as custodians of religious knowledge for lay Muslims and urged readers not to delve into, let alone publicly discuss, difficult legal-theological issues (*masa'il*). The chapter also argues that Deobandi–Barelvi polemics, which exploded at the end of the nineteenth century and the beginning of the twentieth, were precisely the form of public debate about such difficult issues that Thanvi and other Deobandis (though, we will see, not all) were keen to avoid.

The fourth chapter—"Remaking the Self"—shows how Deobandis conceived of Sufism itself, in two complementary ways: as coterminous with the Shari'a, and as a discourse of ethical self-fashioning. The chapter begins by contextualizing the "self" at the center of the reformist public, arguing that the self-fashioning which that individual is called to perform is never a quest for autonomy in the sense of *auto-nomos* (arrogating to oneself one's own law), but an autonomy that simultaneously liberates the self from the strictures of "customs" (*rusum*) and illicit innovations (*bid'at*), and realigns the self around the Sunna, as mediated by living scholar-Sufis. It details how Deobandis saw the crux of the Sufi path as the process of divesting the self of "base" ethical qualities (*akhlaq-i razila*) and embodying "praiseworthy" ones (*akhlaq-i hamida*). The chapter elucidates an all-important concept in Deobandi Sufism: *suhbat,* the "companionship" with Sufi masters by which one acquires the dispositions and affects that aid translating religious knowledge (*'ilm*) into practice (*a'mal*). The corollary to the need for the *'ulama* to make sense of religious knowledge is the need for companionship with living Sufis to make sense of the Sufi path—not only because the most reliable knowledge is *embodied* knowledge, but because Sufi books without a living interpreter harbor complex metaphysical concepts that pose spiritual dangers for the uninitiated. The chapter concludes by illustrating how Deobandis reconceptualized the very definition of Sufi sainthood (*walayat*) by way of Sufi ethics, arguing that any pious Muslim not only can be but *is* a saint (*wali*) by virtue of that piety. This entailed, I will show, expanding the semantic parameters of the concept of the *wali* (connoting "ally," "friend," and "protector") in the Qur'an. Accordingly, they viewed Sufi saints primarily as moral exemplars, not as miracle workers or as conduits for intercession with God.

The fifth chapter—"What Does a Tradition Feel Like?"—examines how "Deobandi" tradition is mediated through scholarly and pedagogical networks, in theory and practice. The first part of the chapter focuses on Qari Muhammad Tayyib (1897–1983), chancellor of the Dar al-'Ulum Deoband for half a century and the foremost theorist of Deobandi identity, arguing that mid-twentieth-century Deobandis like Tayyib developed the concept of the *maslak* as a means of lending ideological and affective coherence to a rapidly expanding global network. Tayyib theorized the *maslak* as a "middle path" between ideological extremes—as, for instance, between those who indulge in "excessive" Sufi devotions and those who dispense with Sufism altogether—and as an embodied discourse one learns to inhabit through the companionship (*suhbat*) of those who already do. The second part of the chapter, shifting from "theory" to "practice," traces the rise of the Tablighi Jama'at, a Deobandi revivalist movement that sought to make individual Muslims mobile "embodiments" (*mujassam*) of the seminary (madrasa) and the Sufi lodge (*khanqah*), effectively translating Thanvi's project of public reform into an actual program—one explicitly based on internalizing the teachings of Thanvi's Urdu primers for lay Muslims, on shunning public debate of controversial legal issues (*masa'il*), and on the replication of a set of reformed affects in others; hence the Tablighi Jama'at's role, by midcentury, in propelling Deobandi tradition across the globe. As Tayyib theorized a global reformist movement, the Tablighis were busy shaping and expanding it.

Accordingly, the sixth chapter—"How a Tradition Travels"—reconstructs how Deoband became a global phenomenon, highlighting the reciprocal relation between the rise of the Tablighi Jama'at in South Africa and the expansion of South African Deobandi scholarly networks. Scholars and students traveled between Deobandi seminaries in India and South Africa as early as the first decade of the twentieth century, but this chapter shows how the Deobandi "brand," as it were, did not emerge in South Africa until the 1960s—a direct outcome, I argue, of the growth of the Tablighi Jama'at in that decade. One of the ironies of the South African context is that the Tablighi Jama'at, which officially is supposed to avoid controversies, became embroiled in internecine polemics and counterpolemics over local Sufi devotions, principally the *mawlud*. The chapter concludes with a brief survey of these polemics.

The seventh chapter—"A Tradition Contested"—shows how this "branding" of Deoband intersected with the volatile context of an emergent Muslim anti-apartheid politics and how public debate about Deobandi critiques of Sufi devotions became inseparable from public debate about the very authority of the Deobandi *'ulama*. The chapter begins with an overview of Islamic resurgence and activism in South Africa in the 1970s and '80s, much of which was animated by the belief that the *'ulama* generally, and the Deobandi *'ulama* specifically, were incapable of challenging, or unwilling to challenge, the state. South Africans, we will see, roundly dismissed Deobandi critiques as theological quibbles that were, at best, irrelevant to the task of liberating South Africa and, at worst, a dangerous capitulation to tyranny. The chapter focuses on the bitter invectives of the South African Deobandi scholar Ahmed Sadiq Desai—a disciple of Thanvi's own closest disciple, Masihullah Khan (d. 1992)—who rearticulated Thanvi's politics in South Africa. With a flashback to 1920s India, we will see how Thanvi felt a deep, affective aversion to Muslim participation in anticolonial politics—one in which Islamic law and Sufi ethics constrained the very conditions of the political. We then see how Desai, in turn, deployed Thanvi's critiques toward Muslim participation in the anti-apartheid movement. For their critics, Deobandi contestations of local Sufi devotions in the midst of this period's social and political upheaval made them seem all the more retrogressive. As Deobandi scholars criticized Muslim activists for mobilizing against apartheid alongside activists of other faiths, and justified that position through Sufi vocabularies, a growing number of Muslims lambasted Deobandis for their alleged collaborationist stance toward the apartheid regime, and articulated their politics through devotional practices like the *mawlud*. Many of these local activists, moreover, defended their activism precisely through transnational politics that Deobandis mostly abhorred, drawing variously on the Shi'i Islamist vocabularies of revolutionary Iran and the nascent transnational discourse of progressive Islam.

1

A Modern Madrasa

In the aftermath of the failed Indian uprising of 1857, the Government of India Act of 2 August 1858 disbanded the East India Company and transferred sovereignty over India to the queen. On 1 November 1858, Queen Victoria issued the following proclamation to her new subjects:

> Firmly relying ourselves on the truth of Christianity, and acknowledging with gratitude the solace of religion, we disclaim alike the right and the desire to impose our convictions on any of our subjects. We declare it to be our royal will and pleasure that none be in anywise favoured, none molested or disquieted, by reason of their religious faith or observances, but that all shall alike enjoy the equal and impartial protection of the law; and we do strictly charge and enjoin all those who may be in authority under us that they abstain from all interference with the religious belief or worship of any of our subjects on pain of our highest displeasure.[1]

While at first glance this may strike some as a policy of benign noninterference, Karuna Mantena argues that it was, far more, a concession to "native inscrutability."[2] Simply put, the British concluded that the events of 1857 had primarily "religious"—rather than social, political, or economic—causes. From 1857 onward, as Ilyse Morgenstein Fuerst demonstrates, "religion" became the primarily lens through which the British understood their Muslim subjects, and any subsequent resistance to British rule was, necessarily, born of purely "religious" motivations.[3]

Demarcating a religious space ostensibly free from interference was a strategy of rule the British had adopted elsewhere. Throughout their colonies, from Ireland to India, the British advanced policies of disestablishment—a rule to which the Church of England at *home* was an exception—facilitating the emergence of "religion" as a private domain of conscience that Muslims and Hindus alike became keen to protect against state encroachment.[4] Some of the British, accordingly, saw the Victorian proclamation not so much as constraining British interference in native religious affairs as consigning religion to a "private" domain that facilitated, rather than restricted, Christian missions. The barrister P. F. O'Malley saw the proclamation as authorizing Christian missionary efforts even by an official of the empire, who is "still left to follow in his *private* capacity the dictates of religious duty, and to assist as he has hitherto done in the great Missionary work."[5]

The proclamation also pointed to a new, albeit tenuous, notion of the "secular" in colonial India. Scholars have long dismissed earlier notions of the secular as the decline of religion. They have also challenged more recent notions of the secular as religion's privatization. Scholars have, most recently, understood the secular as a form of power that distinguishes "religion" from its various others—whether "superstition," "culture," "politics," or something else.[6] Following Robert Cover's dictum that "Every denial of jurisdiction . . . is an assertion of the power to determine jurisdiction and thus to constitute a norm," Iza Hussin sees the Victorian proclamation as a performative act ("juris-*diction*"), declaring which spaces would be marked by "religion" and which would remain under the purview of the state.[7] Post-1857 discourses of official neutrality toward natives' "religion" were in large part discourses that named a range of phenomena—institutions, traditions, forms of knowledge—as "religious." Indeed, as I explore below, the British were willing to support madrasas only if their curricula included "secular," and not only "religious," subjects.

In 1866, just a few years after Victoria's proclamation, the Dar al-'Ulum Deoband was founded, and it soon began to fill this new space marked off as "religious." It was precisely within an emergent colonial modernity that the madrasa as a "religious" space and the *'ulama* as a class of "religious" scholars became entrenched in the very identity of the Deoband movement. This chapter explores a number of questions at the origin of Deoband: Why did a movement that claimed to seamlessly revive Islamic tradition emerge precisely at the height of colonial modernity, with all of its political, epistemic, and psychic ruptures? To what extent is the movement's valorization of "tradition" an outcome of that very modernity? This chapter suggests that it is too simple to view Deoband as "traditional" in some respects (for instance, in terms of accentuating Hadith and Islamic law) and "modern" in others (institutionally and administratively resembling a British college more than a classical madrasa, for example). It proposes, rather, that tradition and modernity are so co-constitutive that Deoband's traditionalism *is* what makes Deoband modern. Deobandi valorization of "tradition"—seen, for instance, in its privileging of "transmitted" knowledge (*manqulat*) above its "rational" counterpart (*ma'qulat*), discussed below—is hard to conceive before colonial modernity and attendant discourses of the Indian secular gave new meaning to tradition itself. Moreover, while the texts that Deobandi scholars study are not modern, the idiom through which they communicate that learning to the public *is*, in part because "the public" itself is largely (though not exclusively) modern—a subject the second and third chapters explore further.[8]

To be clear, I am not arguing that Deoband is solely the product of colonial modernity. For one, such an argument would grossly overstate the extent to which colonialism shaped the lives of the colonized. Much recent literature on colonialism has, in fact, stressed the *limits* of colonial power and imperial reach.[9] More importantly, it would understate the extent to which the Deoband movement is anchored in texts and discourses that long predate colonialism. I see modernity, therefore, not as something that "happened" to the Deoband movement. It is not a reified "thing" that travels from Europe to India, a "virus that spreads from one place to another," in Sanjay Subrahmanyam's words. It is, rather, a "global and *conjunctural* phenomenon."[10]

In highlighting Deoband's modernity, I seek to complicate standard narratives about Deoband specifically, and madrasas generally, both within and beyond the study of Islam. Even a cursory glance at literature on Islam and modernity reveals that the Deoband movement is typically regarded as, at best, a premodern vestige of medieval learning or, at worst, a stridently antimodern force holding back Muslim progress. Fazlur Rahman, among the most influential internal critics of the Islamic intellectual tradition, saw Deoband as "medieval," which meant, for him, that it perpetuated stagnant disciplines of learning that shrouded the "élan of the Qur'an" beneath a culture of commentaries and supracommentaries.[11] While Rahman's approach to Muslim modernity has been formative for rethinking Qur'anic hermeneutics,[12] approaching phenomena like the Deoband movement through this lens obscures the extent to which the movement has been shaped *by* modernity.

I speak of "modernity" here in two distinct but intersecting registers. The first comprises the sum total of new ideas, practices, institutions, and socialities that scholars often call "colonial modernity." In the following, I seek to delineate how Deoband emerged *within* and *against* colonial modernity while heeding Frederick Cooper's warnings against reifying "colonial modernity" as an agent in its own right.[13] The second is modernity as a reflexive attitude, a self-conscious distanciation between past and present, especially insofar as it values the present over the past.[14] Broadly, I show here how Deobandi scholars were profoundly shaped by the first modality of the modern—institutionally, discursively, and in what they regarded as properly "religious"—even as they consciously rejected "modernity" in the second sense. That is, Deobandis did not understand their movement as a "modern" one, let alone *modernist*.[15] Most Deobandis, and certainly the main characters of this book, understood themselves as *anti*-modern.[16] But in making this claim, we must also be attentive to the ways in which Deobandis understood the very category of the "modern" (*jadid*). Ashraf 'Ali Thanvi, for example, conceived modernity in epistemic terms. For him, it was an attempt by certain Muslims to adapt "Islamic" knowledge to Western science. Typified by Sayyid Ahmad Khan (d. 1898), this "modern theology" (*'ilm al-kalam al-jadid*) was anathema to Thanvi, an intellectual capitulation to the modern against which he believed the madrasa should serve as a bulwark.[17] In short, the Deoband movement is ambivalently modern, thoroughly shaped by, and inseparable from, the contexts of its origin at the height of British imperial domination and the changes—social, institutional, technological, political, economic—that it ushered in, *even as* many Deobandi scholars resolutely rejected "modernity" as they construed it.

This chapter makes three main arguments: First, the Victorian discourse on religion and religious institutions after 1857 intersected with, and amplified, Muslim scholars' reimagining of the madrasa as a "religious" space and of the knowledge they had mastered as "religious" knowledge, in contrast to the "useful" secular knowledge promoted by the British. Second, in the wake of Mughal decline and the near evaporation of the traditional patronage networks they had supported, the *'ulama* rebranded themselves as custodians of public morality rather than professionals in the service of the state—a state, of course, that had ceased to exist—that is, a simultaneous de-professionalization *and* privatization of the *'ulama* through which they took on a more active role in shaping individual subjectivities and public sensibilities. Third, as the British attempted to co-opt the judicial administration of Indian Muslims through the British-Islamic legal hybrid known as "Anglo-Muhammadan law," they created a legal and ethical vacuum that early Deobandi scholars sought to fill with a highly personalized, individuated notion of Islamic legal norms, pressed into the service of critiquing Sufi devotions and reformulating Sufism itself as a regime of ethical self-fashioning, for which the fatwa and the short primer on Islamic belief and practice became key instruments. This chapter, then, sets up a framework for understanding how the Deobandi *'ulama* conceived of, and engaged with, nascent Muslim publics—a development described in the subsequent two chapters.

DECLINE AND REVIVAL: FOUNDING THE DAR AL-'ULUM DEOBAND

The Deoband movement emerged in the context of widespread notions that Indian Islam was in a state of abject decline in the nineteenth century. Deobandis were not alone in this view. Narratives of decline, in fact, shaped a wide swath of Muslim intellectual and cultural life in the nineteenth century. The poet Altaf Hussain Hali (d. 1914) mourned the "decay" (*tanazzul*) of India's Muslims in his famous *Musaddas*. The institutions of Muslim greatness had broken down in the face of the West's rise. "The Ummah has no refuge," he mourned, "no qazi [judge], no mufti [jurist], no Sufi, no mullah [scholar]."[18] For Hali's close associate Sayyid Ahmad Khan, India's Muslims had reached a veritable nadir, "the furthest limit of decline, disgrace and baseness."[19]

The opening pages of Rashid Ahmad Gangohi's biography are a veritable litany of decline. His biographer vividly describes the year Gangohi was born, 1828, as one in which Muslims were in the throes of un-Islamic customs and mired in ignorance and superstition: "Over here, drums and sitars crash and clang. Over there, bazaar women dance while someone goes into 'ecstasy' [*wajd o hal*]. Over here, there is grave worship and *ta'ziya* worship;[20] over there God's saints are abused and cursed." The masses had little interest in Islam itself: "The prevailing view was that Islam consisted only of prayer, fasting, and a few beliefs about the afterlife—maidens in paradise, snakes in hell, and worms of the grave." Non-Islamic laws and practices had insinuated themselves into the Shari'a. Fake mystics performed feats of trickery and called them "miracles" (*karamat*). But nothing signified this decline quite like contempt for the *'ulama* and the ignorance of the *'ulama* themselves. "The masses considered themselves self-sufficient and to have no need for the *'ulama*," he writes, "while pseudo *'ulama*, deprived of self-reform [*tahzib-i nafs*], became their servants and paid employees."[21]

These narratives colored the world in which a number of young Muslim scholars converged in the aftermath of the uprising of 1857 to revive Indian Islam from within via a new educational movement. They hailed from a cluster of closely knit *qasbahs* north of Delhi—Nanauta, Gangoh, Thana Bhawan, Ambetha, Kandhla—situated in the fertile plains between the Yamuna and Ganges Rivers, often separated by only a few miles. Their families were interconnected by scholarship, marriage, and Sufi discipleship. Foremost among these men was Muhammad Qasim Nanautvi (1833–1880), upon whose vision the Dar al-'Ulum Deoband was principally founded. "His central goal," as his biographer Sayyid Manazir Ahsan Gilani put it, "was an educational movement through which rays of divine knowledge would shine across India and beyond."[22] This was surely self-evident from the vantage of 1954, when Gilani wrote Nanautvi's biography, long after the Deoband movement had become a global phenomenon. From Nanautvi's vantage, however, it is hard to imagine he could have known how prominent this movement would become.

Nanautvi was born in Nanauta in 1833. In 1843, he went to Delhi to study with Mamluk 'Ali, a scholar who also hailed from Nanauta and who had cultivated close ties to the family of Shah Wali Allah, had been teaching at Delhi College since 1825, and had achieved renown within Muslim scholarly circles of north India.[23] In Delhi, Nanautvi met Rashid Ahmad Gangohi, who had also come to study with Mamluk 'Ali and who would go on to leave a profoundly deep imprint on the Deoband movement. Nanautvi and Gangohi became immensely close. Mamluk 'Ali was not the only mentor they shared. Both became disciples of the Sufi master Hajji Imdad Allah al-Makki. Born in 1817 to a scholarly family in Nanauta, Hajji Imdad Allah also traveled to Delhi in 1833 to study with Mamluk 'Ali and Muhammad Ishaq, a disciple of Wali Allah's son Shah 'Abd al-'Aziz.[24]

The events of 1857 profoundly affected Nanautvi, Gangohi, and Imdad Allah, as they did all Muslims. After the local chief (*ra'is*) of Thana Bhawan was arrested and hanged for allegedly smuggling elephants into Delhi to help the rebels, the town's residents asked Imdad Allah to act as "commander of the faithful" (*amir al-mu'minin*) during the uprising, a role for which the British sought his arrest. Gangohi was implicated, too: Imdad Allah needed someone to carry out Shari'a-based legal judgments in the town and turned to Gangohi. As the uprising was squashed, Gangohi was arrested and served six months in a British jail. Imdad Allah, for his part, had to flee to Mecca to avoid imprisonment.[25] From Mecca he maintained a prolific correspondence with his Sufi disciples back home and frequently received them in Mecca during the Hajj.

Nanautvi was known as an erudite, incisive thinker with a penchant for theology and philosophy—which, as we will see below, distinguished him sharply from his friend and associate Gangohi. One can glimpse the sort of texts a young man involved in Indo-Persian intellectual life would have studied in this period. Before entering Delhi College, he studied works of logic (*mantiq*) and dialectical theology (*kalam*), such as *Mir zahid*, a commentary on a work of logic by Iranian philosopher al-Tafta-zani (d. 1390), as well as Mulla Mahmud Jaunpuri's (d. 1651) *Shams-i bazigha*, an Indian work on astronomy.[26] He also placed himself at the center of inter- and intrareligious polemics of the day, and knew the power of print in carrying out these debates; in 1850 he began working at the influential printing house Matba' Ahmadi, which was devoted to publishing works by Wali Allah and scholars of his circle.[27] He carried out high-profile debates with Dayananda Saraswati, founder of the Hindu revivalist movement Arya Samaj, on the nature of God's omnipotence,[28] and refuted Saraswati's provocative assertion that Muslims' facing the Ka'aba during prayer was a form of idolatry.[29] He critiqued the modern-ist theology of Sayyid Ahmad Khan,[30] and was also a vocal critic of the Shi'a in India and elsewhere.[31]

Nanautvi used to visit Deoband because his father-in-law lived there. During his visits, he stayed in Deoband's Chatta Masjid, where he fre-quently had long conversations with local notables, including Muhammad 'Abid Husain (d. 1912), who would later play an important role in raising money for the new madrasa.[32] The town of Deoband was well placed for locating a new madrasa, situated close to the *qasbahs* from which its early supporters and teachers came. The Madrasa Islamiyya at Deoband, as it was called at first, was formally inaugurated in the Chatta Masjid on 15 Muharram 1283, corresponding to 30 May 1866.[33] (In 1879, the name was changed to Dar al-'Ulum Deoband.)[34] Some of the innovations that Nanautvi proposed were fiercely opposed at first: 'Abid Husain came out against the idea of the madrasa having its own separate building and wanted to continue at Chatta Masjid, but Nanautvi convinced him other-wise—a strikingly novel innovation, since madrasas were traditionally located in mosques or in family homes.[35] In 1874, Nanautvi moved forward with plans to purchase land near the Chatta Masjid for a new campus.[36] Muhammad Ya'qub was the first head teacher (*sadr mudarris*) of Deoband, serving in that role from 1866 to 1886. Like Gangohi and

Nanautvi, he too studied at Delhi College with Mamluk 'Ali, his father, and was known for his mastery of Hadith studies. Like them, he also became a Sufi disciple of Hajji Imdad Allah. And like many other graduates of Delhi College, he went first to a government position, teaching at Government College in Ajmer.[37] The familiarity of Deoband's founding figures with British educational and governmental institutions was evident in the array of "modern" features in this madrasa.

A "MODERN" MADRASA

The Dar al-'Ulum Deoband is a particularly renowned madrasa in a long history of Islamic educational institutions, going back at least to the tenth century, when the first madrasa originated in Khurasan. The madrasa subsequently spread to Baghdad by the mid–eleventh century, to Cairo in the late twelfth century, and eventually to India by the early thirteenth century.[38] In time the madrasa became, along with the Sufi lodge (*khanqah*), the most recognizable and near ubiquitous institution of medieval Islamic society.

Traditionally, madrasas' principally oral mode of learning centered around the memorization of texts. This does not mean that these texts were somehow frozen; instead, as Michael Chamberlain elegantly expressed it, they were "enacted fortuitously in time," and could thus be invoked to serve various needs in various contexts.[39] In the medieval madrasa there was no set curriculum, no slate of exams; students who mastered a given text would get an *ijaza*, a certificate permitting them to transmit those texts in turn. Indeed, during this period it was less important "*where* an individual studied" than "with *whom* one had studied," a system that "remained throughout the medieval period fundamentally personal and informal, and consequently, in many ways, flexible and inclusive."[40] And since they did not charge tuition, madrasas typically depended on charitable endowments (*awqaf*) to sustain themselves.

The Dar al-'Ulum Deoband changed all of this, even as Deobandi scholars sought to retain key features of the oral economy of the transmission of Islamic learning, as chapter 3 elaborates in more detail. Over the course of several years after 1866, Deoband's founders implemented a number of novel innovations: a fixed program of study (based on the Nizami curriculum, discussed below), a slate of exams to gauge students' progress, formal graduation ceremonies, a central library, a salaried faculty, and purpose-built structures for study and instruction, as opposed to mosques or homes. Students would come to Deoband, in theory, not to study with a specific *person*—though the renown of specific scholars *did* attract students from far and wide—but to study *at Deoband* as an institution. In these respects, it bore more resemblance to British colleges in India than the classical madrasa. Indeed, Barbara Metcalf argued that it was at Delhi College that Nanautvi witnessed the advantages of the British administrative approach to educational institutions—ironic given the lengths to which early Deobandis sought to avoid British influence in virtually all other spheres of Muslim public life.[41]

But it was the founders' conscientious decision to rely on individual donations, rather than political or courtly patronage, that most distinguished it as a "modern" madrasa. In the older system of patronage, a donor (*waqif*) was typically rooted in a specific neighborhood or town, was affiliated with a specific family, and knew the beneficiaries of his or her donation.[42] By contrast, Deoband began with a handful of tiny donations from local Muslims. In one narrative told of Deoband's origins, after dawn prayers at the Chatta Masjid, Muhammad 'Abid Husain, who would later become Deoband's first chancellor (*muhtamim*), made a pouch from a handkerchief and went around the neighborhood collecting donations: two rupees here, five rupees there. As a historian of the Dar al-'Ulum observed, "It was strange and novel indeed to establish an educational institution with public donations ['*awammi chande*] that would be free from the influence of the government."[43] Metcalf rightly saw the "participation of people with no kin ties and the system of popular financing" as the twin pillars of the Deobandi approach.[44]

The Dar al-'Ulum was, notably, not a charitable endowment (*waqf*).[45] Nanautvi himself made this a centerpiece of his vision for the institution. In his founding principles for the Dar al-'Ulum, Nanautvi stipulated, first and foremost, that "as much as possible, the workers of the madrasa should always seek to increase donations," and to seek them from the "commoners" (*'awamm*), who would receive divine blessing (*baraka*) for their donations. He urged future leaders of the institution to avoid "assured income," noting the "harms of patronage from the government and the affluent."[46] This model, dependent on individual donors, was easily replicable. The second seminary based on the Deobandi model, Mazahir al-'Ulum, in Saharanpur, was founded a mere six months after the Dar al-'Ulum Deoband.[47] Muhammad 'Abid, meanwhile, remained active in soliciting funds for a new congregational (*jami'*) mosque, begun in 1870, that would accommodate the seminary's growing number of students. This was significant both because the mosque was built with individual donations, and because it broke with the precedent of having only one congregational mosque per city: Deoband already had one, built in the early sixteenth century—a mosque whose Friday *khatib* was appointed by the ruler, a political context that no longer applied after 1857.[48]

It is for all these reasons that Margrit Pernau calls Deoband a "project of the emerging middle class," in which the ongoing importance of birth and lineage was complemented by "piety, asceticism and a willingness to work hard."[49] What Pernau also calls the "privatization of the *ulama*" was premised, in part, on breaking those relationships of patronage and reconstituting the madrasa as a "private" space—but "private" only insofar as it was independent of the state.[50] As the third chapter shows, these "private" *'ulama* were intimately involved in the constitution of new publics. I argue, however, that this valorization of lay Muslim patronage and rejection of government and courtly support are twin manifestations of a broader trend in how the Deobandi *'ulama* began to understand themselves as custodians of lay Muslim sensibilities rather than professionals in the service of the state. This, in turn, depended on etching out a purely "religious" space for the madrasa itself.

CONCEPTUALIZING "RELIGIOUS" KNOWLEDGE, MAKING "RELIGIOUS" EXPERTS

There were other dimensions of the Dar al-'Ulum Deoband that were deeply entangled with colonial modernity. The very idea of the *'ulama* as exclusively (or near exclusively) "religious" professionals was fairly novel. There are antecedents for this notion in the premodern period, of course. As early as the Delhi Sultanate, Zia al-Din Barani (d. 1357) distinguished between the "otherworldly" *'ulama* (*'ulama-yi akhirat*) and those who opted for a "worldly" career (*'ulama-yi duniya*).[51] But under the Delhi sultans, the principal function of madrasas was educating scholars for state employment.[52] The Mughals, too, patronized Islamic educational institutions, which trained the *'ulama* to become civic officials. The most well known example of this mutually dependent relationship between Mughal administration and the *'ulama* was Farangi Mahall, a family of scholars named after the residence (*mahall*) in Lucknow, given to the family by the Mughal emperor Aurangzeb (d. 1707), that had been previously occupied by a wealthy European (*farang*). A member of this family, Mulla Nizam al-Din (d. 1748), created the Dars-i Nizamiyya (the Nizami curriculum) in the early eighteenth century, stressing the rational sciences (*ma'qulat*) to prepare young *'ulama* for work in the civil administration of new princely states that emerged in the wake of the post-Aurangzeb fragmentation of Mughal power.[53] The *ma'qulat* included subjects such as logic (*mantiq*), philosophy (*hikmat*), dialectical theology (*kalam*), rhetoric, and astronomy, distinguishing them from the "transmitted" sciences (*manqulat*)—Hadith studies, Qur'an exegesis (*tafsir*), and Islamic law (*fiqh*). As Mulla Nizam al-Din designed it, the Nizami curriculum contained only one work on Hadith: the *Mishkat al-masabih*.[54]

Scholars during this period did not see the *manqulat* and *ma'qulat* as rival discourses of knowledge—let alone seeing the one as "religious" and the other as "secular," as Yoginder Sikand has noted—but as complementary parts of the same whole.[55] This complementarity has roots that stretch back long before the colonial period, as Jamal Malik observes. Ibn Khaldun (d. 1406), for one, distinguished between "traditional" (*naqliyya*) sciences (studies of the Qur'an and Sunna) and "philosophical" (*'aqliyya*) sciences. While emphasizing the *manqulat*, Shah Wali Allah, too, believed the *ma'qulat* allowed scholars to "strengthen faith through rational proofs," in Malik's words.[56] While the two are conceptually distinct, Ebrahim Moosa has rightly noted their deep interdependence. Architects of the Nizami curriculum understood the *ma'qulat* to provide the intellectual resources for comprehending the *manqulat*.[57] The *ma'qulat* were regarded to be useful for training individuals for careers in administration because they developed critical intellectual skills. One historian of Islamic education in India argues that the whole point of the *ma'qulat* was "exercising the mind" (*zehni mashq*).[58] Philosophy and logic were not studied as ends in themselves, but were understood by the *'ulama* as "tools" for "mental exercise" (*zehni varzish*).[59]

In Deoband's early years, Nanautvi seems to give this complementarity at least partial credence. In 1873, he wrote that a student at the Dar al-'Ulum would "attain proficiency in all the rational and transmitted sciences [*'ulum-i 'aqliyya o naqliyya*]. God willing, they will have the capacities to acquire all the ancient and modern sciences [*'ulum-i qadima aur jadida*]. The reason for this is that in these madrasas ... religious knowledge alone is insufficient. Rather, we also deal with subjects that hone the intellect, just as in previous times."[60] This is not a view shared by Nanautvi's principal co-collaborator in the founding of Deoband, Rashid Ahmad Gangohi. For Gangohi, the *manqulat* was not only properly "religious" knowledge but the *only* knowledge worth knowing. He dismissed the *ma'qulat* as useless, if not dangerous. When he became *sarparast* ("patron," in a spiritual rather than financial sense) of the Dar al-'Ulum in 1879, following Nanautvi's death, Gangohi began to shape the Deobandi curriculum according to his vision.

Born in 1829 in the northern Indian village of Gangoh, Gangohi went to Delhi in his youth to study Hadith with the prominent Hadith scholar Shah 'Abd al-Ghani (d. 1878). He was also a Sufi master of the Chishti and Naqshbandi orders.[61] The next two chapters examine Gangohi's work in detail.[62] For now, I wish to underscore how Gangohi left his mark on the Deoband movement in his insistence that the *manqulat* take precedence over the *ma'qulat*, to the near complete exclusion of the latter.[63] Gangohi's distaste for the rational sciences was famous. Gangohi once tried to convince his Sufi disciple Khalil Ahmad Saharanpuri to leave his post at a madrasa after it introduced philosophy and astronomy, but relented when he learned that Saharanpuri would not have to teach it.[64] Gangohi himself completed the entire Nizami curriculum as a student in Delhi, including all the subjects that were customary at the time: logic, philosophy, mathematics, astronomy. But when he began teaching, he abandoned the rational sciences, seeing them as sources of "unbelief and associating God with others" (*kufr o shirk*). Gangohi once explained to a student that the *ma'qulat* was rife with statements that would invoke God's anger when uttered, even by those who did not believe a word of them. The student protested, however: "But sir, what can we do? We are compelled [to study them], for without them we will not get jobs." Gangohi replied, "If someone offered you a hundred rupees a month to carry a basket of outhouse waste back and forth across the bazaar, would your dignity permit you to take this job?" The student was evidently silenced.[65] This was not merely a matter of dignity, however. The possibility that a student might inadvertently utter a statement of infidelity (*kufr*) was a matter of salvation or damnation. It was for similar reasons that he discouraged Muslim parents in Saharanpur from sending their children to schools run by Christian ministers because the students were expected to read Christian books and sing hymns. In an 1883 fatwa, drawing on Hanafi scholar Ibn 'Abidin, Gangohi argued that deliberately expressing a statement of unbelief (*kalimat-i kufr*), even in jest, rendered one an unbeliever (*kafir*). Even parents who allowed children to attend such schools were toying recklessly with unbelief, he said, reasoning from a principle in Mulla 'Ali al-Qari's (d. 1606) commentary on the Hanafi *Fiqh al-akbar*: "Approving of *kufr* is itself *kufr*" (*al-rida bi-l kufr kufrun*). His point is simply that words have ontological consequences—whether they are proclaimed in a missionary school or a madrasa—and thus Muslims needed to approach the rational sciences with the utmost circumspection.[66]

Changing British policies toward the patronage of Muslim scholars was yet another context for this new validation of "religious" knowledge over "rational" knowledge. Initially, the British took over the patronage that had begun to wane with the decline of Mughal power. They relied extensively on native munshis (scribes) literate in Persian, the administrative and literary language of the Mughal empire.[67] When Muslims in Calcutta petitioned Warren Hastings, governor-general of Bengal, to establish the Calcutta Madrasa in 1780, they did so by reminding him that the nawabs of Bengal, who preceded the British, had patronized Islamic learning. Hastings was motivated in supporting Muslim learning by both the expediency of rule and an admiration for "Oriental" learning and culture. As Thomas Metcalf put it, it was a "mixture of scholarly curiosity and administrative convenience."[68]

But as numerous scholars have shown, Hastings's patronage was also bound up with his belief that Muslims and Hindus needed to be governed by their own texts, for which the 'ulama and Hindu pandits would serve as intermediaries and interpreters. Hastings's vision was first articulated in the Judicial Plan of 1772, which stipulated that "the laws of the Koran with respect to Mahometans and those of the Shaster with respect to Gentoos [Hindus] shall be invariably adhered to," even though they did not yet understand the extent to which Islamic law was based on more than the Qur'an, nor, as Rosane Rocher points out, did they "know the extent of the content of the shastra (canonical literature), nor were they familiar with Sanskrit."[69] Still, this reflected the idea that India's people were intrinsically religious and were therefore to be governed by their scriptures. As East India Company merchant Thomas Twining put it, "[T]he people of India are not a political, but a religious people. . . . *They* think as much of their religion as *we* of our Constitution. *They* venerate their Shastah and Koran with as much enthusiasm as *we* our Magna Charta."[70]

The belief that Indians are inherently religious implied, for many, that the East India Company ought to support religious institutions as a key mechanism of governance.[71] This "Orientalist" position, insisting that the British should actively promote Islamic learning and the Persian language as a means of creating imperial functionaries, prevailed until it was eclipsed by the "Anglicist" position in the 1830s, which saw Islamic (and Hindu) learning as utterly inferior to European learning.[72]

Drawing on support from evangelicals and utilitarians, this position was exemplified most famously by the oft-cited Minute of Macaulay in 1835. The most vocal critic of the Orientalist position was Charles Trevelyan, who inveighed against government support for Arabic and Persian, calling for the swift replacement of instruction in these languages with English:

> Buried under the obscurity of Sanskrit and Arabic erudition, mixed up with the dogmas of religion, and belonging to two concurrent systems made up of the dicta of sages of different ages and schools, the laws are at present in the highest degree uncertain, redundant, and contradictory. . . . The expositors of the law are the muftis and pundits; men, who deeply imbued with the spirit of the ancient learning to which they are devoted, live only in past ages, and are engaged in a perpetual struggle to maintain the connection between the barbarism of antiquity and the manners and opinions of the present time. Their oracular responses are too often the result of ignorance, pedantry, or corruption.[73]

The Deoband movement responded to the destruction of patronage networks with a new discourse of authenticity, centered on reconstituting "severed" links to medieval disciplines of learning and the moral life of the individual Muslim. Carl Ernst describes this process as a shift "from a local inflection of universalist Islamicate learning under aristocratic patronage to a defensive posture of authenticity articulated by a new class of religious scholars under the pressure of foreign colonial rule."[74] The transition was not immediate, and never uniform. Gangohi's biography is full of stories about Sufi disciples of his who studied at Deoband and then went on to work in civil administration. At one point he mused, "When we were students, anyone who studied Arabic would be highly valued for the top administrative posts." Gangohi's uncle pressured him to take a government post, but relented when he "realized I would never agree to work for the British."[75]

The shift away from employing the ʿulama as scribes and administrative personnel is essential for understanding the concomitant shift *toward* the new, self-appointed role of the ʿulama as stewards of public morality, exemplified by the Deobandis but evident among their rivals as well. However, I do not wish to suggest that precolonial ʿulama were unconcerned with public morality, in India or elsewhere. The role of the inspector of markets (*muhtasib*) would be one such example. Kristen Stilt demonstrates how the Mamluk-era *muhtasib* was essentially the public face of the law, "as much a part of the legal landscape as the judge or mufti," tasked not only with ensuring fair and equitable trade but also with making sure market patrons attended congregational prayer and maintained the fast during Ramadan.[76] In India, the *muhtasib* under Aurangzeb policed public behavior such as wine drinking and gambling.[77] The difference between these efforts and those of the Deobandis was that the latter were mediated by a new print culture, as will see in chapter 3.

THE SHIFTING TERRAIN OF ISLAMIC LAW

But the other major impact of the end of British patronage was that it left a vacuum in the administration of Islamic law. In the decades before the founding of Deoband, the British ceased to patronize Islamic learning and began to regard a madrasa education as "useless" knowledge, precisely as Deobandis began to defend the madrasa as a purely "religious" institution and Islamic learning as valuable precisely *because* it did not serve the utilitarian calculus of the state; indeed, they said, learning was an act of worship that led to one's salvation in the next world. At the same time, a parallel process emerged: as the Orientalist argument for governing Muslims according to their (ostensibly) sacred texts gave way to the Anglicist argument of governing according to British laws and norms, so, too, did that shift create a space in which the Islamic law itself was reimagined—never completely, I note below—as a moral discourse of reform rather than a juridical process located in the courts of qazis (judges), which had effectively ceased to exist.[78]

We can further understand how the British sought to govern "natives" through their respective texts by detailing how that philosophy of rule affected Islamic law. As noted above, the British aimed to rely principally on what they deemed "canonical" texts, which they regarded as more reliable than actual "native" experts on those texts. The East India Company regarded the traditionally fluid and context-specific nature of Islamic law to be fickle and unreliable (even though fatwas would be solicited by, and used in, British criminal courts until 1832, when their use was abolished).[79] Thus, in 1778, East India Company judge and famed Orientalist scholar William Jones (d. 1794) called for a "complete Digest of Hindu and Mohammedan laws, after the model of Justinian's inestimable Pandects," one that would make the "Pandits and Maulavis" superfluous. At first, Jones proposed relying on the *Fatawa-yi Alamgiri*, a primer on Hanafi law compiled under the Mughal emperor Aurangzeb (d. 1707).[80] But ultimately the *Hidaya* ("Guidance"), an abbreviated manual on Hanafi law by the twelfth-century Transoxianan jurist Marghinani

(d. 1197), became the basis of what the British called "Anglo-Muhammadan law." Marghinani never purported to summarize Hanafi law in toto, but only to provide a convenient primer for Hanafi law in his time and place.[81]

But the text's concision and brevity were precisely the qualities that attracted the architects of Anglo-Muhammadan law. In Charles Hamilton's introduction to his 1791 translation of the *Hidaya,* he posited, at once, the immutability of Islamic law's textual sources *and* the fickle caprice of the Muslim jurists who interpret them:

> [I]t is impossible, in the infinite variety of human affairs, that the text of the KORAN, or the traditionary precepts of the Prophet, would extend to every particular case, or strictly suit all possible emergencies. Hence the necessity of *Mooftees,* whose particular office it is to compound the law and apply it to cases. The *uncertainty* of this science, in its judicial operation, is unhappily proverbial in all countries. In some, which enjoy the advantage of an established legislature, competent at all times to alter or amend, to make or revoke laws, as the change of manners may require, or incidental occurrences render necessary, this uncertainty arises pretty much from the unavoidable mutability in the principles of decision. Of the *Mussulman* code, on the contrary, the principles are fixed; and being intimately and inseparably blended with the religion of the people, must remain so, as long as they shall endure.[82]

Thus the British saw Islamic law as at once too rigid (a "code") *and* too loose, fixed by "ancient" texts but haphazardly applied by its specialists.[83] Hamilton concludes that the "*Mussulman* code" is so "intimately blended with their religion that any attempts to change the former would be felt by them as a violation of the latter."[84]

The British quest for uniformity and universalism undermined the context-specific nuance and flexibility of Islamic law in part by introducing "the state" as a legal entity in Islamic legal proceedings. Governor Hastings was appalled that Hanafi law permitted relatives of a murder victim to pardon the perpetrator or to claim blood money. It was "a law of barbarous construction, and contrary to the first principle of civil society, by which the state acquires an interest in every member which composes it, and a right in his security."[85] In this manner, the British reformulated Islamic criminal law from a conflict between two parties to a conflict between a defendant and the state.[86] There were yet other ways they changed Islamic criminal law. British jurists found Islamic evidentiary standards too strict, they rejected the requirement that witnesses be of "upright" (*'adl*) reputation, and they strongly favored incarceration over corporal punishment.[87] But above all, they sought to reorient Islamic law around the principle of relying on the precedent of prior legal decisions (*stare decisis*), utterly foreign to Islamic legal reasoning.[88] We see this especially in post-1857 efforts to isolate and remove "native lawyers" (i.e. muftis) and rely instead on the decision of courts. The English barrister William Morley argued, in 1858, that India's laws needed to be restructured around this principle: "In no instance is the maxim '*stare decisis*' so imperative . . . as when applied to the laws administered in India."[89] In 1860—just six years before the Dar al-'Ulum Deoband would be founded—the Indian Penal Code abolished the last vestige of Islamic criminal law.[90] By 1864, even "native lawyers" were no longer consulted; for the time being, English judges would consult the texts directly without the help of Muslim jurists.[91] (Deobandi fatwas, meanwhile, show that the Dar al-'Ulum's muftis could tolerate the idea of a non-Muslim *appointing* a Muslim judge, but the judge himself had to be a Muslim; a British judge would not do.)[92] What Hallaq has called "the rigidification of Islamic law," an "attempt to remold Islamic law in the image of the concision, clarity, and accessibility" of English law, was more or less complete.[93] This does not mean, of course, that such a system functioned well. Realizing that "the presence of Kazis . . . is required at the celebration of marriages and the performance of certain other rites and ceremonies," the government passed the Kazis Act of 1880, once again permitting the government to appoint qazis, first in Madras and later, by 1894, in the North-Western Provinces, the heartland of the Deoband movement.[94] There is little evidence, however, that many qazis were actually appointed. The fact that, as late as 1933, Ashraf 'Ali Thanvi petitioned the government to appoint qazis in every district to adjudicate divorces for women trapped in unhappy marriages but without recourse to a judge suggests a persistent dearth of qazis.[95]

For all intents and purposes, nevertheless, the absence of a full-fledged legal apparatus created a vacuum that Deobandis sought to fill by giving legal advice directly to individual Muslims through fatwas.[96] By the mid to late nineteenth century, muftis began to issue legal opinions on the authority of a particular madrasa.[97] They also issued fatwas in substantially larger numbers than previously through the widespread use of print. The Dar al-'Ulum Deoband established a Dar al-Ifta' in 1892, whose "main goal was religious education of the masses so that common Muslims could understand legal issues [*masa'il-i shar'iyya*]," even though, as we will see in chapter 3, Deobandis also debated how much the masses should know.[98] But famous muftis issued their own collected volumes of fatwas, which, like all texts at this time, benefited from the availability of mass printing. Rashid Ahmad Gangohi's collection, in particular, was critical in establishing the juro-ethical stance of the Deobandis on a variety of issues. Fatwas were traditionally solicited by qazis; now they were solicited primarily by individual Muslims, as well as some fellow 'ulama, who sent renowned 'ulama like Gangohi their questions about proper belief and practice. The fatwa became a tool of mass moral reform, "a form of the care of the self," linking "selves to the broader practices, virtues, and aims" of Islamic tradition.[99]

And unlike muftis of the past, Gangohi and his generation of muftis rarely cited works of fiqh, and often gave their fatwas without any explanation of their legal reasoning at all, typically providing nothing more than a relevant quotation from the Qur'an or Hadith. Gangohi would provide legal reasoning in proportion to the learning of the one who requested the fatwa, depending on whether it was requested by a lay Muslim or one of the 'ulama. "Gangohi's proficiency in deriving and extracting rulings on legal issues [masa'il] was incomparable in his day," his biographer writes, and "it was his practice to issue fatwas in accordance with the understanding of the person requesting it. Whether to commoners ['awamm], the elite [khawass], or the ignorant [juhala'], he wrote and spoke to all according to their proficiencies and capacities."[100] One could argue that the very lack of juristic reasoning in these fatwas points to their broad audience, who would have had presumably little use for such reasoning.

"USEFUL" SECULAR KNOWLEDGE, "USELESS" RELIGIOUS KNOWLEDGE

In the Religious Endowments Act (Act XX) of 1863, the government formally divested itself of any control over "religious" endowments or institutions—with some initial legal ambiguity about what constituted "religion" from the vantage of the state. It mandated that the government "divest itself of the management of Religious Endowments" and relinquished any control over religious endowments' finances or leadership, but reserved the right to continue supervision of the "secular" aspects of any endowment that was "partly of a religious and partly of a secular character."[101] The act was intended to replace the Bengal Regulation XIX of 1810 and the Madras Regulation VII of 1817, in which the Board of Revenue effectively served as patron of temples and mosques—regulations that came under fire from evangelicals who criticized the idea that the British should be actively involved in patronizing "heathen" religious institutions. Nile Green has argued that the state's retreat from involvement in "religious" affairs created a vacuum that was filled (always tenuously) by a new religious "marketplace."[102] Thus, we can understand the period from 1780 to 1863 as one in which the British effectively replaced Mughals in patronizing Muslim law and education, and then gradually created a vacuum by *withdrawing* that support, culminating in the 1863 Religious Endowments Act.[103]

It was not only legally and discursively that Deobandis came to see the madrasa as a space impervious to state intrusion. It was also physically removed. As mentioned, while Deoband was only a train ride away from Delhi, the *qasbah* certainly afforded Deobandis less scrutiny than they would have had in the city that would soon become, by 1911, the imperial capital. Deoband was largely beyond the radar of colonial surveillance until the early twentieth century, insofar as it occupied a sphere of "religion" that had already been "rendered distinct from 'politics.'"[104] The colonial archive reflects the relative indifference of the state toward Deoband, until Deobandi *'ulama* became actively involved in anticolonial politics. When the Dar al-'Ulum Deoband *did* come under scrutiny for the political activities of several prominent Deobandi scholars—a subject to which I return in the final chapter—the institution tried to deflect such attention by reassuring British officials that the institution was purely "religious" and not at all "political." As Deobandi scholars began to support the civil disobedience movement of Gandhi, the British pressured the Nizam of Hyderabad, who had begun contributing annually to the institution beginning in 1887, to discontinue his support.[105] In response, no less a political figure than Husain Ahmad Madani, then head teacher (*sadr mudarris*) of Deoband, wrote:

> I have to state that the Dar-ul-Ulum School, from the time it was brought into being, devoted its attention *solely to imparting religious teaching* and the propagation of the Muhammadan religion. It silently did its duty in this field. . . . In these days when political and other movements grew in India, the Jamiat-ul-Ulma declared the policy of the Dar-ul-Ulum on platforms and by means of articles published in various newspapers. The local Officers and the Governor of the Provinces were appraised that the Dar-ul-Ulum adhered to its old policy of keeping *aloof from politics,* and confined its activities only to imparting religious teaching, and so far as it could be imagined, no suspicion attached to the working of its Dar-ul-Ulum and to the policy it followed.[106]

This was, to be sure, a strategy on Madani's part to deflect suspicion away from Deoband, but it points to a larger assumption about the madrasa as an "apolitical" space. By the early twentieth century, then, it seems, the mutual exclusivity of religion and politics was self-evident. Deobandis not only promoted their institution as purely "religious," but the memory of it ever being anything *but* religious had become blurry. Thus, Maulvi Rahim Bakhsh of Bhawalpur concluded, after a visit to Deoband in 1908, that "the instruction in this seminary, in accordance with the *older style of the East,* is *purely religious [khalis mazhabi]*"—even though this "style" was, in fact, quite new.[107]

The transition of the *'ulama* from "worldly" state-employed professionals to "otherworldly" religious experts is mirrored in the transition from a madrasa education as "useful" knowledge to "useless" knowledge. That is, as a madrasa education was rebranded as "religious," it ceased to be "useful." The discourse on useful knowledge goes back to the origins of the British presence in the subcontinent. The very first sentence of Hamilton's translation of the *Hidaya* is an encomium for empire, praising it for "the diffusion of useful knowledge."[108] But it is especially the product of utilitarians' critiques of Indian learning generally, and their fierce opposition to supporting "Hindoo" and "Mahomedan" institutions of learning specifically. The Education Despatch of 1854 was perhaps the definitive call for supplementing, if not replacing, "Asiatic learning" with "useful" knowledge. It was nothing less than "one of our sacred duties to [confer] upon the natives of India those vast moral and material blessings which flow from the general diffusion of useful knowledge, and which India may, under Providence, derive from her connexion with England."[109] But this attitude had already borne real consequences for decisions surrounding the funding and patronage of Islamic educational institutions. Thirty years before the Despatch, James Mill lambasted the use of government funds for "native" colleges in an 1824 letter to the revenue department: "The great end should not have been to teach Hindoo learning or Mahomedan learning, but useful learning." In establishing "[s]eminaries for the purpose of teaching mere Hindoo, or mere Mahomedan literature," he continued, "you bound yourselves to teach a great deal of what was frivolous, not a little of what was purely mischievous, and a small remainder indeed in which utility was in any way concerned."[110] With the retreat of British patronage under way, Muslims in Calcutta pleaded in 1835 to keep the Calcutta Madrasa open, defending madrasa education as "useful" precisely *because* it would lead to government work. They praised the British for their support of "kazee[s]," for the use of "futwahs in trials," and defended the Madrasa on the Anglicist's terms:

"Through the establishment of the Mudrissa, many students are annually instructed in *useful knowledge,* and thence proceeding into the interior obtain high appointments in the cities and zillahs [districts] of Hindoostan."[111]

Despite such pleas, support for madrasas diminished and madrasa education was increasingly condemned as "useless" *because* it was essentially religious. Colonial authorities believed that *primary*-level religious education (e.g., in village *maktabs*) could be the basis of overcoming Muslims' "backwardness" and forming loyal subjects, so long as it taught a mix of "religious" and "secular" subjects.[112] In December 1867, a little over a year after the madrasa at Deoband was founded, the British government approved a grant of fifty rupees per month to the Mahomedan Female School in Bangalore "on condition that the ordinary branches of secular knowledge should be regarded as an essential part of the education course in that institution," insisting on "secular reading and writing" in addition to "Alcoran."[113] Even this concession to religious subjects was too much for some British administrators. In June 1858, a director of public education in the Punjab reported going through "all the old Persian books . . . prohibiting everything which is grossly indecent on one ground, and everything which pertains to religion on another ground." The same director criticized the local policy of hiring teachers from madrasas to teach in newly established public schools, and providing funds for schools connected to mosques: "[W]hile proclaiming our principle of religious neutrality, and our desire to spread secular education, we [are] propagating Muhammadanism." Accordingly, he ordered "all village schools to be removed from the precincts of mosques and other buildings of a religious character [and] the disuse of all books of a religious character in the schools."[114] Here, secularity is defined partly through *subjects* of study, partly through *spaces* of study.

Madrasas that taught only "religious" subjects could not qualify for government support; hence an 1872 survey of the North-Western Provinces classified such schools as "indigenous (unaided)," meaning they received no government funding. Among the "indigenous" schools surveyed were the then-new seminaries of Dar al-'Ulum Deoband and Mazahir al-'Ulum Saharanpur.[115] In the same year, a commission led by Sayyid Ahmad Khan called for Muslims to establish schools where "useful knowledge might be taught along with religion."[116] But the madrasas of the "old system," the report averred, listing the Dar al-'Ulum Deoband as a prime example, were "altogether *useless* to the nation at large, and . . . no good can be expected from them."[117] The Indian Education

Commission of 1882 encouraged local Muslim schools (*maktabs*) to add "secular" subjects, but as late as 1892 a report in Bengal lamented that the "course of instruction" in such schools "does not go beyond the mere mechanical repetition of the Koran" and does not impart "any real practical education."[118]

In a searing indictment of this approach to "indigenous education," published in 1883, the Orientalist G. W. Leitner, the principal of Government College Lahore, argued that such disrespect for religious learning forced the *'ulama* to withdraw into enclaves defined principally by their distinction from "secular" education. Due to British meddling, the cultivation of "sacred classical languages" was monopolized by a "priestly class" who "withdrew into the background." "By the elimination of the priestly classes from our educational councils," he concludes, the British "introduced a social *bouleversement,* in which neither birth nor traditional rank, nor the reputation of piety, liberality, or courage, seemed to weigh with Government . . . against the apparently more practical usefulness of the supple *parvenus* who began to monopolise official favor."[119]

Leitner's view was not universal among his contemporaries. An 1885 report on the North-Western Provinces and Awadh concluded that "no special measures on behalf of Muhammadans are required, as Mussalman education in these provinces is by no means in a backward state."[120] Nevertheless, Leitner's diagnosis might illuminate why scholars like Gangohi "withdrew into the background" and saw the madrasa as just such an enclave. In a letter written in 1884, soon after becoming patron of Dar al-'Ulum and a year after Leitner's study was published, Rashid Ahmad Gangohi inverted the calculus of "useful knowledge," writing that it is, in fact, *philosophy*—an important feature of the *ma'qulat*— that is useless. "Philosophy is a useless thing. No conceivable benefit [*nafa'*] can be gained from it. Three or four years are wasted on its study. It dulls the minds of men and distracts from religious matters." "Thus," he goes on, "this wicked art has been removed from the madrasa and has not been taught at the Deoband madrasa in the last year," though he surmises that some teachers continued to teach it clandestinely.[121] If Gangohi is correct, the shift away from the *ma'qulat* at Deoband was abrupt indeed, for as Leitner himself observed, the Deoband curriculum still included numerous works on logic, astronomy, geometry, and mathematics as late as 1882.[122] Other Deobandis, too, proudly defended the anti-utilitarianism of the madrasa. Khalil Ahmad Saharanpuri's relatives wanted him to learn English and get a position in the government. "God saved me from learning English and gave me the fortune of religious knowledge [*'ilm-i din*]," he declared.[123] In an essay written in 1912, Ashraf 'Ali Thanvi, likewise, concluded that the madrasa should be "a purely religious school. It should neither be influenced by, nor mixed with, worldly concerns," for to mix "worldly and religious aims would ultimately lead to a worldly orientation."[124]

The point is that Thanvi was already operating in a colonial episteme in which a religious/secular binary was hegemonic, for even attempts to describe the mutual imbrication of the "religious" and the "secular" in *pre*-colonial Muslim education were bound by the inevitable recourse to that binary. As a 1936 study of Islamic education before the British put it: "Education was regarded as a preparation for life *and* for life after death. Hence it was that religion was at the root of all study: Every *maktab* and *madrasah* had a mosque attached to it, and in every mosque there were separate classes for the instruction of students in sciences other than religious, so that secular instruction might go hand in hand with religious instruction."[125] Noting that the secular and religious go "hand in hand" still presupposes the distinction itself.

Muslims in India and elsewhere, of course, have pushed back against such a stark epistemic breach between the religious and the secular in Muslim education. In 1927, the British convert to Islam Marmaduke Pickthall castigated madrasas that shun "modern" knowledge under the pretext of calling it "secular," for, in his view, Islam reveres *all* knowledge as "religious." "Most Muslims nowadays speak of religious education as something quite apart from education as a whole, as if it meant the teaching of Fiqh [law] only," he wrote. "From the proper Muslim standpoint, all education is alike religious. . . . In a real Muslim school, there would be no separate 'religious' education. . . . No terms such as 'secular' and 'religious' exist in proper Muslim phraseology."[126]

From a historical perspective, Pickthall had a point. As Muhammad Qasim Zaman has shown, while the notion of "useful" (*nafi'*) knowledge certainly has some precedent in medieval Islamic societies, the notion of the madrasa as "purely religious" does not. It is an "eminently modern" one with "little precedent in medieval Islamic societies."[127] It is, I would argue, an example of how the discourse of modernity *produces* its other. As Ebrahim Moosa argues, "The very success of the secular public square anticipates and requires the emergence of an exclusive religious sphere. Hence the madrasas fill that exclusive religious sphere with consummate ease and enable the discourse of individual religious salvation to morph into identity politics."[128] Just as the first Deobandis conceived of the madrasa as a "religious" space set against colonial secularity and considered themselves as "religious" experts, whose signature distinction was the mastery of knowledge for which colonial authorities had no use, they also looked beyond the madrasa to emergent publics of lay Muslims whose salvation they took it upon themselves to safeguard. That is the subject of the next two chapters.

2

The Normative Order

The previous chapter examined how the *ulama* of the Deoband movement conceptualized the madrasa as an enclave of religious knowledge
and the *ulama* as custodians of Muslim public life, tasked with filling
the political and legal void left by the decline of Muslim power in India
and reviving Indian Islam by revitalizing the religious lives of individuals. In this sense, the "inward turn" that Barbara Metcalf and Francis
Robinson have described is only half of the story.[1] The other half, the
story of the next two chapters, is a simultaneous *outward turn* toward
emergent Muslim publics. Deobandi scholars sought to harness new lay
Muslim readers of Urdu to their project of reforming Muslim subjectivities. But this new public of readers was also situated within, and
partly intersected with, a simultaneously emerging public of the colonial crowd. Before we examine these new publics in the following chapter, we will look in this chapter at why Deobandi scholars were compelled to turn outward in the first place.

This outward turn was fixated on maintaining what I call the normative order and vigorously critiquing perceived threats to it: innovation
in religious matters (*bid'a*), and beliefs or practices that compromise the
integrity of God's oneness (*shirk*). This chapter begins with a brief overview of the sources on which early Deobandis based their theorization
of *bid'a* and *shirk*. It then shows how and why they saw two major
devotional practices—the celebration of the Prophet Muhammad's

birthday, and various devotions that surrounded the tombs of Sufi saints—as the predominant sources of normative disorder.

THEORIZING THE NORMATIVE ORDER: *BID'A* AND *SHIRK*

For the Deobandis, there were two fundamental threats to the normative order revealed by God in the Qur'an and elaborated by the Prophet Muhammad in his words and deeds, the Sunna: illicit innovation in religion (*bid'a*), and associating God's divine qualities with other entities (*shirk*). They recognized two primary sites in Muslim public life where these dual theological dangers proliferated: devotions in praise of the Prophet Muhammad, and devotions on behalf of the Sufi saints.

Deobandis conceived of *bid'a* as altering, adding to, or subtracting from the *din*, a word usually translated as "religion" but which fundamentally connotes "debt" and "obligation"—a semantic range captured by Qur'anic references to the "day of judgment" (*yawm al-din*)—and which in time came to be understood as the sum total of ritual obligations that bind humans to God, as revealed by God in the Qur'an and elaborated through the Prophet's words and deeds (the Sunna): hence *din* as "religion."[2] *Bid'a* can also be understood as setting up any counternorm that competes with or simulates the normative order of the Qur'an and Sunna.[3] What makes *bid'a* insidious is that lay Muslims (the *'awamm*) confuse normativity, assuming for instance that nonobligatory aspects of religious practice are obligatory. This conception of *bid'a* has roots in the premodern period. The Andalusian jurist al-Turtushi (d. 1126), for example, worried that supererogatory fasting—completely permissible in principle—would lead lay Muslims to assume that it was obligatory, like the fasting during Ramadan.[4] We will see Ashraf 'Ali Thanvi make a similar comparison between obligatory and nonobligatory fasting below.[5] But though the idea has premodern roots, Deobandis became focused on *bid'a*—defining it, cataloging it, combating it—to an extent that has few, if any, premodern precedents.[6]

The second major threat to the normative order is *shirk* (from the Arabic root "to participate or associate"). *Shirk* is commonly thought of as polytheism, but that is not entirely accurate. Polytheism is, of course, an example of *shirk*, but one need not posit other gods besides God to commit *shirk*. Rather, *shirk* is the idea that any of God's attributes (e.g., God's knowledge) are "associated" with any entity other than God—for instance, the notion that a saint may have superhuman knowledge. Believing this does not make the saint a god as much as it makes the saint *godlike*. As we will see, a saint may *in fact* have superhuman knowledge, but that knowledge is granted by God. It is *believing* that the saint possesses that knowledge independently of God that is the hallmark of *shirk*. *Bid'a*, then, is a belief or practice that overlaps or competes with the *din*. *Shirk*, analogously, is to believe that some entity overlaps or competes with God's essence and attributes. *Bid'a* is to compromise the integrity of the *din*. *Shirk* is to compromise the integrity of *tawhid*, the oneness of God's divinity.

As mentioned above, the Deobandis were not the first to theorize *shirk* and *bid'a*. They were influenced by a number of scholars of the premodern era who wrote extensively on these issues. One of them was the Andalusian scholar Abu Ishaq Ibrahim al-Shatibi (d. 1388), whom the Deobandis read, studied, and cited.[7] Shatibi defined *bid'a* as "an invented path in religion that emulates the Shari'a and is intended to be followed in striving toward the obedience of God," or is "intended to be followed with the same intentions as the Shari'a."[8] Shatibi is clear that mere *newness* does not constitute *bid'a*, whether good or bad. For this reason, he rejects earlier definitions of *bid'a* that theorized it in terms of *temporality* rather than normativity—that is, as whatever came after the Prophet, as opposed to what simulates or competes with the *din*.[9] This is also the reason he rejects other scholars' classifications of *bid'a* into "good" (*hasana*) and "bad" (*sayyia*), a dichotomy that pre-supposes a temporally defined conception of *bid'a*. Deobandis, too, rejected this distinction as conceptually incoherent. "A *bid'a* can never be 'good' [*hasana*]," Gangohi wrote. "What you call 'good *bid'a*' is, in fact, the Sunna," by which Gangohi means something new that has been substantiated through the normative legal sources.[10] For Muhammad Shafi', too, the Hadith "All innovation [*bid'a*] is misguidance, and all misguidance is in the Fire" is ample scriptural evidence for discarding any notion of a "good" *bid'a*.[11]

What defines *bid'a*, for Shatibi and for the Deobandis who drew upon his work, is that it is an innovation *in* religion that also *resembles* religion—a distinction that Shatibi illustrates with his distinction between "real" (*haqiqi*) and "relative" (*idafi*) *bid'a*.[12] "Real" *bid'a* consisted of innovations that cannot be substantiated in any way through the four sources of law in Sunni jurisprudence: Qur'an, Sunna, consensus (*ijma'*), and analogy (*qiyas*). "Relative" *bid'a* consisted of acts that may be permissible (*mubah*) or even recommended (*mandub*) in one context, but become *bid'a* when people confuse their normative status—for example, by treating a merely permissible act as recommended. Raquel Ukeles described Shatibi's category of "relative" *bid'a* as "the gray area between *sunnah* and *bid'ah*" brought about by "changing an occasional practice to a regular practice, or an optional practice to a required practice."[13] The significance of this, for Deobandis generally and especially for Thanvi, cannot be overstated. The difference between "real" and "relative" *bid'a* might be thought of as the difference, as Thanvi once put it, between those who are "sacrilegious [*bad dini*] and disobedient [*mo'anid*]" in committing *bid'a*—that is, those who innovate intentionally and maliciously—and those who come from a place of "sincere" (*mukhlis*) motives, who innovate by accident.[14] The latter becomes, in many ways, more of a preoccupation of the Deobandis precisely because it insinuates its way into public life, often through the best of intentions.

Shatibi's normativity-based conception of *bid'a* is also the one elaborated by Muhammad Isma'il (d. 1831), by far the most important figure for understanding how Deobandis conceived of the normative order. As we will see, Gangohi, like other early Deobandis, referenced Muhammad Isma'il's works and urged his followers to read them. At the same time, Muhammad Isma'il's works challenged the very interpretive hierarchies on which the *'ulama* staked their claims to lead the masses toward salvation—in ways this chapter hopes to make clear.

Muhammad Isma'il was born in 1779 in Delhi into the Wali Allah family of scholars: his father was Shah 'Abd al-Ghani, one of Shah Wali Allah's sons. He received the standard religious education that others in his family received, but his life was changed irrevocably when in 1819 he met Sayyid Ahmad Barelvi (d. 1831), the foremost activist for Islamic revival in early-nineteenth-century India.[15] Born in 1786, Sayyid Ahmad was also close to the Wali Allah family, becoming Shah 'Abd al-'Aziz's Sufi disciple and student in 1806. From an early age, Sayyid Ahmad began to attract a following of Muslims anxious about the perceived decline of Indian Islam.[16] He preached across the Ganges Delta from 1818 to 1821 and took his scores of followers on the Hajj from 1821 to 1823.[17] Upon returning, he called for jihad against the Sikhs, who had banned the call to prayer in the Punjab and desecrated mosques.[18] In 1831 Sayyid Ahmad and Muhammad Isma'il were both killed fighting Sikhs at Balakot (in what is now northwestern Pakistan).[19]

Muhammad Isma'il's real impact, however, was in his writings, some of which are among the earliest examples of Urdu in print. He composed his work at the cusp of a shift from Persian to Urdu as the language of the Muslim elite, which would also become the primary language of

Deobandi works.[20] Muhammad Isma'il wrote his most important and widely read treatise, *Taqwiyyat al-iman* (Strengthening the faith), in "simple Urdu" (*salis Urdu*), from which "both the elites [*khawass*] and the commoners ['*awamm*] can derive some benefit."[21] These dual tropes of simple language beneficial to elite and commoner alike continue to animate Deobandi thought into the present.[22]

Much has been written about Muhammad Isma'il, and I intend to touch only on the two aspects of his legacy that are most important for understanding Deoband: first, his discourse on *bid'a* and *shirk;* and second, his radically populist hermeneutics, which called individual Muslims to reject any forms of authority other than the Qur'an and Sunna and to study the Qur'an and Hadith directly, without mediation by religious elites. I argue that the Deobandi project was animated by the former even as it tried to constrain the latter.

The argument of *Taqwiyyat al-iman,* written around 1824,[23] was deceptively simple but had immense repercussions for the religio-political imaginary of Muslims in British India: *tawhid,* the absolute unity of God, is diametrically opposed to *shirk,* associating another person or thing in any way with God. Isma'il identified four fundamental forms of *shirk:* association with God in knowledge (*ishrak fi-l 'ilm*), association with God in power (*ishrak fi-l tasarruf*), association with God in worship (*ishrak fi-l 'ibadat*), and association with God in matters of custom or everyday life (*ishrak fi-l 'adah*). Later Deobandi scholars would adapt this typology of *shirk* in their own works for lay Muslims.[24] "Association" with God in knowledge informed debates about whether the Prophet Muhammad has knowledge of the "unseen realm" (*ghayb*)— that is, suprahuman knowledge. "Association" with God in power led into debates about whether there are theoretical limits to God's sovereignty—namely, whether God could produce additional prophets of Muhammad's stature or even tell a lie, and whether to suggest that God is somehow *incapable* of doing so is itself akin to denying his limitless omnipotence. The last two categories are the most salient here: "association" with God in worship and in customary practices covered those Sufi practices that bore a dangerous similarity to the worship accorded solely to God, or customary practices that resembled acts sanctioned by the Sunna—such as the reverence bestowed upon the Prophet Muhammad during the *mawlud* or in the act of granting him salutations, or upon the Sufi saints during their death-anniversary festivities. *Shirk* is not simply polytheism: "*Shirk* is not simply to equate some entity with God or consider it on par with God. It is also *shirk* to see in entities other than God the attributes that God has specified for Himself, the acknowledgment of which is one of the marks of servanthood."[25] As a later Deobandi scholar, Muhammad Manzur Nu'mani, elaborated, it is God that has endowed medicine with the power to heal and water with the power to quench thirst. *Shirk* is, analogously, to believe that anything, even medicine, has an intrinsic power apart from God. *Shirk* is, in this sense, mis-assigning agency. It is the assumption that dead saints have agency, or that an amulet for curing an illness has agency, or that astrological predictions exercise agency over the future.[26]

If *shirk* is the preoccupation of *Taqwiyyat al-iman*, Muhammad Isma'il theorizes *bid'a* principally in other works, especially *Izah al-haqq fi ahkam al-mayyit wa al-darih* (Elucidating the truth about the rules concerning the dead and tombs). In the broadest sense, just as *shirk* is the opposite of *tawhid*, so *bid'a* is the opposite of the Sunna. Isma'il begins this text by citing a number of Hadiths pertaining to *bid'a*, including "Whoever innovates [*ahdatha*] something in this matter [*amr*] of ours that is not part of it will have it rejected." Isma'il says the two key words in this Hadith are "innovates" and "matter." "Innovation" describes anything that is utterly new. Like Shatibi, he calls *bid'a* only that which is both new and unable to be substantiated from the normative legal sources. As for "this matter of ours"—that refers to the *din*. From this we get a two-part conception of *bid'a* very similar to Shatibi's "real" and "relative" *bid'a*. The first he calls "literal *bid'a*" (*bid'a asli*), "anything that is invented [*muhadas*]." That is, in other words, the literal definition of something newly invented. "The second," which he calls "figurative *bid'a*" (*bid'a wasfi*), "is to add to, subtract from, or alter the form of the Shari'a."[27] The latter is the one about which he expressed the deepest concern, for a whole range of things—studies of Arabic grammar, or Sufi litanies (*adhkar*)—are not "parts of the religion" (*ajza' al-din*), but "if someone considers them to be part of the religion, that act necessarily becomes *bid'a for that person*."[28] Overall, then, Muhammad Isma'il conceived of *bid'a* in three ways: first, as a practice that directly opposes or invalidates the Sunna; second, as a practice done with the same intent or regularity as the Sunna but not part of it—in other words, creating a kind of false or counter-religion alongside the Sunna; and third, making anything non-obligatory obligatory, or vice versa.

Muhammad Isma'il initiated a comprehensive critique of all forms of earthly authority—so comprehensive, in fact, that it sidelined even the *'ulama*. The Qur'an and the Hadith alone, he believed, should be the sole sources of authority for Muslims. One can see Isma'il's exclusive reliance on the Qur'an and Hadith in the very structure of the book: each section begins with a brief quote from the Qur'an or Hadith, on which his radical critique of *bid'a* and *shirk* rests.

What is radically novel about Muhammad Isma'il's approach to the Qur'an and Hadith is the idea that they are transparently simple to understand and require no mediation, whether by the *'ulama* or by any other figures of authority. *Taqwiyyat al-iman* opens with a stunning passage worth reproducing at length:

> In the present age, people have chosen myriad paths. Some follow the customs of their ancestors, while some follow the ways of holy ones [*buzurg*]. Some offer the self-proclaimed sayings of the scholars [*'ulama*] as their proof, while some pry into religious matters under the pretext of using their intellect [*'aql*]. The best path is to refrain from meddling in what has been revealed [*naql*] with our intellect and, instead, take the Qur'an and Hadith, fountains that nourish the soul, as the standard by which to assess the sayings of the holy ones, the decisions of the *'ulama,* and the customs of one's community, accepting what conforms and rejecting what does not.
>
> It is common today for people to believe that the Qur'an and Hadith are difficult to understand and require a whole lot of knowledge, that we are so ignorant that we are unable to understand them and incapable of acting on them, and that only the saints [*awliya' Allah*] are capable of such acts. This is absolutely baseless, for God has said that the Holy Qur'an is clear and manifest: 'We have sent down to you verses that are clear proofs, and no one disbelieves them except the transgressors' [2:99]. Understanding this is not difficult, nay it is easy. *Acting* on it is difficult, because it is difficult to control the self [*nafs*], and thus the disobedient give it no credence. It is not necessary to have a lot of knowledge to understand the Qur'an and Hadith because the Messengers were sent to bring understanding to the ignorant and knowledge to those without it, as God says: 'It is He who sent among the illiterate a messenger of their own, who recites to them verses and purifies them, who teaches them the Book and Wisdom. Truly before this they were clearly in error.' [Qur'an 62:2] . . . If someone says that understanding the Qur'an is only for the *'ulama* and acting on it is only for the holy ones, then they trample upon this verse and disregard God's glorious bounties.[29]

There are several aspects of this passage worth noting here. First, the notion that the Qur'an is easy to understand was radical in its implications for individual Muslims. It opened the floodgates of a populist hermeneutics, dismissing the importance of both the intellect and scholarly experts in understanding the text. Of course, the Qur'an is not always easy to understand and even occasionally highlights its own opacity, hence the legal distinction between verses that are clear

(*muhkam*) and those that are ambiguous (*mutashabih*).[30] Later
Deobandis stressed that the Qur'an is actually *difficult* to understand.
"If exacting the right meaning from the Holy Qur'an were so easy,"
Muhammad Zakariyya Kandhlavi (d. 1982) wrote, "then why was it
necessary for prophets to be sent? The Qur'an could have been hung
from the Ka'aba and people could have taken from it what they wish.
The prophets were sent because through their deeds divine guidance
was given perfection and form."[31]

Second, even the *'ulama* fall under his critique of all forms of authority beyond the Qur'an and Hadith. This is precisely why India's own
Salafi movement, the Ahl-i Hadith, found inspiration in Muhammad
Isma'il for its rejection of the Islamic legal schools.[32] Third, *Taqwiyyat
al-iman* invokes the Qur'an and Hadith in support of its arguments, but
conspicuously avoids citing any medieval Islamic legal or theological
authorities. The text, in short, encapsulates a certain scripturalist impulse
that would animate later Deobandi discourses even as it stood in tension
with them as Deobandis attempted to retain that legal and theological
edifice.

The corollary to a Qur'an so transparent that it requires no intermediary to understand it is a God so powerful—indeed, a God with an utter
monopoly on power—that no one can intercede between humans and
God, because any would-be intermediaries, such as the saints (*awliya'*),
are as powerless as the average believer: "Think about those who associate God with others [*mushrik*], who call upon the holy ones [*buzurg*]
and implore them to fulfill their desires. These holy ones do not control
even a mote of creation or have the slightest share in it, let alone are they
pillars of divine power."[33] God is so powerful that he could, if He wished,
instantaneously upend and subvert every law of the universe and even
every article of Islamic faith, replacing them with an entirely new system.
In one of the most striking passages of the text, Isma'il writes: "Truly the
power of this Shah of Shahs is so great that in an instant, solely by pronouncing the command 'Be!' God could create millions of prophets,
saints, djinn, and angels equal to Gabriel and Muhammad, or in a single
breath, can turn the whole universe upside down and bestow upon it a
wholly new creation"—the essence of Isma'il's controversial doctrine of
imkan-i nazir.[34] Muhammad Isma'il articulated a stark and radically
polarized vision of divine sovereignty in which human beings, including
all prophets and Sufi saints, are utterly powerless before God's majesty,
thereby undercutting the very possibility of saintly intercession between
God and humankind. The sovereign, in this vision, is the sole power

capable of deciding on the exception to otherwise immutable rules and laws. The sovereign by definition transcends the law, simultaneously dictating the law and exempt from it.[35]

It is important to clarify that the semantics of sovereignty in *Taqwiyyat al-iman* are quite different from theorizations of God's sovereignty by twentieth-century Islamists, such as Qutb and Maududi, who used the neologism "*hakimiyya*" to connote the *political* valence the word carries in English—quite explicitly in Maududi's case, who inserted the English word "sovereignty" into the Urdu text in *Islam ka nazariyya-i siyasi* (The Islamic view of politics) of 1939, leaving no doubt about the word's intended meaning. Maududi took Qur'anic statements such as "[A]uthority [*al-hukm*] belongs to God alone" (12:40) to mean that society and state must be governed exclusively by God's laws, not "manmade laws"—a notion more or less foreign to the medieval exegetical tradition, as Muhammad Qasim Zaman has shown.[36] Muhammad Isma'il, too, invokes Qur'an 12:40, but does so to argue that God alone ought to be worshipped—a reading that aligns more with exegetes like Tabari (d. 923) than it does with Maududi.[37] When Isma'il wants to convey God's "authority," he uses words like *tasarruf* ("holding, disposing, possessing") and *ikhtiyar* ("discretion, disposal, management") to describe God's utter and complete control over the universe.[38] To convey God's "power," he uses words like *taqat* ("power, capability") and *saltanat* ("dominion, rule"). The latter, of course, *does* have a political connotation, but not so much in the way Isma'il uses it, which again takes the form of a critique of *shirk*: "No one is a partner or associate in God's power [*saltanat*]."[39] The distinctly modern neologism *hakimiyya* does not appear at all in the text. This does not mean, of course, that Isma'il's theorization of divine power does not have political *implications*. But it is important, nonetheless, to distinguish between Isma'il's notion of divine sovereignty, centered around a critique of *shirk*, and notions of divine sovereignty that emerged much later.

Muhammad Isma'il was by no means the only one advancing powerful critiques of *shirk* in India in the early nineteenth century; similar claims arose, for instance, out of the work of Khurram 'Ali Bilhauri, whose *Nasihat al-Muslimin* of 1813 suggested that "[i]n the same way that the heathens worship the idols, Muslims started worshipping the tombs of the saints whom they believe to be as powerful as God." Like Muhammad Isma'il, Khurram 'Ali was intent on disabusing the Muslim masses of their ill-informed notions of agency and intercession, putting forth a typology of *shirk* similar to Muhammad Isma'il's. He memorably describes the act of calling for help upon any entity other than God (e.g., a saint) as being as ineffectual as cupping water from a river in one's hand and calling upon the water to come into one's mouth.[40]

But Muhammad Isma'il, more than any other early-nineteenth-century reformist thinker, impacted the first generation of Deobandis. No early Deobandi internalized this reformist impulse more than Rashid Ahmad Gangohi. For Gangohi, "*Taqwiyyat al-iman* is a magnificent, utterly true work, strengthening and reforming the faith, and the entire meaning of the Qur'an and Hadith is contained in it."[41] He regarded Muhammad Isma'il as a "saint of God" (*wali Allah*).[42] Yet, despite Gangohi's unqualified praise, his collected fatwas reveal just how controversial Muhammad Isma'il's propositions were to many Muslims. Several people requesting them inquired whether it was permissible to call Muhammad Isma'il an "unbeliever" (*kafir*),[43] and in fact several prominent *'ulama* under the guidance of Fazl al-Haqq Khairabadi (d. 1861) did exactly that.[44] Gangohi, expectedly, condemns declaring Muhammad Isma'il an unbeliever with the justification that he is a saint (*wali*). He echoes his intellectual predecessor in still other ways, defending the controversial notion that God is capable of lying (*imkan-i kizb*) and that God could create other prophets on par with Muhammad (*imkan-i nazir*), offering the explanation, like Muhammad Isma'il, that God is capable but would never do so.[45] And like Muhammad Isma'il, he steadfastly denies that Muhammad had "knowledge of the unseen" (*'ilm-i ghayb*), a staple of Sufi perceptions of the Prophet as a man of unparalleled knowledge of this world and the next.[46] Gangohi also endorses Muhammad Isma'il's stark vision of divine sovereignty. The relationship between God and the created world is like that between a potter and a pot: a potter creates a pot but also has the power to break it at will.[47] But it is Isma'il's analysis of *bid'a* that is critical for our purposes here. Indeed, Gangohi once reprimanded a young Ashraf 'Ali Thanvi for his insufficient understanding of *bid'a,* for which he recommended that Thanvi read Muhammad Isma'il's *Izah al-haqq fi ahkam al-mayyit wa al-darih*.[48] While the next two chapters will outline ways that the Deobandis attempted to constrain the populist hermeneutics that Isma'il unleashed, the remainder of this chapter will show how these same Deobandis adopted, and adapted, Isma'il's interrogation of *bid'a* and *shirk* in their critiques of celebrating the Prophet Muhammad's birth celebration (*mawlud*) and the Sufi saints' death anniversaries (*'urs*).

THE *MAWLUD:* HOW SHOULD ONE LOVE
THE PROPHET?

No form of devotional practice became the object of incessant debate and critique more than the *mawlud,* the celebration of the Prophet's birthday, against which Deobandis deployed the theorization of *bid'a* they inherited from Muhammad Isma'il. Known variously as *mawlud, mawlid* or *milad* (in Arabic, "birth"), the celebration of the Prophet Muhammad's birthday (the 12th of the Islamic month of Rabi' al-Awwal) has been a perennial flashpoint within modern South Asian Islam. It has, in fact, been contested from various quarters since at least the thirteenth century, and remains so today, with renowned institutions such as Al-Azhar issuing legal opinions on the practice.[49] Arguments for and against the *mawlud* proliferate in fatwas, in scholarly studies, and on the internet.[50] Nevertheless, the celebration is widely observed in nearly every country in which Muslims live.

A typical *mawlud* entails reading stories about different events in the Prophet's life, reciting the Qur'an, sending benedictions (Arabic, *salawat;* Urdu, *durud*) upon the Prophet, and singing poems of praise (*na't*) in honor of him. Many wealthy Indian Muslims even endowed *mawlud* festivities in their wills.[51] Shah Wali Allah, notably, vividly recounted the *mawlud* that he attended during his Hajj pilgrimage in 1730–1731, where he described seeing visions of the Prophet's spiritual light (*nur*) during the event, in unmediated form: "I saw his blessed and holy spirit clearly and manifestly, not only from the world of spirits [*'alam-i arwah*] but directly from the imaginal realm [*'alam-i mithal*]."[52] By no means limited to Sufis, the *mawlud* has long been intimately linked to Sufi practices, especially accompanying Sufi musical assemblies (*sama'*) as well as narrative accounts of his birth, virtues, and superhuman qualities, such as his primordial light (*nur*).[53]

Deobandi scholars were also not the first to criticize *mawlud* festivities. Many early condemnations of *mawlud* festivities were based simply on the fact that they did not exist in the Prophet Muhammad's era, nor did he celebrate his own birthday. Even its supporters concede that the earliest documented celebrations of the *mawlud* are from much later— possibly as late as the twelfth century.[54] Even in the twelfth century, one critic bemoaned "the taking of hashish, the gathering of young men . . . [and] the singing of [songs] arousing longing for worldly pleasures."[55] In the sixteenth century, the legal legitimacy of standing in honor of the

Prophet, known as *qiyam,* was debated, with some denying its legality and others seeing it as a natural display of love and emotion for the Prophet.[56] Jalal al-Din Suyuti's (d. 1505) *Husn al-maqsad fi 'amal al-mawlid* (The good intention of celebrating the mawlid) defended the practice as a "good innovation" (*bid'a hasana*) provided that it remained within certain normative parameters.[57] Muhammad ibn 'Abd al-Wahhab (d. 1792), founder of the Wahhabi movement, opposed the practice, but his views on *mawlud* and other alleged innovations did not become entrenched in the Hijaz until long after his death; even in the late nineteenth century, as Deobandis such as Gangohi were issuing fatwas against the practice of standing in reverence of the Prophet (*qiyam*) during the *mawlud,* a Hanafi mufti of Mecca issued a polemic in support of the *mawlud,* insisting that *not* standing for the Prophet was sinful—precisely the sort of claim, as we will see below, that Deobandis came to see as one of the clearest marks of *bid'a.*[58]

Deobandi critiques of the *mawlud* begin largely with Gangohi, who issued many fatwas on the celebration. "This festival," one of them concludes, "did not exist in the era of the Prophet Muhammad, in the era of the pious Companions, in the era of the Followers, or the Followers of the Followers, or in the era of the founders of the Islamic legal schools [*mujtahidin*]. It was invented some four hundred years later by a king[59] whom most historians regard as immoral [*fasiq*]."[60] The practice of standing in respect of the Prophet (*qiyam*), the theological implications of which we will examine below, only exacerbates its iniquities. What if the *mawlud* is free of *qiyam*? In response to this question, Gangohi simply declared: "Holding a *mawlud* gathering is not permissible under any condition."[61]

Besides, Gangohi says, most of the masses attend *mawlud* gatherings not for the purpose of remembering God (*zikr*) but for entertainment. And while they justify these gatherings with the claim that it increases the love for the Prophet, in fact, most of the stories they tell are based on weak, unsubstantiated Hadith narrations. "In truth," he concludes, "any good that is acquired through illicit [*ghayr mashru'a*] means is, in itself, impermissible."[62]

And yet, Gangohi approved lectures about the Prophet's birth and virtues, even small gatherings for that purpose. He was frequently asked how to perform *mawlud* "properly." On one occasion (unfortunately undated), he sent Khalil Ahmad Saharanpuri, one of his most accomplished Sufi disciples, to conduct a *mawlud* at the request of a certain "Sultan Jahan," likely Sultan Jahan, Begum of Bhopal from 1901 to

1926, who had extensive contact with Deobandi scholars in her court—in particular, graduates of Mazahir al-'Ulum, where Khalil Ahmad Saharanpuri taught.[63] When the *mawlud* commenced:

> [First] Khalil Ahmad read the verse "There has come to you a Messenger,"[64] and explained it, after which he discussed . . . some current innovations [*bid'at*]. After expounding on some events and details of the Prophet's birth from *Tavarikh-i habib Allah* [Stories of God's beloved],[65] the *mawlud* was finished. Many were very displeased toward the owner of the house, saying, 'You invited us to your home and then you disgraced us.' But in reality, this *mawlud* was beneficial. Some of the people present thought that those who reject the *mawlud* reject every aspect of it, but many were disabused of this notion.[66]

Saharanpuri himself summarized all the features of the customary *mawlud* that Deobandis disdained, adding that, were these features to be removed, such a *mawlud* would cease to be a *bid'a*—precisely the type, in other words, that he performed for Sultan Jahan:

> We [Deobandis] reject the impermissible things that have become associated with . . . *mawlud* assemblies in India: lecturing from weak [Hadith] narrations, men and women mixing together, extravagance in lighting candles, believing the assembly is obligatory, shaming and declaring unbelievers of those who do not participate, and other things prohibited by the Shari'a. If the *mawlud* assembly were free of such things, how could we say that recalling the noble birth is impermissible and an innovation [*bid'a*]?"[67]

The debate over *mawlud* took an especially contentious turn in the last two decades of the nineteenth century, however, with the 1887 publication of Saharanpuri's *Al-Barahin al-qati'a 'ala dhalam al-anwar al-sati'a* (Definitive proofs on the darkness of al-Anwar al-Sati'a), a response to 'Abd al-Sami' Rampuri's *Al-Anwar al-sati'a* (The dazzling lights). Rampuri, a disciple of Imdad Allah, wrote *Al-Anwar al-sati'a* in response to Gangohi's (and others') criticisms of *mawlud* and *'urs*.[68]

Saharanpuri, a disciple and close associate of Gangohi's, believed that the most theologically alarming facets of the *mawlud* were the belief that the Prophet was present (*hazir*) at the gathering and the act of standing (*qiyam*) in his alleged "presence." Critiques of standing (*qiyam*) during the *mawlud*, to be sure, long predate the Deobandis. The crux of these critiques was the participants' specification of the *mawlud* as the only context in which one stands in respect of the Prophet. Shah 'Abd al-Ghani, son of Shah Wali Allah and father of Muhammad Isma'il, had asked why it is only during the *mawlud* that people tend to stand in respect of the Prophet: "Who says that it is impermissible to remember the Messenger of

God while standing? Our objection is that if standing is to show respect, then what is the reason for standing *only* when recalling the Prophet's birth and not at other times? In fact, if the Prophet's birth is recalled in any place other than a *mawlud* assembly, then no one stands up."[69]

Saharanpuri built upon these prior interventions. *Al-Barahin al-qati'a* is a lengthy text, with multiple lines of argument; here I will discuss only those aspects of his argument related to standing during the *mawlud*. First, before addressing the details of the *mawlud* itself, Saharanpuri begins by clarifying that recollecting the Prophet's birth is an acceptable and even laudable act. This is something he demonstrated in practice with his own celebrations of the Prophet's birthday, as we have just seen. He then critiques the metaphysical basis for believing the Prophet is present at the *mawlud* gathering. Rampuri had compared the Prophet's presence to the ubiquity of sunlight, for "just as the sun is everywhere within the first Heaven," he says, "the Prophet's spirit [*ruh-i nabi*] is in the seventh Heaven, the 'Illiyun."[70] "How is it unreasonable to believe," he therefore asks, "that, from there, his blessed sight is cast upon the earth, or some parts of it, and the lights of the Muhammadan effulgence [*faizan-i ahmadi*] grace every pure gathering like the rays of the all-encompassing sun?"[71] For Saharanpuri, this is a flight of poetic fancy that treads dangerously into polytheism. He takes the Qur'anic pronouncement, "There is nothing like Him" (42:11), to mean that any quality belonging to God—seeing all, hearing all, knowing all—belongs to Him and Him alone. Assuming that the Prophet is present at the *mawlud* assumes that he has these divine qualities.[72] Third, Saharanpuri delves into the act of standing itself, which he deems a *bid'a* on the basis of how it is specified both for the *mawlud* only (an argument others had made prior to him), as well as for specific times within the *mawlud* that were meant to correlate with the birth of the Prophet. Fourth, responding to Rampuri's assertion that standing is neutral with respect to the law (*mubah*), Saharanpuri writes: "Yes, the act of standing [in and of itself] is absolutely neutral [*mubah*]. And honoring the Pride of the World [the Prophet Muhammad], Peace be upon Him, is praiseworthy [*mustahabb*]. But the way the ignorant engage in both with such diligence [*taqayud*] and specificity [*takhsis*], the way the masses regard them as a Sunna and a necessity [*wujub*], makes the act *bid'a* and reprehensible [*makruh*]."[73] Finally, standing is also an aspect of the Salat prayer—in other words, of the basic ritual commands of Islamic worship. Saharanpuri reasons that the commandment to stand for God's sake in the Qur'an—"Stand up for God, obedient" [*wa qumu li-Allahi qanitina*] (Qur'an 2:238)—renders the act of standing in reverence an intrinsic act of worship, which he defines as "standing, with hands folded, in humility." The act begins to border dangerously close to *shirk* when it is coupled with the belief in the Prophet's suprahuman knowledge.[74]

We can glimpse the impact of Saharanpuri's text in a letter that Hajji Imdad Allah sent to him from Mecca in July 1890, three years after the publication of *Al-Barahin al-qati'a*. As the preeminent Sabiri Chishti master of the nineteenth century, Imdad Allah mentored the first generation of Deobandis, including Muhammad Qasim Nanautvi and Rashid Ahmad Gangohi. In this letter, Imdad Allah was concerned with the effect of that publication on public sentiment and—a subject to which we return in the next chapter—the public's capacity to understand its content:

> From cities and kingdoms across India—Bengal, Bihar, Madras, Deccan, Gujarat, Mumbai, Punjab, Rajputana, Rampur, Bhawalpur—newspapers have arrived one after another, stirring up grief and shock. Hearing all this has made this poor faqir extremely sad. The cause is *Barahin-i qati'a* and other books. The fires of *fitna* have been kindled by the refutation of *Anwar-i sati'a*, which *'ulama* everywhere have defended. (I shall remain neutral on the matter.) . . . Your refutation of every sentence showed such arrogance that—I seek refuge in God—you have even said that God is capable of uttering a lie. This affliction has been so world-shattering that noble *mawluds* have been subdued and this issue has reached every city and town, even reaching the Two Holy Cities—May God increase their nobility and honor!—and other countries. . . . My friend, this is an issue for which the understanding of the masses ['*awamm*] is deficient. I fear it will lead to suffering and strife. Publicizing these issues is against the public interest [*maslahat*] and against the Shari'a.[75]

This is the context for the publication of Hajji Imdad Allah's *Faisala-yi haft mas'ala* (A decision on seven controversies) in 1894. Hajji Imdad Allah regarded the *mawlud* as a matter in need of urgent resolution, ranking it first out of the seven controversies he addresses in the book.[76]

Before outlining Imdad Allah's approach to the *mawlud*, it is crucial to comment on his relationship with Gangohi and the Deoband movement.[77] Though he took on hundreds of disciples throughout his life, he was not a scholar ('*alim*), a status that did not always keep him from opining on legal matters. But Imdad Allah saw precedents in Islamic history for his role as a non-'*alim* among the *'ulama*. "God grants to some of his servants who are not technically *'ulama* the tongue [of another]," he explained, and just as "the tongue granted to Shams Tabrizi was Maulana Rumi, who elaborated upon the knowledge of Hazrat Shams Tabrizi in great detail, similarly, Maulana Muhammad Qasim Nanautvi is my tongue."[78] Nanautvi saw their relationship in a similar light; he once quipped that Imdad Allah was not a "scholar" (*maulvi*) so much as a "scholar-maker" (*maulvi-gar*).[79] Imdad Allah was deferential to the *'ulama*: "I am ignorant," he once told a group of *'ulama*. "You are *'ulama*. In my heart is only what has alighted there, and I have explained it thus; if there is any error in it, anything in conflict with the Qur'an and the Sunna, please do not hesitate to tell me. Otherwise, on the Day of Judgment, I will say, 'I told them to explain it but they did not clarify the matter.'"[80] His Sufi lodge, Khanqah Imdadiyya, in the northern Indian town of Thana Bhawan, was a hive of scholarly activity, a place where Qur'an, Hadith, and Islamic law (*fiqh*) lessons took place, even before Thanvi took up residence there.[81]

But at times Imdad Allah opined on legal matters beyond his expertise, for which Gangohi gently admonished his Sufi master. Once a disciple of Imdad Allah's had just returned from the Hajj and said to Gangohi that Imdad Allah gave him permission to attend a *sama'* musical assembly. When Gangohi heard this, he said, "This must be incorrect. But if he is stating the truth, Hajji Sahib [Imdad Allah] is incorrect. In such matters it is Hajji Sahib's duty to consult us. And in matters regarding the reformation of the self, it is our duty to follow him."[82] Gangohi made it clear that Imdad Allah needed to refrain from issuing legal advice, since he did not have the expertise to do so. On one occasion, he heard disturbing rumors from Mecca. Someone who had been on Hajj with Imdad Allah reported: "We went to see Hajji Imdad Allah in Mecca, and someone there asked Hajji Imdad Allah for a fatwa for which women would be released from the obligation of performing the Hajj because of the hardships of the journey." The man goes on to say that they stopped Imdad Allah as he prepared to issue the bizarre ruling. In light of such reports, Gangohi states: "I wrote to Imdad Allah several times asking him not to openly discuss religious controversies [*masa'il*] but only to explain simple facts that the people can grasp."[83]

Even if the Deobandis did not believe he had sufficient legal knowledge to opine on legal controversies or issue fatwas, Imdad Allah's ability to *intuit* truths about the world was renowned, such that Ashraf 'Ali Thanvi believed Imdad Allah had experienced the unity of all being (*wahdat al-wujud*) and had a direct apprehension of the divine names. On one occasion, upon hearing the verse "There is no God but Him! To Him belong the most beautiful names," [Qur'an 20:8] Thanvi says, "Hazrat

Imdad Allah was so overpowered by God's oneness [*tawhid*] that he witnessed the unity of being [*wahdat al-wujud*] as if it were right in front of him."[84] Gangohi and Nanautvi would become, for *their* disciples, the rare paragons of the scholar-Sufi, those who mastered both the inner and outer dimensions of Islam. Imdad Allah saw Gangohi and Nanautvi as individuals in whom the "inner" (*batin*) and "outer" (*zahir*) were seamlessly united:

> Whoever feels love and devotion toward me should regard Maulvi Rashid Ahmad [Gangohi] and Maulvi Muhammad Qasim [Nanautvi], in whom the inner and outer perfections are united, as my equal, or in fact as residing at a higher level than me. Although on the surface the matter is quite the opposite [given that Imdad Allah was their master], they stand in my place and I stand in theirs.[85]

An oft-repeated analogy to describe the master–disciple relationship in Sufism is that the disciple must be like a corpse in the hands of a corpse washer.[86] How is it then that Gangohi could disagree with his own master, Imdad Allah, and do so openly? As Gangohi's biographer sees it, once a disciple reaches the stage at which he possesses his own connection to God (*sahib-i nisbat*), he can disagree openly with his master. Gangohi had attained this stage, and struck a balance between respect for Imdad Allah and fidelity to the law.[87] Gangohi described his relationship to Imdad Allah, which encapsulates his thinking on the primacy of legal knowledge over experiential, intuitive knowledge, in the following terms: "No one becomes a discile to let a Sufi master—who [in this case] is not even a scholar—judge the validity or invalidity of what one has studied and learnt; or to force the established rulings of the Qur'an and Hadith into accord with the master's dicta. . . . If one's master commands something that is contrary to the commands of the Shari'a, the disciple should not accept it; indeed, it would be the disciple's obligation to show the master the right path."[88]

This complicated relationship is the context in which we must understand Imdad Allah's attempted intervention in *Faisala-yi haft mas'ala*. Imdad Allah begins by telling his readers that there are inherent virtues in remembering the Prophet's birthday. Imdad Allah himself confesses to attending the *mawlud* because of the blessings (*barakat*) one acquires. But, he says, there are a number of major debates about the *mawlud*: whether the Prophet's spirit is present during the event, whether it can be celebrated only on the date of the Prophet's birth (12 Rabi' al-Awwal) or on any day, and whether the *mawlud* is a religious commandment.

Do any of these constitute *bid'a*? Imdad Allah makes it clear that he opposes *bid'a*, which he defines simply as "bringing into the religion [*din*] that which is not part of it."[89] Imdad Allah, crucially, did not believe that setting a specific time for the *mawlud* is a *bid'a*. What makes assigning a date illicit is then believing it to be *obligatory*.[90] Later Deobandis, too, will insist that to regard a merely permissible (*mubah*) or even a commendable (*mustahabb*) act as mandatory (*wajib*) is probably the most egregious form of *bid'a*. Like Gangohi, and like Thanvi some years later, he is clear that no one ought to insist on others participating *as if* celebrating the Prophet's birthday were a ritual commandment. But this point applies not just to the *mawlud* as a whole but, equally, to standing in honor of the Prophet (*qiyam*), because of the assumptions about his omnipresence associated with it:

> Some criticize those who do not stand in respect of the Prophet during *mawlud*. This is incorrect. In the view of the Shari'a, standing is not essential, and according to the jurists, even a praiseworthy [*mustahabb*] action becomes sinful when it is demanded. . . . [Moreover] it is plainly objectionable to believe that one cannot attain merit [*sawab*] if a date for the *mawlud* is not appointed, or if standing in respect of the Prophet is not performed, or if sweets are not arranged. Such a belief is a transgression of the limits of the Shari'a, just as it is reprehensible to regard a permissible [*mubah*] act as forbidden. In both cases, there is a transgression of limits [*ta'addi-yi hudud*].[91]

One can see Imdad Allah grappling with Gangohi's criticisms, especially in his definition of *bid'a*. But, he says, there is also a transgression of limits from those who condemn others for believing that the Prophet is present. Implicitly responding to Gangohi, Imdad Allah states in no uncertain terms: "To regard the belief that the Prophet graces the *mawlid* with his presence as unbelief [*kufr*] and associating God with others [*shirk*] is beyond the pale. Both logic ['*aql*] and tradition [*naql*] testify to the possibility of his presence, and it *has* actually happened on occasions." Moreover, one can clearly imagine that the Prophet can be present without him requiring knowledge of the unseen ('*ilm-i ghayb*): there are many examples, he reminds readers, of God granting superhuman knowledge to his creation.[92]

Ultimately, Imdad Allah resists condemning the whole *mawlud* because of these relatively minor infractions. This is, he says, quoting a line from Rumi's *Masnavi*, like "burning one's rug because of a single flea."[93] Imdad Allah asserts that differences over issues such as *qiyam* are akin to differences within branches of law (*fiqh*)—an argument we will see Thanvi make below before Gangohi forced him to renounce it.[94]

(Gangohi's view on this was that Imdad Allah heard differing views on *mawlud* from various *'ulama*, and thus *assumed* it was akin to an issue concerning the "branches" (*furu'*) of the law (*mas'ala far'iyya*), about which a degree of different views is acceptable, whereas in fact it is an issue of belief (*mas'ala i'tiqadiyya*), about which there can be no dispute.)[95] Imdad Allah closes his discussion of the *mawlud* with a call for conciliation. Partisans to this debate should consider the different viewpoints over the *mawlud* "like the differences between Hanafis and Shafi'is. They should meet and greet each other and continue to show love to one another. They should especially avoid criticism and debate in public because it is beneath the dignity of the Muslim scholar's profession."[96]

Ashraf 'Ali Thanvi, too, believed that a *mawlud* like the one conducted by Khalil Ahmad Saharanpuri was not only permissible but spiritually beneficial. Most others, however, were not. Indeed, Thanvi offered perhaps the most systematic Deobandi treatment of the *mawlud*, one that reveals the textures of Deobandi understandings of *bid'a*. We have already encountered Thanvi several times, but it is necessary at this point to provide a bit of background on this crucial figure. Thanvi was born in 1863 in Thana Bhawan, a small northern Indian town not far from Deoband. His father managed the estate of a wealthy landowner in Meerut but wanted a religious education for his eldest son and sent Thanvi to the Dar al-'Ulum Deoband, where he began his studies in 1878 and graduated in 1883.[97] Thanvi made his first Hajj pilgrimage in 1884, where he took on Hajji Imdad Allah as his Sufi master, and a second in 1893, where he spent some six months with Imdad Allah. Upon returning to India, he taught at Madrasa Faiz-i 'Amm in Kanpur until finally returning to Thana Bhawan in 1897, where he taught, wrote, and lectured from the Sufi lodge, Khanqah Imdadiyya, where Imdad Allah had lived before his exile in Mecca. In Thana Bhawan, Thanvi met with hundreds of disciples in person, maintained an active correspondence with many more via mail, issued fatwas, and wrote prolifically on Islamic law and ethics, Qur'an, and Sufism.

Thanvi struggled to reconcile the conflicting stances of Imdad Allah and Gangohi—both men dear to him—on *mawlud* and other issues, though ultimately the legal proclivities of Gangohi took precedence. Thanvi expressed this ambivalence during a lecture recorded by his disciple Muhammad Shafi':

> I used to think a *milad* [i.e., *mawlud*] assembly, which is fundamentally concerned with recollecting the Prophet, was a praiseworthy and joyous occasion. In fact, even if certain evils and common errors had become included in

it, I believed it was necessary to remove them, but that one should not abandon such a praiseworthy act altogether. In essence, this is the way [*maslak*] of our master, Hajji Imdad Allah. Because of his incredible kindness, love, and tenderness, I also felt this way. This was also the way of most of the Sufis. Maulana Rumi, too, felt this way, as when he said: "Don't burn your rug because of a single flea."[98]

Here Thanvi cites the same line from Rumi that Imdad Allah cited when he argued against dispensing with the *mawlud* over what he thought were minor objections.

But Thanvi goes on to explain that Hanafi law does not condone this approach: "According to the way [*maslak*] of the Hanafi jurists, when some act is praiseworthy [*mustahabb*] in principle but does not fulfill the objectives of the Shari'a [*maqasid-i Shari'a*], and evils or innovations become connected with it, or even the fear of evils or innovations, this praiseworthy act must be abandoned completely. But one must not abandon a praiseworthy act that *does* fulfill Shari'a objectives on account of the presence of evils. Rather, those evils must be removed." So, he elaborates, even praiseworthy acts that facilitate adherence to the Shari'a—the congregational prayer, for example, or teaching and reciting the Qur'an—have occasionally become corrupted by evils (*munkarat*) and innovations (*bid'at*). The law dictates that every effort be made to remove any corruptions from such acts. But when otherwise praiseworthy acts that do *not* facilitate adherence to the Shari'a become corrupted by evils and innovations—of which *mawlud* is the prime example—the law dictates that Muslims should abandon the practice altogether.[99]

Citing Shatibi, Thanvi illustrates this principle with a story known as the Pledge of the Tree. In 628, the Prophet Muhammad assembled his followers outside of Mecca, hoping to enter the city to make an '*umrah* pilgrimage to the Ka'aba while the Muslims were still at war with the Meccans. He sent 'Uthman ibn 'Affan, who would later become the third caliph, to negotiate their entry. After some time, when 'Uthman did not return, they feared he had been killed and the Companions gathered under a tree, where they pledged to avenge him. After the event, Companions of the Prophet made a habit of gathering there because of the spiritual blessings (*baraka*) that emanated from the site. 'Umar, during his reign as second caliph (r. 634–644), "felt that this tree, under which the Prophet accepted the Pledge and for which the Qur'an mentions God's satisfaction [Qur'an 48:18], should be cut down," Thanvi explains, "even though the Companions who had started to gather there were not doing anything impermissible." It was the mere "*danger* of evils [*munka-*

rat] becoming associated with it" that compelled 'Umar to cut down the tree.[100] 'Umar's decision, Thanvi says, illustrates the Hanafi legal principle of preemptively obviating the spiritual dangers of any devotional practice that does not serve a broader function within the legal economy of the Shari'a: "Hazrat Gangohi adhered to this Hanafi *maslak,* and did not permit participation in the *milad* festival on account of the evils and innovations connected to it." But in a startling confession, Thanvi admits that this strictness conflicts with his personal disposition toward Sufi participation in the *mawlud.* He goes on:

> At one time, Hazrat Gangohi and I disagreed on this matter, but in the end, because of the strength of the legal proofs [*dala'il*] against it and in the interest of preserving the religion, he elected to take the more cautious and safer *maslak,* but I did not believe that the *maslak* chosen by the noble Sufis was baseless . . . *I do not oppose* or hold in suspicion those noble Sufis who participate in *milad* assemblies that are free of evils and innovations.[101]

The "legal proofs" (*dala'il*) against *mawlud* to which Thanvi refers were, in his view, comprehensive and decisive. Thanvi argued that the *mawlud* was a *bid'a* according to the Qur'an, the Hadith, and the consensus (*ijma'*) of the Ummah, as well as by analogy (*qiyas*) with similar prohibitions in the Qur'an and Sunna—in other words, with respect to every source of Islamic law. As for the Qur'an, Thanvi cites the verse "Do they have partners [with God] who have made lawful for them some religion without God's permission?" (41:21). "The verse makes it clear," Thanvi says, "that it is blameworthy and reprehensible for anyone to prescribe in any religious matter, without God's permission, meaning without a legal rationale [*dalil-i shari'*]."[102] From the Hadith, too, Thanvi argues that *mawlud* is an innovation, referencing in fact the same Hadith that Imdad Allah cites in *Faisala-yi haft mas'ala*: "Whoever innovates in this matter of ours, that which is not part of it will be rejected." A Hadith from Muslim ibn al-Hajjaj, likewise, forbids specifying ritual actions in such a way that they take the form of a faux commandment: "Do not single out the night of Jum'a [Thursday night] among other nights for prayer, and do not single out Friday among other days for fasting, unless your regular fast happens to fall on that day." The Prophet, Thanvi explains, wanted to protect the delicate relationship between the temporal normativity assigned to Friday, the day of congregational prayer, and prayer and fasting as prescribed ritual acts of worship. God did not command the Muslims to fast on Friday; therefore, no one ought to make a habit of doing so, unless another commanded fast (e.g., Ramadan) overlaps with that day. In other words, do not fast on Friday *because* it is Friday. In the same way, while "in itself, [remembering] the Prophet's birth has blessings [*barakat*] and virtues [*fazilat*]," he is clear that "specifying the Prophet's birthday for a festival ['*eid*] is neither prescribed by tradition [*manqul*], nor a specification that arises out of habit [*takhsis 'aadi*]," but in fact those who practice it "consider it to be part of the religion [*din*]."[103] In a commentary on the same Hadith elsewhere, he spells out the argument in even more detail: "It is forbidden by the Shari'a, when the Shari'a does not specify [concerning a practice], to believe that a practice should be performed in a certain way, to intentionally perform it a certain way consistently or inconsistently, even if there is no intention of specification, or to delude the masses into thinking there is a specification, even unintentionally or inconsistently. Today, it is not only the masses ['*awamm*] that have been afflicted with this evil; many of the elites [*khawass*], especially the Sufis, have been as well."[104] For example, if a Sufi abstains from meat as a way of disciplining desire, that is perfectly fine. If he or she regards such abstinence as *in itself* a religious duty, that of course is a clear *bid'a*. However, even for those who abstain for valid reasons, Thanvi counsels them to eat meat occasionally so as not to appear to regard it as forbidden when it is clearly permissible.[105]

Thanvi elaborates on his hermeneutics of *bid'a* in his analysis of the *mawlud* in *Islah al-rusum* (The reformation of customs), published in 1893. Thanvi argued that there are essentially three kinds of *mawlud*: The first kind of *mawlud* assembly, Thanvi tells us, is permissible without any reservations whatsoever. This is a case in which some individuals gather "by chance" to discuss the life, birth, and virtues of the Prophet Muhammad. "The Prophet explained his own life and perfections in this way," says Thanvi. They have not been forced or compelled to gather for this *mawlud,* and they do not engage in any prohibited acts.[106] The second is completely impermissible: in this gathering, "sweet-voiced" boys sing fabricated tales, bribes and other forms of illicitly earned money are exchanged, and the organizers spend enormous sums for food and lighting in the pursuit of local fame and prestige. Moreover, participants pressure others to attend and ridicule those who do not, often skip the compulsory daily prayers, and believe the Prophet Muhammad to be literally present at the gathering.[107] Significantly, though Thanvi concedes that not all *mawlud* gatherings of this type contain every one of these iniquities, he insists that such a gathering is completely impermissible if even *one* of them is present. We have already seen how, with Gangohi, the presence of one impurity infects the whole: "This type of assembly is impermissible because of these unlawful elements, and participating in it is also unlawful. Nowadays most *mawluds* are of this type. If perhaps not *all* of these unlawful elements are present, by necessity, some of them are, and a single unlawful element renders the whole unlawful, as is obvious."[108]

The third kind of *mawlud* is described as follows:

> There is neither the informality of the first kind nor the forbidden elements of the second kind. Although this form also has stipulations, they are *halal* and permissible [*mubah*]. For example, the stories told are sound [*sahih*] and reliable, the storyteller is trustworthy and is not seeking fame, and the money involved is *halal* as well. There are no decorations, and money is not wasted. The dress of the participants and the ablutions are in accordance with the Shari'a, and if by chance something contrary to the Shari'a happens, then the lecturer refuses it on the basis of "commanding the good" and explains necessary rules in accordance with the situation. If there is poetry, it is not set to music, and its subject matter remains aligned with the Shari'a and is not excessive. There is no hindrance in completing the required acts of worship, and the intention of the organizer is pure and only for the sake of seeking blessings and love for the Prophet. . . . The attendees do not consider the Prophet to be omnipresent and a knower of the unseen ['alim al-ghayb]. This assembly, in which such caution is taken, is rare.[109]

He goes on to explain the legal hermeneutic that informs his approach to the *mawlud*, which effectively summarizes the entire Deobandi stance on *bid'a*. First, he says, it is expressly forbidden to "consider an unnecessary matter necessary or to act on it with the same or higher degree of persistence than one accords to necessary and obligatory acts, or to consider it blameworthy to forgo this action or to censure those who do."[110] The Shari'a forbids "restricting, stipulating, specifying, or making mandatory" any particular belief or action if it simulates or mimics the normativity of the law. This is a succinct formulation of the same principle that appears in both Imdad Allah and Gangohi: to perform any action with the same degree, consistency, or intentionality that one is expected to grant Sunna acts is prohibited. Thus, Thanvi relates a Hadith in which Ibn Ma'sud observed the Prophet occasionally leaving his prayer from the left side, even though he had said leaving from the right side was recommended. The point, Ibn Ma'sud says, is that one must not extrapolate a commandment from something merely recommended.[111] In the same way, the Shari'a forbids even slight alterations of what has been commanded, even if arising from the best of intentions. Someone who prays five cycles (*rak'at*) during Salat, when he or she is supposed to pray only four, will get credit for none—even if that person thinks that he or she is doing "extra" prayers.[112] It is important to highlight the element of intentionality here. There is no harm in someone spontaneously standing (*qiyam*) while recollecting the Prophet's birth, especially in an ecstatic state (*hal*) born out of love for him. It is when those recollecting the Prophet's birth treat standing as an article of faith that *bid'a* arises.[113]

Second, even one violation of the Shari'a renders an otherwise legitimate act reprehensible. There is, in other words, a metonymy between an illicit part and otherwise licit whole. "A permissible [*mubah*] action," he writes, "in fact, even a praiseworthy [*mustahabb*] one, becomes unlawful and prohibited if combined with an unlawful action."[114] Thanvi offers the example of attending a dinner when invited: a Sunna and praiseworthy act in principle, it becomes repugnant if forbidden (*haram*) activities take place.

Third—perhaps the most important point for understanding Deobandi social interventions into Sufi practices: "As it is a commandment to save other Muslims from harm, if the elite [*khawass*] engages in some unnecessary action that corrupts the belief of the masses ['*awamm*], then this action will become reprehensible and prohibited for the elite as well. The elite should abandon such an action."[115] The inference here is that the elite, who are supposed to understand the rationale behind what is prohibited and what is accepted, must be cautious regarding what they say and how they conduct themselves in public view.

Fourth, that which was appropriate in the past may no longer be so today: "It is possible for something that was once lawful to be no longer regarded as such; for, at that time there was no reason to deem it reprehensible, but now a reason to deem it reprehensible has arisen. Or something that is permitted in one place may be prohibited in another."[116] Here Thanvi invokes a legal principle known as "corruption of the times" (*fasad al-zaman*), which deems acts that are permissible in principle to be no longer permissible because of a perceived "corruption" (*fasad*) in the wider society. As others have noted, this principle granted jurists enormous latitude in prohibiting certain acts because it relied on a subjective judgment about a law's social context.[117] We will see Thanvi make similar claims about the Sufi saints' death anniversaries (*'urs*) and the Sufi musical assembly (*sama'*).

The fifth and final point concerns one of the most oft-cited justifications for a particular action in terms of Shari'a: whether it has some "benefit" to the masses. Thanvi approaches this logic with extreme caution. "If an action contrary to the Shari'a has some benefit or public good [*maslaha*]," he argues, "but attaining this benefit or good is not necessary in terms of the Shari'a, or there are other means of attaining it, or these actions are done with the *intention* of attaining the benefit, or after seeing the benefit then the masses will not stop such an action— then it is not permissible."[118] Thanvi largely rejected the use of the legal category of *maslaha* and condemned the abuse of this legal stratagem as "*maslaha* worship" (*masalih parasti*).[119]

So, for example, if someone attends a lecture on the Prophet's life and teachings and, say, feels an urgency to donate food, money, or clothing to the poor, or perhaps even becomes so emotionally over-whelmed that he or she stands up, there is no harm in this *so long as* it does not become a habit, and one is not doing it solely for the "benefit" of aiding the poor but only for the pleasure of God. It is not that Thanvi opposes helping the poor, to be sure; but doing so *for that reason* is objectionable, since the only motive for such a gathering should be worship. And one must not appoint a time for it, nor insist that others do it; it must be purely spontaneous.[120]

In 1915, Thanvi delivered a sermon on the Prophet's birthday in the main mosque in Thana Bhawan, titled *Al-Surur bi-zuhur al-nur* (Joy at the appearance of the light). This sermon, we can assume, represents what Thanvi described as the third type of *mawlud*: devoid of *bid'a* and sound in every way. He began the sermon with a long panegyric on the Prophet's birth, expounding on Qur'an 21:107: "We have not sent you [Muhammad] except as a mercy to the worlds." Thanvi sees this verse as the basis for Sufi understandings of the Prophet as Light (*nur*). "To be a mercy for the worlds, the Prophet had to be created before them, and this existence is his Light. The Prophet's Light was created before all else."[121] Indeed, the Prophet's birth is an occasion of "joy and mirth" (*farah wa surur*), but one that veered toward excessive forms of veneration.[122] The sermon becomes an extended critique of forms of *bid'a* that take place at these gatherings. Fundamentally, he says, any new innovation since the Prophet's era can be categorized in one of two ways. The first is some-thing that actually facilitates the goals and intentions of the Shari'a. This category includes "the composition of religious books, and the establish-ment of madrasas and Sufi lodges [*khanqahs*]." In the Prophet's time, he goes on to say, these innovations were not needed. Such was the affective power of the Prophet's message and personality that his Companions became living embodiments of that message. It is only in subsequent cen-turies that the need for religious books, seminaries, and Sufi lodges arose. The second category, of which the *mawlud* is the prime example, is the mirror image of the first. The rationale (*sabab*) behind celebrating the Prophet's birthday is joy at his birth. The Prophet's Companions shared that joy, Thanvi argues, but they did *not* innovate the actual practice of *celebrating it*. "They had the rationale [*sabab*] for celebrating the Prophetic birth, but neither the Prophet nor the Companions celebrated it. Can we say—God forbid!—that their understanding was limited? If the rationale was not present, then we could say they had no cause for it. But the rationale for *milad* [i.e., *mawlud*] was there, and neither the Prophet nor the Companions celebrated it." In the first category, there was no initial rationale for it, but the rationale emerged later as a means of fulfilling Shari'a commandments, whereas in the second, there was a rationale for it, and the early Muslims still did not innovate the practice despite this evident rationale. They did not have a reason (*sabab*) for madrasas and innovated them when the need arose. They *did* have a reason for *mawlud* celebrations and did *not* innovate them despite it. "This," he says, "is the basis for distinguishing Sunna from *bid'a*."[123]

GRAVE DANGER: VISITING SAINTS' GRAVES (*ZIYARAT*) AND CELEBRATING THEIR DEATH ANNIVERSARIES (*'URS*)

For Sufis, especially of India's own "indigenous" Sufi order, the Chishtiyya, the Indian subcontinent is what Thomas Laqueur calls a "necrogeography." Saintly bodies anchor the spiritual landscape, their shrines orient pilgrimage routes, and their death anniversaries give shape to the passing of time. Above all, saints *do* things for their devotees. This is what Laqueur calls the "work of the dead"—work that is inseparable from the spaces their bodies occupy.[124] For these reasons, Engseng Ho described the grave as a "dense semiotic object" with the power "to create communities based not on revelation but on something autochthonous and incipient in the grave complex."[125] For the Deobandis, this semiotic density disrupted the correct understanding of divine sovereignty. Any grave, in theory, could channel these disruptive forces. With its magnetic pull on lay Muslims, a Sufi saint's grave was all the more threatening in this regard. Combine the spatial dimension of the grave with the temporal dimension of the saint's death anniversary—in short, *doubly* disruptive—and one can begin to understand Deobandi attitudes toward the *'urs*.

Literally meaning a "wedding" (i.e., the day the saint "wedded" his beloved, God), the *'urs* is typically celebrated at the saint's grave on the day of his death. The 'urs has deep roots in central Asia and Anatolia. Jalal al-Din Rumi's (d. 1273) 'urs was already being celebrated in the early fourteenth century. The 'urs celebration seems to have come to India as Sufis fled central Asia in the wake of the Mongol invasions of Khurasan.[126] Nile Green has cautioned against the dominant view of the 'urs as a "narrowly 'popular' devotionalism."[127] "If anything," argues Green, "saint worship emerged at the top of the social spectrum and trickled down from there."[128] Indeed, the *Baburnama* records that the first Mughal emperor, Babur (d. 1530), visited Sufi saints' shrines and circumambulated them.[129] Akbar (d. 1605), likewise, visited the shrine of Mu'in al-Din Chishti some fourteen times, patronizing the shrine and donating the massive cauldron used to prepare food for pilgrims.[130] In 1640, the daughter of Mughal emperor Shah Jahan, Jahanara, wrote of walking "seven times around the illuminated tomb" of Mu'in al-Din Chishti and "kissing the ground" nearby.[131]

Sufis considered visiting saints' graves an important part of spiritual pedagogy. In the same era as Jahanara, Muhammad Chishti (d. 1630) described the etiquette of visiting graves for the average Sufi: "As for visiting your master's grave, when you draw near do not go too quickly, nor too slowly, but go at a moderate pace. If there is no harm in doing so, circumambulate the grave. . . . When you circumambulate, recite the *takbir* ["*Allahu akbar*"] and the Fatiha [sura 1 of the Qur'an], then say, 'O master!'" Kissing the grave and rubbing the dirt near the grave are also acceptable, if not expected, forms of showing one's reverence.[132]

But beyond Mughal elites and Sufi adepts, saints' shrines became sites of popular veneration as well. In the mid–eighteenth century, Muhammad Najib Qadiri Ajmeri observed in his *Makhzan-i a'ras* (Treasury of death anniversaries) just how widespread offering food to the saints and distributing it to other pilgrims was during this time.[133] Observations of Delhi during the reign of Muhammad Shah (d. 1748) reveal a robust culture of saint veneration in and around the city, as recorded in Dargah Quli Khan's *Muraqqa-yi Dihli* (Delhi scrapbook). Khan ornately described the shrine of Nasir al-Din Chiragh-i Dihli (d. 1356)—among the most prominent disciples of Nizam al-Din Awliya', who supported circumambulation of saints' tombs[134]—and the festivities that took place there:

> The radiance of his miracles [*karamat*] is a burning lamp for the destitute. The air [of his tomb] is the envy of the rose in assuaging the hearts of the needy. Truly he is not only the Lamp [*chiragh*] of Delhi, but the eye and lamp of all of India. Pilgrimage to his blessed tomb is performed on Sunday. In the

month of Diwali, the crowds are especially large, and on every Sunday of Diwali, pilgrims are blessed with good fortune. Near the shrine is a fountain where people bathe and are completely cured of old illnesses. Hindus and Muslims alike make pilgrimage to the shrine. From morning till night, caravans of pilgrims arrive. Spread out in the shade of every tree and beneath every wall, people are filled with mirth and cheer by spectacles strange and wondrous. In every place there is music and merriment. Sounds of the barrel drum and Jew's harp echo from every corner. Such pomp and splendor are especially present during his blessed 'urs.[135]

One can sense in this evocative description, in particular, the baroque array of beliefs and practices that had come to define the Sufi shrine.

As with the *mawlud*, Imdad Allah believed that contentions surrounding the 'urs pertained to particular aspects of it, not the practice as a whole, which he wanted to preserve. Besides giving an opportunity for pleading for the mercy of the dead, Imdad Allah explains, the 'urs provides a means for Sufis to meet one another and for Muslims to find potential Sufi teachers.[136] Like the debate about the *mawlud*, debate about the 'urs revolved around whether the Shari'a sanctions setting aside a specially appointed day for Muslims to come together at the tomb of a saint to honor him—not around the merits of visiting saints' tombs generally.[137] Some 'ulama cite the Hadith "Do not make my grave a site for an 'Eid" to argue that it is forbidden to have fairs and festivities at the tomb and to decorate it with pomp and display. These 'ulama believe that the purpose of visiting tombs is recollection of the afterlife, but the meaning of this Hadith, he explains, is *not* that gathering at a tomb is forbidden; otherwise the caravans to Medina for visiting the Holy Cemetery would also be forbidden. "The truth is that visiting tombs is permissible, whether individually or in a group," he submits, "as well as conveying merit upon the dead through Qur'an recitation or [distributing] food, and it is established that this is a social good [*maslaha*]."[138]

Deobandis agreed with Imdad Allah on many of these points, and did not oppose visiting saints' graves categorically. In fact, many believed visiting the graves of saints within their Sufi lineage (*silsila*) was an important aspect of spiritual training. Deobandi works abound with references to the spiritual energy that graves emit. Khalil Ahmad Saharanpuri, for example, enjoyed paying his respects to the founder of the Chishti Sabiri lineage, 'Ala al-Din 'Ali Sabir (d. 1291). But he was not above criticizing even the familial caretaker (*sajjada nishin*) of the shrine during his visits. Once the caretaker brought him two green handkerchiefs to place on the shrine and various sweets to leave nearby. The caretaker was stunned when Saharanpuri not only rejected the offerings but lectured him on the impropriety of making such offerings. On another occasion, Saharanpuri and Thanvi visited the shrine of Mu'in al-Din Chishti in Ajmer. One of the attendants in Ajmer was vexed when Saharanpuri sat down near the tomb and went into a meditative state (*muraqaba*), because it conflicted with the custom in that part of the shrine of prostrating and circumambulating. The attendant was horrified when Khalil Ahmad sat in this state for so long that other pilgrims began to get offended.[139]

Above all, Deobandis have taught that graves—all graves—are meant to be sites of reflection on mortality. Mahmud Hasan Gangohi (d. 1996) described the proper etiquette for visiting the grave of one's parents:

> When one goes to the grave, he should think of the high positions they held, the buildings they owned, and the houses they once owned. They possessed orchards and cars. Some of them had children; some had extensive knowledge, and today all of them are in their graves. They had not taken anything of the world along with them into the grave. The only thing that they had taken along was their actions. If their actions were good then they will be in a good condition, and if their actions were evil then they will be in a miserable condition. May God shower His mercies on these people. Reflect over this in order that your love for the world decreases.[140]

We see similar sentiments in Muhammad Zakariyya Kandhlavi's *Maut ki yad* (Remembrance of death), a collection of Hadiths, with short commentaries, that pertain to death and dying—a Sufi meditation on the futility of any deed that is not motivated solely on attaining the pleasure of God.[141]

Gangohi, too, visited saints' graves. But as we have already seen, the public persona of Deobandi scholars was an important part of decisions to avoid certain practices. Gangohi once enjoyed going to the grave of his ancestor 'Abd al-Quddus Gangohi (d. 1537).[142] "Initially I went often and would sit close to it," explained Gangohi, "but because of the innovators, I abandoned this practice. Nowadays I feel restless in my urge to visit the grave, but I won't go because the descendants [of 'Abd al-Quddus at the shrine] will say that I am inclining toward them—in other words, inclining toward *bid'a*. For this reason, I am content to send him my salutations from here and have no desire to go there."[143]

Here, Gangohi demonstrates in practice one of the principles for understanding *bid'a* that Thanvi articulated in theory: that it is incumbent on the elite (*khawass*) to abandon a practice that corrupts the masses ('*awamm*)—indeed, even one that is permissible in principle. The generation before Deoband may have been less strict about this. A story is told about the Hadith scholar Shah Muhammad Ishaq of Delhi (d. 1845), grandson of Shah Wali Allah and revered among Deobandis, visiting the shrine of Mu'in al-Din Chishti. One of his disciples in Ajmer learned that he planned to pass through the town and intended to visit the shrine. The disciple learned of his impending visit and asked Muhammad Ishaq not to come, since he had been preaching against visiting saints' shrines around the town and worried that if his master came to Ajmer, it would nullify the lessons he had preached. Muhammad Ishaq responded: "Khwaja Sahib [Mu'in al-Din] is one of our great masters. I will not be able to pass through and not visit him. When I come to Ajmer, give a sermon in which you explain that I am in error in coming to Ajmer and that there is no need for this sort of action. Say this in front of me and do not think I won't be able to endure it. I will admit my error and you will avoid doing the harm that worries you so."[144]

If Muhammad Ishaq's love for Mu'in al-Din was such that he was willing to make an example of himself of what *not* to do, Gangohi was far more apprehensive about his public persona, and would adhere to the normative order even if it went against his own master's suggestions. When Gangohi visited Imdad Allah in Mecca, Imdad Allah invited him to attend a *mawlud*. Gangohi replied, "No, Master, I cannot go. In India, I prevent people from going to this. If I participate, the people back home will say that I gladly went to a *mawlud* here." The author of the anthology in which both of these stories appear adds: "Now, look! Who could be more beloved and honored than one's Sufi master. Yet among the followers of the religion [*din*], its preservation is more essential [than love for one's master]. When there is a contradiction between the two, preference was given to the religion."[145]

Gangohi's aversion even to *appearing* to countenance controversial Sufi devotions extended to his treatment of his students. Whenever the *'urs* of his ancestor 'Abd al-Quddus Gangohi was being held in Gangoh—which he had tried, unsuccessfully, to stop—Gangohi would become unsettled and irritable. One of his students came to visit him in Gangoh, but accidentally came during the *'urs*. Gangohi snubbed him, and the student was nonplussed as to why he received such treatment. When he realized the *'urs* was the reason behind Gangohi's irritability, the student said, "Master, I have no attraction to the *'urs*! By God, I did not come to Gangoh for this reason and I had no idea that the *'urs* is being celebrated here nowadays." Gangohi replied, "Although your intention was not to participate in the *'urs*, there were two men on the road coming to the *'urs* and you were the third. According to the Prophet, whoever supports a gathering is part of it."[146]

But Gangohi's main grievance was with the social practices that had coalesced around the *'urs*. Gangohi specifically forbade leaving food at tombs on an appointed day or a specific occasion—a line of reasoning similar to Muhammad Isma'il's belief that anything done with a pre-scribed time encroaches upon the Sunna: "Distributing food on an appointed day is without the slightest doubt an innovation, even though one may still incur divine favors, and a fixed *'urs* is against the Sunna, and therefore an innovation. Distributing food only at an unappointed time is permissible."[147]

He also vehemently opposed circumambulating Sufi shrines, during *'urs* or on any other occasion. Gangohi rebutted an (unnamed) author who asserted that circumambulating shrines is permissible because "the fundamental principle of all things is that they are permissible until a legal rationale [*dalil*] is produced to prove they are forbidden [*haram*]. . . . With respect to circumambulating saints' graves, it is not permissibility that is in need of proof. Rather, it is the impermissibility that must be proven." The author argues that Qur'an 22:29—"circu-mambulate the Ancient House"—commands Muslims to walk around the Ka'aba during the Hajj but does not *limit* Muslims to circumambu-lating the Ka'aba, adding that circumambulating the Ka'aba is an act of "worship" (*'ibadat*) whereas circumambulating saints' tombs is mere "reverence" (*ta'zim*).

Gangohi's rebuttal is clear and incisive. Likewise citing the Qur'an— "We designated for Abraham the site of the House, saying 'Do not asso-ciate anything with Me and purify My House for those who walk around it, for those who stay there[148] and those who bow and pros-trate'" (22:26)—Gangohi argues that God made circumambulation (*tawaf*) a ritual act on par with prostration (*sajda*), both of which must be "purified" of association with anything other than God. This is a clear textual proof (*nass*) that circumambulation is *intrinsically* an act of worship. Elsewhere, the Qur'an states: "He has commanded that you worship none except Him" (Qur'an 12:40). Taken together, these verses prove incontrovertibly that circumambulation is an act of worship, and that any act of worship is for God alone: "The only permissible rever-ence [*ta'zim*] for the saints is that which is not specified for God." Finally, he concludes, the hermeneutic principle animating the original inquiry—"The fundamental principle of all things is that they are permissible until a legal rationale is produced to prove they are forbidden"—applies *only* to matters for which there is no clear textual reference (*nass*) in the Qur'an or Sunna. Thus, he reasons, the author misapplied a core legal principle. He concludes by inverting the logic of the original inquiry: when we are speaking of worship, it is not the case that anything is permissible until proven to be impermissible; rather, is it *permissibility* that must be proven.[149]

Ashraf 'Ali Thanvi reiterates the same distinction between reverence and worship in *Hifz al-iman* (The preservation of faith), one of his most incisive critiques of Sufi devotions, published in 1901. Thanvi argues that prostration as reverence is analogous to prostrating toward someone as a form of salutation (*tahiyyat*), an action that appears in stories of past prophets, including Adam and Joseph. This form of prostration, however, was abrogated by the revelation to the Prophet Muhammad. Substantiating it today would require a proof (*dalil*) from the Qur'an or Hadith, but no such proof exists.[150] Thanvi cites a Hadith from Abu Dawud attributed to Qays bin Sa'd, who saw Persians prostrating themselves to a governor at Al-Hira and then told the Prophet he was deserving of this. The Prophet replied, "If you passed by my grave, would you prostrate yourself before it?" Qays replies, "No." The Prophet says, "Then do not do this."[151] The form of prostration the Prophet proscribes here, Thanvi says, is to bow as a salutation. The other form, prostration as worship, is clearly *shirk*. All the proof we need, Thanvi says, is the Prophet's negative response to Qays, which simultaneously proscribes *both* prostration as "reverence" in any capacity and prostration toward graves specifically. If prostrating toward a grave is reprehensible, "prostrating toward a living saint is even more reprehensible." Thanvi also adduces a proof from Ibn 'Abidin: "As for kissing the ground in front of scholars ['*ulama*] or chieftains, this is forbidden, and both the one who does it and the one who approves it are sinners because it resembles idol worship." He concludes: "When simply kissing the ground is forbidden by virtue of its resembling worship, prostrating resembles it even more so, and in this narration [from Ibn 'Abidin], worship and reverence both fall under the same legal precept: prostrating in this manner is infidelity [*kufr*]."[152]

Thanvi then takes up the question of circumambulating (*tawaf*) a saint's grave. He begins his argument with the Hadith "Circumambulation of the Sacred House is like Prayer." "Prayer's most salient feature is that it is worship. Thus, whatever resembles this feature is also worship," he reasons. "The meaning of this Hadith is that just as prayer is worship, so circumambulating is worship, and worship of anything other than God is forbidden [*haram*] and infidelity [*kufr*]. This is proven from absolutely clear textual referents [*nusus*]." Circumambulation, again, is *intrinsically* an act of worship, one that has been specified only for the Ka'aba. Circumambulating anything else is forbidden.[153]

Like Gangohi, Thanvi, too, believed that there is a value in visiting graves. They remind the visitor of his or her own mortality.[154] But Thanvi knew all too well the emotional tug of the dead and its threat to *tawhid*. In *Bihishti zewar* (Heavenly ornaments), Thanvi lists tomb-based devotions first in his catalogue of impermissible innovations—which, he explicitly states, is arranged in order of their danger to the normative order:

> To hold fairs at graves with all manner of pomp, to light lamps at graves, for women to go to graves, to put sheets over graves, to build permanent grave-stones, to revere graves excessively to win the favor of elders, to kiss or lick a *ta'ziya* or grave, to rub the dirt of graves, to circumambulate or bow before graves, to perform the daily prayers in direction of graves, to make offerings of sweets, rice, or cakes at graves, to keep *ta'ziyas* or flags, to offer them salutations, or offer them halva or cakes.[155]

Thanvi is firm in his belief that one cannot attend *'urs* gatherings without being adversely affected by the moral corruption that pervades them; even if one attends with the best of intentions, it will induce in him or her a "propensity toward sin."[156]

Thanvi lists off several other factors that, combined, shape his judgment against the *'urs*. He submits that among the worst kinds of *'urs* are those that entail musical assemblies (*sama'*), and that these are "never, ever permissible according to the statements of the great Sufi masters."[157] Thanvi also rejects the common practice of traveling to a tomb for the sake of fulfilling some oath.[158] Covering tombs with shrouds or decorating them with lights is equally repugnant, as is making offerings of food or other items near the shrine.[159] But what of those who make the argument that shrine-based offerings actually benefit the poor, who are able to partake of the food offered? Thanvi rejects this notion immediately as a legal "trick" (*hila*) since, he submits, the real intention of those who offer such things has nothing to do with feeding the poor; their intention is solely to glorify the shrine and its saint. If they really want to feed the poor, why do so at a Sufi shrine? The same logic, as we saw previously, informed his views on *mawlud*.

Aside from this litany of moral dangers and theological risks, visiting saints' shrines (*ziyarat*) and celebrating their death anniversaries also encourage the public to believe that the saints are able to intercede with God on behalf of those who visit. Gangohi argued that there are three different types of calling on any entity other than God: The first is to "pray [du'a] to God to carry out a task on account of the sanctity [hurmat] of such-and-such a person." This is unanimously understood to be permissible, even at the graveside of a saint. The second kind is to say directly to the dead, "Please do this task for me," whether at the grave or elsewhere. This is unequivocally shirk. The third is to go near the grave and to say, "Such-and-such person, please pray [du'a] for me that God fulfills this task." The legality of this, he goes on to explain, is up for debate, hinging on whether the dead are able to hear, about which the 'ulama differ.[160] As for Thanvi, if the sense of intercession (tawassul) that one has in mind when visiting a tomb is that saints have some direct leverage over the mechanics of the universe, this is a polytheism no different from the idol worship that God sent down the Qur'an in order to abolish.[161]

But what if the sense of intercession is not about the saint's power, but rather about the saint's knowledge? The masses visit these tombs with the expectation that the saint will be able to bestow on them some insight into the future—for example, whether their children will reach a certain age. This, too, is deeply problematic for Thanvi. If one implies that the saint is essentially omniscient, then this is plainly shirk. But if one implies, by virtue of the proximity that the saint has to God, that somehow God conveys this knowledge to the saint, perhaps that is not shirk, says Thanvi, but such a view is unnecessary. In the latter case, why not just go directly to the source of such knowledge—in other words, to God?[162]

The Qur'an itself states that asking for help (isti'ana) should be directed toward God and God alone, as Deobandi Qur'an commentaries readily point out. A single verse from Sura al-Fatiha, in fact—"You alone we worship, and you alone we ask for help" (Qur'an 1:4)—makes this explicit. For Muhammad Shafi', "the secret [raz] to the Qur'an is Sura al-Fatiha, and the secret to Sura al-Fatiha is 'You alone we worship, and you alone we ask for help.'" Shafi' explained that calling upon a saint as if the saint had power to fulfill some request independently of God, or even as if God had granted such power to the saint, is to associate God's power with others (shirk). But, he elaborates, the Qur'an itself is replete with stories of the prophets' miracles (mu'jizat). Are these events not evidence that God channels his power through the prophets? Yes, but those powers are temporarily channeled through the prophets in the same way electricity is channeled through a fan. A fan cannot run independently of the power that makes it move.[163] Similarly, one of Thanvi's students, Muhammad Idris Kandhlavi (d. 1974), author of the famed Qur'an commentary Ma'arif al-Qur'an (Sciences of the Qur'an), too saw this verse as a lynchpin of Qur'anic theology.[164] In seeking help from an entity other than God, whether or not one is guilty of *shirk* hinges on the belief of the one seeking help. Believing that a saint, for example, possesses powers of intercession *in essence* (*mustaqil bi-l dhat*) is unequivocally *shirk*. It is even *shirk* to believe that God has bestowed that power onto the saint. But suppose someone does not believe such things, but still prostrates toward the saint's grave or takes a vow (*nazr*) in the saint's name? This, says Kandhlavi, effectively *treats* the saint *as if* he had such powers, something he calls *shirk* in everyday practice (*a'mal*), if not necessarily belief (*i'tiqad*). *Shirk* in practice does not render one a non-Muslim, but it is a slippery slope toward becoming one.[165]

At first glance, it may seem that Deobandis sought to flatten the hierarchies of the medieval Sufi cosmos so that individual Muslims could, at least in theory, commune directly with God without any mediators. But I think we misread Deobandi texts if we assume they sought to purge Islam from all forms of hierarchy. As we will see in the fourth chapter, they sought to replace a saintly hierarchy based on miracles (*karamat*) with one based on moral distinction. For centuries, Sufis had varied roles in the spiritual lives of their disciples, but Deobandis opposed the role of what Arthur Buehler called the "mediating shaykh." As the "sole intermediary between Prophet and disciple," the mediating shaykh stands in contrast to the "directing shaykh," who guides "the daily lives of initiated disciples." As Buehler explains, "While the activities of a directing-shaykh enable disciples to arrive near God themselves, the mediating-shaykh 'transmits' the disciples' needs to Muhammad, who then in turn intercedes with God."[166]

In all of these variegated critiques of saints and their graves, one might assume that Deobandis shared the same antipathy toward shrines that motivated Wahhabis to destroy them across Arabia—a process that began in Muhammad ibn 'Abd al-Wahhab's own day but culminated with the 1926 leveling of the Jannat al-Baqi' in Mecca, a cemetery containing graves of some of the earliest Muslims. But the Deobandis were never willing to anathematize even Muslims who participated in some of the practices they believed were *shirk;* in fact, they pushed back against those who did, as the Deobandi Qur'an and Hadith scholar Shabbir Ahmad 'Usmani (d. 1949) made clear before an audience of Arab *'ulama* during a June 1926 conference in Mecca, convened by 'Abd al-'Aziz ibn Sa'ud, then king of Najd and the Hijaz, but soon to be, as of 1932, the first king of the newly formed Kingdom of Saudi Arabia.[167] The conference included *'ulama* from across the Muslim world, part of a series of conferences in the summer of 1926 in Mecca and Cairo whose ostensible aim was continuing the discussions about the caliphate that had been raging across the Muslim world since the end of the First World War.[168]

'Usmani had been invited in part because of the scholarly reputation he had acquired in the Middle East on the basis of his famed Hadith commentary, *Fath al-mulhim*. On 25 June, 'Usmani and other *'ulama* discussed "the construction and destruction of tombs and holy places."[169] Ibn Sa'ud himself began the discussion by arguing that one who engages in *shirk* is also, necessarily and by definition, an unbeliever (*kafir*), adducing two verses from the Qur'an that, he submitted, applied to any "worshipper of tombs" (*'ibad-i qubur*): "We only worship so that they bring us nearer to God" (39:3), and "We found our fathers following a religion and we followed in their footsteps" (43:23)—both verses being the excuses that those who insisted on worshipping other gods, in addition to God, gave to the Prophet.[170] Ibn Sa'ud drew on the same story we saw Thanvi cite earlier, about 'Umar cutting down the tree that certain Companions had begun to revere. While Thanvi adduced the story to illustrate the hazards of practices like the *mawlud*, for Ibn Sa'ud it justifies *leveling* graves, even—or especially—those of the Companions.[171] Other *'ulama* at the conference had argued that anyone prostrating before a tomb is a polytheist (*mushrik*) on account of that action's ostensible similarity to idol worship. The upshot of these assertions was that such people could be legitimately killed. 'Usmani respectfully but firmly disagreed, proceeding to defend those who prostrate before tombs on this point. 'Usmani argued that there is a considerable degree of difference (*ikhtilaf*) among the *'ulama* on issues such as "prostrating before tombs, hanging lamps around them, or placing sheets over them. We regard these acts as innovations [*bid'at*] and detestable [*munkar*], and we have always waged jihad of the pen and tongue against them, but we have never believed it permissible to take their wealth or spill their blood."[172]

For a Deobandi scholar to defend so-called grave worshippers before an audience of Saudi *'ulama* is remarkable. For one, it reminds us of the need to resist the facile usage of terms like "Wahhabi" to describe Deobandis. Shabbir Ahmad 'Usmani's audience before *actual* Wahhabis is perhaps just the most salient example of why this label is problematic.[173] Most Deobandis have rejected the label. Khalil Ahmad Saharanpuri's summary of Deobandi belief argued that the core feature of Wahhabism is the rejection of following a single legal school (*taqlid*), on account of which the Deobandis are hardly Wahhabis, but also lamented that the scope of the label had expanded to include anyone who criticizes shrine-based practices.[174] As we will see in the final two chapters, Deobandis' critics have deployed the label "Wahhabi" loosely and haphazardly, with little attention to the genealogy of the term, grouping together Deobandis who have actively critiqued Wahhabism with Deobandis who have offered them at least tacit praise.[175]

Indeed, in this period, Deobandis did not carry out their critique of normative disorder through an assault on Sufis or their shrines, though the conclusion of this book takes up the question of Deobandi culpability for Taliban attacks on Sufi shrines in Pakistan in recent years. Their critique was primarily, though never exclusively, textual in nature, carried out through short critical pamphlets, primers on belief and practice, published sermons, and Qur'an and Hadith commentaries. The following two chapters turn to the Muslim publics that these texts harnessed toward the remaking of Muslim self and society.

3

Remaking the Public

The previous chapter examined how Deobandis theorized what I have called the normative order by way of the forces that militate against it: *bid'a*, "innovations" within revealed religion (*din*) that contravene or simulate it; and *shirk*, beliefs or practices that compromise the oneness of God's being (*tawhid*). It showed how they saw certain popular devotional practices, especially the celebration of the Prophet Muhammad's birthday and the Sufi saints' death anniversaries, as sites where both *bid'a* and *shirk* proliferate. But their concern about these devotions was not so much that they threatened the normative order in and of themselves—though certain beliefs associated with them certainly did—as what the lay Muslim masses, the *'awamm*, tended to assume about them: for example, assumptions about the Prophet's presence at the *mawlud* or the saint's intercession at the *'urs* (which Deobandis deemed to be *shirk*), or the assumption that specific rules for the *mawlud* had to be followed or that the *'urs* could be carried out only on a certain day (which they deemed to be *bid'a*). The problem was that the masses, for the most part, were simply *unaware* of the normative order. The question this chapter takes up is twofold: why, precisely, did Deobandis see the Muslim public as a site of normative *disorder,* and how did they understand the task of reforming it? The former question, we will see, hinges on a notion of the "masses" (*'awamm*) that Deobandis inherited from a precolonial social and intellectual hierarchy between *'amm* (common) and *khass* (elite)— the latter, in this context, signifying the *'ulama*—that was itself in the process of becoming muddled, if not collapsing altogether, especially as it intersected with, but was never reducible *to,* ideas of the public as a collectivity of "rational" (*'aql-mand*) individuals reading religious texts in private, as opposed to the irrational energies of the colonial crowd. But there were other ways in which the public was in a state of flux. For one, Deobandis encouraged Muslims to distinguish themselves from non-Muslims—in everyday habits, demeanor, clothing—through denunciations of "imitating" (*tashabbuh*) non-Muslims. And yet, by contrast, the difference between *'amm* and *khass* was becoming *less* distinct as lay Muslims read and studied religious texts independently of the *'ulama* or became "middling" *'ulama* with their encouragement.

As for the second part of the question—*how* to do reform—Deobandis grappled with an array of approaches to carrying it out. Should the *'ulama* go to the sites where those in need of reform tend to congregate, such as the Sufi shrine and the *mawlud* assembly, and preach to them directly, even with all the risks of abuse and slander from an unsympathetic audience? Or should one write reformist texts, which will reach far more people, but without the intimacy of the sermon and with all the attendant hermeneutical risks of print? This chapter will show how Ashraf 'Ali Thanvi shifted abruptly, at Gangohi's instigation, from the first strategy to the second, from a tactic of mingling amid the (disorderly) masses and preaching to them directly to a tactic of harnessing the power of print to reform individuals through the written word.

THE PUBLIC AND THE CROWD

To understand how Deobandis understood the public, perhaps paradoxically, as both a source of normative disorder *and* the site through which to reform it, we must explore the nature of the late colonial public itself. The turn of the twentieth century was, of course, a period of sweeping social and political change in India. During this period, "new markets, new communications, and new networks linked individuals to larger arenas, and brought former strangers into new settings that stimulated new styles of social interaction."[1] Scholars such as Manu Goswami and Marian Aguiar have illustrated the effects of new technologies—in particular, the Indian railway—in producing new forms of collectivity and even the very notion of India as a geographic imaginary.[2] The Dar al-'Ulum Deoband was founded in the immediate aftermath of three major technological innovations—the postal service in 1854, rail travel in 1859, and the telegraph in 1865—that profoundly altered public life.³ The first railway station at Deoband opened in 1869, connecting Deoband to Delhi in the south and Saharanpur in the north.⁴ Railway travel in India "reinforced and made visible internal differentiations along class, gender, and 'respectability' lines" and "enabled the translation, over time, of these different perspectives into systematic and comprehensive visions of the political and social world."⁵

But aside from connecting Deoband with cities and towns across North India—and eventually, by steamship, across the Indian Ocean—these new technologies also contributed to the very forms of social intercourse that Deobandis saw as a source of normative disorder, as in facilitating mass pilgrimage to Sufi shrines. The railway was critical to the celebration of the *'urs* of Shah Barkatullah of Marahra, for instance—a Sufi saint especially important for the Barelvis. Custodians of the shrine would advertise the event up and down the railway route and string lights from the station to the shrine.⁶ Likewise, the first railway service to Ajmer began in 1879, profoundly changing the scale of the pilgrimage to the *'urs* of Mu'in al-Din Chishti—now one of the largest gatherings of Muslims in the world, in some years rivaling the Hajj.⁷ An 1892 guidebook for visiting Ajmer, *Sair-i Ajmer* (Traveling to Ajmer), gave detailed instructions for getting from the train station to the shrine of Mu'in al-Din. Significantly, the author of the guidebook was a Hindu and wrote the book partially for Hindus visiting the shrine, as well as for Muslims.⁸ Just a few years later, in an 1898 letter, Thanvi lamented the "mixing" (*ikhtilat*) of crowds—Muslim and non-Muslim, men and women, youth and adult—that took place at these shrines.⁹ Thanvi preferred the solitude of his *khanqah,* as did Gangohi, whose distaste for "the public [*jalvat*] and crowds of people [*izdiham-i khalq*]" was well known to his students and disciples.¹⁰

This period, of course, was also one of grave prognoses about a then-nascent mass society. Gustave Le Bon's *La psychologie des foules* (The psychology of crowds) of 1895 theorized the mimetic contagion of crowds in ways that bear a striking resemblance to Thanvi's view, seeing in the urban crowd "a collective mind [in which] the intellectual aptitudes of individuals, and in consequence their individuality, are weakened."¹¹ Similarly, for Thanvi, the customs (*rusum*) that proliferate in crowds and mass society "are of the sort that have spread like a tempest among otherwise intelligent [*samajh-dar*] and rational [*'aql-mand*] people. . . . The only explanation for this is that these customs have become such common practice among the people that they have cast a veil upon their rationality [*'aql*]."¹²

The crowd, then, was a source of normative disorder not only because of the tendencies of the masses to elevate merely permissible actions to obligatory ones—the most salient mark of *bid'a*—or to misunderstand the agency of saints—a telltale mark of *shirk*. The crowd also harbored intrinsic forces of disorder and disruption. The disruptive affect of the crowd was one of the main reasons for which Thanvi believed that the Sufi musical assembly known as the *sama'* needed to be abandoned, despite the fact that the *sama'* was the "preeminent symbol" of India's most prominent Sufi order, the Chishtiyya.[13] In classical Sufi pedagogy, the goal of the *sama'* is ecstasy, known as *wajd*. Though *wajd* is generally considered a "state" (*hal*) of the Sufi path, as opposed to a "station" (*maqam*), meaning it was achieved not through one's own volition but through divine favor, *sama'* was nevertheless a technique for effecting it. For Thanvi, the *sama'* occupies a liminal space between a public of reformed individuals and the crowd. Its danger was precisely in its tendency to devolve into a mere "crowd" when the visceral affect of ecstatic bodies prevailed over emotional restraint. This is the essence of Thanvi's argument in *Haqq al-sama'* (The true Sufi musical assembly), published in 1899, in which Thanvi redeploys arguments from al-Ghazali's *Ihya' 'ulum al-din* to argue that the *sama'* of his day was no longer a viable pedagogical option for Sufis. He draws on al-Ghazali's three-part typology for the conditions of the *sama'*: time (*zaman*), place (*makan*), and participants (*ikhwan*).[14] *Zaman* means the time of the *sama'* should not conflict with other religious duties, such as the five daily prayers. *Makan* means it should not take place in a public setting "with people coming to and fro, in which some sort of tumult [*hangama*] may distract the heart." *Ikhwan* means that all members of the assembly must be sincere in their spiritual purpose, for if even a single "ostentatious Sufi" joins and proceeds to "feign ecstasy and tear his clothes, the spiritual grace [*lutf*] of the gathering vanishes."[15] If this was the case in al-Ghazali's time, says Thanvi, "now consider our times":

> The majority of participants are people for whom *sama'* is detrimental. . . . Even if there happens to be present among them a pious person who is a servant of God, then he neither possesses adequate external knowledge of the Shari'a, nor is he an expert in the inner knowledge [of the Sufis]. He does not understand the subtle points [of *sama'*], nor is he aware of the terminologies and subtleties of the mystics to enable him to interpret the verses he hears. He is unable to reconcile the Law [*Shari'a*] and the Truth [*haqiqa*]. On account of his ignorance, he will accept any corrupt thoughts occurring to him. Whether it be an illicit innovation [*bid'a*] or unbelief [*kufr*], he is not concerned as long as he derives pleasure. Thousands are involved in clear unbelief because they misunderstood poetry sung during a *sama'* gathering.[16]

Thanvi, once again, applies the principle that the *sama'*, too, needs to be left behind if it corrupts the masses: "There are many actions that may be permissible [*mubah*] or even recommended [*mandub*], but they are forbidden because there is a risk of them corrupting the masses ['*awamm*]. For this reason, the legal scholars have completely forbidden the *sama'*, for its corruption is overpowering [*ghalib*]."[17]

In short, the *sama'* is permissible in theory, but not its "modern" forms, insofar as now "the audience comprises members of the general public ['*awamm al-nas*]." "Such a thing is, in and of itself, neutral [*mubah*] with respect to the law," he writes, "but is impermissible in light of the well-entrenched habits of today's public. In the present age, *sama'* has become a pastime, a source of entertainment for the masses."[18]

But *sama'* was also dangerous because the public is not equipped to understand the occasional ecstatic utterance (*shath*; pl., *shathiyat*) of a participant in an ecstatic state (*hal*). It is, in fact, that very state of ecstasy that absolves someone of any legal or theological infractions that the utterance might entail. Sufi devotional practices are not the only context in which the public encounters ecstatic utterances they do not understand; they often encounter them in tales of saintly miracles, which Gangohi deemed especially dangerous.[19] Ideally, any discussion of ecstatic utterances would take place within the safe confines of the Sufi lodge, the only place where Thanvi was comfortable discussing difficult theological puzzles. Even there, he remained circumspect. On one occasion, he discussed what is undoubtedly the most famous ecstatic utterance in the history of Sufism, Mansur al-Hallaj's "I am God!" (*ana al-haqq*). "Various people have claimed divinity [*khuda'i*], but Husain ibn Mansur [al-Hallaj] should not be compared to them," he begins, absolving Hallaj of any legal ramifications for his claim. "For his claim to divinity," Thanvi continues, "was made in an ecstatic state [*hal*], and otherwise he professed servanthood ['*abdiyat*] because he performed his prayers." He continues: "But someone asked [Hallaj] once, 'When you are God, to whom do you pray?' He answered, 'I have two forms, one external [*zahir*] and the other internal [*batin*]. My external form prostrates to my internal form.' This, too, is an abstruse riddle [*ramz-i ghamiz*]."[20] Commenting on Hallajian aphorisms was something best done in the intimate setting of the *khanqah*.

The Sufi in ecstasy, in other words, was a moral and legal danger to those surrounding him. The Sufi might say things that ought not be repeated, and the state of ecstasy itself had a contagious energy that tended to affect others. That affect was magnified in public settings where the noninitiated gathered to gawk at sacred devotions that they regarded as mere entertainment. However—and this point cannot be overemphasized—Deobandis were by no means antipathetic toward all forms of social affect. On the contrary, the next chapter will show how the affective energy (*faiz*) of pious bodies—an energy that coalesces around bodies both living and dead—has a transformative salutary power, without which the disciplinary project of self-reformation would be a *merely* intellective one. Deobandis do not, therefore, conform neatly to the narrative of modernity by which the public is gradually divested of affect—a presumption based, in turn, on seeing rationality and affect as intrinsically at odds.[21] On the contrary, the Deobandis believed that reformed publics are brought into being precisely *through* the affective powers of the virtuous body. Moreover, the very same technologies that were a source of normative disorder also permitted madrasa students to travel great distances to study at Deoband or Saharanpur, and permitted Sufi masters and their disciples to communicate via mail, which was especially important for Thanvi.[22] We must not overemphasize this point, of course; we should avoid imputing the rise of new publics to a sort of techno-determinism. After all, Sufi masters and disciples communicated via letters in the Mughal era, too, long before the British arrived.[23] These shifts were perhaps more quantitative than qualitative. The broad point is simply that, from the Deobandis' perspective, the same technologies that enabled illicit innovations (*bid'a*) to proliferate also provided new means to reform them.

PUBLICS AND POLEMICS

By Thanvi's time, as we will see below, the "public" to which Deobandis addressed their reformist energies was primarily a discursive one: a community of like-minded readers of Urdu religious texts. In some respects, Deobandis rearticulated the distinction in classical liberalism between the public—dispersed across space, linked through texts, brought together via rational deliberation—and crowds—present in a particular space, intrinsically irrational, vulnerable to the vagaries of mass affect.[24] The individual at the center of the Deobandi public was the reformed lay Muslim: emotionally restrained, disciplined in his or her sensibilities, meticulously following the Sunna in all aspects of daily life. If such an individual lay at the center of an imagined public configured through the circulation of reformist texts, that individual's foil was the lay Muslim who attended all manner of mass gatherings, whether lavish weddings or saints' death anniversaries, heedlessly shunning ritual obligations like the daily prayer.

In other respects, however, the Deobandi public is quite different from classical liberalism's. As the next chapter explores further, Deobandis' understanding of the self was not premised on a Kantian autonomy from priestly authority, relying on the "public use of one's reason in all matters."[25] The individual at the center of the Deobandi public was not, in other words, represented by bourgeois individuals "pursuing their own self-interest, conversing, debating and deciding independently without regard to loyalties or obligation."[26] As we saw, Deobandis *did* believe that rationality (*'aql*), with which humans are naturally endowed, played a key role in the ability to distinguish divinely revealed normativity from its multiple competitors, but this rationality was not reasoning for reason's sake, the Kantian *Räsonieren,* "a use of reason in which reason has no other end but itself."[27] If, in the Kantian public, "ideas are presented on their own merits by self-reflective moral subjects rather than . . . preachers, judges, and rulers," in the Deobandi public, reflective moral subjects re-form their sensibilities around an authoritative structure that ultimately emanates from the Sunna and is mediated by the *'ulama.*[28]

But there is yet another difference between the (idealized) liberal public and the Deobandi public, one relevant to the discussion here. By the early twentieth century, the Deobandi public had already been shaped by a culture of polemics—polemics that circulated textually, but were also occasionally staged in actual public fora: in other words, a culture that was simultaneously mediated by reading publics *and* the mass affect of crowds. This sort of staged debate, known as a *munazara* ("disputation," from the Arabic root "to look at or evaluate"), was a popular form of public argument and, indeed, mass entertainment.[29] The *munazara* was typically a person-to-person debate, held at a certain time and place and before an audience, such as a noteworthy *munazara* that took place between *'ulama* and Christian missionaries at Agra in April 1854 over the nature of revelation.[30] These are not debates that one or another of the interlocutors would "win."[31] They were, to borrow from Jesse Lander's description of polemic generally, forms of "discursive calcification," a "hardening of partisan identities and ideas."[32] Yet although polemics are "polarizing," they are also "pluralizing" in the sense that they open up the space of polemic to incorporate what Michael Warner calls "onlookers": "the agonistic interlocutor is coupled with passive interlocutors; known enemies with indifferent strangers."[33] The *munazara* was public in a spatial sense, then, but was also informed by the discursivity of texts. The reading publics that Deobandis addressed were already partly defined by the caustic polemics and counterpolemics that preceded them, exchanges that strain any presumptions about rational debate embedded in the liberal notion of the public. These were, in short, reading publics *already* enmeshed in the politics of the crowd.

Some Deobandis seemed inclined toward the view that the *'ulama* had a responsibility to proclaim the truth, in all its complexity and regardless of the public impact, and accordingly saw the *munazara* as an efficient means of doing so. Often the *munazara* was staged between Muslims and non-Muslims, as with Nanautvi's participation in a series of famous debates in 1876 and 1877 between Hindus, Muslims, and Christians over the nature of God.[34] But at other times, the *munazara* was staged between Deobandis and their Muslim rivals, especially the then-emerging Barelvi school led by the fiery Ahmad Raza Khan. In 1889, Khalil Ahmad Saharanpuri was invited to participate in a *munazara* in Bhawalpur over the row that ensued after the publication of *Barahin-i qati'a* (The conclusive proofs). Over the course of several days, Saharanpuri and his main opponent, Ghulam Dastagir, went back and forth over the possibility of God telling a lie (*imkan-i kizb*), a debate that Saharanpuri "won" so decisively that other Deobandis called him "Master of the Debaters" (*Sayyid al-Munazarin*).[35]

Barahin-i qati'a is probably the most salient example of a Deobandi text that embodies the culture and spirit of the *munazara* and exemplifies the overlap between reformed readers and colonial crowds. While many were discomfited by the sudden insertion of theological and legal issues (*masa'il*) into public debate, both in staged *munazaras* and in published texts styled like them, Saharanpuri seemed less concerned about these risks. In the wake of its publication, a certain Ya'qub 'Ali Khan, who taught Ahmad Raza Khan's father but whose views inclined toward Muhammad Isma'il's, approached Saharanpuri. "This issue about the possibility of [God] lying, which is synonymous with divine power, is beyond the comprehension of most scholars [*maulvis*], let alone the masses," he said. "Only an intelligent and extremely learned *'alim* can understand it. Scholars inclined toward *bid'a* are causing a fuss over this issue among the masses and making them anxious about it. They make the masses suspicious of the pious [*ahl-i haqq*] and stir up mischief. You should not have written about this issue." Saharanpuri replied that it was a necessary response to 'Abd al-Sami' Rampuri's critiques of Gangohi, and that he therefore had a responsibility to publish it. Besides, when the Prophet ascended to heaven and came back, he was ridiculed by those who could not understand it. Would it have been better, he asks rhetorically, if the Prophet had remained silent?[36]

A few years after the publication of *Barahin-i qati'a,* the mutual disdain that had begun to grow between Deobandis and the then-nascent Barelvi movement reached a fever pitch. In February 1906, Ahmad Raza Khan presented a series of Deobandis' allegedly heretical statements to *'ulama* in Mecca and Medina, and published these statements, along with these *'ulama*'s responses, in his *Husam al-haramayn 'ala manhar al-kufr wa al-mayn* (The sword of the two sanctuaries [Mecca and Medina] upon the throat of unbelief and falsehood). There is no room to analyze this text here, and others have done so in depth.[37] The main point is that Khan accused key Deobandis of unbelief (*kufr*), citing reasons such as Deobandis' belief that God's omnipotence theoretically encompassed God's ability to lie (*imkan-i kizb*).[38] He concluded with the following verdict: "By the consensus [*ijma'*] of the Ummah," the Deobandis—along with adherents of other movements, like the Ahmadis—are "disbelievers [*kafir*] and apostates [*murtad*] and out of the fold of Islam."[39] Khan saw the Deobandis as purveyors of strife, tearing at the very fabric of the Ummah. "The creed [*mazhab*] of the Sunna is a stranger to Hindustan," he wrote, ominously. "The darkness of tribulation [*fitan*] is in the ascendant. Evil is on the rise."[40]

Imdad Allah was deeply distressed by the rifts that had formed because of these polemics, among his disciples as well as in the public at large. He hoped *Faisala-yi haft mas'ala* (A decision on seven controversies) would be a balm for the wounds of "Muslims generally, but especially for those close to me"—which included disciples that were then in the process of polarizing along "Deobandi" and "Barelvi" lines. Imdad Allah saw no good in "fighting and altercation" (*niza' o jidal*). "My wish," in fact, "is that my friends do not bother with publishing any responses to this, because I have no desire to engage in debate [*munazara*]."[41] This aversion to the *munazara* was partly a plea to protect the public. For Imdad Allah, there was nothing positive to come out of involving the masses in these controversies. If scholars insist on discussing the possibility that God could lie or create other prophets, they should do so in "private conversation" (*zaban-i khalwat*) and never before a public audience. And if one *must* write about these issues, Imdad Allah says, one should do so in Arabic, lest the masses read it and feel the need to debate these issues among themselves.[42]

Thanvi arguably had more in common with his mentor Imdad Allah on this issue than he did with Saharanpuri. For Thanvi, "it is the way of the Sufi masters to forsake debate [tark-i mubahasa], even when they are right."[43] Below, we will see how Thanvi took a middle path between the aggressive, confrontational approach of Saharanpuri and the conciliatory, irenic approach of Imdad Allah. At the same time, he thought that many misunderstood *Faisala-yi haft mas'ala,* taking it to be an endorsement of *mawlud, 'urs,* and other practices. "This is absolutely not true," Thanvi wrote in 1898. For these people, "[Imdad Allah's] intention was to proclaim the truth to the masses. They believe I am guilty of hiding the truth while others have been freed from doubt and uncertainty. Yet it is clear that these widespread and common issues have led to all kinds of corruption in the belief and practice of the masses, and particularly the ignorant masses in India, as any intelligent writer can plainly see."[44] In any tension between conciliation and informing the masses of their errors, Thanvi always gave preference to the latter.

FLUID PUBLICS: THE DEOBANDI PUBLIC BETWEEN 'AMM AND KHASS

There is yet another crucial lens through which to understand Deobandi efforts to reform the public—in fact, the principal lens through which they understood the public itself: *'amm* and *khass.* The hierarchy of common (*'amm*) and elite (*khass*) is one that had been established, if often challenged, across the span of centuries. The meanings of *'amm* (in Arabic, "general") and *khass* (in Arabic, "specific," "particular") have shifted across historical, social, and legal contexts. In most contexts, the hierarchy was a hermeneutic one. One need not scour early Islamic texts to find such hierarchies. Ja'far al-Sadiq (d. 765), the sixth imam of the Shi'a and a major influence on Sufism, opens his Qur'an commentary with the following typology of readers: "The Book of God has four things: literal expression ['ibarah], allusions [isharah], subtleties [lata'if], and realities [haqa'iq]. The literal expression is for the commoners ['awamm], allusion is for the elite [khawass], the subtleties are for the saints, and the realities are for the prophets."[45] If such a theological hierarchy was defined in terms of knowledge, the *'amm*/*khass* distinction was also often a spatial one. The Mughal court, for instance, distinguished between the public audience hall (*divan-i 'amm*) and the private audience hall (*divan-i khass*), the latter conferring political capital on those who could access it.[46] In some contexts, the "elite" (*khawass*) would have been defined primarily in terms of class; throughout the nineteenth century, the *ashraf* ("nobility," denoting, in principle, Muslims of non-Indian ancestry, but a status that one could also earn) were, at this time, in the process of merging with a nascent "middle class."[47]

But for the *'ulama,* the *'amm/khass* distinction is most often a scholarly one: *khass* designates those who are defined by their mastery of religious knowledge (*'ilm-i din*); *'amm* designates everyone else. We have already seen numerous times how that comparative lack of religious knowledge is the source of normative disorder among the masses. But in the late nineteenth and early twentieth centuries, Deobandis strived to change the *'awamm* in two ways: they encouraged, even demanded, that the *'awamm* distinguish themselves from non-Muslims, and at the same time, their efforts to foster religious knowledge among the *'awamm* blurred the very hierarchies on which their identity as *'ulama* were based. Stated differently, they sought to foster distinction on the horizontal axis between Muslims and others, while they blurred it on the vertical axis between *'ulama* and laity.

Let us consider the first axis. Deobandis encouraged Muslims to distinguish themselves from non-Muslims in their demeanor, habits, daily routines, and dress. Nowhere is this more evident than in Deobandis' warnings against "imitation of the unbeliever" (*tashabbuh bi-l kuffar*). This concept, to be sure, did not begin with the Deobandis. It is one that Indian reformists invoked long before the Deoband movement—Sayyid Ahmad Barelvi once rebuked Muhammad Isma'il for attending a Hindu fair (*mela*)[48]—but is also a concept that has been invoked in various contexts for centuries.[49] But it preoccupied Deobandis to a significant extent. Gangohi was especially vocal in calling out what he saw as "Hindu" or "Christian" elements in Muslim devotional practice, which was for him prima facie evidence of its normative illegality.[50] The circumambulation of tombs, for instance, is "impermissible as it *necessitates resemblance with idol worshipers,* who engage in the same activity around their idols."[51] Lighting candles, hanging lamps, and leaving food at shrines also resembled polytheist practices and Hindu idolatry.[52] Gangohi was averse to ostensibly Christian and Jewish practices as well: "Kissing tombs is the practice of the Jews and Christians, and is thus forbidden."[53] Gangohi and Saharanpuri both opposed the *mawlud* for, among other reasons, its ostensible resemblance to non-Muslim religious practices.[54] The parallel with Christmas was the obvious one, but Gangohi also noted its resemblance to Shi'a commemorations of 'Ashura as well as the Hindu celebration of Krishna's birth, the *janmasthami*, which entails reading stories about Krishna's birth, analogous to the stories of the Prophet Muhammad's birth recounted in the *mawlud*.[55] Gangohi also asserted that the belief that the Prophet's soul descends from the world of spirits (*'alam-i arvah*) to the material world (*'alam-i dunya*) each year on his birthday bears similarities (*mushabahat*) to Hindu beliefs about the annual rebirth of Krishna.[56]

These admonitions went beyond devotional practice. They also concerned everyday social exchanges. Gangohi discouraged Muslims from doing business with Hindus, urged Muslims not to attend Hindu lectures and rallies, and criticized Muslims who retained trappings of "Hindu" custom and lifestyles. One fatwa permits the use of copper pots, which he associates with Hindus, so long as it is not done out of imitating (*tashabbuh*) unbelievers (*kuffar*).[57] A similar fatwa banned Muslims from wearing "Hindu" and "English" clothing.[58]

But Gangohi was not uniformly opposed to anything vaguely resembling "Hindu" belief and practice. He had no problem with the Sufi practice of holding the breath (*habs-i dam*) during meditation, as he explained to Thanvi, who was concerned about its potential similarity to Hindu yogic practices. Gangohi saw the matter as legally neutral (*mubah*), and, he adds, both yogis and Sufis adopted the practice because of its benefits in purifying the body through the regulation of bodily heat—central to both Chishti and Qadiri meditative practice, he notes. Its utility, then, precedes its adoption by both communities; it is not the case that Sufis adopted the practice *from* yogis.[59]

Ashraf 'Ali Thanvi, too, was determined to educate Muslims on the dangers of "imitation" (*tashabbuh*), couched within a broader conscientiousness about what he calls the signs (*shi'ar*) and marks (*'alamat*) of Islam in public space. Like Gangohi, he critiqued certain devotional practices for their resemblance to non-Sunni practices. He believed the distribution of sweets during *mawlud* may have derived from the Shi'i practice of distributing sweets on the 10th of Muharram.[60] But Thanvi's anxiety about public distinction informed how he perceived Muslims' sartorial choices and personal comportment as well. Thanvi explained the legal status of public distinction with the following analogy: suppose a man fills an empty liquor bottle with water and drinks it in public. He is not consuming liquor, to be sure; nonetheless "he is a criminal and, from the perspective of the Shari'a, a sinner, because he appears [*tashabbuh*] to be among the consumers of liquor."[61] This is why Shari'a norms mandate "distinguishing the Muslim community [*qawm*], the maintenance of difference in our clothing, our manners, our way of speaking, and our behavior." Whereas the Shari'a requires certain forms of Muslim distinction in any context—for example, the beard—some are mandated only in specific contexts. Thus, he says, "in our country, wearing coat and pants, wearing *gurgabi* [a type of shoe], tying a *dhoti* [worn by Hindu men around the waist], and women wearing the *lahanga* [a kind of skirt] are all things that are purely the characteristics of other communities [*aqwam*]."⁶² For Muslims to wear English dress in England was perfectly acceptable, as indeed he conceded that some did; but wearing such clothing in India was forbidden, precisely because it compromised public distinctions between Muslims and others.⁶³ Even printing the Qur'an might unwittingly perpetuate illicit forms of imitation. In 1917 Thanvi responded to a question about the permissibility of printing an English translation and commentary on the Qur'an, with the Arabic and English side-by-side in parallel columns. Thanvi regarded this, with no explanation, as "an imitation of non-Muslims" and said that the Qur'an must come at the top of the page, with the English translation below it and the commentary at the bottom.⁶⁴

At the same time that Deobandis encouraged Muslims to differentiate themselves from non-Muslims (and from non-*Sunni* Muslims), they also encouraged Muslims to become "like" the *'ulama*. By Thanvi's era, the distinction between lay Muslims and *'ulama* had also become more fluid. This was partly due to the very reformist activities that the Deobandis implemented. Those whom Thanvi purports to initiate into this rarefied scholarly discourse become part of a sort of quasi public of "middling" scholars—not quite the scholarly "elite," but not entirely "common" either, a group he describes with the Urdu word *mutawassit* ("middling," "midway," "intermediate").⁶⁵ Besides, Thanvi was clear that many of the *'ulama* would benefit from reading reformist texts as well, not just the laity. But Thanvi also sought to open a space for Muslims to go beyond what they could learn from these texts. These texts represented, to be sure, a *minimal* effort needed to shore up the reformed subjectivities he sought to cultivate. He hoped that these texts would inspire some Muslims to become *'ulama*. In fact, Thanvi abbreviated the madrasa curriculum in an attempt to make the core features of a madrasa education available to lay Muslims:

> If one has a desire for Arabic but little time, one can read only the necessary books. After a curriculum has been abbreviated accordingly, what once entailed ten years will take only two and a half. Do not be alarmed at this

novelty, and do not say earlier *'ulama* were wasting their time since what now takes two and a half years used to take ten. For my intention is not that *the very same* instruction that took ten years will now take two and a half, but we can conclude that a man, after such instruction, will become firm in his religion [*din*] and can become a scholar [*maulvi*] of moderate skill. Of course, his knowledge will not be vast, but if he so desires, he will have the ability to expand it.[66]

Completing this abbreviated curriculum would make someone a "middling scholar" (*mutawassit 'alim*), an opportunity he extended to women in *Bihishti zewar* (Heavenly ornaments), assuring them that "you will become within three years, God willing, a *maulvi*, a scholar of Arabic, and join the ranks of the *'ulama*. You will be able to give lectures on Qur'an and Hadith, just like the *'ulama*. You will be able to give fatwas, just like the *'ulama*. You will be able to teach Arabic to children, just like the *'ulama*."[67]

HOW TO DO REFORM: PRINT, PUBLICS, AND RELIGIOUS KNOWLEDGE

Whether someone who simply reads reformist texts in his or her spare time, or someone aspiring to become a "middling" *'alim*, the individual was the central node in a reformist matrix that linked individuals to families, families to towns, and towns to the wider reading public of reformist literature. The introduction to *Bihishti zewar,* one of the most widely printed books in South Asia, makes this abundantly clear, linking the moral health of the individual with the moral health of the Muslim body politic in explicit terms. Thanvi explains why he composed the book: "The cause of the devastation" in which Indian Muslims find themselves "is women's ignorance of religious knowledge, which in turn ruins their beliefs, deeds, social transactions, character, and public life. . . . The reason is that corrupt belief leads to corrupt ethics, corrupt ethics to corrupt actions, corrupt actions to corrupt social dealings, and corrupt social dealings lead to corrupt public life."[68]

Though Thanvi saw the reformist text as the primary instrument of effecting reform, this had not always been the case. Evidence suggests that he gradually came around to this strategy from an earlier inclination to reform individuals by going directly to them. In a series of letters between Gangohi and Thanvi in May and June of 1897, Gangohi admonished Thanvi for attempting to reform the *mawlud* in Kanpur by engaging with its participants directly. The correspondence began after

Thanvi received word through a mutual acquaintance that Gangohi was angry at him. Gangohi wrote to him, saying, "I overheard that you may be guilty of things I consider *bid'a*. . . . This is difficult for me to believe." It becomes clear, in Thanvi's response, that the rumor to which Gangohi refers is that Thanvi had participated in a *mawlud*. A despondent Thanvi wrote back to defend his participation in the *mawlud* in the following terms:

> Where I was living then [in Kanpur], there were many assemblies [*majalis*] where people undoubtedly transgressed the limits. Initially people were opposed to my objections. After three or four months, I took my first journey to the Hijaz, and Hazrat [Imdad Allah] said to me: "There is no need to be so strict. Wherever the practice exists, do not object to it. Wherever it is absent, do not introduce it." After my return [to Kanpur], I would participate [in such assemblies] upon request with a resolve to reform [*islah*] the beliefs of the people. Thus, I always spoke on these various occasions and explained clearly that if they believed these actions to be essential, they became *bid'a*. . . . By virtue of how deeply rooted these habits are, I have no hope of upturning them. Yet if I did not participate at all, there would be no hope of reform. Another reason I participated is that I saw how few people came to sermons, but people of all different tastes and persuasions would come out in droves for these assemblies. This afforded me an opportunity to offer advice and counsel [*pand o nasa'ih*], reform their beliefs, and rectify their actions. Hundreds, even thousands, of people repented of their corrupt beliefs and evil deeds and became righteous. Many Shi'a became Sunni. Usurers, drinkers, and people who did not pray were corrected. In short, I gave sermons [*wa'z*] under the pretext of giving lectures [*bayan*]. Finally, I saw that it would not be possible to remain at these assemblies without participating. Upon even a slight objection [to participating], I would be called a Wahhabi and be degraded and abused verbally and physically.[69]

Later on in the letter, he submits: "If participation is truly against the pleasure of God and His Prophet, then Hazrat Imdad Allah's approval of it needs explanation. The masses are having doubts about their respect for and connection to the *'ulama*. To remedy this, I feel confident that there is room in the Shari'a [for participation in these assemblies]."[70] But he offers to quit his employment at the madrasa in Kanpur if Gangohi urges him to do so.

In his response, Gangohi excuses Imdad Allah for his lack of knowledge of legal niceties, and concedes that Thanvi followed him out of the love and respect he has for the master. But he says that Thanvi's participation in the *mawlud*, even for the purposes of reforming it, demonstrates an incomplete knowledge of *bid'a*, for which he chastises Thanvi and urges him to read Saharanpuri's *Barahin-i qati'a*.[71] He ends the letter with a gentle admonition, giving his disciple the space to arrive at the conclusions he had made abundantly clear: "I will not interfere with the methods you wrote about. Do whatever you deem appropriate and prudent. I approve of any method for freeing God's creatures [*khalq-i khuda*] from an innovator [*mubtadi*'], so long as you avoid any severity that could be cause of disorder [*fasad*]."[72]

But Thanvi seems to have taken Gangohi's advice to heart. The fact is that he did quit teaching in Kanpur soon after this exchange with Gangohi, taking up residence at Imdad Allah's *khanqah* in Thana Bhawan, where he would spend most of the rest of his life.[73] And indeed, these years coincided with the publication of a number of short primers on Islam and succinct critiques of popular devotions and customs, including *Islah al-khayal* (The reformation of thought) in 1901, and *Bihishti zewar* in 1905. Thanvi did not stop writing for the rest of his career. I do not want to suggest that this exchange with Gangohi was the sole reason for his shift to writing, or that his writing began only afterward. In fact, Thanvi began writing reformist literature while still in Kanpur. *Islah al-rusum* (The reformation of customs), though not a "primer" per se, was composed as early as 1893. His first true primer on Islamic belief and practice was likely *Ta'lim al-din* (Instruction in the religion), published in Kanpur in July of 1897—a mere two months after these letters were written.[74] Unless Thanvi wrote *Ta'lim al-din* in a matter of weeks (not altogether impossible for a writer as prolific as he), he likely began it beforehand. Regardless, the letters and the subsequent relocation to Thana Bhawan heralded a shift to print as his preferred medium of reform.

Though Thanvi came to see the task of reforming Muslim practices like *mawlud* and '*urs* as one that could be best accomplished through religious texts written for lay Muslim readers of Urdu, the aim was never *only* about reforming these practices. The salvation of the masses, under the strain of colonial modernity, depended on endowing them with a certain degree of religious knowledge, empowering them to reform themselves and then others. This attitude toward knowledge and salvation was not new to Thanvi. It has roots in the Qur'an itself, of course. As Franz Rosenthal put it, "Right from the start, the student of the Qur'an finds himself confronted with the thought presented forcefully and inescapably that all human knowledge that has any real value and truly deserves to be called 'knowledge' is religious knowledge."[75] Thanvi called on Muslims not only to acquire essential religious knowledge, but to ponder the very notion of reform (*islah*) and how it related to their everyday choices.[76] This core knowledge was so critical, in fact, that

Thanvi regarded its pursuit as a "binding duty" (*farz-i 'ayn*) upon all Muslims individually. This was not a new idea either; al-Ghazali, too, as Thanvi would have known, had argued that a certain degree of religious knowledge was a binding duty—especially what is necessitated by Islamic belief, worship, and social conduct (*mu'amalat*).[77] The difference between al-Ghazali and Thanvi, here, is not the content of their views, but the context.

To this end, Thanvi composed numerous short primers that sought to convey just enough knowledge to prepare Muslims to navigate the fluid public life of colonial modernity and, most importantly, attain salvation. One of these primers, *Hayat al-Muslimin* (The life of Muslims), begins with a Hadith of Ibn Majah—"Seeking religious knowledge is compulsory upon every Muslim"—and explains: "This Hadith establishes that every Muslim—whether male or female, city dweller or villager, rich or poor—must acquire religious knowledge. And 'knowledge' does not only mean reading Arabic. In fact, it means learning about the faith, whether through reading Arabic books or reading Urdu books, whether inquiring among reliable *'ulama* or listening to reliable lecturers."[78]

As numerous scholars have documented, the rise of large-scale lithographic printing in nineteenth-century India introduced a world of print across multiple vernaculars.[79] This included the rapid expansion of Urdu-language presses and Urdu book markets, which was in part due to British privileging of Urdu as an administrative lingua franca over more "regional" languages like Punjabi.[80] In the rise of Urdu print, we can also see the concomitant emergence of Urdu reading "publics"—in the dual, overlapping senses of an *'awamm* that had a voracious appetite for books, *and* a "public" that had begun to refer to itself using that very term. Thus, in the 1880s, journalist and novelist Abdul Halim Sharar began to speak of a nascent *"Islami pablik"* in Urdu.[81] Soon thereafter, the Urdu novelist Ratan Nath Sarshar began to use the word "public" (*pablik*) in Urdu to signal a new category of reader that, he believed, the category of *'awamm* did not adequately capture.[82]

However, Thanvi and other Deobandis use the terms *'amm* ("common," "mass") and *'awamm* ("commoners," "masses") predominantly to refer to these readers. Within the Deoband movement at least, it was Thanvi, primarily but not exclusively, who tapped into these new markets in the first two decades of the twentieth century with short, introductory texts on Islam.[83] These texts would typically cover worship (*'ibadat*), belief (*'aqida*), ways of life (*mu'asharat*), social relations (*mu'amalat*), Sufism (*tasawwuf*), and the rights (*huquq*) due to different members of a properly ordered Muslim society—one's spouse, one's children, one's parents, one's friends. They also typically included sections on Sufism and the importance of resisting *bid'a*, the latter typically with minimal commentary, as in *Bihishti zewar*: "God and his Messenger have laid out for their servants all aspects of religion [*din*] in the Qur'an and Hadith. It is improper to introduce anything new into religion. Such a thing is called *bid'a*."[84]

This minimalist approach to explaining *bid'a* is found throughout other Deobandi texts written for lay audiences. Mufti Muhammad Kifayat Allah's *Ta'lim al-Islam* (Instruction in Islam), to take a prominent example, combined core principles of belief and practice alongside Deobandi reformist perspectives in a deliberately simple question-and-answer format:

> *Question:* After unbelief [*kufr*] and associating others with God [*shirk*], what is the greatest sin?
>
> *Answer:* After *kufr* and *shirk*, innovating in religion [*bid'a*] is the greatest sin. A *bid'a* is anything that does not have a foundation in the Shari'a [*asl-i Shari'at*]—that is, has no basis in the Holy Qur'an or Noble Hadith, did not exist in the time of the Messenger of God, his righteous Companions, the Followers, or the Followers of the Followers,[85] and for which adhering or abstaining is understood as a religious deed. *Bid'a* is a very bad thing. The Messenger rejected *bid'a* and called those who commit it destroyers of religion. He said that all *bid'a* is sin and all sin leads to hell.
>
> *Question:* What are some of the acts that are *bid'a*?
>
> *Answer:* People have devised thousands of *bid'as*. Here are a few: constructing permanent [*pukhta*] graves; constructing domes over graves; holding the *'urs* or lighting lamps at graves; putting sheets of cloth over graves; assembling to eat at the home of the deceased; including the *sehra* [a floral garland attached to a groom's headgear] or the *baddhi* [a floral garland worn around the waist] in marriage ceremonies; adding conditions and qualifications to any otherwise permissible and desirable acts that have no basis in Islam.[86]

It is important not to overstate the distinction between reformist texts for fellow *'ulama* and for lay Muslims. There was surely some overlap between the two. By and large, Thanvi's texts on law and Sufism were written for *'ulama* and Sufi disciples, respectively (though these were often one and the same). His texts for lay Muslims concerned Islamic belief and practice, and while they might hint at more technical legal issues, they deliberately avoided delving into them. But we can partly identify which texts he intended for lay Muslims by the fact that *he* identifies them as such. Thus, he marketed *Hayat al-Muslimin*—a primer published in 1928, covering the importance of religious knowledge, reciting the Qur'an, the life of the Prophet, the rights (*huquq*) due to others, how to pray, how to fast, Muslim marriage, and other topics—as a primer for lay readers, a "treasure house sufficient for the well-being and success of Muslims in this world and the next."[87]

But print, of course, came with certain hermeneutic risks. To mitigate them, Thanvi urged lay readers of these texts to consult the *'ulama* at every turn:

> Those who are able to read Urdu, or able to learn to read Urdu easily, should consult reliable Urdu religious books. . . . To the extent it is possible, these books should be studied lesson by lesson with a properly knowledgeable person, and if such a person is unavailable, you may study the books on your own, but whenever you do not understand something or there is some doubt, make a mark with your pencil. Then when a properly knowledgeable person is available, inquire [about what you do not understand] and then impart that knowledge to others, whether in the mosque or in an assembly room. Then at home, share the knowledge with your wife and children. . . . Those who cannot read Urdu should have a literate man read to them so they can hear these books and inquire about religious issues. . . . Whenever you are about to do some deed, whether religious or worldly in nature, and do not know whether it is good or bad in terms of the Shari'a, then it is necessary to ask a pious *'alim* and to bear in mind what he says, and to tell it to other men and women. If you don't have the time to go directly to such an *'alim,* send him a letter, along with a self-addressed envelope so that he can respond to you easily and quickly.[88]

As Francis Robinson observed, for the Indian *'ulama*, "[t]he printed book was designed to reinforce learning systems that already existed, to improve them, not to transform them. No one was to read a book without the help of a scholar."[89]

Thanvi applied the same principle to reading the Qur'an: it should be done only under the supervision of a qualified scholar. The very idea of *studying* the Qur'an, as opposed to knowing by heart a number of key suras for recitation in the five daily prayers, was still relatively novel in Thanvi's era, at least from the standpoint of the *'ulama*. In the previous chapter, we saw how Muhammad Isma'il advanced the notion of the Qur'an as easy to understand and accessible to all. While Deobandis benefited from the revivalist impulse behind Isma'il's call for individual Muslims to engage with their scripture more directly, a Qur'an that needs no human mediation marginalizes the *'ulama,* who are trained in its proper interpretation. The abundance of mass-printed Qur'an translations magnified these hermeneutic risks. We see Thanvi grappling with this dilemma as he advises individuals to read the Qur'an, even in translation, but to do so, again, alongside a trained scholar. "Instruction in the Holy Qur'an is desirable, and in fact commanded, for all Muslims, young and old, commoners ['awamm] and the elites [khawass] alike. This includes instruction from translations for non-Arabic-speaking commoners." There are a few principles that must be adhered to, however: "The instructor should be a full-fledged scholar ['alim-i kamil] and a wise sage [hakim-i 'aqil] who discusses the translation and selects topics to interpret in accordance with the understanding of the learner. The instructor should be easy to understand, soft in tone, and not conceited about himself or his knowledge, so that he does not make mistakes in interpretation [tafsir] or have the audacity to interpret the Qur'an from his own opinion [tafsir bi'l ra'e]."[90]

This effort to police the boundaries of interpretation was at least partly an effort to preserve the place of the 'ulama as custodians of Islamic tradition. But it was also born of a real fear of the untrained masses engaging in wild speculation about matters beyond their comprehension—whether concerning the Qur'an, Islamic legal issues (masa'il), or ecstatic utterances (shathiyat) of the Sufis—and thereby imperiling their very salvation. This is nowhere more evident than in Thanvi's discussion of the Islamic legal concept of the ratio legis, known as 'illa (Arabic, "reason"). In the principles of Sunni jurisprudence (usul al-fiqh), there are two substantive sources of the law (Qur'an and Sunna) and two methodological sources: analogy (qiyas), and consensus (ijma') of the 'ulama. Qiyas allows the derivation of a new legal verdict (hukm) by analogy with an existing one in the Qur'an, Sunna, or consensus. A paradigmatic case illustrating this process is Islamic law's prohibition of intoxicants. The Qur'an explicitly forbids wine (Qur'an 5:90) but not other intoxicants—for example, liquor. In jurists' prohibition of other intoxicants, wine consumption is the original case (asl), other intoxicants are the new case (far'), and preventing intoxication is the "reason" or "rationale" ('illa) that links the original case and the new case, yielding the legal verdict (hukm) of prohibition. But actual cases were rarely so clean-cut. Sometimes cases presented multiple possible 'illas. Even the very process of determining what constituted an 'illa in a particular case had its own name—ta'lil ("ratiocination")—derived from the same Arabic root.[91] Deriving a legal verdict in a situation for which the Qur'an and Sunna do not offer clear proofs was a delicate matter indeed. "While standing at the core of shar'i epistemology," writes Kevin Reinhart, "the *'illa* is the most problematic link in the epistemological chain because there is no objective procedure for its determination."[92] Getting it wrong is to tamper with God's will.

Therefore, Thanvi asserts, only a *mujtahid*—one qualified to engage in independent legal reasoning (*ijtihad*) from the scriptural sources—was permitted to derive new laws by way of analogy. As far as he was concerned, neither he nor anyone else alive in his day, moreover, was a *mujtahid*.[93] He saw the derivation of the law as an epistemically sensitive process that could go horribly wrong in the hands of someone ill qualified. What if, he speculates, someone were to decide that the *'illa* for the Qur'anic prohibition of adultery (*zina*) is to avoid confusion about bloodlines? Would it, then, become permissible to fornicate with a woman who is barren? The very idea, of course, is an abomination.[94] If even the *'ulama* were susceptible to this sort of wayward legal reasoning, what of the masses? "There is an illness these days in that the masses search for the rationales [*'illat*] behind rulings [*ahkam*]," which was in turn part of a broader "mass illness, in which everyone wants to be . . . a *mujtahid*."[95] This is why "the rationales [*'illat*] for legal rulings [*akham-i shar'iyya*] should never be discussed in front of lay Muslims."[96] For Thanvi, discussing the *'illa* before the public was a veritable invitation for lay Muslims to form their own legal "verdicts" on contentious issues, something only the *mujtahid* is qualified to do—not average *'ulama*, not even Thanvi himself, let alone the masses. Thus, he urged lay Muslims not to inquire about the reasons behind legal rulings, and urged the *'ulama* not to discuss the reasons behind legal rulings publicly.

Two clarifications about Thanvi's stance are important here. First, as Fareeha Khan has convincingly shown, despite Thanvi's rhetoric about the utter absence of *ijtihad* in his time, he was a *mujtahid* in every way but in name. Thanvi's *ijtihad* ranged from rulings on contracts to rulings on parental rights (*huquq al-walidayn*) that diverged markedly from Hanafi precedent. Khan argues that Thanvi fits the classic ranking of the jurist qualified to do *ijtihad* within the legal issues pertaining to a given school (a *mujtahid fi'l masa'il*), if not the higher rank, one qualified to make decisions on new issues not covered by the school's founder (a *mujtahid fi'l madhhab*)—the founder, in this case, being Abu Hanifa. Calling his decisions "*ijtihad*" would have run afoul of the Deobandis' carefully crafted image as staunch defenders of traditional legal conservatism (*taqlid*).[97]

Second, and more germane to our purposes here, Thanvi was also stretched between his impulse to curtail public debate about knotty legal and theological issues and his awareness that the public was *already* debating such things and that he should therefore at least intervene to mitigate the damage. He did not always manage that tension well. A case in point is the rather odd book *Al-Masalih al-'aqliyya li-l ahkam al-naqliyya* (The rational benefits of transmitted rulings), published in 1916, in which Thanvi systematically offers "rational" explanations for a whole array of Islamic beliefs and practices, from prayer and fasting to dietary restrictions and criminal penalties. (To take one example, pork, he says, is forbidden because pigs naturally tend to consume impurities [*najasat*], which are then transmitted to the one consuming it. While Thanvi does not offer such commentary, one can imagine him fielding a question about whether pork would then become permissible for a Muslim if a pig were raised in such a way as to ensure that the animal consumed no impurities. This is precisely the risk of offering "rational" explanations for legal rulings.)[98] Zaman persuasively argues that Thanvi was under great pressure to appeal to the "rational" sensibilities of an English-educated readership, and that this text stands in tension, if not outright contradiction, with what he says elsewhere.[99] Let me return momentarily to the adultery example I just discussed. In *Al-Masalih al-'aqliyya li-l ahkam al-naqliyya*, Thanvi provides a rational reason for forbidding adultery, the very thing we just saw him caution against. He provides two reasons, in fact: First, adultery has a deleterious effect on the social order (*intizam-i tamaddun*); it is liable to provoke anger and retaliation on the part of the families involved. Second—and notably, given the discussion above—adultery mixes bloodlines (*khalt-i nasab*).[100]

Is this not a direct contradiction with what we just saw above? To be fair, nowhere in this text does Thanvi say that he is offering the reader legal rationales (*'illat*) for what the Shari'a mandates; he is offering "rational," one might even say quasi-sociological, explanations for what is already clear and incontrovertible. In other words, one *must* abide by the Qur'anic prohibition on adultery, but if explaining to an inquisitive reader that prohibiting adultery has the added benefit of avoiding confusion in patriliny and the social discord that accompanies it, then so be it. And these are the very readers for whom he says he writes this book in its preface. "In our era," Thanvi writes, "the effect of modern education [*ta'lim-i jadid*] is that many people have developed a desire and a taste for looking into the benefits [*masalih*] [of legal rulings], and although the real cure for this would be to halt such investigations, given the harms that arise from them, experience shows most people will reject such advice, with the exception of certain sincere students among the common people." And to ensure no reader takes the book to have any legal import whatsoever, "these benefits are not indicated [within the textual sources], nor are they the basis for the rulings themselves." He then clarifies that the basis for writing such a book at all was partially that Shah Wali Allah's *Hujjat Allah al-baligha* (The conclusive argument from God), a book that also explored the "benefits" (*masalih*) of God's revelation, had been translated into Urdu—a worrisome development for Thanvi, since it was never intended for a mass readership.[101] In a sense, then, Thanvi is trying to get ahead of a problem that had already started to fester.

Thanvi fully understood that he was walking a hermeneutic tightrope. He was trying to attract certain "educated" readers—skeptical of the 'ulama, perhaps even disaffected toward religion in general—with "commonsense" (*afham-i 'amma*) explanations for what religion commands of them, yet attempting to undercut their attraction to such explanations at the very same time. Once again, we see Thanvi simultaneously struggling to bring certain readers into his orbit through the power of print, while insisting that relying on print alone is harmful. The mediation of the 'ulama is vital.

Islamic law was by no means the only subject on which Deobandis fought to curtail public misunderstanding, nor was Thanvi the only Deobandi to undertake this effort. The same ambivalence about public knowledge informs their Hadith commentaries as well, as Joel Blecher shows. In his commentary on Hadiths related to discretionary punishments (*ta'zir*) in the application of criminal law, Anwar Shah Kashmiri (d. 1933) accepted that Hanafi traditions permitted enormous latitude in interpreting such punishments. Nevertheless, to obviate the possibility that "the general public would deliver severe punishments without proper training," Kashmiri was clear that only a "traditionally trained expert" could interpret the law. As Blecher notes, Kashmiri's concern was about, for instance, "an overzealous husband or father taking the law into his own hands, beating his spouse or his child abusively."[102] As we have seen time and again, whether with respect to basic belief and practice or to the interpretation of the Shari'a, Deobandis believe that the public is adrift without the 'ulama.

Most Deobandis situated their approach to what the public *can* know and *should* know between the rarefied interpretive hierarchies of most premodern scholars and the hermeneutic populism of figures like Muhammad Isma'il. This always unstable balance ended up conjuring specific Muslim publics as much as it shaped preexisting ones, for if the likes of Imdad Allah were hesitant to involve the masses in controversial matters, later Deobandis bring these very same publics into being by virtue of calling them toward their normative ideals. We have seen how Deobandis—above all, Ashraf 'Ali Thanvi—became invested in the task of educating Muslim publics *just enough* to know the spiritual dangers of *mawlud, 'urs,* and other practices, but not so much that the public arrogated to itself the wherewithal to arrive at its own conclusions about these practices without the input of the *'ulama*—a delicate balancing act indeed. Thanvi and others sought to achieve this task by educating Muslim publics on a mass scale in the basics of Islamic belief and ritual practice. In the next two chapters, we will see the tension between these opposing forces—the impetus toward lay Muslim revival through endowing individual Muslims with religious knowledge, and the countervailing impetus toward constraining their interpretation of the very same knowledge—play out in two complementary ways.

First, we will explore in the following chapter how Deobandis' Sufi pedagogy, at the nexus of the law (*shari'at*) and the Sufi path (*tariqat*), included a similar ambivalence about "studying" Sufism through books. Just as one should "study" the Qur'an only under the supervision of a scholar, one should embark on the Sufi path only under the tutelage of a Sufi master. And just as lay Muslims have no business discussing Islamic legal issues (*masa'il*), they also have no business discussing ecstatic utterances (*shathiyat*) of the Sufis or reading Sufi poetry, replete as these works are with abstruse metaphysical concepts, like the "unity of being" (*wahdat al-wujud*), that can lead to the very speculation that, in turn, leads to *shirk*. Then, in chapter 5, we will examine yet another iteration of this ambivalence as it emerged in the origins of the Tablighi Jama'at, a revivalist movement that grew out of Deobandi reform. We will see how the movement's founder, Muhammad Ilyas, built an organized program that essentially translated Thanvi's teachings into practice, combining Sufi ethics (shorn, to some extent, of actual Sufi orders) with a modicum of religious knowledge—one that encouraged lay Muslims to reform themselves and then seek out others to reform, under the (at least partial) supervision of the *'ulama,* while *discouraging* discussion of legal issues and other controversial matters.

4

Remaking the Self

The previous two chapters detailed how Deobandi scholars theorized the normative order and how Muslim publics were, at once, the source of normative disorder and a site where that disorder could be remedied. That remedy entailed endowing "common" Muslims with the religious knowledge necessary to correct erroneous beliefs, perform core ritual duties, and recognize risks to salvation: illicit innovations in religion (*bid‘a*), and associating God's attributes with entities that are not God (*shirk*). The previous chapter described this process as remaking the public. The current chapter builds on that argument by homing in on the self at the center of that public, and the ethical fashioning in which that self was called to engage. Deobandis conceived this self-fashioning almost exclusively through the vocabularies of Sufism. And just as Deobandis believed one could not fully embrace religious knowledge without the aid of religious scholars (*‘ulama*), so, too, they believed that one could not fully embody Sufi ethics without the companionship (*suhbat*) of Sufi masters. The need for living, in-the-flesh *‘ulama* and for living, in-the-flesh Sufi masters were two sides of the same coin. It was the centripetal, anthropocentric force that counterbalanced the centrifugal force of an increasingly bibliocentric economy of knowledge. For the Deobandis, the self is best cultivated by way of other selves.

By "self," in this context, I refer to the *nafs*—translated variously as "lower soul, carnal soul, appetitive soul, self, lower self, impulsive self, instinctual self, [or] ego"—the transformation of which Sara Sviri described as the "*sine qua non* [of] Sufism."[1] In many ways the *nafs* is analogous to the Freudian *id*, and in fact mid-twentieth-century Arab psychoanalysts made that comparison explicit, drawing on classical Sufism to better understand Freud.[2] Remaking the public was a call for the individual to take the *nafs* both as an object of introspection (*muhasaba*) and purification (*tazkiya*), *and* as a quasi-autonomous subject doing the inspecting and purifying. I describe this as a *quasi* autonomy because the self called to interrogation is not directed toward the telos of vanquishing authority but, paradoxically, toward reaffirming it. The subjected self is reoriented around the authoritative structure of the Sunna, as mediated through and interpreted by Sufi scholars, at the very same time that it is liberated from competing modes of subjectivation, whether false customs (*rusum*) or illicit innovations (*bid'at*).

This notion of self and selfhood is, then, arguably quite different from what Immanuel Kant famously called for in the opening lines of "An Answer to the Question: What Is Enlightenment?": "Enlightenment is mankind's exit from its self-incurred immaturity. Immaturity is the inability to make use of one's own understanding without the guidance of another."[3] The Deobandi self is one that comes to fruition precisely *through* deference to the authority of the *'ulama* for the acquisition of religious knowledge and deference to the Sufi master for turning that knowledge into action. The autonomy that the Deobandi self seeks to achieve is autonomy *from* the constraints that customs and illicit beliefs place on one's agency. As the authority of these diminishes through the work of self-reformation, the authority of the Sunna replaces it *at the very same time,* instantiated in the bodies of other reformed selves. These are not two separate processes. Autonomy as *auto-nomos*—arrogating to oneself (*auto*) one's own law (*nomos*)—was never the goal of Deobandi disciplines of the self. To relinquish oneself from the clutches of faux normativities was always already to give oneself over to the formative power of the Sunna. It is not, then, an "autonomy" in the conventional sense of (mere) self-determination.[4] It may be useful, rather, to situate Deobandis' notion of autonomy within the broader genealogies of the self-governing individual that J. Barton Scott explores in his study of reformist Hinduism. On one hand, the Deobandi notion of autonomy bears more than a passing resemblance to the liberal ideal of the self-governing individual, with its critiques of the constraints that "customs" place on individual agency. On the other hand, it stands in stark contrast to this liberal ideal as an "exit from priestcraft"—that is, a self liberated from religious authority. As Scott demonstrates, this liberal ideal was always something of a fiction. It was, to borrow Charles Taylor's phrase, a "subtraction story," premised on the false (but still powerful) idea that once you "subtract the priest . . . you find 'modern man' just waiting to be free." This story ignores, of course, the extent to which liberal selfhood is "the contingent product of the modern social imaginary rather than its antecedent source."[5] But more importantly for our purposes, the liberal ideal of selfhood overlooks the extent to which the self is formed through relations with other selves. Against this Kantian "fantasy" of the autonomous self, Scott sees in Gandhi's writings a "model of ascetic self-rule [that] entails obedience, asking that the subject inhabit a norm or rule that by definition precedes him," a model that "implies relationality . . . that entwines the subject with others."[6]

Foucault famously described Stoic philosophies of self-care as an "intensification of the relation to oneself by which one constituted oneself as the subject of one's acts."[7] While Deobandis certainly took the self as an object of *intense* introspection and discipline, it is important not to imagine the Deobandi self as solipsistic, or one conjured entirely through the act of introspection itself. In his study of Stoic spiritual exercises, Pierre Hadot recognized that self-mastery is a process that transpires through dialogue, and dialogue is always embedded in a community.[8] Sajjad Rizvi's application of Hadot to Islamic philosophy could just as well describe ethical self-formation in Deobandi Sufism. Rizvi describes the insufficiency of the written word without a human mediation or an interpretive community: "The written word is an *aide-mémoire* for the spoken word," which is in turn predicated on "the revealed word, encoded in a sacred book, requiring a spiritual master to initiate and explicate."[9] We will see below how the pursuit of self-mastery, then, takes shape through the tutelage of a Sufi master, and comes to full fruition, ideally, in a community of other reformed selves within the disciplined sensoria of the Sufi lodge (*khanqah*). This sort of self-fashioning is premised on the notion that it is not "belief, discussion or persuasion . . . [that] transforms a person, but practice—action, repetitive behavior, and physical habits. It also points to a process, an on-going practice, the fulfillment of which in this life is impossible."[10] The self, then, is a project. The goal of fashioning the self, which always takes the Sunna as the ultimate reference point, is never complete; rather, one approaches that goal asymptotically, the way a curve approaches a line.

This is, then, an ethical discourse that one accesses through the study of the Qur'an and the Sunna and by observing and imitating the pious exemplars of the Sufi tradition, who were its living embodiments. This understanding of ethics, it should be noted, is different from ethics as the deduction of universally normative laws through the rational faculties, associated most notably with Kantian philosophy. Deobandis believe their values to be universally normative, of course, but they derive those values from participating in a *tradition*. It is an ethics based not just on assenting to metaphysical claims about truth, but equally on embodying pious dispositions in accord with the Prophetic model—or, more precisely, how that Prophetic model has been filtered through centuries of commentary. It is an *"imitatio Muhammadi,"* as Annemarie Schimmel put it, yet never *mere* passive imitation, since these pious dispositions must be actively internalized.[11] Such subjectivation is "the production of a morally and socially bounded individual self through a process of inward reflexivity,"[12] yet for the Deobandis such mastery is never in the abstract: mastery of the self is not an end in itself, but a means of freeing one from the constraints of this world, constraints that distract human beings from the sole reason they were placed on this earth—namely, to worship God and express gratitude (*shukr*) for his beneficence. In the case of Deobandis' Sufi ethics, the cumulative power of their own "tradition" exerts itself upon this discourse of self-transformation.

SUFI ETHICS OF LIFE

Deobandis use two terms that connote "ethics:" *akhlaq* and *adab*. *Akhlaq* derives from the semantic root that connotes "creation" and sees the ethical as an attunement to the highest ideals for which God created human beings, especially worship. The word is translated variously as "ethics," but also "disposition" and "character." Similarly, with its semantic connotations of "disciplining," *adab* connotes "civility," "etiquette," and "character." Deobandis have called *adab* the essence of Sufism. Zafar Ahmad 'Usmani declared that "[t]he entirety of Sufism is *adab*,"[13] while Rashid Ahmad Gangohi deemed *adab* its "most fundamental" aspect.[14] He elaborated on this idea elsewhere, in what is a veritable summary of the entire Deobandi approach to Sufism:

> The Sufi's knowledge is knowledge of the inner [*batin*] and outer [*zahir*] aspects of the religion [*din*] and of the power of certainty [*yaqin*]. This is the highest form of knowledge. The reality of the Sufi is the adornment of character [*akhlaq*] and remaining perpetually turned toward God. Sufism is the adornment of the self with God's ethics, the eradication of one's will, and absorption in seeking the satisfaction of God. The Sufi's ethics are identical to those of the Prophet Muhammad, in accordance with what God has said: "Truly [Prophet] you are of great character [*khulq*]" [Qur'an 68:4].

Gangohi goes on, in this statement, to describe the Sufi's character in detail:

> The Sufi's character is as follows. The Sufi regards himself as the lowliest, which is the opposite of pride. The Sufi is kind in dealing with God's creation and patient with people, is gentle with others, shuns wrath and anger, sympathizes with others and lets them take precedence. With abundant compassion, the Sufi respects what is due to others above what is due to himself, is generous, forgiving of faults and mistakes. . . . *The entirety of Sufism is, in fact, character [adab].*[15]

Numerous Deobandi works on Sufism describe the self as an ethical work in process that entails the divestment of harmful traits (*akhlaq-i razila*)—among them love of the world (*hubb-i dunya*), love of fame (*hubb-i jah*), greed (*hirs*), pride (*takabbur*), hypocrisy (*riya*), lust (*shahvat*), and envy (*hasad*)—and the adoption of virtuous ones (*akhlaq-i hamida*)—God-consciousness (*taqwa*), gratitude (*shukr*), patience (*sabr*), love (*muhabbat*), asceticism (*zuhd*), humility (*khushu'*), and others. This discourse long predates the Deoband movement. Sufis have understood these as stages (*maqamat*) on the Sufi path for centuries. For al-Qushayri (d. 1072), "Sufism means to take on every sublime moral characteristic from the life of the Prophet and to leave behind every lowly one."[16]

Ethics is, therefore, the space where law and Sufism converge. This mutual imbrication of inward and outward is the basis for the assertion that law (*Shari'a*) and the Sufi path (*tariqa*) are interconnected and, indeed, mutually constitutive. Even Shahab Ahmed's description of Sufism as "*para-nomian*"—"*beside, beyond* and *above* law," as opposed to *against* it—does not do justice to the mutually imbricated nature of Sufism and law in Deobandi understandings of them.[17] This ethical work is achieved, inwardly, when one becomes conscientious of God at every waking moment, which is reflected, outwardly, by performing the core ritual obligations of a Muslim naturally and reflexively. For Gangohi, this is the internalization of law and the process of removing any dissonance between the legal injunctions and their performance:

> Knowledge of the law ['*ilm-i Shari'at*] and knowledge of Sufism ['*ilm-i tariqat*] are the very same thing. The law and Sufism are also the same. When someone knows the commands of the Shari'a, he has knowledge of the law. When someone knows the essence of the command, he has knowledge of Sufism. To perform a duty or necessary deed against the will of the self [*nafs*] is to act in line with the law. When sincerity [*ikhlas*] and love for the reality of God completely encompass the depths of the heart, that is called Sufism. So long as knowledge and practice are in conflict with one another, Shari'a will dominate. When the conflict dissipates, that is Sufism.[18]

The ultimate point of Sufism is to make worship come naturally. Worship (*'ibadat*) requires two things: knowledge of the religion (*'ilm-i din*), and a "longing for, desire for, and *delight* in worship." The latter is fostered through Sufism.[19]

The corollary to Shari'a and Sufism as outer and inner manifestations of the same ethical imperative is that Sufism can be derived directly from the scriptural sources by which we know the Shari'a—namely, the Qur'an and Hadith. Thus, one of Thanvi's treatises, *Haqiqat al-tariqa min al-sunnat al-aniqa* (Realities of the Sufi path derived from the elegant Sunna), derives Sufi ethics through a commentary on 330 individual Hadith narrations.[20] Each is labeled with several categories depending on the particular "benefit" (*fa'ida*) that the narration offers. For Thanvi, Sufi ethics are contained in, and derived from, the Qur'an and the Hadith. These are the ethics that the Sufi masters embody, and which one acquires through companionship with them or, failing that, through reading stories about them:

> After correcting one's beliefs and reforming one's external [*zahiri*] actions every Muslim is obligated to reform his or her internal [*batini*] states. Innumerable verses in the Holy Qur'an and endless narrations in the Hadith attest to this duty. And yet people are heedless of this, bound by sensory desires. Who does not know that the Qur'an and Hadith stress acquiring virtues such as asceticism [*zuhd*], contentment [*qana'at*], humility [*tavazo'*], patience [*sabr*], gratitude [*shukr*], love of God, acceptance of fate, trust [*tawakkul*], surrender to God [*taslim*], and expressly forbid qualities such as love of the world, greed [*hirs*], pride [*takabbur*], hypocrisy [*riya*], lust [*shahvat*], anger, envy [*hasad*], and contempt? . . . This is the meaning of reforming one's internal actions and the fundamental purpose of the Sufi path [*tariqat*], and it is proven without the slightest doubt that this is *a required duty* [of all Muslims].[21]

I return to the theme of Sufism as a "required duty of all Muslims" below. For now, I want to note two important points relevant to the passage above. First, one of the aims of disciplining the self was the proper regulation of the emotions that arise from the *nafs*, not necessarily their elimination, which Deobandis understood to be impossible, in any case. Thanvi and other Deobandis follow al-Ghazali here, as they do on many matters. For al-Ghazali, certain predilections of the *nafs* had to be properly regulated and channeled; thus, anger (*ghazab*), for example, is the basis for courage (*shaja'at*).[22] Thanvi used these Ghazalian insights in his sermons, preaching that anger at sin is an emotion the drives the work of reform.[23]

Second, expounding on the mutual imbrication of Sufism and Shari'a was also a rhetorical strategy for arguing against Sufism's new critics. Thus, one could also see Thanvi's *Haqiqat al-tariqa min al-sunnat al-aniqa* as a rebuttal to Salafi critics of Sufism that, ironically, substantiates Sufism solely through the Hadith, at once challenging their view on Sufism *and* reaffirming Hadith-centered modes of rhetoric and argument. By the first two decades of the twentieth century, when Thanvi was writing and publishing his most important work, Muslim modernists on the one hand, and Wahhabis on the other, had leveled vicious accusations against Sufism. Thanvi understood that he had to demonstrate that Sufism is rooted firmly in the Qur'an and Sunna if he hoped to counter Sufism's most hostile critics. One way of defending Sufism was to show meticulously how the Qur'an and Hadith are wellsprings of Sufi ethics. Thanvi, like other Deobandis, argued that what we now call "Sufism" and what we call "law" (*fiqh*) were not yet disaggregated in the era of the Prophet:

> Shari'a is the name for the collection of rules from which all inward and outward actions derive. In the terminology of the ancients the word "*fiqh*" had a meaning synonymous with Shari'a. . . . Then in the terminology of the present, the part of Shari'a connected to outward actions became "*fiqh*" and the part connected to inward actions became "Sufism," and the paths for these inward actions is called "*tariqat*."[24]

The very distinction between the two emerged only as a "convenient means of describing the inner and outer dimensions" of the same thing. Treating them as *actually* separate "is an error of the ignorant, which today has even infected the learned."[25] To disabuse the reader of the notion that this is simply self-evident, Thanvi notes with a good deal of irony that "extreme" Sufis and "superficial" (*khushk;* literally, "dry") *'ulama* actually both hold the same erroneous notion: that Sufism is not to be found in the Qur'an and Sunna:

> The principles of Sufism exist in the Qur'an and the Hadith, yet people seem to think Sufism is absent from them. Of course, that is wrong. Extreme Sufis and superficial *'ulama* alike believe that Qur'an and Hadith are free of Sufism. Both are wrong. The superficial *'ulama* say Sufism does not exist, but this is delusional. . . . The extreme Sufis say that the Qur'an and Hadith are only about external matters, that Sufism is inner knowledge for which—God forbid!—the Qur'an and Hadith are not necessary. In short, both groups believe that the Qur'an and Hadith are devoid of Sufism. One group thinks they can ignore Sufism; the other, the Qur'an and Hadith.[26]

Yet, even though Shari'a and Sufism are mutually interdependent, Deobandis have been clear that the acquisition of core religious knowledge must take precedence over embarking on the Sufi path, for if the aim of Sufism is moral cultivation, the aim of religious knowledge is avoiding eternal damnation. In some sense, Thanvi seemed more concerned about "extreme" Sufis than the *'ulama* who rejected Sufism altogether. Such *'ulama,* though profoundly misinformed, were still likely to enter paradise, whereas such Sufis imperiled their salvation by collapsing the very distinction between Islam and unbelief (*kufr*).[27] This is why the choice of a Sufi master educated in Islamic law was critical: "If the seeker is a scholar [*'alim*], he will be aware of the requirements of the religion [*din*]. If the seeker is not a scholar, he should search for a master who will first correct his beliefs and instruct him in legal matters [*fiqhi masa'il*]."[28] For this reason, Gangohi insisted on not accepting a Sufi pledge (*bai'at*) from any prospective disciple who was still a student. He rebuffed even Ashraf 'Ali Thanvi's request for *bai'at* while Thanvi was still a student at Deoband. He would, however, accept the pledge from a lay Muslim who was *not* a student—the implication being that, for the student, acquiring religious knowledge takes precedence over self-reform, whereas for the lay Muslim, anything at all is better than nothing.[29] Ashraf 'Ali Thanvi, too, would not normally accept the Sufi pledge from prospective disciples while they were still students, though he did occasionally make an exception for outstanding disciples.[30]

CONTAGIOUS PERFECTION: CHANNELING PROPHETIC AFFECT THROUGH COMPANIONSHIP (*SUHBAT*)

Deobandis have argued that, in the lifetime of the Prophet Muhammad, what would come to be known as Sufism and what would come to be known as Shari'a had not yet been disaggregated. This is less an argument about history—certainly, speaking about "Sufism" *avant la lettre* is anachronistic—as much as it is an argument about the Prophet himself, who seamlessly and powerfully embodied Sufism and Shari'a.

We can see this in how Deobandis understand an all-important Sufi concept, *ihsan,* meaning "goodness" or "excellence" but, in its core semantic root, also linked to the concept of beauty. *Ihsan* and Sufism are often simply equated, as in Muhammad Manzur Nu'mani's *Din o shari'at* (Religion and Shari'a): "In the prophetic Hadith, the perfection of *din* is called *ihsan, which we call Sufism.* In common parlance, it can be explained this way: one's heart attains the same degree of certainty and assurance that one attains from the direct experience of reality, in which there is no room for doubt about its veracity."[31] When one attains *ihsan,* he continues, this heart-certainty infuses every breath with God-consciousness.

This idea goes back to the roots of the Deobandi movement. Gangohi, who taught his disciples that "Sufism is fundamentally another name for *ihsan,*" explained *ihsan* in terms of prophetic affect. The affective power of the Prophet Muhammad's presence was such that an unbeliever who recited the testament of faith (*kalima*) before him would attain *ihsan* instantly. After the Prophet's death, the Companions and the Followers still retained that power, but it had begun to diminish. The first Sufi masters invented spiritual techniques to recover that power, but as that first generation became a distant memory, Sufis took these techniques to be ends in themselves rather than tools for re-creating that prophetic affect, which is part of the origin of *bid'a.*[32] Elsewhere, Gangohi explained *ihsan* as a constant introspective gaze, one that reflects the visceral cognizance that God sees what one does at every moment: "One should maintain this inward gaze (*muraqaba*) at all times. In short, apprehending God's presence with every deed, one should discover what pleases God and do that, and discover what dis-pleases God and avoid that. This is the nature of *ihsan.*"[33]

This prophetic affect is channeled genealogically from Sufi master to disciple, in principle extending back to the Prophet himself, as Sufi *silsilas* (initiatic chains) often do. But what is being transmitted is not merely esoteric knowledge or mystical insight but that very affective power that the Companions felt in the Prophet's presence, which is connoted in the concept of "companionship" (*suhbat;* from the Arabic *suhba*). *Suhbat* has roots in the traditional transmission of knowledge in premodern Islamic education. A student training to become a jurist would undergo a period of "fellowship [*suhba*]" with a master. A *sahib,* "fellow," was the student who became a constant companion of a particular master. Both terms are linked semantically to the Companions (*sahaba*) of the Prophet Muhammad, who learned from observing his model (*sunna*) and whose observations of the Prophet's behavior became an important part of the Hadith.[34] Similarly, for the Sufis, *suhbat* is an "intimate spiritual com-munication between human hearts," mirroring and complementing the genealogical transmission of knowledge, a genealogy that originates with the Prophet Muhammad himself. The Naqshbandi Sufi Mirza Jan-i Janan

(d. 1781) experienced this prophetic *suhbat* directly in an ecstatic moment during a Hadith lesson. The affective power of hearing the Prophet's words was like "companionship [*suhbat*] with God's messenger. . . . I experienced the Prophet's divine energy [*tawajjuh*] and spiritual countenance [*altafat*]." In this moment, he says, "[t]he meaning of 'The religious scholars ['*ulama*] are heirs of the prophets' became clear."[35]

Gangohi, too, taught that this prophetic companionship was at the core of Sufism. Sufism provided the spiritual resources to experience what it would have been like to be one of the Companions. In a letter to a disciple, he described this companionship in terms of divine effulgence (*faiz*):

> The ultimate aim of all the Sufi paths—once you have reached this summit there is nothing else beyond it—is this: Why did the Companions of the Prophet give up all their wealth and prestige? What did they see? It was that they had acquired certainty [*yaqin*] through the divine effulgence of companionship [*fuyuz-i suhbat*] of the Prophet Muhammad, passing away [*fana'*] from the world and subsisting [*baqa'*] in the afterlife, acquiring certainty in the truth of the Maker. Afterward this became the basis for every action. What made Sayyid 'Abd al-Qadir Jilani, Khwajah Mu'in al-Din Chishti, and Baha al-Din Bukhari [Naqshbandi] so great? This very same certainty.

Establishing this connection (*nisbat*) is the reason God sent the Prophet, Gangohi says—a connection that illuminates the Ummah horizontally through his *suhbat* and vertically through time as that *suhbat* is channeled by the Sufi saints, connecting generation to generation, which Gangohi calls the "light of certainty" (*nur-i yaqin*).[36]

This prophetic affect can be ascertained through companionship with Sufi saints, but in a critical concession to a bibliocentric economy of knowledge, Deobandis taught that one could get glimpses of it from reading *stories* about the saints. Thus, an introduction to Thanvi's *Hikayat al-awliya'* (Stories of the saints) by one of his disciples explains how the milieu into which the Prophet Muhammad was sent was one of utter ignorance (*jahalat*) in which every individual was governed entirely by lust and passion, how there was no distinction between truth and falsehood, and how tribal sentiment ('*asabiyya*) prevailed over human relations. The Prophet Muhammad changed all this solely through the spiritual power (*faiz*) of his very presence (*suhbat*). This power had such "force of influence and quickness of effect that after just a short time, it reached people everywhere." The author of the introduction adds: "The Sufi masters know well the secret [*raz*] of this power, and that companionship of the righteous [*suhbat-i nek*] is absolutely necessary for the reform [*islah*] of their students and followers . . . a notion corroborated everywhere in their writings, words, and letters." But these Sufi masters also know that "many are incapable of leaving one's family and occupation to undergo strenuous travel and to spend one's wealth and provisions" to seek out their companionship. "For this reason, the stories [*hikayat*] and discourses [*malfuzat*] of these noble ones are compensation for those deprived of their presence."[37]

Stories, then, allow readers to experience at least a glimmer of the spiritual energy (*faiz*) that the Sufi masters ultimately inherit from the Prophet himself. Like everything else for Deobandis, *faiz* (from the Arabic *fayd*, "flood") can be easily misunderstood. *Faiz* is the energy that emanates from holy bodies, objects, and spaces, whether a saint's shrine or a sacred text. It adheres to objects but also penetrates bodies. Central to Sufi cosmology and psychology, *faiz* has been understood by Sufis to be a divine emanation that travels through the subtle centers (*lata'if*) of the cosmos, which are reflected in the subtle centers (*lata'if*) of the body. Unsurprisingly, twentieth-century Sufis have often compared it to electricity. For Ahmad Sirhindi (d. 1624), the Prophet Muhammad's perfect intimacy with God meant that he was also a perfect embodiment of this divine emanation, one that the saints can also experience in proportion to their own intimacy with God.[38] Ibn al-'Arabi understood *faiz* to be a cosmic reverberation of the act of creation itself, and thereby a continuous self-disclosure (*tajalli*) of God.[39]

It will be no surprise, then, that Gangohi would be apprehensive about the ability of the masses to understand this phenomenon without the appropriate training. *Faiz* "can be experienced at the shrines of saints," he says, "but it is never permissible to sanction this for the masses." One can learn about *faiz* according to one's spiritual capabilities and intellect, but "for the masses, to explain these matters is only to open up the door to unbelief [*kufr*] and associationism [*shirk*]."[40] Thanvi elaborated: "Some ignorant people believe that the Sufi masters have the ability to administer divine grace [*faiz*] however they wish." But "when even the Prophet did not have this power"—citing a Hadith in which the Prophet clarified a verse from the Qur'an, "Indeed, [Muhammad,] you do not guide whomever you like" (28:56)—"how could anyone else?"[41]

Faiz is, then, simultaneously a powerful tool of spiritual self-formation and a potential source of normative disruption. This is why, among many other reasons, Thanvi opposed the "study" (*mutala'a*) of Sufism without the guidance of a Sufi master—for mere study was "insufficient to reform one's character," and many benefits of the Sufi path are simply inaccessible without the "companionship of an expert" (*mahir ki suhbat*) in Sufism.[42] But he also made concessions to those who did not have time to stay at a Sufi lodge or take up a disciplinary relationship (*islahi ta'aluq*):

> The thing around which reform [*islah*] ultimately revolves is the companionship [*suhbat*] of those who have already experienced reform, and serving and obeying them. When their literal companionship [*suhbat-i zahiri*] is not feasible, then one can experience their spiritual companionship [*suhbat-i ma'navi*] by studying their lives, tales, and teachings, which will be, to a certain extent, a sufficient substitute. This is the secret as to why the authoritative texts [*nusus*] urge the companionship of the good and warn against companionship of the evil. This is also why there are stories of God's faithful everywhere throughout the Qur'an and Hadith.[43]

Deobandis understood that the need for *suhbat* placed a sort of intrinsic limitation on their quest for public reform, for not everyone had the time to seek out a Sufi master. To overcome this dilemma, Thanvi argued that companionship in the same physical *space* as the Sufi master, while ideal, can be replaced by a sort of companionship mediated by mail. This is why he spent part of every day responding to letters written by the hundreds of disciples who lived across India. The Sufi adept should "spend a few days with his master if he has some free time, and if he does not, this spiritual instruction can be carried out remotely—for instance, by means of letters if the disciple [*murid*] is unable to reach the master in person."[44] Failing that, the core principles of Sufism could be grasped through reading introductory books on Sufism. But books never replace the master. In most cases, in fact, "[b]ooks may be beneficial, but they are *for the master*. Disciples do not benefit from studying books, but may study them at the master's discretion," said Thanvi, adding rhetorically: "Is your *book* a perfect human being [*insan-i kamil*]—that is, a master? Do you resolve difficulties [on the Sufi path] with reference to your books?"[45]

The beginning of Sufi pedagogy is the pledge (*bai'at*) to the Sufi master. Traditionally, the pledge was followed by a long period of study and spiritual training with the master, usually at a Sufi lodge (*khanqah*). Thanvi, as is well known, took on hundreds of Sufi disciples, many of whom did come to his *khanqah* in Thana Bhawan, where upon arrival they were asked to fill out a form on which they provided their name, home country or region, current address, occupation, whether they had given *bai'at* to others and, if so, to whom, whether they had read any of

Thanvi's books or heard his sermons, their purpose in desiring *bai'at*
with him, and other details.[46] To others he gave spiritual guidance
through written correspondence.

But the Deobandis also saw the Sufi pledge as a crucial tool in the
work of both individual and public reform. Thanvi saw *bai'at* as a critical
instrument in the project of religious reform (*islah-i din*).[47] Biographies of
Deobandi scholars abound with stories of middle-class people who
underwent dramatic conversions after taking *bai'at*. One of Khalil Ahmad
Saharanpuri's disciples, a certain Muhammad Yasin, wore English clothes
and managed a tavern in Bombay before pledging himself to Saharanpuri.
After taking the pledge, he gave up his job and his English clothes. A
friend saw him and asked, "Are you Mister Muhammad Yasin?" He
replied, "I am no longer a 'mister.' Just Muhammad Yasin."[48] For Gangohi, the Sufi pledge was a pledge for self-rectification, a "renewal of
repentance" (*tajdid-i tauba*)—not the transmission of esoteric insight
from master to disciple. For Gangohi, even the desire to be part of a spiritual lineage (*silsila*) missed this fundamental point. His biography records
the basic text that he would read out loud while giving a *bai'at*, which the
prospective disciple would have to repeat after him:

> I believe in God, His Angels, His Books, His Prophets, and in fate, that all is
> from God whether good or bad, and that there is life after death. I repent
> from unbelief [*kufr*], associationism [*shirk*], innovation [*bid'a*], and all other
> sins. I promise not to lie, steal, fornicate, or slander. I commit to pray five
> times daily, fast during Ramadan, perform the Hajj if I can afford it, and pay
> the charity [*zakat*] if required. If I omit something, I will repent immediately.
> I am taking *bai'at* at hands of Rashid Ahmad into the Chishti, Naqshbandi,
> Qadiri, and Suhrawardi lineages.[49]

SUFISM IS FOR EVERYONE

Remaking the self around the Sunna through the tools of subjectivation
provided by Sufi pedagogy is also a way of remaking Sufism itself into a
tool of mass reform. This is why one of the refrains we see again and
again in Deobandi texts is that Sufism is for all Muslims, or even that it is
obligatory. Like other ideas we have discussed, the idea of Sufism as a
"compulsory" part of a Muslim's ethical life is not completely new to
Deobandis. One of the Deobandis' foremost influences, Qazi Sanaullah
Panipati (d. 1810), also taught that "pursuing the Sufi path is compulsory
[*wajib*]." And like Deobandis, Panipati accentuated ethical divestment of
qualities like envy, malice, ostentation, the desire for fame, and love of
self.[50] But Deobandis elaborated on the idea extensively. In some sense,

the very possibility of regarding Sufism as "obligatory" presupposes distilling Sufism down to its ethical core. Thanvi made this point explicitly in letters to his disciples. As he explained to one, "The Sufi pledge [*bai'at*] is not obligatory, but reform of one's actions [*islah-i a'mal*] is obligatory, and giving precedence to what is obligatory [*taqdim-i wajib*] is obligatory."[51] Though the master–disciple relationship is by far the *best* way to accomplish reform, requiring all Muslims to undergo a Sufi initiation would be impractical. But requiring self-reform for all is an extension of Deobandis' understanding of Sufism as ethics. Sufism as ethics is, ipso facto, Sufism for everyone. Thus, Thanvi's *Bihishti zewar* (Heavenly ornaments) sums up a litany of ethical qualities any young woman should have—repentance (*tauba*), fear of God (*khauf*), patience (*sabr*), gratitude (*shukr*), trust in God (*bharosa*), love of God (*mahabbat*), contentment (*raza*), sincerity of intention (*sidq*), and introspection (*muraqaba*)—as qualities that should be adopted by "every Sufi disciple, indeed, *every Muslim.*"[52] One of Thanvi's most important disciples, Masihullah Khan, echoes his master in maintaining that "it is incumbent for every Muslim to become a Sufi. Without Sufism, in reality, one cannot truly be called a complete Muslim."[53]

In terms of his approach to educating lay Muslims, Thanvi's Sufi pedagogy mirrors his legal pedagogy: just as a little bit of knowledge goes a long way to ensure that a Muslim understands correct belief and practice, even a small amount of Sufi knowledge, ideally from a living Sufi master, but from books if a master is unavailable, can go a long way in cultivating conscientious piety. And just as Thanvi is wary of lay Muslims opining on legal matters beyond their comprehension, he is also wary of Sufi adepts misinterpreting individual experiences as visionary insight (*kashf*). The problem is that far too many enter the Sufi path with the hope of having a vision or mystical experience. Thus, Thanvi attempted to constrain lay readers from pursuing the Sufi path for the express purpose of experiencing *kashf*. If such an experience happens to come along, it is a gift from God, but it is not an end in itself.[54]

Thanvi saw leniency on the part of the master, at least early on, as a core facet of Sufi pedagogy. "The Sufi masters know that too much severity can make people hold back from what is good," Thanvi conceded. "Many people are too weak to abandon sinful practices all at once. This ability must be developed in stages."[55] His biographer confirmed this as part of his basic temperament: "God granted Hazrat [Thanvi] with a mild disposition. On every issue he always preferred ease [*suhulat*] for himself and for others. He would never make matters unnecessarily difficult."[56]

Part of making Sufism "easier" was making it more palatable to modern sensibilities. One of the classic Sufi techniques of disciplining the self (*nafs*) was known as *mujahada* ("striving"), which entailed depriving the body of basic desires—typically food, sleep, conversation, and social interaction. Thanvi replaced the older Sufi practice of "abandoning" (*tark*) these desires with a "reduction" (*taqlil*) in them.[57] He regarded deliberately subjecting oneself to physical extremes to be self-indulgent. Speaking about the bodily rigors to which some Sufis subject themselves during spiritual exercises (*riyazat*), Thanvi asked, "On any path there is an easy way and a hard way. Why not choose the easy way?" He compared self-imposed "hardship and severity" to walking to the next town to draw water for ablutions (*wudu'*) when there is plenty of water nearby.[58]

With this in mind, Thanvi's *Qasd al-sabil* (The purpose of the path) proposed a simplified program for those interested in Sufism. The very first thing anyone should know about Sufism, he says, is that it is the art of translating knowledge (*'ilm*) into practice (*a'mal*). Religious knowledge can be attained from consulting a scholar (*'alim*) or, if necessary, from reading books. The next step is repentance (*tauba*) for sins and the search for a Sufi master. The Sufi master should have knowledge, be pious, have no desire for worldly gain, and should not prove his holiness through miracles (*karamat*). The Sufi adept, too, must be motivated solely for the pleasure of God, not by a desire for miracles or mystical insight (*kashf*).

Qasd al-sabil breaks down this "simplified" Sufism into four programs: for non-scholars (*'awamm*) who have no worldly responsibilities (*dunya ke kam*), for scholars who have no worldly responsibilities, for non-scholars who have such responsibilities, and for scholars who have such responsibilities. Both programs for non-scholars entail daily *zikr*—literally, "remembering," denoting the recitation of phrases and litanies that aim to remind the Sufi of God. The main difference between the program for non-scholars who have worldly responsibilities and those who do not is that the latter should "go to spend time with one's master" if possible, and if not, should at the very least avoid associating with other people and cultivate seclusion. Both groups of non-scholars should "learn about legal issues [*masa'il*] that are absolutely necessary" and "when encountering any new issues [*masa'il*], consult a scholar, and if one's Sufi master is also a scholar, that is best."[59] As for *'ulama*, those who have worldly commitments should engage in *zikr* daily, and lecture to non-scholars only on essential subjects, and whenever lecturing should do so "clearly, softly, and without severity."[60] A scholar who has no worldly commitments should strive to spend "some free time, at least six months," in the company of his master. The main difference between the two categories of *'ulama* is that the latter should spend nearly all their waking hours in prayer and *zikr*.[61]

What Sufi adepts should read also depends on their status. For the *'ulama* he recommends al-Ghazali's *Ihya' 'ulum al-din* (Revival of the religious sciences). For non-scholars, he recommends reading al-Ghazali's *Tabligh-i din* (Propagating the faith), a condensed version of the *Ihya'*. Thanvi reveres this book, in particular, for its efficiency and accessibility in conveying Sufi ethical principles: parts three and four, respectively, enumerate the negative ethical characteristics (*mazmum-i akhlaq*) that a pious Muslim must eliminate from the self (e.g., excessive food, excessive speech, anger, envy, love of wealth, love of fame, love of the world, pride, ostentation)[62] and the positive ones (*akhlaq-i mahmuda*) that a pious Muslim must adopt (e.g., fear of God, asceticism, patience, gratitude, sincerity, trust in God, love, contentment, and remembrance of God).[63]

Importantly, though, Thanvi says there are some Sufi texts that non-scholars should avoid, including the *Masnavi* of Rumi, the *Diwan* of Hafiz, and any other books in which a Sufi's mystical states (*kaifiyat*) are recorded, for "the common man is not capable of understanding these books."[64] But, just as the *'ulama* should not discuss legal issues (*masa'il*) in front of the masses, Sufis should also avoid discussing finer points (*daqa'iq*) of Sufism in front of them, "for they may think that what they hear is opposed to the Shari'a."[65]

ANYONE CAN BE A SAINT

The ultimate implication of both a "simplified" Sufi path for busy, middle-class Muslims and the notion of Sufi ethics as "obligatory" is a reorientation of the very idea of Sufi sainthood around ethical criteria— ethics that anyone, common (*'amm*) or elite (*khass*), can embody and inhabit. Deobandi works are replete with the idea that any Muslim can be a "saint" (*wali*). The final section of this chapter will explore how Deobandis have theorized sainthood itself through what I call "ethical sainthood." To do so requires a brief digression into the history of the concept of Muslim sainthood itself.

Some premodern understandings of Sufi sainthood saw the saint (*wali*) as almost ineffably rare. For the fourteenth-century Persian Sufi 'Ala ad-Dawla al-Simnani (d. 1336), the *wali* was so rare that there are only seven in the world at any given time. The *wali,* in fact, constitutes part of the very fabric of existence. Indeed, the very word for existence (*kawn,* from the root K-W-N) comprises the K (*kaf*) of the divine command "Be!" (*Kun*), the W (*waaw*) of sainthood (*walaya*), and the N (*nuun*) of prophecy (*nubuwwa*).[66]

By the early twenty-first century, in a point of stark contrast, Deobandis defined the *wali* in a near inverse of Simnani's conception. When asked "What is the distinguishing characteristic of the saints [*awliya'*] of God, in light of the Holy Shari'a?" a mufti of the Dar al-'Ulum Haqqaniyya responded: "Every Muslim who conforms to the Shari'a, is sober and abstemious, and avoids sins both major and minor is one of the saints [*awliya'*] of God and is among God's friends [*Allah ke doston*]."[67] How can we explain such wildly divergent views of the parameters of Sufi sainthood?

The word *wali* is derived from an Arabic root that connotes "nearness" or "proximity," as well as "guardianship" and "protection." Thus, the *wali* is said to possess proximity to God, and by virtue of this proximity, the *wali* has the ability to guard and protect. Scholars of Islam have long pointed out the pitfalls of translating the Arabic *wali* as "saint," in part because of the absence of any canonization process in Islam comparable to that of Catholicism, a view particularly associated with Bryan Turner.[68] But many scholars of Sufism have also defended translating *wali* as "saint." Critiquing Turner, Vincent Cornell writes, "If a *wali Allah* looks like a saint, acts like a saint, and speaks like a saint, why not call him a saint?"[69] Many, perhaps most, Sufis throughout history have understood the *wali* to be, at minimum, extraordinary. For Scott Kugle, it is the saints' status as individuals "set apart" from society that gives them social power *in* society, especially by way of relics that metonymically stand in for the saint's body and channel that power—what Kugle calls the "cultural logic of sanctity."[70]

By contrast, Deobandis' ethical sainthood does not so much invert or collapse saintly hierarchies as realign those hierarchies around the principal criterion of moral rectitude. Deobandis argue that any pious Muslim not only can be, but *is,* a saint, simply by virtue of that piety, and as saintly believers, Muslims excel over others only in degrees of piety. Deobandi scholars developed this idea quite gradually, by creatively appropriating and expanding a classical Sufi distinction between a "general" sainthood (*walayat 'amma*), common to all believers, and special sainthood, or sainthood of the elect (*walayat khassa*).

The concept of a "general" or "common" sainthood emerged out of early Sufis' engagement with the polyvalence of the term *wali* in the Qur'an itself. One of the earliest to suggest a dual meaning of the term *wali* was the Hanafi Sufi-scholar Abu Bakr Muhammad al-Kalabadhi (d. 990 or 994). Kalabadhi distinguished "two kinds of sainthood [*walaya*]": "The first is going out from God's enmity [*'adawa*], and this is common to all believers [*'amma al-mu'minin*]. It is not necessary that one be aware of it or realize it, and it has a general sense, as in the phrase 'The believer is the *wali* of God' [*al-mu'min wali Allah*]." The phrase seems also to be an allusion to Qur'an 2:257: "God is the *wali* of those who believe"—a verse in which *wali* conveys the sense of "ally." However, Kalabadhi continues, the second type of *wali* "is chosen and made [by God], and it *is* necessary that one be aware of it and realize it. When one has this [status], he is saved from self-regard, and does not become vain. He is withdrawn from others, and takes no pleasure in seeing them. He is saved from the temptations of humanity, although human nature [*tab' al-bashariyya*] remains within him. He is not tempted by the pleasures of the self [*nafs*], and thus is not tempted in his faith, although natural temptations may remain. This is the special *walaya* from God toward his servant."[71] In Kalabadhi's short, enigmatic depiction of two degrees of *walaya*—friendship, allyship—the first degree applies to all believers, the second only to a select few, who are aware of their status. The latter have tempered the self (*nafs*) to an extent that they are at least partially free from pleasures that tempt the "average" believer. For our purposes, this demonstrates, at the very least, that even as early as Kalabadhi, what distinguishes the "special" (*khass*) *wali* is an ascetic mastery of the self (*nafs*). Deobandis' "ethical sainthood," in other words, was not created out of whole cloth.

There are other premodern sources for the distinction between "common" and "special" *walaya*, and again, efforts to understand Qur'an 2:257 are often the impetus for the distinction. At the beginning of *Nafahat al-uns* (Breaths of intimacy), a collection of Sufi saints' biographies by the Persian poet 'Abd al-Rahman Jami (d. 1492), we find a similar contrast between a common *walaya* (*walaya 'amma*) and a special *walaya* (*walaya khassa*). Like Kalabadhi, he also references Qur'an 2:257. Jami writes, "Common *walaya* is shared among the entirety of believers, for God says: 'God is the *wali* of those who believe.' The *walaya* of the elect," on the other hand, "is special by virtue of its connections to the masters of the Sufi path."[72] But Jami quickly moves on to his biographies of great saints. I would like to suggest that his brief, even perfunctory, commentary on the two degrees of *walaya* is born of a necessity to recognize the semantic range of *wali* in the Qur'an, but that he did so by a point in the history of Sufism at which the "true" meaning of the *wali* was clear: it meant the great saints, and only the great saints.

One may speculate that Jami's *Nafahat al-uns,* which "would later become one of the most influential Naqshbandi Sufi texts imported to Mughal India,"[73] may have had some impact on Ahmad Sirhindi's (d. 1624) distinction between what he calls lesser sainthood (*walayat-i sughra*) and greater sainthood (*walayat-i kubra*). Lesser sainthood has three stages of its own. The first, Sirhindi says, is that of "common Muslims," who "follow the lofty Prophetic example" but who have not yet "calmed the self [*nafs*]." Calming the *nafs* confers a "degree of sainthood" (*bi-darajah walayat*). The second level corresponds to "those on the Sufi path who concentrate on the refinement of character." The third degree is a "special sainthood" (*walayat-i khassa*), in which the self has become "tranquil and free of struggle and rebellion."[74] What Sirhindi then calls the "greater sainthood" (*walayat-i kubra*) is characterized by complete subjugation of the self.[75]

While Deobandis certainly read Sirhindi—though I have not encountered any Deobandi commentary on this *particular* passage—there are other, more direct, venues through which Deobandis took up the distinction between levels of *walaya.* Qutb al-Din Dimashqi (d. 1378), whom Gangohi translated into Persian, also saw in Qur'an 2:257 the basis for two classes of *wali.*[76] Dimashqi, like Kalabadhi, understood "common sainthood" (*walayat 'amma*) to denote those who avoid God's "enmity" ('*adawa;* Urdu, '*adavat*):

> A *wali* is a friend [*dost*] of God. Friendship [*dosti*] with God is to have faith [*iman*] in him. As God says: "God is the *wali* of those who believe" [Qur'an 2:257]. Some masters [*akabir*] divide *walayat* into two kinds. The first is *walayat-i 'amma,* which is avoiding God's enmity ['*adavat*] and hatred [*dushmani*]. God's enmity is unbelief [*kufr*] and hypocrisy [*nifaq*]. This form of *walayat* applies to the entire community of believers. As God says: "God is the *wali* of those who believe. He takes them out of darkness and into light" [Qur'an 2:257]. The second kind is *walayat-i khassa,* which applies to those who achieve a constant and permanent state of obedience [to God] without deficiency [*kotahi*] or indolence [*susti*].[77]

One more source will suffice to demonstrate the range of texts that Deobandis invoked in their thinking about sainthood. Muhammad

Zakariyya Kandhlavi—among the most important Deobandis of the mid–twentieth century, and one who will loom large in subsequent chapters—drew on Ibn Taymiyya's (d. 1328) discussion of sainthood. Like Kalabadhi and Dimashqi, Ibn Taymiyya, too, defines *walaya* as the opposite of enmity (*'adawa*), insofar as, he notes, *walaya* connotes proximity to God and enmity connotes distance from God.[78] He divides all people into three groups: those who are dominated by their ego (*zalim li-nafsihi*) and ignore God's commands completely; those who shun what is forbidden and carry out what is commanded (*muqtasid;* literally, "one who adopts a middle course"); and finally, those who "excel in goodness" (*sabiq al-khayrat*), who not only shun what is forbidden and carry out what is commanded but also shun what is abominable (*makruh*) and embrace what is lawful (*masnun*). The latter two groups are among the "saints" (*awliya'*) referred to in Qur'an 10:62: "Surely the *awliya'* of God shall not fear, nor shall they grieve." Thus, he says, "the *awliya'* of God are the pious believers [*al-mu'minun al-muttaqun*], but these are divided into the general [*'amm*], who take the middle course [*muqtasidun*], and the special [*khass*], who excel in goodness [*sabiqun*]."[79]

Ibn Taymiyya's notion that prayer and piety are the primary criteria for identifying the saint is one that Deobandis embrace and expand. We see this, above all, in Thanvi. Thanvi, too, references this distinction between a "common" and "special" *walaya*. Commenting, like Ibn Taymiyya, on Qur'an 10:62–63—"Truly the *awliya'* of God shall not fear, nor shall they grieve. Those who have faith (*amanu*) and remain pious (*yattaquna*), for them are glad tidings, in this life and in the afterlife"—Thanvi says:

> Two pillars of *walayat* are noted [in this verse]: faith [*iman*] and piety [*taqwa*]. Those who have attained degrees of faith and piety have also attained the rank of *walayat*. If the lowest stage of faith and piety has been attained, by means of correct beliefs and deeds, the lowest stage of *walayat* is also attained, which all believers have acquired. This is called general sainthood [*walayat-i 'amma*]. And if the highest degree of faith and piety has been attained, then the highest degree of *walayat* has also been attained. This is called special sainthood [*walayat-i khassa*]. And—*technically speaking* [*istilahan*]—this is who we call a saint [*wali*].[80]

The only difference between the first kind of *wali* and the second, he then adds, is that the latter possesses "complete faith" (*iman-i kamil*) and "complete piety" (*taqwa-yi kamil*).

There is a cognizance here, on Thanvi's part, in a text that would have been read mostly by fellow Sufis and Sufi disciples, that the latter is what Sufis typically mean when they speak of the *wali*. This is, "technically speaking," Sufi sainthood. But it was important, for Thanvi, that average Muslims could aspire to a saintly life. Thus, in *Bihishti zewar,* a book written explicitly for lay Muslim women, as noted above, Thanvi writes:

> When a Muslim worships faithfully, avoids sin, maintains no love for this world [*dunya*], and obeys the Messenger in every way, then he is a friend of God [*Allah ka dost*] and God's beloved. Such a person is called a *wali.* Sometimes they achieve deeds that others are unable to achieve. These deeds are called miracles [*karamat*]. However high a rank he may achieve, a *wali* is never able to equal a prophet. However beloved by God he may become, a *wali* is duty-bound to the Shari'a as long as he remains within his senses. He is not excused from prayer, fasting, or any other obligatory form of worship. It is not correct for him to commit any sin. Anyone who acts contrary to the Shari'a is unable to be a friend of God [*Allah ka dost*].[81]

Here Thanvi lays out a starkly minimalist definition of the *wali,* the contours of which we have seen in the texts discussed above. To be sure, many earlier theorists of sainthood also believed that the *wali* was constrained by the Shari'a, but noting this so explicitly here is, I submit, part of Thanvi's broader project of public reform. For him, it is essential that readers of *Bihishti zewar* understand that although the saints are "special," they are so only to the degree that they excel in embodying Muslim legal and ethical norms.

We encounter this "flattened" conception of Sufi sainthood in numerous other Deobandi works. Muhammad Kifayat Allah defined the saint simply as "a Muslim who obeys the commands of God and His Messenger, worships abundantly and refrains from sins, loves God and His Messenger more than everything in the world, and is close to God and His Messenger."[82] Muhammad Manzur Nu'mani's *Islam kya hai* (What is Islam?) makes this even more explicit: "This little book contains the essence of the whole of Islam. All the lessons of the Qur'an and Hadith have been collected in its twenty chapters, such that a common man ['*amm admi*] can not only be a good Muslim, but can also become a perfect believer [*mu'min-i kamil*] and a saint of God [*wali Allah*] also."[83]

It is no coincidence, I suggest, that these sentiments appear in texts that Deobandis wrote for a lay Muslim audience. In later Deobandi works, the notion that anyone *can* be a saint merges with a notion that everyone *must* be a saint, for if Sufism is defined as ethics, and ethics are obligatory, sainthood itself—at least the "common" variety—becomes obligatory. A contemporary Pakistani disciple of Thanvi's, Hakim Muhammad Akhtar (d. 2013), makes this point explicitly:

[Becoming] a friend of God [*Allah ka dost*] is an individual duty [*farz-i 'ayn*], binding upon every Muslim. To be a scholar ['*alim*] of the religion, or to memorize the Qur'an, or be a mufti, is a general duty [*farz-i kifaya*] [incumbent on the Muslim community as a whole]. In any given town, some will memorize the Qur'an or become a religious scholar, and so that general duty will be fulfilled. But becoming . . . God-fearing and abstaining from sin is a duty for every Muslim. One who recites supererogatory prayers [*tahajjud*] by night, who performs the required acts of worship by day, but does not save himself from sin is not a *wali* of God. But one who does not recite the supererogatory prayers or perform supererogatory acts of worship, and only fulfills those duties emphasized in the Sunna, yet is *free of sin*—he is a *wali* Allah.[84]

Akhtar states that being pious and free of sin is obligatory for all Muslims. He then says freedom from sin is what defines the *wali*. Therefore, it follows that all Muslims *qua Muslims* are *awliya'*.

Kelly Pemberton has argued that Deobandis undercut the intercessory roles of Sufi masters and Sufi saints alike by making "fundamental texts, teachings, and tenets of Islam available to all, and simultaneously encouraging the idea that on the basis of such knowledge each individual must develop the ability to make informed decisions about what constituted 'correct' and 'incorrect' matters of faith, rather than relying solely upon the dictates of spiritual guides."[85] I would argue that this is half correct. There is no doubt that Deobandis emphasized "correct" belief and practice, nor is there any doubt that they made strategic use of print to convey these reforms. But I believe it is clear that the Sufi master, as conduit of Prophetic *faiz* and human interpreter of the normative order, is never replaced by the text. In the next chapter, however, we will begin to explore how this delicate balance between books and bodies begins to wear thin as the Deoband movement becomes a global one. We will see how mid- and late-twentieth-century Deobandis like Muhammad Taqi 'Usmani begin to see the text as the defining feature of an expanding Deobandi tradition—one that, however, also conjures a tradition that still resonates on the level of an affective allegiance to its masters: a tradition that, for 'Usmani, is "felt" (*mahsus*) in the body as much as it is apprehended by the mind..

5

What Does a Tradition Feel Like?

Up to this point, we have explored how the Deoband movement mobilized a newly found urgency toward public reform among a closely knit community of *'ulama* in colonial north India, one that sought to draw lay Muslims away from the enticements of devotional practices whose multiple forms of *bid'a* and *shirk* threatened Muslims' salvation, and toward a renewed engagement with religious knowledge (*'ilm-i din*) and a Sufi ethics of self-formation nurtured through the master–disciple relationship and communities of like-minded persons. We saw how these *'ulama*, most notably Ashraf 'Ali Thanvi, composed simple primers on "correct" belief and practice for Urdu readers to attain these objectives, at the same time that he sought to constrain readers' sense of interpretive independence by urging them not to delve into complicated legal issues (*masa'il*) and to consult the *'ulama* whenever they were doubtful about something they had read. For Thanvi and others, books were increasingly necessary, but never *sufficient*, as a mean of acquiring religious knowledge. Knowledge was never meaningful in and of itself, but only insofar as it was applied to self-reform (*islah-i nafs*) and implemented in practical life (*a'mal*).

This chapter delineates how this delicate balance became strained, and how Deobandis sought to mitigate those fissures as Deoband itself became a global movement. From this point forward, the book shifts its focus away from the major themes and architects of Deobandi thought and toward the growth of Deoband as a movement and a network. In particular, this chapter queries the notion of "tradition" discussed in the introduction—namely, how tradition is configured in a global network bound together by the circulation of books and bodies, and what makes that tradition cohere—or fail to cohere. To that end, the chapter examines two pivotal sites for understanding how Deoband became global. The first is the career and writings of Qari Muhammad Tayyib (1867–1983), who presided over the Dar al-'Ulum Deoband as chancellor (*muhtamim*) from 1928 to 1980—the decades in which Deobandi madrasas were founded in countries as far-flung as the United Kingdom, South Africa, Trinidad and Tobago, and the United States. In the work of Tayyib, I argue, the concept of the *maslak* ("path" or "way") becomes a central category for theorizing the coherence of Deobandi tradition, and its centrality increased *precisely* as Deoband became global. In other words, as the network expanded across borders, its scholars increasingly reflected on exactly *what* linked the network together and *how*.

The second site for understanding Deoband as a global phenomenon is the rise of the Tablighi Jama'at—of which, not coincidentally, Tayyib became a staunch advocate. Now the world's largest Muslim revivalist movement, the Tablighi Jama'at ("Preaching Party") promotes *tabligh*—derived from the Arabic root "to convey," but here meaning "preaching" or "proselytization"—between Muslims, as opposed to proselytization of non-Muslims. A core argument of this chapter and the following one is that the Tablighi Jama'at is an extension of the very logic of Deoband's program of public reform—emphasizing correct belief, personal piety, and the virtues of companionship (*suhbat*) while striving to avoid contentious issues (*masa'il*)—and an engine of Deoband's presence in public life, one energized by Deoband's network of seminaries but functioning independently of it. Like its relationship with the reading public itself, Deoband's relationship with the Tablighi Jama'at has been an ambivalent one. As we will see, the founder of the Jama'at, Muhammad Ilyas, sought to strike the very balance between lay Muslim knowledge and deference to the *'ulama* that Thanvi advocated—*'ulama* who, importantly, had serious qualms about the very notion of an organized movement of lay religious revival. If this chapter demonstrates how the Tablighi Jama'at was an agent of Deobandi mobility in theory, the following one demonstrates that point in practice, showing how public consciousness of "Deoband" in South Africa was inextricably linked to Tablighi missions in the 1960s, even though Deobandi scholars had lived and taught there largely under the radar as early as the 1920s, simply as *'ulama* rather than as "Deobandi" *'ulama*. It is no accident, additionally, that some of the most adamant defenders of the Tablighi Jama'at were Deobandis who were based in South Africa or spent time lecturing, teaching, and training Sufi disciples there.

We will also see here how both Tayyib and Ilyas understood the seminary (madrasa) and Sufi lodge (khanqah) as dual, complementary spaces of moral discipline and formation. They understood them, as did Deobandis before them, as "sacred" spaces imbued with affective power by and through which the normative order could be inculcated in the hearts and bodies of students. In this sense, they approached the seminary and Sufi lodge as zones of spatial normativity—in essence, as nomoi. Carl Schmitt argued that the concept of nomos cannot be reduced either to "law" or "norm"—the latter probably its closest cognate in English.[1] Rather, the word has a spatial quality, meaning "both 'to divide' and 'to pasture,'" a meaning ultimately derived from the jurisdiction that comes from cultivating land.[2] For Schmitt, "Nomos is the measure by which the land in a particular order is divided and situated; it is also the form of political, social and religious order determined by this process. . . . In particular, nomos can be described as a wall, because, like a wall, it, too, is based on sacred orientations. The nomos can grow and multiply like land and property: all human nomoi are 'nourished' by a single divine nomos."[3] Nomos, then, is inextricably bound up with space and place. In a broader sense, this makes it useful for understanding the spatiality of the maslak, as well as limitations of the word "law" for understanding Deobandis' juro-ethical discourse as a set of normative dispositions.

As we saw in the first chapter, this is in no small way the outcome of the demise of Islamic law as it was exercised before colonialism, and the concomitant impulse to cultivate the space of the seminary as a "religious" refuge—one in which learning was an act of devotion, free from the utilitarian calculus of "useful knowledge." But this moral order could itself be rendered mobile in the bodies of the teachers, students, and wandering preachers (tablighis) who, quite literally, embodied that order. The space of the Sufi lodge, too, complemented the seminary by cultivating in practice the legal norms that seminary students came to understand discursively. And just as the space of the seminary was a refuge, we have seen how Deobandis understood the spaces of the market, the railway station, the shrine—all places where crowds congregate—as spaces bereft of the nomoi that governed the seminary and Sufi lodge, which made the embodiment of those nomoi in one's demeanor, speech, clothing—in short, in the entire complex of social relationships—all the more essential. There was something, in short, that inhered in the very space of the seminary and Sufi lodge, such that it defined the character of those who dwelled in them. Thanvi captured this sensibility in telling the story of a police officer assigned to a case of theft at a seminary in Kanpur. The officer told the shocked students and teachers, "I'm sorry, but madrasa students steal things, too." Thanvi responded to the event differently, with a sardonic retort: "A madrasa student is never a thief . . . though a thief may be a madrasa student."[4]

THEORIZING A GLOBAL *MASLAK:* QARI MUHAMMAD TAYYIB (D. 1982)

In Arabic, the word *maslak* means "way" or "path," but in South Asia, the term has come to denote the features that define a given school, sect, or movement. Thus, Deobandis have their *maslak,* Barelvis have theirs, as do the Ahl-i Hadith, and so forth. Scholars have, therefore, understood the concept almost entirely through the prism of sectarian distinction.[5] By contrast, I argue that, for the Deobandis, the *maslak* is as important for defining *internal coherence* as it is for defining external difference. For the Deobandi *'ulama,* the *maslak* is more than a set of beliefs; it is best understood as a comprehensive juro-ethical discourse, a discipline oriented around the cultivation of specific affects. It is a normative world that one comes to inhabit through proximity to the bodies of those who already do. Moreover, this chapter will show how these two processes of boundary making cannot be separated: one defines and constitutes the other.

Qari Muhammad Tayyib (d. 1982) was the seminal theorist of the Deobandi *maslak.* The grandson of Muhammad Qasim Nanautvi, he was chancellor of the Dar al-'Ulum Deoband for over half a century, from 1929 to 1982. He was the Sufi disciple of both Husain Ahmad Madani and Ashraf 'Ali Thanvi, who designated him as a *khalifa,* giving him the authority to initiate others.[6] Tayyib promoted the Dar al-'Ulum Deoband and the Deoband movement not only in his written work but in numerous lectures across the Middle East and Africa in the 1960s.[7] Like the other Deobandis we have seen, he believed that knowing the law could not be understood outside of a carefully cultivated ethical sensibility, the paragons of which were the founding jurists (*mujtahidin*), who were endowed with a direct intuition (*'ilm-i ladunni*) of divine norms—a subtle critique of Salafis and others for whom, Tayyib suggests, the return to independent reasoning (*ijtihad*) was not only a false panacea but a mechanical process devoid of the law's ethical underpinnings.[8]

The central text in Tayyib's oeuvre is *Maslak-i 'ulama-yi Deoband* (The way of the Deobandi scholars), written in 1975. This was not the first time that a Deobandi scholar attempted to summarize what Deobandis believe. The earliest effort to do so was Khalil Ahmad Saharanpuri's *Al-Muhannad 'ala al-mufannad* (Sword upon the disproved), composed in Arabic in 1907 in response to queries from Arab *'ulama* on what Deobandi scholars believed, in the wake of Ahmad Raza Khan's declaration of unbelief (*takfir*) against the Deobandis in 1906.[9] Significantly, however, Saharanpuri does not describe Deobandis as having a "*maslak*."[10] The *maslak*, again, becomes for Tayyib a means of making sense of a tradition rapidly becoming global.

Maslak-i 'ulama-yi Deoband puts forth two basic, complementary arguments: that the Deoband movement is comprehensive, unifying all aspects of traditional Islamic law, theology, and Sufism; and that it avoids any "extremes," tracing a middle path between, for example, those who indulge in excesses of Sufi piety and those who reject Sufism as a whole. It is what he calls a "middle" (*mutawassit*) way that privileges following past legal precedent (*taqlid*) over independent reasoning (*ijtihad*), and a "sober" Sufism over excessive Sufi devotions. While Tayyib does not explicitly make such a connection, he invokes a symbolism of the "middle" that has been animated by numerous currents in Islamic theology, as for example in Sunni theologians' claims to avoid the "extremes" (*ghuluw*; lit., "exaggeration") of those who took Qur'anic descriptions of God's "face" and "hand" literally, and those who "stripped God of all attributes" altogether.[11] For Tayyib, this middle path strives to avoid any form of "excess" (*tafrit*) or "extremism" (*ghuluw*) and is consistently "balanced" (*mu'tadil*). Part of this balance is what Tayyib calls Deoband's "comprehensiveness" (*jami'iyyat*), the idea that the movement is grounded fundamentally in the Sunna and the moral rectitude of the Prophet's Companions, which are in turn channeled simultaneously through the transmission of discursive knowledge and through Sufism's chain of initiatic relationships that originated with the Prophet himself. "The People of the Sunna and Community [*Ahl-i Sunna wa-l Jama'a*] adopted the very same path of comprehensiveness [as the Companions]," Tayyib asserts. "This comprehensiveness was transmitted, link by link, until . . . it passed on to the Dar al-'Ulum Deoband, which in turn transmitted it to the Deobandi *'ulama*. This comprehensiveness became their distinctive trait."[12]

Tayyib's argument also positions Deoband against its rivals, both the Ahl-i Hadith, who dismissed the entire edifice of Islamic law, and the

Barelvis, who typify the devotional "excess" (*tafrit*) that Deobandis shun. In assimilating Deoband to Sunni Islam itself, Tayyib is not just maneuvering rhetorically against the Barelvis, who *also* call themselves the Ahl-i Sunna wa-l Jama'a; in fact, he sees in this phrase a convergence of the diachronic and synchronic—of transmitted norm (*sunna*) and imagined community (*jama'a*)—one that signifies Deoband as a *living* tradition, anchored in time and space.

Tayyib begins his discussion of the centrality of Sufism to the Deoband school with the standard conceit that we have seen throughout this book: Sufism is, in its very essence, a matter of personal character and inner purification, and cannot be separated theoretically or practically from the Shari'a:

> The Deobandis believe that perfecting one's ethics [*takmil-i akhlaq*] and purifying one's self by taking initiation and being in the presence of Sufi masters are beneficial and necessary forms of spiritual guidance. However, the Sufi path [*tariqa*] is not a path different from the Shari'a, which is transmitted from one heart to the next. The Sufi path is simply the internal and ethical dimension of the Shari'a, the path of reforming the heart [*islah-i qalb*], principles of which are firmly established by the Qur'an and Sunna.[13]

Sufis go astray, Tayyib submits, when they forget the stipulations of the Shari'a and become mired in "excessive" practices:

> In the view of the Deobandi *maslak*, the holy saints among the esteemed Sufis are like the spirit [*ruh*] coursing through the Ummah from which it derives its inner life [*batini hayat*], which is the very root of life. Thus the Deobandi *maslak* understands that love and respect for the saints is vital to preserving faith [*iman*], but extremism [*ghuluw*] in love for them or in certain beliefs must not result in their deification. It understands that honoring the saints is a moral duty, but this does not mean worshipping them, prostrating toward or circumambulating their graves, taking oaths on them, or making sacrifices for them.[14]

Rather than objects of worship, the Sufi saints are the most perfect embodiments of a certain disposition (*mizaj*) that one can attain only in their presence. It is a disposition that one acquires not only through reading texts (though texts certainly contain a wealth of knowledge that can guide one toward perfected piety) but also through person-to-person relationships: "The Deobandi *maslak* . . . neither idolizes people, nor regards mere religious education as sufficient in and of itself; neither people, nor books, nor pure intellection is sufficient on its own, nor reliance solely on the words and deeds of persons."[15] Similarly, elsewhere Tayyib describes the *maslak* as "a collection of principles, rules, narratives, and biographies. These are transmitted through texts, but texts must involve the lived companionship of the righteous. Only then can one cultivate the *maslak*." [16]

But whereas Thanvi made certain reluctant *concessions* to an increasingly bibliocentric economy of knowledge, Tayyib seems to envision a more equal complementarity between books and bodies. Indeed, in the twentieth century, Deobandi tradition increasingly became stitched together in large part—one could argue *primarily*—through networks of texts and their readers. But can books *replace* bodies in channeling the *maslak?* Tayyib engaged this question in the last book he wrote, published posthumously. [17] By that point, the Deoband movement had reached an extent probably unimaginable even to Thanvi's generation, let alone Gangohi's and Nanautvi's. Tayyib still envisioned the global Deobandi network as a movement whose ultimate fount is the thought of Ahmad Sirhindi and Shah Wali Allah as channeled through Nanautvi and Gangohi. But he posited three forms of "connection" (*silsila*, a term usually used to describe Sufi initiatic lineages) to that original fount of inspiration that compelled Deobandi *'ulama* across the globe—teaching, preaching, and writing:

> The *'ulama* of Deoband comprise not only the circles of instruction and teaching, preaching and proselytization, the giving of fatwas and issuing of legal decrees, and the writing and editing of texts connected to the Dar al-'Ulum Deoband, but also comprise all the *'ulama* whose thought originates with Ahmad Sirhindi and Shah Wali Allah and who adopt the taste and disposition [*zawq o mashrab*] of Muhammad Qasim Nanautvi and Rashid Ahmad Gangohi. . . . The *'ulama* of madrasas in Bengal and Assam, or the hundreds of madrasas in other parts of India that are connected through teaching [*ta'limi silsila*] . . . those that are connected through preaching [*tablighi silsila*], spreading out across the countries of the world, or connected through writing [*tasnifi silsila*], whether they are in Europe, Asia, Africa, or America—all are, properly called, "Deobandi *'ulama*." [18]

But one can discern a subtle shift toward the importance of *texts* for the coherence of the movement. In the preface to that book, the contemporary Pakistani Deobandi scholar Muhammad Taqi 'Usmani continues, like Tayyib, to comprehend the *maslak* in terms of the delicate interrelationship between books and bodies. But there is a new emphasis on books in mediating that tradition across space:

> Look into the authenticated books [*mustanad kitab*] on the beliefs of the Ahl-i Sunna wa-l Jama'a and you will find the beliefs [*'aqa'id*] of the Deobandi *'ulama*. Study the authenticated books that are taught on Hanafi

law and the principles of jurisprudence, and there, too, you will find the legal track [*fiqhi maslak*] of the Deobandi *'ulama*. Research the authenticated and sound [*musallam*] books on ethics [*akhlaq*] and goodness [*ihsan*], and especially their chapters on Sufism and purification of character, and there you will find the very origin of the Deobandi *'ulama*. . . . To know their *maslak*, study the authenticated books of detailed Qur'an commentaries, the sound commentaries on Hadith, Hanafi law, belief and theology, Sufism, and ethics—which all the *'ulama* of the Ummah regard as well authenticated and trustworthy.[19]

'Usmani then puts a slight new inflection on the dynamic of textual and embodied knowledge, introducing a new term for one who can speak for Deobandi tradition: an "interpreter" (*tarjuman*). 'Usmani defines the true "interpreter" of Deobandi tradition as much by what he is not as what he is. A madrasa student will experience some of the spiritual effulgence (*faiz*) that permeates the madrasa, but unless he masters the *textual* tradition, he cannot be called an "interpreter" of it. He still contends, conversely, that one may study all the books of the tradition, but unless one has spent time in the companionship (*suhbat*) of its living embodiments, in that case, too, one cannot be an "interpreter."[20]

There are other ways in which 'Usmani accentuates the bibliocentric over the anthropocentric: he has called for Sufi *texts* to be taught in Deobandi seminaries. To put this into context, it is necessary to briefly explain why they are not part of the curriculum already. Tayyib's explanation was that the disposition (*mizaj*) of Sufism permeates the madrasa by virtue of the Sufi bodies that dwell there. Sufism is in the madrasa but is not *of* it. It is not a formal part of the madrasa curriculum, but it pervades madrasa studies on an informal level. There is, simply put, no need for Sufi *texts*. Besides, as we have seen, Deobandis have urged students to take up Sufi training only after they have completed their studies. Thanvi, for his part, suggested that Sufi lodges (*khanqahs*) should be *attached* to seminaries in order to obviate the illicit Sufi practices that, he believed, arise in stand-alone Sufi lodges.[21]

There are historical reasons for the absence of Sufi texts in the seminary curriculum that predate Deoband. The curriculum Shah Wali Allah taught at Delhi's Madrasa Rahimiyya included Sufi texts. In fact, the "chief attention in [Madrasa Rahimiyya] was given to mystic literature."[22] When Mulla Nizam al-Din created the Nizami syllabus, he removed Sufi texts in order to emphasize "training capable administrators for Muslim states rather than specialists in 'religion,'" according to Francis Robinson.[23] Even though Deobandis largely retreated from serving as government functionaries, as we saw in chapter 1, Sufi texts did not reappear in the curriculum, in part because Deobandi seminaries treated training in Qur'an, Hadith, and law (*fiqh*) as a *prerequisite* for taking Sufi initiations—first the madrasa, *then* the *khanqah*.

'Usmani, by contrast, has called for a return of Sufi texts to the madrasa curriculum, submitting that Sufism was not part of the Deobandi syllabus for a simple reason: the moral nurturing that comes from the presence of a Sufi master was once easy to obtain, but the moral decadence of the present day has thoroughly compromised the ability to gain this nurturing through the companionship (*suhbat*) of a Sufi alone. Hence he calls for reintroducing Sufi texts to madrasa syllabi:

> Sufism and ethics [*akhlaq*] were not included in madrasa course work because the very environment of the madrasa trained one in ethics and the Sufi path, and for anything else attachment to a Sufi master would be sufficient. Nowadays it seems necessary that books on Sufism and ethics should be included in the foundations of madrasa course work. To this end, select parts from Ghazali's *Bidaya al-hidaya*, *Arba'in*, and *Ihya' 'ulum al-din*, Suhrawardi's *'Awarif al-ma'arif*, Thanvi's *Al-Takashshuf*, and so on can be incorporated at different levels of course work.[24]

Among the most necessary reforms, 'Usmani submits that "every madrasa [should] make Sufism and moral excellence [*ihsan*] part of the curriculum. . . . The teachers and administration of every madrasa should establish a spiritual link with a Sufi *shaykh* for the purpose of reform and training."[25] He further recommends reading groups to study the lives of Deoband's great Sufi-scholars:

> Teachers and students should be required to meet together even once a week to study the sayings and lives of the great elders of the religion [*din*], especially the great *'ulama* of Deoband. In this way, Hazrat Thanvi's *Arvah-i salasa* [a collection of stories of saints], *Tazkirat al-Rashid* [the biography of Gangohi], *Hayat-i Qasimi* [a biography of Nanautvi], *Tazkirat al-Khalil* [the biography of Saharanpuri], *Hayat-i Shaykh al-Hind* [the biography of Mahmud Hasan], *Ashraf al-savanih* [a biography of Thanvi], and *Aap biti* [the autobiography of Muhammad Zakariyya Kandhlavi] should be studied collectively to yield their benefits.[26]

'Usmani's call to reincorporate classic Sufi texts and the biographies of Deoband's founding figures into madrasa curricula reveals an anxiety about whether Deoband's traditional approach to teaching Sufism—by "example" rather than by text—is effective. But it also points to a new consciousness about the roles that these principal "interpreters" of Deobandi tradition have played in defining it.

'Usmani is not the only mid- or late-twentieth-century Deobandi to lament the separation of Sufism and the seminary. For Muhammad Shafi' (d. 1976), the overspecialization of both *'ulama* and Sufis has led each group to neglect the other:

> On one side, the *'ulama* began to neglect remembrance of God [*zikrullah*] and pondering the afterlife. Love for God and the Messenger, which is a requirement of perfect faith [*iman-i kamil*], too began to decline. On the other side, the Sufis became ignorant of the religious sciences, and their care for the Sunna and Shari'a began to diminish. The madrasa and the *khanqah* became rivals heaping blame upon one another. The madrasa regarded knowledge of a few legal questions to be height of understanding, the *khanqahs* a few litanies and supererogatory prayers. The madrasa lost touch with internal matters [*a'mal-i batin*], the *khanqah* with the Shari'a and Sunna, such that Sufism became a few customs [*rusum*] with no basis in the law and prophetic model.[27]

For Shafi', the Dar al-'Ulum Deoband was founded to fill this gap between the legal and the mystical—a "fusion of the madrasa and the *khanqah*." To convey this point, Shafi' relates how Mahmud Hasan commemorated the construction of the first mosque on Dar al-'Ulum Deoband's campus by penning a Persian chronogram, "I saw a *khanqah* in this madrasa" (*dar madrasa khanqah didam*), corresponding to the year 1910, when the mosque was finished.[28]

In some sense, this new emphasis on Sufi texts and the biographies of prominent Deobandis is an attempt to articulate a Deobandi imaginary that *can* function independently of the madrasa and *khanqah*. It is, put differently, a means of recuperating the affective dimension of a *maslak* increasingly mediated by texts. This mediation, of course, does not *replace* bodies. Tayyib, 'Usmani, and other mid- and late-twentieth-century Deobandis still consider experiencing the companionship of other pious bodies the sine qua non for acquiring the shared "temperament" (*mizaj*) and the "taste" (*mazaq*) that define what it is to be a "Deobandi." These teacher–student and master–disciple relationships overlap and work inter-changeably in the formation of pious selves. 'Usmani explains that the *maslak* of Deoband is a "feeling" that one ascertains not through rational deliberation, but only through the companionship (*suhbat*) of other schol-arly and saintly bodies. It can be "felt" (*mahsus*) but "not easily described," just as "one can smell a rose, but cannot readily describe the scent. . . . In the same way, the 'temperament' and 'taste' of their companionship can be grasped but cannot be logically articulated [*mantiqi ta'bir na mumkin hai*]."[29] Similarly, Deoband's very origins in the Wali Allah tradition cannot be grasped through "rational thought or deliberation, or through intellectual investigation. It is, rather, inspirational [*ilhami*]."[30]

I want to suggest—in simultaneously situating the *maslak* as a "temperament" that one acquires through physical proximity to other bodies *and* as a concept that subsists prior to or beneath logic or cognition—that Tayyib, 'Usmani, and others are attempting to disabuse Deoband's critics of the notion that the *maslak* is a rote list of beliefs, as it has sometimes been described. And there is good reason for such a move. The fact is that, as many Deobandi scholars are willing to concede, there is little difference between the Deobandi and Barelvi *maslaks* if approached through the lens of discursive tradition or "belief" alone. In one of the most widely read Deobandi polemics on Deobandi–Barelvi difference, Muhammad Yusuf Ludhianvi states that there are few, if any, substantial differences between Deobandis and Barelvis in terms of "belief." Both are Hanafi in law and Ash'ari or Maturidi in theology, and both affiliate with the same Sufi orders: Qadiri, Chishti, Suhrawardi, and Naqshbandi.[31] But in saying they are nearly identical, it is the "*nearly*" that concerns these scholars. For the Deobandis, the Barelvi scholars' insistence on what Deobandis see as a near deification of the Prophet Muhammad, ascribing to him suprahuman knowledge and omnipresence, is the crux of what distinguishes the two. As Pierre Bourdieu pronounced in *Distinction*: "Social identity lies in difference, and difference is asserted against what is closest, which represents the greatest threat."[32] But it is precisely this *relative* lack of difference in terms of belief that leads Deobandi scholars to explain the *maslak* in affective language. Not only is the *maslak* configured through the presence of scholarly and saintly bodies; those bodies must be the *right* ones—in other words, properly reformed bodies. Not just any body will do. In other words, it is this affective language that helps to articulate how difference works in a way that explicitly cannot be reduced to mere belief. It is this unstated, even emotional, bond between Deobandi bodies that makes the network cohere internally and differentiates it externally. The theorists of the Deoband movement, then, sought to narrate a tradition at the intersection of books and bodies, at the nexus of real and imagined companionship. The global "interpreter" of the Deoband movement is what Constance Furey calls "the relational subject, formed and enacted through sustained affiliations and intense encounters."[33] This theorizing was an effort, I submit, to offset the centrifugal forces of Deoband's own disparate geography with the centripetal forces of shared affect.

MOBILIZING DEOBANDI BODIES: THE TABLIGHI
JAMA'AT AND DEOBAND'S GLOBAL EXPANSION

Just before departing for his second Hajj in 1925, Muhammad Ilyas, who would soon establish the Tablighi Jama'at, traveled just south of Delhi to a region called Mewat. He went to establish a number of Qur'anic schools for the Meos, the traditional inhabitants of the area. The Meos had long been regarded by the north Indian *'ulama* as, at best, nominally Muslim. Ilyas hoped these schools would counteract the efforts of Hindu activists to "reconvert" the Meos. He was soon disap-, pointed. The *'ulama* who taught in these schools could reach only a fraction of the Meo population. According to Ilyas's biographer, Abu al-Hasan 'Ali Nadvi, Ilyas began to think of the Meos as sheep (*bheron*) and the local *'ulama* as their often ineffectual shepherds (*chupan*). The problem, Ilyas said, is that when the shepherd herds the sheep from one direction, they wander off in the other. When the shepherd herds them from the other direction, they wander off yet again.[34] At this point, he had something of an epiphany: what if it were possible to teach the sheep not to wander? But this question begged another: if the sheep are taught to herd themselves, as it were, what becomes of the shepherd?

The second part of this chapter concerns the fate of the shepherd in this pedagogical arrangement. Ilyas, like Thanvi, attempted to navigate a precarious liminal space between the careful guidance of the *'ulama* on the one hand, and independence from them on the other. In this sense, the Tablighis have represented another side of the delicate balance between books and bodies, between competing forces within Deobandi tradition that Tayyib and 'Usmani also attempted to comprehend, if not control, as we just saw.

Born in 1885, Muhammad Ilyas went to Gangoh at the age of eleven or twelve to study with Rashid Ahmad Gangohi. After Gangohi died in 1905, Ilyas went to Deoband, where he began his formal studies, graduating from the Dar al-'Ulum Deoband in 1910. After finishing at Deoband, Ilyas went to Saharanpur, where he continued his studies under Khalil Ahmad Saharanpuri and taught at Mazahir al-'Ulum. It was his father, in fact, who had preached among the Meos long before Ilyas. His father came from a wealthy family, but renounced his inheritance to take up residence at a mosque in the Nizamuddin district of Delhi (so named because of the shrine of Nizam al-Din Awliya' located there). When their father died in 1898, maintenance of the mosque fell to Ilyas's brother, who continued his father's work among the Meos. The mosque became associated with this mission in Mewat. Upon the death of his brother in 1917, Ilyas in turn took up residence at the mosque. The mosque would become, and remains, the global center (*markaz*) of the Tablighi Jama'at.[35]

One of the debates among scholars of the Tablighi Jama'at is whether and to what degree Sufism informed, and continues to inform, the movement. It is certainly the case that, today, a Tablighi need not be a Sufi, and vice versa. But there was considerable overlap between Ilyas's efforts and those of other Deobandis to reform lay Muslim publics by encouraging Sufi initiations. Khalil Ahmad Saharanpuri visited Mewat in 1925 to support Ilyas's proselytization efforts, where his biographer claims he initiated hundreds of Meos into the four Sufi orders (Chishti, Qadiri, Suhrawardi, Naqshbandi) that predominate among Deobandis. In undertaking their pledge (*bai'at*) to him, Khalil Ahmad asked the Meos to utter the Islamic testament of faith (*kalima*), repent for their sins, and say, "We pledge not to commit an act of unbelief [*kufr*] or polytheism [*shirk*] or innovation [*bid'a*]. We will not steal, commit adultery, lie, or slander. . . . We will not commit major or minor sins, or if we do, we will repent immediately. We are being initiated into the Chishti, Naqshbandi, Qadiri, and Suhrawardi orders at the hands of Khalil Ahmad."[36]

How much these mass initiations transformed those who underwent them is impossible to say. But the pledge itself speaks to a continuity not only between Deobandi reform and organized *tabligh,* but also organized *tabligh* and Deobandi Sufism. Regardless, Ilyas turned his revival efforts into a formal program, founding the Tablighi Jama'at in 1927. From the beginning, his focus was on reinvigorating the piety of Muslims, especially those, like the Meos, whom he believed were weighed down by un-Islamic customs and beliefs. He developed a program that became known as the Six Points (*che batein*): first, correctly pronouncing and understanding the meaning of Islamic testament of faith (*kalima tayyiba*), which cultivates a "passion" (*jazba*) for fulfilling the commands of God; second, learning to pray (*namaz*) correctly and with reflection, which brings one's "entire life" (*puri zindagi*) into conformity with the commands of religion; third, the pursuit of religious knowledge (*'ilm*) and recollecting God (*zikr*) at all times; fourth, respect for other Muslims (*ikram-i muslim*); fifth, purification of intention (*ikhlas-i niyyat*)—that is, doing all things solely for the pleasure of God and desire for the afterlife; and sixth, freeing up one's time (*tafrigh-i waqt*) for the task of reforming others.[37] The methodology of the program centered on the preaching mission (*gasht;* lit., "going round"), which participants are called to do with a troop (*jama'at*) one night a week, three nights a month, forty days a year, and for one hundred twenty days once in a lifetime.

For Ilyas, the question as to the fate of the shepherd in the narrative above points to an enduring ambivalence at the heart of the Tablighi mission, at least at its origins. How would this new movement position itself vis-à-vis the Deobandi *'ulama* from whose reformist project it emerged? Would these *'ulama* engage in *tabligh* alongside the untrained, unlettered masses? Would they merely advise? Or would they remain aloof entirely? Many scholars have assumed that the Tablighi Jama'at emerged seamlessly from Deobandi discourses. It did emerge from them, to be sure, but it was hardly seamless. The tension I explore here came to a head when an array of *'ulama* decided that too many unqualified members had been permitted to give public speeches. The movement's leader at the time, Ihtisham al-Hasan, was concerned upon reading, in 1967, that Qari Muhammad Tayyib had said that the "current form of *tabligh* at Nizamuddin," headquarters of the movement, "is not in accord with the Qur'an and Hadith, nor in conformity with the *maslak* of the true *'ulama*."[38] We will see, at the end of this chapter, how Tayyib ultimately came around to being one of the movement's most fervent supporters.

The latter part of this chapter argues, first, that Muhammad Ilyas sought to push the boundaries of what roles the *'ulama* should have among newly mobilized Muslim publics, which necessarily also became a rearticulation of *'ulama* authority and an expansion of the spaces where that authority staked its claims. It argues, second, focusing on Thanvi's reactions to the movement, that initial misgivings among the *'ulama* about mass *tabligh* gave way to a more sanguine position that saw the task of moral reform outweigh concerns about the movement's methodology. Thanvi saw lay preaching as an opportunity to advance a program of Islamic reform in public contexts. But I will argue, along the lines we have seen throughout this book, that in projecting their authority in lay venues, the *'ulama* compromised that authority *in the very act* of extending it. The ensuing debate coalesced around the management of this tension—namely, how to engage the masses in doing what traditionally only the *'ulama* did without undercutting the very reason for their existence. The Tablighi Jama'at, then, is an embodiment of Deoband's sociology of public knowledge: the masses should know just enough to fulfill their core Islamic ritual duties, but not so much that they publicly debate religious topics beyond the purview of their expertise.

To begin with Ilyas's views on the 'ulama, Ilyas advanced the view that the dual spaces of Deobandi reform—the madrasa and the *khanqah,* the seminary and the Sufi lodge—had become too insular, incapable of competing with other forms of newly mobilized public religiosity. An abiding dissatisfaction with the reach of both is part of his own self-narrative. As he describes it, he began teaching at Mazahir al-'Ulum in Saharanpur but quickly grew disillusioned with the fact that his students became *mere 'ulama*—invested in the vocation but not in its spirituality. "After they studied with me," he said, "they would become *'ulama* and choose occupations like those that are common nowadays. Some would study medicine [*tibb*] and then open clinics, some would take a university examination and work in a school or college, some would remain in the madrasa for additional studies, and nothing else beyond this. Upon reflecting on this, my heart recoiled from madrasa teaching."[39] Having become dissatisfied with the madrasa as an institution for developing the ethical character of students, Ilyas then attempted to achieve this through Sufism. He relates how his disciples progressed rapidly on the Sufi path, but soon people began coming to him seeking amulets to ensure a pregnancy, or prayers for success in a court case, and so on. "Upon reflection, my attention turned from this as well," he said. "I determined that the proper way to use the internal and external [*batin aur zahir*] capabilities that God has given us is to use them toward the work for which the Prophet used his own capabilities, and that work is to bring others toward God. . . . This is our movement."[40] But he added, "If this work is done, a thousand times more madrasas and a thousand times more *khanqahs* will be established, and every Muslim will in fact become an embodiment [*mujassam*] of a madrasa and *khanqah.*"[41]

What is he attempting to do here? Why transcend the madrasa and *khanqah* only to return to them? Much like the Deobandi reformist project as a whole, Ilyas attempted to unite madrasa education and a disciplined Sufi ethics, orienting both around discourses of self-reform (*islah*). Ilyas saw Sufi ethics and Islamic law converge in the very bodies of individual Muslims. This is, of course, precisely why he made the acquisition of knowledge ('*ilm*) and the typically Sufi practice of recollecting God (*zikr*) key components of his "Six Points" and saw them working in tandem.

It was, then, Ilyas's vision literally to *mobilize* Deoband's reformist project; not everyone, he says, can attend a madrasa or study at the feet of a Sufi master. The question then becomes how one can combine these two forms of disciplinary self-formation into a single body *and* render that body mobile. Ilyas saw the bodies of the 'ulama as living instantiations of the knowledge transmitted from the Prophet—affect that can, in turn, be transmitted to the lay Muslims who spend time with the 'ulama and then be transmitted to others, for, as he says of the 'ulama, "their bodies [ajsam] carry forth prophetic knowledge ['ulum-i nubuwwat]."[42] In other words, the bodies of the 'ulama link Deobandi tradition across space, just as their transmission of the Sunna binds them through time. For the Tablighis, the affectivity of bodies in motion becomes replicable through the process of revival itself. This is not unlike the relationship between self and world that J. Michelle Molina adroitly reconstructs in her study of early modern Jesuit missionaries, whose practices of disciplinary introspection compelled them to go into the world to replicate those experiences in others—a "devotional labor undertaken to control the passions [that] simultaneously activate[d] movement."[43]

Other Deobandi scholars, Mahmud Hasan Gangohi (d. 1992) foremost among them, vigorously defended the notion that the Tablighi Jama'at provided a service to the faith that the madrasa and khanqah alone were simply unequipped to provide. In the next chapter, Mahmud Hasan Gangohi will become crucial for understanding the spread of the Tablighi Jama'at to South Africa. Born in 1907 in Gangoh, he graduated from Deoband in 1930, where he studied Hadith under Husain Ahmad Madani.[44] He became interested in Sufism from reading Thanvi's Qasd al-sabil (The purpose of the path; discussed in chapter 4), and became a Sufi disciple of Muhammad Zakariyya Kandhlavi, who would later make Gangohi a khalifa (one authorized to initiate others).[45] By 1964 he was appointed chief mufti at the Dar al-'Ulum Deoband,[46] and in 1966 he became rector of Mazahir al-'Ulum Saharanpur.[47] Gangohi made numerous visits to South Africa for the purpose of lecturing and accepting Sufi initiations, making an extended stay from 1984 to 1986.[48] His Sufi initiates have included major South African Deobandi scholars.[49]

Mahmud Hasan Gangohi was involved with the Tablighi Jama'at from its inception, accompanying Muhammad Ilyas on some of his initial preaching expeditions in Mewat.[50] Gangohi appealed to Qari Muhammad Tayyib when Tayyib was still skeptical of the group, eventually converting him to the movement and persuading Tayyib to speak before a Tablighi gathering in Saharanpur.[51] He aligned the mission of the Tablighi Jama'at in the same tradition of public engagement that Thanvi advocated for the 'ulama, identifying the Tablighi gathering as a third site, after the madrasa and the khanqah, for disseminating religious knowledge and fashioning moral selves. Mahmud Hasan Gangohi saw the organization as providing reform to those who do not have the time or inclination to attend a seminary or sit with a Sufi master:

> The fundamental point is that learning religion [*din*] is required of everyone. To this end, books are written and published, seminaries are established, a syllabus is formulated for them and its system of study is arranged, Sufi lodges are established, preachers are provided to lecture at gatherings, and libraries are founded. Various methods are chosen to make it easy to acquire religion, on the condition that none of them violates the Shari'a. One of these is the Tabligh Jama'at. Not every person is able to acquire the religion from a seminary, nor does every person have time to read through an entire syllabus, nor does every person even have the intellectual capacity to do so. The same situation applies to the Sufi lodge. Not every person is able to acquire religion through books. . . . Among the countless Muslims, how many are able to benefit from the seminaries and the Sufi lodges? And those who benefit from gatherings and sermons are even less in number. Irreligiousness [*be dini*] is so prevalent that it was necessary to find a method of promoting religion that could also be both prevalent and simple.[52]

At the same time—again, showing Thanvi's imprint—Gangohi said the Tablighi Jama'at cannot replace the *'ulama*, and in fact, "those involved in the *tabligh* parties have a responsibility to grant the utmost respect to the seminaries and the Sufi lodges and to consult with them in their own reform [*islah*]."[53]

But surely the model was based on something of a paradox: Ilyas made it clear that the movement was needed precisely because many people no longer had the time or initiative to attend a seminary or take initiation with a Sufi master. Yet somehow those participating in *tabligh* were meant to "embody" the madrasa and *khanqah*. Would he or she not then embody only an incomplete or attenuated form of those institutions? His solution to this problem, albeit a tenuous one, was to have participants visit the seminaries to seek guidance of the *'ulama*, even with the understanding that they might be turned away.[54] Thus he admonishes, "Even if the *'ulama* do not show interest in the work of *tabligh*, do not cast suspicions on them, but realize that they have not yet fully grasped the nature of this work."[55]

He seems, then, to have understood the epistemic limits of his organizational model. The core mission of *tabligh*, he said, would be to instill in individuals a zeal for religious knowledge, which would in turn compel them to seek out the *'ulama*. But the *'ulama* must be taught to anticipate these roving bands of pietists. Thus, he states, "the *'ulama* are to be told that this work attempts only to instill the desire for religion among the masses and prepare them to learn it. Only the *'ulama* and the reformers [*sulaha'*] can provide further instruction and training in it."[56] This effort would not only compel lay Muslims to seek out the *'ulama*, but would also persuade the *'ulama* to adopt a more public role, to emerge from what Ilyas saw as the confines of the madrasa and engage with the public directly.[57] In some sense, then, Ilyas's view was the mirror image of Thanvi's: whereas Thanvi spent much of his career attempting to convince lay Muslims to take charge of their own salvation in seeking religious knowledge but to consult with the *'ulama* at every step, Ilyas spent much of his career attempting to convince the *'ulama* to take seriously his movement of lay piety, which must have appeared to many *'ulama* as dangerously, if not brazenly, independent of them.

As late as 1944, in a speech to a group of *'ulama* in Delhi, Ilyas still framed his work in terms of *'ulama* opposition, even at this comparatively late point in his career. Even though, as he puts it, "it has been my burning desire to explain my mission" to the *'ulama*, "this desire has so far remained unfulfilled." The *'ulama* still prefer "to stand aloof."[58] The dominant rhetorical trope in this speech, as in others, is that this "religious work" is nothing new. He is, in fact, seeking to offset the novelty of this particular form of *organized* proselytization by declaring it a mere return to the prophetic pedagogy of the Prophet's Companions. That is, what appears to be new is in fact very old indeed.

So far, we have explored how Ilyas viewed the *'ulama* generally. How did Ilyas view Thanvi? And how did Thanvi view Ilyas's fledgling movement? Thanvi was, in fact, the one scholar whose blessing Ilyas desired more than any other. It was his "heart's desire" for his movement that "the teachings be [Thanvi's] and the method of *tabligh* be mine, so that thereby his teachings may become well known."[59] By this point, Thanvi was the most authoritative Deobandi scholar of the interwar period, and Ilyas knew that Thanvi's imprimatur would give the movement the impetus it needed. Thanvi's own reformist literature was used by Ilyas and others early in the movement, and indeed, we know from the biographies of scholars such as Masihullah Khan Sherwani that numerous students read Thanvi's reformist texts at the feet of Ilyas.[60]

Ashraf 'Ali Thanvi had been engaged in *tabligh* efforts of his own in the early 1920s. He came to Mewat in 1922, even provisionally *encouraging* celebrations of the Prophet's birthday under the assumption that such practices would ease the transition into a more "orthodox" Islam.[61] Thanvi soon thereafter published *Islahi nisab* (Reformist program), a series of short primers aimed partly at engaging the *'ulama* in teaching the masses and partly at engaging the masses toward acquiring religious knowledge. What is noteworthy about these efforts is that they are 'ulama-led. He shared Ilyas's view that the 'ulama had to become more publicly engaged; where he differed, at least initially, was in how to involve lay Muslims in this project of reform. Thanvi believed that, for one, only the 'ulama should engage in organized preaching. The Dar al-'Ulum Deoband itself had, as of 1910, made this a part of its overall training of 'ulama, establishing a department of preaching (tabligh) to counter Hindu prose-lytization, especially among the Arya Samaj.[62] Thanvi's initial response to rumors of organized tabligh was accordingly harsh; he called the efforts a "new fitna." If they were not even ready to listen to the 'ulama, he said, how could they possibly be ready to do the work of tabligh themselves?[63] Ilyas later sent a group of Tablighis to Thana Bhawan to visit Thanvi and seek out his approval, and as numerous sources rather triumphantly report, Thanvi declared, "If one wanted to see the Companions of the Prophet, one should see these people [i.e., the Tablighis]."[64] What prompted this change?

For one, Thanvi was deeply disturbed by reports that the Arya Samaj was pressuring Meos to apostatize, and Thanvi saw apostasy (irtidad) as a far greater fitna than organized tabligh itself.[65] But even if he had qualms about organized lay preaching, he was adamant that the masses should, or *must*, work to reform others: that is, they must do tabligh. At its core, for Thanvi, tabligh simply means actively striving to reform oneself and others, starting with one's own family. In this sense, as he elaborated in a sermon at Thana Bhawan in May 1923, tabligh must not be solely the prerogative of the 'ulama; it is the responsibility of all Muslims.[66] He states in jest that if one thinks of tabligh as something only the 'ulama should do, then one might as well ask the 'ulama to fast and pray on one's behalf as well, for tabligh is no less obligatory than fasting and praying.[67] But Muslims must consult with the 'ulama in the process of doing tabligh. Here, too, Thanvi seeks to keep the 'ulama at the center of the reformist nexus. "Reading books on medicine does not make one a physician. Possessing the means to heal is what makes one a physician. Likewise, reading books on Qur'an, Hadith, and law alone does not give one true knowledge. This is merely the recollection of words. To possess true knowledge, something above and beyond books is necessary," he explained. "This is the companionship [suhbat] of the people of God [ahl-i Allah], who are, nowadays, usually the 'ulama."[68]

Thanvi notes that the act of tabligh is rooted in the Qur'an itself, though the term does not appear there. "Commanding the good and forbidding the evil" (*amr bi'l ma'ruf wa nahy 'an al-munkar*) is Than-vi's point of departure, citing Qur'an 3:110: "You are the best of nations who has been raised for mankind. You enjoin the good and forbid the evil."[69] But the Qur'an also provides the model for *how* lay Muslims should engage in reforming others. From the verse "Call [others] to the way of your Lord with good wisdom and instruction, and debate with them in a better way" (16:125), he argues that Muslims should offer "gentle advice [*narm nasihat*] ... in a manner without blame or reproach." Likewise, as Qur'an 25:63 proclaims, "When the ignorant address them, they reply peacefully."[70]

In seeking to delegate responsibilities for doing *tabligh* between lay Muslims and scholars, Thanvi carefully differentiated between four types of *tabligh*: that which is addressed to individuals, that which is addressed to the masses, that which gives "general" advice on religion, and that which gives "detailed" advice. *Tabligh* to individuals—for example, parents giving children instruction on the proper performance of prayer or the Hajj—is obligatory upon all Muslims, whereas *tabligh* toward the masses is permissible only by the *'ulama*. Likewise, discussing major issues of the religion—prayer, fasting, and so on—is the responsibility of all. Preaching to the masses and discussing legal issues (*masa'il*) is permissible only by the *'ulama*.[71] Accordingly, Thanvi lists several conditions for non-*'ulama* doing *tabligh*. In brief, first, one must begin with absolute sincerity (*ikhlas*); doing *tabligh* for any purpose other than conveying religious knowledge—for example, fame or compensation—is strictly forbidden. Second, one must show compassion (*shafaqat*) and gentleness (*narmi*). Third, one must simply do *tabligh*; one should not lecture on the *rules* of *tabligh*. Fourth, he says, one should be modest and give specific forms of religious advice. One should not lecture about matters outside of one's expertise, or lecture to crowds.[72]

As with nearly everything in the Deoband movement, of course, these concerns had precedents in the premodern period. Jonathan Ber-key has explored similar concerns among medieval *'ulama* about popu-lar preachers who resorted to stories (*qisas*) of dubious authenticity to convey religious knowledge, often to the chagrin of the *'ulama*. These *'ulama* voiced concerns about the masses' capacity to understand theo-logical matters invoked in these stories, as when Ibn al-Jawzi insisted that popular preachers avoid discussion of God's attributes, for if even the *'ulama* could not agree on such issues, "the ignorant common per-son" (*al-'ammi al-jahil*) stood no chance of understanding them.

Another expressed concern about popular preachers' references to anthropomorphic language, such as a Hadith pointing to God creating Adam "in his own image" (*'ala suratihi*).[73]

Similarly, even as Ilyas sought to channel *'ulama* authority as a salutary force in Islamic public life, he did so with minimal recourse to the Islamic legal tradition, preferring instead to reach individuals through the Qur'an, Hadith, and edifying stories of the Companions—a rhetorical stratagem of the movement generally. Thanvi, as we have seen, was deeply wary of public discourse becoming unfettered from legal norms. He wanted to reach the masses, but was apprehensive about mass affect. These dual concerns remained an undercurrent in Tablighi works well into midcentury. Muhammad Zakariyya Kandhlavi, for example, enjoined the *'ulama* to engage the masses publicly, yet confessed:

> The masses have made it their business to form opinions of their own on religious controversies [*masa'il*]. Why do they find it necessary to arbitrate over differences among the men of knowledge [*ahl-i 'ilm*], over intellectual issues and reasoning, when they lack the capacities to do so? In such arbitrations and decisions, they ought to follow the true *'ulama*, whose sound beliefs and piety are born of experience and whose credentials as men of God are established. But this is not their intention. Their intention is to engage in disputes. In such assemblies, in such public discourses, the masses find no gratification unless others are reviled, unless others are criticized, unless others are publicly disgraced. The masses find assemblies in which religious topics are explained in a straightforward manner to be dull [*phika*] and insipid [*be maza*].[74]

That is, the masses want disputation (*munazara*), not religious lectures. They want entertainment, not edification.

But in weighing the risks of popular preaching with the need for mass reform, Deobandis mostly gave a preference to the latter. Sometime in the late 1960s, no less a figure than Qari Muhammad Tayyib gave an impassioned speech in defense of the Tablighis.[75] In Tayyib's view, the Tablighis are a direct extension of the entire Deobandi philosophy of companionship (*suhbat*) with the pious. Like Gangohi and others, he referenced the Prophet's ability to turn an idolater into a Muslim instantaneously through the affective power of his mere presence. The history of Islam is, for Tayyib, the nostalgic attempt to re-create that affect and apply it to the task of self-reform (*islah-i nafs*).[76] As other Deobandis note again and again, Tayyib, too, comments that the best means of self-reform is through finding a Sufi master to be one's guide. But what if a master is unavailable? The Tablighi Jama'at, he suggests, offers the most elegant solution to that problem. To illustrate this idea, Tayyib drew on al-Ghazali, who proposed four means for doing self-reform when one cannot find a master. The four-part typology moves inward from society to complete solitude: first, one should seek companionship with other "men of God" (*suhbat-i ahl Allah*) to aid in self-reform; second, if such companionship is not possible, one should find pious friends (*intikhab-i dost*); third, if one cannot find such friends, one should let the fault-finding of one's enemies guide one toward awareness of what needs to be reformed; finally, one should engage in self-reform through rigorous self-interrogation (*muhasaba*). "Suppose one says, 'I am on a mountaintop. I have neither the companionship of a master, nor friends, nor enemies. How am I to reform myself'?" Tayyib asks rhetorically. Paraphrasing al-Ghazali, he replies that such a person can still spend time every day in introspection and gratitude (*shukr*).[77] But Tayyib brings his argument back around to the Tablighi Jama'at: they exemplify all four forms of self-reform. "So when one goes out for *tabligh*, he is in the company of holy men, and he is amid good friends who prevent one another from doing evil."[78] Even the accusations of "Wahhabi" and "innovator" (*bid'ati*) that Tablighis receive, he adds, are opportunities for introspection. "You will ponder: what are my weaknesses and faults, and how can I mitigate them?"[79] Lastly, the Tablighis engage in daily self-interrogation (*muhasaba*). At the end of each day, they ask, "How much good did I do, and how much evil?"[80]

There is no reason to doubt Tayyib's sincerity here. But grafting al-Ghazali's rhetorical device onto the Tablighi Jama'at feels artificial, a call to an ideal rather than a description of actual realities on the ground. From the vantage of many Muslims whom we will discuss in the final two chapters, Tayyib's third point—about the Tablighis' enemies—was the most germane to their experience. In 1970, only a year or so after this speech, the first major Tablighi–Barelvi clash in South Africa would take place. Whether those involved took Tayyib to heart and saw these events as opportunities for introspection is impossible to know. Regardless, that story—one involving a bitter, internecine conflict between subcontinental rivals in a very different context—is the one to which we now turn.

6

How a Tradition Travels

That Islam is a global religion is obvious. What is less obvious is precisely *how*. In the previous chapter, we saw Qari Muhammad Tayyib, chancellor of the Dar al-ʿUlum Deoband and the preeminent theorist of Deobandi tradition, attempt to grapple with what made Deoband cohere as a movement across time and space, precisely as the movement began to expand beyond the Indian subcontinent. Tayyib deployed the concept of the *maslak* to lend coherence to Deobandi tradition, so long as the individuals in its ambit were involved in one of the three key modalities of the movement: teaching, writing, and preaching. We have also seen how Ashraf ʿAli Thanvi sought a balance between the anthropocentrism of teaching (whether by the *ʿalim* or the Sufi master) and the bibliocentrism of writing—always regarding the latter as subservient to the former. And we saw how he, Tayyib, and others came around to accepting the Tablighi Jamaʿat as a mass mobilization of the seminary (madrasa) and the Sufi lodge (*khanqah*).

This chapter details how the Deoband movement expanded to the locale outside of South Asia where it has established a presence greater than in any other place: South Africa. It will show how Deoband's mobility was configured partly through the migration of individual Sufi-scholars from India to South Africa (and, eventually, from South Africa to India), and partly through the global rise of the Tablighi Jamaʿat. It will argue, moreover, that the Tablighi Jamaʿat, more than the movement of individual scholars, became the principal engine behind the global migration of Deobandi contestations over the Sufi devotional practices we saw in chapter 2. These roving contestations were, in turn, inseparable from both the global rise and the highly local iterations of the Deobandi–Barelvi rivalry, which took on an especially bitter hue in the South African context.

This chapter begins with a brief overview of Islam in South Africa in order to set a scene for the gradual rise of the Deoband movement, beginning with Deobandi *'ulama* councils in the 1920s, the first branches of the Tablighi Jama'at in 1960, and the first Deobandi Dar al-'Ulum in South Africa in 1973. One of the reasons that a Dar al-'Ulum was not established in South Africa until 1973 is that local *'ulama* born in South Africa still tended to travel to Indian seminaries well into the latter half of the twentieth century. This chapter and the next explain how several prominent Deobandi scholars—Masihullah Khan, Mahmud Hasan Gangohi, Qari Muhammad Tayyib, and Muhammad Zakariyya Kandhlavi, all of whom were students and/or disciples of Rashid Ahmad Gangohi or Ashraf 'Ali Thanvi—were instrumental in establishing a Deobandi presence in South Africa through their repeated visits to the country and their initiations of scores of South Africans into their Sufi orders, many of whom went on to establish or teach in Deobandi madrasas there.

Finally, the chapter details the emergence of Deobandi–Barelvi polemics in the 1970s. Transpiring in mosques, at lectures, and in assembly halls, and through the circulation of short pamphlets and broadsides, these polemics rehashed points of contention—over *mawlud*, *'urs*, *bid'a*, whether God can lie (*imkan-i kizb*), whether God can create additional Prophets after Muhammad (*imkan-i nazir*), and others. They rehashed these arguments mostly in English and with little of the texture or hermeneutical complexity of the texts we examined previously and, for the most part, did not adapt or apply these polemics to local South African contexts.

In this and the next chapter, I will suggest ways that these polemical circulations constitute the very forms of public debate over theological issues that scholars like Thanvi hoped to curtail. Moreover, the fact that the Tablighi Jama'at was central in instigating these polemics suggests a certain compromising of its initial commitment to avoid these issues and perhaps a straying from Thanvi's exhortation for Tablighis to offer "gentle advice [*narm nasihat*] . . . in a manner without blame or reproach."[1] As the final chapter will argue, Tablighis' quarrels with Barelvis brought both movements under critical scrutiny from South African Muslims who were not ideologically or politically invested in either group, and who regarded them as politically retrogressive squabbles with no bearing on local exigencies. In the broadest sense, the fate of Deobandi thought in South Africa shows how a tradition interpellates multiple publics as it travels, some of which function as counterpublics militating against not just the debates themselves but the very *terms* of debate. It also shows how the careful control that Thanvi sought to maintain over the circulation of the Deobandi public was unhinged in at least two ways—first, by the movement of those publics into new locales, where they met new forms of resistance, and second, by elements intrinsic in the circulation of the public itself, especially via texts. In this sense, centripetal forces of Deobandi "tradition"—articulated through the *maslak,* emphasizing bodies as the mediators of books—gave way to the centrifugal, even chaotic, forces of a global movement.

ISLAM(S) IN SOUTH AFRICA

The three-and-a-half-century-old story of Islam in South Africa is less well known to most readers than the story of Islam in South Asia. A brief overview will familiarize readers with this history, as well as provide context for the clashes we will see later in this chapter and the next, both within Muslim communities of Indian descent and between Muslims of Indian and "Malay" descent, as Cape Muslims have traditionally been called.

In 1652 the Dutch colonial administrator Jan van Riebeeck established Cape Town as a waystation for ships traveling between the Netherlands and Dutch trading posts in the East Indies. Situated along a natural harbor at the tip of southern Africa, Cape Town was settled by Dutch farmers and merchants who relied on slave labor. From the outset, the Dutch imported slaves from other parts of its empire to work in the Cape, many of whom were Muslim.[2] The Dutch severely curtailed the practice of Islam in the Cape colony; Muslims were unable to build mosques, madrasas, or cemeteries, or engage in any Sufi practices.[3] The arrival of Shaykh Yusuf in 1694 marks the emergence of the first major figure in Cape Muslim history, though even in the era of Shaykh Yusuf there was no substantial Muslim community in the Cape. Exiled by the Dutch for fomenting unrest and fighting against the Dutch in Indonesia, Shaykh Yusuf was forcibly settled at Zandvliet, outside of Cape Town, where he wrote treatises on Sufism in Malay, Bughanese, and Arabic.[4] It was another political prisoner, Imam Abdullah ibn Kadi—popularly known as Tuan Guru—

who worked to institutionalize Islam in the Cape. After the British took over control of the colony and liberalized some restrictions on Muslims, a free black slave established the first mosque in South Africa in 1795, known as Auwal Masjid. Tuan Guru served as the first imam.[5]

In 1795 the British took Cape Town as part of a larger campaign to secure global trade routes during their war with revolutionary France. The Dutch reclaimed Cape Town in 1803 and granted religious freedoms to Cape Muslims the following year. The British once again seized the Cape in 1806 and ceased the import of slaves in the following year, effectively ending the import of Muslim slaves.[6] With their new freedom to practice Islam openly (albeit with some restrictions), Cape Muslims built a cemetery and a number of small madrasas.[7] The period from 1770 to 1840 saw a sharp growth in the Muslim population of the Cape, and by 1840, Muslims were one-third of a Cape population of roughly twenty thousand.[8] Historians have argued that Sufi orders provided a sense of *communitas* for freed slaves, who were generally barred from Christian congregations, thereby swelling the ranks of the Cape's Muslims.[9]

Two forms of devotional practice—celebrating the *mawlud*, and visiting local saints' tombs known as *kramats* (from the Arabic *karamat*, meaning "miracles")—were and remain especially central to Islam in the Cape. The *mawlud* has been practiced in the Cape since as early as 1772.[10] The Cape has long had numerous *mawlud* clubs ("moulood jamaahs"), each with its own name.[11] Cape *mawluds* have distinctive features that exist perhaps nowhere else, such as the practice called *rampie-sny*, the "cutting of the orange leaves," in which women and girls cut the leaves of orange plants into small strips, which are scented with rose and lemon oils and then wrapped into small bundles using colorful kite paper.[12] These sachets are then distributed among the participants. The *kramats* comprise a circle of tombs that dot the hills and mountains surrounding Cape Town. A 1938 survey of the *kramats* described them as a "Holy Circle" surrounding the Cape.[13] Among the most important is the *kramat* of Sheikh Yusuf, whose annual festival routinely attracts over forty thousand pilgrims.[14] In 1982, on the occasion of the 'urs of 'Abd al-Qadir Jilani (d. 1166), founder of the Qadiri Sufi order, the Cape Mazaar Society was founded to preserve these tombs.[15]

The history of Cape Muslims—or Cape "Malays," as some would later call them[16]—would eventually intersect in numerous ways with the history of Muslims from India who began to arrive on the shores of Natal, then a British colony on the east coast of South Africa, in 1860.

MUSLIM MIGRATIONS IN THE INDIAN OCEAN

In the nineteenth century, millions of Indians migrated to work in far-flung parts of the British empire, the engine of the modern South Asian diaspora.[17] While there were centuries-old networks that linked coastal cities along the Indian Ocean rim, the advent of the steamship and the regularization of British shipping lines in the mid–nineteenth century facilitated new movement of vast numbers of people between India and Africa.[18] India became a "nodal point from which peoples, ideas, goods, and institutions—everything that enables an empire to exist—radiated outward."[19]

Indians first arrived in Natal as indentured servants in 1860, and shortly thereafter the first "passenger" Indians began to arrive, so called because they paid for their own passage to Africa—as opposed to indentured Indians, whose passage was paid by their employers in exchange for a fixed (and often brutal) labor contract. Beginning in the 1880s, both indentured and passenger Indians began to fan out across southern Africa, entering the Boer-controlled Zuid Afrikaanse Republiek (later the Transvaal) and the British-controlled Cape. Between 1860 and 1911, when importation of Indian labor ceased, over 150,000 Indians entered southern Africa.[20]

Significantly, among those on the first ship to arrive was the Sufi Badshah Peer, regarded as the founding saint of Indian Sufism in South Africa. Another Sufi, Shah Goolam Muhammad, known as Soofie Saheb, is credited with establishing Badshah Peer's legend.[21] Habib Ali Shah of Hyderabad sent the young Soofie Saheb, his initiate in the Chishti Sufi order, to Durban to propagate Islam in Africa. Upon arrival in 1895, according to narrations of Soofie Saheb's students, he intuitively knew that a great "holy man" had recently died and sought out his grave. After finding the site along the banks of the Umgeni River in Durban, he established a shrine, mosque, and Sufi retreat (*khanqah*) that remains among the country's most important Sufi institutions today.[22]

Of the passenger Indians, almost 80 percent were Muslim.[23] Many hailed from Gujarat and were roughly divided into two "ethnic" groups: Memons, a merchant community from Kathiawar, a coastal peninsula within Gujarat; and Bohras (not to be confused with the Dawoodi Bohras, a Shi'a sect), mostly from the city of Surat (and hence often called Surtis). Accordingly, wealthy Gujarati Muslims founded mosques along largely ethnic lines in the 1880s. In 1881 a Memon merchant financed Durban's Grey Street Masjid, one of South Africa's largest, whereas Bohra traders financed the West Street Masjid in 1885.[24] The trustees that managed the mosques were also defined in terms of ethnicity; Memons exclusively oversaw the Grey Street Masjid until 1905, when a Bohra successfully challenged that arrangement in court and forced the trustees to include at least two Bohras. Still, these mosque committees wielded enormous influence in establishing new mosques and defining their ideological slant. In the Transvaal they were typically elected, and in Natal often appointed for life, allowing the patronage of wealthy Muslims to shape religious infrastructure.[25]

These "ethnic" divisions also constituted divisions over normative Islamic piety. The Memons were more inclined toward popular Sufi devotions, tracing their origins to a descendant of 'Abd al-Qadir Jilani and maintaining close links to the annual 'urs of Mu'in al-Din Chishti at Ajmer, India.[26] They began observing 'urs and mawlud almost immediately upon arrival; in March 1877, they petitioned the government to exempt the "period of the Moulood Sharif" from the evening curfew that applied to all Indians.[27] The Surtis, on the other hand, were "giving up their former spiritual guides and transferring their reverence to the new preachers who have become the leaders in religious matters," preachers described as "Wahhabi," in the words of a contemporary observer.[28] These divisions, while far from seamless, presaged the ethnic contours of Deobandi–Barelvi polemics in later decades, and more specifically, the efforts of "Deobandi" and "Barelvi" mosque committees to exclude the other from prayers at their respective mosques, as this chapter further explains below.

Indian Muslims spread into the interior, especially after the discovery of gold in the hills of the Witwaterstrand in 1886, prompting a massive influx of labor into what would become Johannesburg. Indians in Natal and the Transvaal (roughly corresponding to the current province of Gauteng) faced severe restrictions on their religious practice. The Boer-governed Orange Free State, centered at Bloemfontein, completely prohibited any Indians from living in its borders, while the Zuid Afrikaanse Republiek, centered at Pretoria, forbade nonwhites from owning land except in rare circumstances.[29] This is of course the context for the early career of Mohandas Gandhi, who established the Natal Indian Congress in 1894 to petition the government on behalf of Indians and in 1906 developed his philosophy of satyagraha at Phoenix, near Durban.[30] The "Indian Question" became even more vexing after the 1910 formation of the Union of South Africa, based on a political compromise between Boers and the British. Almost immediately the leadership imposed a detailed racial hierarchy upon all aspects of economic, social, and political life in South Africa. Most whites favored repatriation for so-called Asiatics; D. F. Malan's Asiatic Bill of 1925 declared Indian properties and businesses "unsanitary" and advocated Indians' return to India.[31]

Despite these restrictions, Indian Muslims continued to seek ways to build new mosques. Some migrated to Cape Town, where they enjoyed relatively more freedom; the Quawatul Islam Mosque was the first Indian mosque in Cape Town, built in 1892.[32] A second wave of Indians, mostly Konkani speakers who tended to share the Shafi'i legal school with the majority of the Cape's Muslims, came to the Cape directly from Bombay. Even after Indian immigration to Natal and Transvaal ceased in 1911, the Cape continued to allow Indians to immigrate.[33] It was during the interwar period, and especially in the 1920s, that the beginnings of a Deobandi presence in South Africa could first be discerned.

THE ARRIVAL OF DEOBANDI SCHOLARS

Deoband has been a global phenomenon nearly since its inception. Whether through figures such as Hajji Imdad Allah teaching scores of Deobandis in the Hijaz or through graduates of Deobandi madrasas fanning out over the British empire, Deobandis moved, like millions of other Indians, through the global networks established by the British empire.[34] The connection between Deoband and South Africa dates back to at least as early as 1910. In that year, the Dar al-'Ulum Deoband–based journal *Al-Qasim* commented on the large number and quantity of donations coming from Muslims in South Africa: "The orbit of [Dar al-'Ulum's] influence is so wide that it has even reached South Africa, and especially Johannesburg." Some South African madrasas had managed to contribute nine hundred rupees.[35] "It gives us utmost joy and delight to announce our sympathy with these madrasas and believe this affinity our scholars have established with these madrasas in South Africa will continue to progress.... This is that spiritual proximity [*qurb ruhi*] that even a great physical distance cannot break."[36] Unfortunately, it does not elaborate on the precise source of these donations, only that they came from Johannesburg.

But Johannesburg was also the location of the first institution founded by a Deobandi in South Africa: the Jamiatul Ulama Transvaal. In 1922 a group of *'ulama* formed the Jamiatul Ulama Transvaal to provide Islamic guidance on religious and Islamic legal matters to local Muslims in the Transvaal. In its creation, Abdulkader Tayob posits an effort by Transvaal *'ulama* to assert their authority against increasingly powerful mosque committees.[37] However, in its first incarnation the Jamiatul Ulama was ineffectual for the most part. Some years later, in 1935, a young graduate of the Dar al-'Ulum Deoband, Mufti Ebrahim Sanjalvi (d. 1983), revived it. Sanjalvi arrived in Durban from Bombay in 1932 and migrated to Johannesburg in 1934. Sanjalvi announced in the Gujarati-language *Indian Views* that his organization would field questions from Muslims on matters of Islamic belief, ritual, and law.[38] The Jamiatul Ulama Transvaal was thus primarily an advisory body of *'ulama* that worked to standardize local madrasa curricula and provide consultations on issues such as *zakat*, prayer, fasting, and so on. It did not engage in Deobandi polemics, nor did it identify as a "Deobandi" organization.

The Jamiatul Ulama Transvaal was closely linked to the Waterval Islamic Institute outside of Johannesburg, founded in 1940 by Muhammad bin Musa bin Isma'il Mia. Mia was born in South Africa in 1904 into a family of Gujarati merchants, and graduated from the Dar al-'Ulum Deoband in 1925 or 1926.[39] At Deoband, Mia studied with one of the preeminent Deobandi Hadith scholars of the twentieth century, Anwar Shah Kashmiri (d. 1933).[40] Kashmiri began his career teaching at the Dar al-'Ulum Deoband but left in 1927 on account of his support of a student group that had grievances with the administration. Mia stepped in to convince Kashmiri to move from Deoband to his ancestral home at Dabhel and teach at a new Deobandi madrasa he was instrumental in founding, the Jami'a Islamiyya in Dabhel.[41] The Jami'a Islamiyya Dabhel became famed within South African Deobandi circles of Gujarati descent for the fact that Anwar Shah Kashmiri, Yusuf Binnori, Shabbir Ahmad 'Usmani, and other prominent Deobandis taught there. It was through the initiative of the Jamiatul Ulama Transvaal that Kashmiri's vast commentary on the Hadith collection of Bukhari, *Fayd al-bari 'ala Sahih al-Bukhari*, was published.[42]

The Waterval Islamic Institute was primarily involved in translating Tablighi texts into English, especially those of Muhammad Zakariyya Kandhlavi,[43] and facilitating the construction of mosques and madrasas.[44] The Jamiatul Ulama used these texts in the curricula it managed for local madrasas.[45] Still, the Waterval Islamic Institute, like the Jamiatul Ulama, was a "Deobandi" institution only to the extent that its founders and many *'ulama* associated with it studied at Deoband. It was not a Dar al-'Ulum, meaning it was not preparing students to become *'ulama*. In another sense, the public seems not to have associated the institute directly with Deoband. A May 1963 obituary of

Maulana Muhammad Mia, Waterval's founder, does not mention his time at Deoband at all.[46]

SOUTH AFRICAN *TABLIGH* AND THE FOUNDING OF DAR AL-'ULUMS

The Mia family maintained close links to the man who would eventually establish the first Dar al-'Ulum in South Africa, Qasim Sema. Sema was born in South Africa in 1920. Muhammad Mia encouraged him at a young age to pursue advanced Islamic studies in India. He arrived in Dabhel to study at Jami'a Islamiyya with Yusuf Binnori. Mia secured Qasim Sema employment in Simlak, near Dabhel—at Majlis 'Ilmi, which Mia founded.[47] Sema returned to South Africa in 1944, where he became a founding member in 1955 of the Jamiatul Ulama Natal, designed to provide for Muslims in Durban services similar to those of the Jamiatul Ulama Transvaal.[48]

Sema became, alongside a Gujarati businessman, Ghulam "Bhai" Padia, a tireless advocate for the Tablighi Jama'at in South Africa. In December 1960, Bhai Padia and Sema instigated the formation of the first Tablighi party (*jama'at*) in South Africa.[49] Sema approached Hajji Suleiman Seedat, custodian of the Soofie Saheb mosque in Ladysmith, for permission to have the first South African Tablighi gathering (*ijtima'*) at that site. Soofie Saheb had arranged the construction of this mosque, Ladysmith's first, before he settled in Durban.[50] The first South African *ijtima'* was held there in 1961.[51] The Tablighi Jama'at reached the Cape as well in the early 1960s. In 1966 Bhai Padia and a Pakistani scholar, Mufti Zayn al-'Abidin, initiated the first Cape Town branch (*jama'at*) of the Tablighi Jama'at, and two years later, in 1968, an *ijtima'* was held at the Muir Street Mosque, which remains the center of Cape *tabligh*.[52] By the late 1960s, the Tablighi Jama'at was firmly established in the Cape. One report describes its work in the townships,[53] while another gives a list of dates and times when *jama'ats* from Durban would be visiting the Cape's mosques.[54] By the end of the decade, a public discussion had formed around whether the Tablighi Jama'at's methods were appropriate for the task of proselytizing in a country where Muslims made up such a tiny minority.[55]

The rise of Tablighi activity in South Africa was part of a larger global expansion of the movement during the 1950s and 1960s. Muhammad Ilyas's son, Muhammad Yusuf, became the second leader of the Tablighi Jama'at upon his father's death in 1944 and worked to spread the movement beyond South Asia, a decision that Marc Gaborieau traces to an *ijtima'* held in 1945, with the first preaching parties traveling to Arab countries such as Egypt, Syria, and Iraq. In the mid-1950s Tablighi preaching parties began to make inroads into southern Africa.[56]

The Tablighi Jama'at also fed the need for Deobandi Dar al-'Ulums in South Africa, which was also, in part, a practical accommodation to South Africans who did not wish, or were not able, to travel to India or (what was then) West Pakistan to become *'ulama*. (As a reminder, a Dar al-'Ulum has typically been defined as an institution that trains *'ulama*, as opposed to a local madrasa, where Qur'an, basics of Islamic belief and practice, and so on are taught.) Today there are at least ten Deobandi Dar al-'Ulums in South Africa.[57] The first was the Dar al-'Ulum Newcastle, founded in 1973 by Qasim Sema (d. 2007). It is important to note that this relatively late date for the first Dar al-'Ulum may strike some as surprising, given that Deobandi scholars had been in South Africa for at least five decades at this point. But the "late" founding of Dar al-'Ulum Newcastle has more to do with the willingness of South African Muslims to travel abroad for their training.

The Dar al-'Ulum Newcastle illustrates several crucial points about Deobandi Dar al-'Ulums in South Africa. First, from the outset, the Dar al-'Ulum Newcastle was closely aligned with the Tablighi Jama'at, as discussed previously. Second, soon after it was established, its administration found it necessary to teach Shafi'i law, since a large number of non-Hanafi, non-Indian students began to enroll from the Cape. This is remarkable in light of the considerable ink Deobandis in the subcontinent had spilled by this point in defending the Hanafi school from Ahl-i Hadith and other critics, and in light of the place that mastery of Hanafi law has in the Deobandi curriculum.[58] Although it is located in the Natal highlands, southeast of Johannesburg, in a region where most of the Muslims were, and remain, of Indian origin, the prestige of being the first Dar al-'Ulum in South Africa drew students from the Cape region, where the Shafi'i school of law has historically dominated, deriving largely from the centuries-old links with Southeast Asia.[59] Because of the rising number of students coming from sub-Saharan Africa, the Dar al-'Ulum Newcastle has, since 2007, begun to incorporate texts in Maliki jurisprudence into its curriculum as well.[60]

This accommodation of the Shafi'i school certainly applies all the more to Deobandi seminaries founded in the Cape region itself, such as Qasim al-'Ulum, founded in 1997 by students of Qasim Sema in the Cape Town township of Mitchells Plain. Because its students are almost exclusively Coloured Muslim ("Malay") students from the Cape, Qasim al-'Ulum teaches Shafi'i law in addition to Hanafi law. As a former student and current instructor explained, "We broke from the Indian tradition. . . . We changed that system to fit local needs. Our graduates are meant to serve the local community."[61] The director of Qasim al-'Ulum credited Qasim Sema with introducing instruction in more than one legal school to South Africa.[62] Much of the institution's literature revolves around defending adherence to one legal school while promoting the equality of all four.[63] In its curriculum, the madrasa teaches Shafi'i commentaries on each of the six canonical Hadith collections. Qasim al-'Ulum accommodates Muslims of the Cape in language as well, providing instruction in English and Arabic, rather than Urdu, the standard language of instruction of the Dar al-'Ulums in Natal and Gauteng.

One of the markers of a Dar al-'Ulum's international prestige is the publication of a collection of fatwas under its aegis. While many Deobandi seminaries in South Africa field questions on religious matters from the general public (and, in fact, Durban-based Deobandi scholar Ebrahim Desai maintains a popular website, www.askimam.com, and runs a Dar al-Ifta' that receives requests from all over the world), by far the most extensive fatwa collection in South Africa is the one published by Dar al-'Ulum Zakariyya, founded in 1983 in honor of Muhammad Zakariyya Kandhlavi, discussed below. The Dar al-'Ulum Zakariyya first began issuing fatwas in 1987, and established a Dar al-Ifta' (an institution devoted to this service, usually with multiple muftis) in 1992.[64] In this collection, too, the accommodation of Muslims who follow Shafi'i law is on full display. Most of the questions from Shafi'is pertain to matters of ritual and worship: prayer, fasting, purification, and so on. Understandably, many questions pertain to contexts in which Hanafis and Shafi'is regularly interact, such as mosques, or that pertain to marriages in which the husband follows one school and the wife another. One person wants to know the Shafi'i opinion on wiping the neck as part of *wudu'* (ablutions in preparation for prayer).[65] Another seeks advice on whether a Shafi'i praying behind an imam should recite the Fatiha during Salat.[66] Fatwas on Shafi'i matters draw on jurisprudence by major Shafi'i scholars, most notably Nawawi. However, most explanations of complex legal matters, especially those central to Deobandi thought, such as *bid'a*, rely primarily on texts by Hanafi scholars (such as Ibn 'Abidin) or on non-Hanafi scholars whose work has been especially important within Hanafi circles (such as Shatibi). We must note that, for the muftis of Dar al-'Ulum Zakariyya, incorporating

Shafi'i law into its fatwas in no way dilutes these Deobandis' commitment to Hanafi law, or to the principle of following one school (taqlid). To underscore the latter point, the head mufti of the seminary, Mufti Raza al-Haq, reminds his (Hanafi) readers that "answers to questions given in accordance with Shafi'i law should only be followed by Shafi'is."[67]

A DEOBANDI BRAND EMERGES

But to understand precisely when a public awareness of the Deoband movement began to emerge in South Africa, we need to go back to the 1960s. Well into the 1960s, even though there were prominent Deobandi scholars and a fledgling Tablighi movement, there was little consciousness of a "Deobandi" identity. The polemics that would divide South Africa's Muslims in the 1970s and 1980s, discussed below, had not yet emerged. For instance, an organization known as the Universal Truth Movement (UTM), supported largely by Deobandi 'ulama, collaborated with Barelvi scholars and even endorsed local mawlud celebrations. Founded in 1958 by Ismail Abdur Razzack and Qasim Sema,[68] the UTM had the primary purpose of translating the Qur'an into African languages and printing pamphlets introducing Islam to a wide, mostly non-Muslim audience. They also raised funds for sending South African students to Deobandi Dar al-'Ulums in India and Pakistan; during Qari Muhammad Tayyib's visit to South Africa in 1963, the UTM beseeched him to set up special language training in Urdu and Persian for African students at Deoband. But notably, the UTM translated and published a major Barelvi scholar's introduction to Islam, Abdul Aleem Siddiqui's *Elementary Teachings of Islam,* and hosted an annual *mawlud* program that the organization viewed as an opportunity for interreligious discussion and reflection: "Everywhere in the country Muslims hold the Mouloodun Nabi. The significance of the Prophet Day Celebrations held by the UTM lies in the fact that prominent speakers from all races and religious denominations are given an opportunity of expressing their view on the Holy Prophet's life. The value of this interchange cannot be over-emphasized for it brings in its wake true harmony and tolerance amongst different people."[69] What are we to make of this ostensibly "Deobandi" organization—which hosted Deobandi scholars, raised money for Deobandi students, and was cofounded by the scholar who founded the first Deobandi Dar al-'Ulum in South Africa, Qasim Sema—sponsoring an annual *mawlud?*

There is other evidence that the Deoband movement had not yet become the contentious "brand" that it would soon become. Coverage of Deobandi chancellor Qari Muhammad Tayyib's monumental visit to South Africa in 1963, just over a month after Muhammad Mia died, mentioned little about his connection with Deoband. Tayyib made his first trip to South Africa with great fanfare, visiting Johannesburg and Cape Town. He visited Johannesburg first, receiving an official reception from the city's mayor.[70] In Cape Town, he was welcomed by hundreds of Muslims at a ceremony that featured speeches by the mayor of Cape Town and Sheikh A. Najaar of the Muslim Judicial Council, who delivered a lengthy panegyric upon Tayyib's arrival.[71] Tayyib gave his first lecture at the Habibia Mosque in Athlone, which was then, and remains now, a "Barelvi" mosque.[72] Tayyib praised Cape Muslims for their "steadfastness" in Islam and noted that Yusuf Karaan, then of the Muslim Judicial Council, was a graduate of Deoband. Yet astonishingly, on the very same page is coverage of a *mawlud* where Yusuf Karaan was billed as the main speaker (though it does not indicate whether Tayyib attended).[73]

But if Deoband had not acquired a public image in South Africa by Tayyib's visit in 1963, this would all change suddenly in the middle of the decade. During Tayyib's visit, a prominent Durban-based businessman, A. M. Moolla, asked Tayyib whether it is permissible for Muslims living in a non-Muslim state to participate in interest-bearing business transactions, known as *riba,* which Islamic law customarily forbids. Tayyib assured Moolla an official response in the form of a fatwa from the Deoband Dar al-Ifta', which was finally issued in 1966. The fatwa argued that Hanafi law permitted Muslims to collect interest in an "abode of war" (*dar al-harb*), where the standard rules governing the taking of interest do not apply, and that South Africa was just such an "abode."

The Deoband fatwa was, by all measures, a scandal for many South African Muslims, with Muslim newspapers in Cape Town, Johannesburg, and Durban registering the negative sentiment. "Alas, with a reckless disregard for the preservation of pure, unadulterated Islam, the Muftees of Doeband [*sic*] have issued a Fatwa decreeing that South Africa is Darul-Harb," complained one letter in Cape Town's *Muslim News.* "How has the amorphous entity called public opinion reacted to this Fatwa?" asked another. "The Muslims have treated it with scorn . . . . Doeband [*sic*] must take note that any assault by them to thwart the holy spirit that rages within the Muslims here in South Africa will discredit them forever."[74] Even the Jamiatul Ulama Transvaal opposed the fatwa—a stunning rejection of the Dar al-'Ulum Deoband by one of its satellite institutions—with Ebrahim Sanjalvi arguing that a ban on *riba* was unequivocally clear in the Qur'an and that this clearly took precedent over any Hanafi legal concession for *riba* in a so-called abode of war.[75]

Fatima Meer, a prominent anti-apartheid activist and author, regarded the fatwa as a "dangerous pronouncement, capable of producing serious and damaging moral, material and political consequences for South African Muslims and to the cause of Islam."[76] Meer challenged Tayyib's use of the concept of *dar al-harb,* arguing that the concept has "not the least authority either in the Quran or in the Hadith."[77] As far as Meer was concerned, Tayyib defined South Africa as a *dar al-harb* solely because Muslims are not the "ruling majority," and not "on the grounds of its governmental policies of inequality and racial discrimination which conflicts with the fundamental Islamic concept of universal brotherhood."[78] Meer's critique was motivated far less by the notion of Deobandis legitimating *riba* as it was by their labeling South Africa an "abode of war," which undercut the interracial and interreligious alliances that activists like Meer were forging. It was also, importantly, a critique of the *'ulama* generally, an example of modernist approaches to the Qur'an that were popular among midcentury South African Muslim intellectuals—for example, those involved in the Arabic Study Circle, discussed below. Features of this approach included criticism of the authority of *'ulama,* and the promotion of lay Muslims reading and understanding the Qur'an directly.[79] This was a major trope of critiques that came to full fruition in the 1970s and '80s.

POLEMICAL PUBLICS: DEOBANDI-BARELVI POLEMICS IN THE 1970S AND '80S

In the 1970s and '80s, a series of public confrontations and highly charged polemics ensued between Deobandis and Barelvis, which in turn were inextricably linked to the South African Tablighi Jama'at and its antagonists. Ebrahim Moosa has argued that "[t]he mileage that the school of Deoband has gained out of its links with the Tablighi Jama'at in the South African context in terms of its own spread and authority, is unmistakable. The fortunes of the Deoband School in this region will to a large extent follow that of the Tablighi Jama'at."[80] The first of these public events took place early in the history of Deobandi–Barelvi polemics and precipitated a long public debate about *bid'a* in the Cape as well as in Durban. It began in 1969 when a popular Gujarati preacher, Muhammad Palan Haqqani, embarked on an extended speaking tour of southern Africa, preaching against celebrations of the Prophet Muhammad's birthday, visits to Sufi saints' graves, and offers of salutations to the Prophet Muhammad, among other practices. Haqqani was not trained as an *'alim* but was associated with Deobandi scholars, especially Muhammad Zakariyya Kandhlavi, who endorsed his lengthy book *Shari'at ya jahalat* (Shari'a or ignorance), published first in Gujarati in 1962 and then in Urdu in 1965.[81]

The Arabic Study Circle of Durban hosted Haqqani in Durban, and it is not difficult to see why his views appealed to them, at least at first. *Shari'at ya jahalat* opens with an impassioned call for Muslims to study the Qur'an directly, one reminiscent in many ways of Muhammad Isma'il's *Taqwiyyat al-iman* (Strengthening the faith), discussed in chapter 2. "Today we keep the Qur'an in our homes to ward off evil spirits. We tie verses up to put them in amulets, or stir them into a liquid [to drink]. We come up with ignorant interpretations and lead guileless people astray, or recite [the Qur'an] solely to gain the spiritual rewards [*sawab*]," Haqqani implores. "Yet we don't apply its guidance to our lives."[82] And, like Muhammad Isma'il's, his book draws almost exclusively on Qur'an and Hadith.[83]

But the book also denounces celebrating saints' death anniversaries (*'urs*), the Prophet's birthday (*mawlud*), and other devotional practices, and accuses Barelvis directly of staging public debates (*munazara*) solely to rile up ignorant crowds by accusing their opponents of unbelief.[84] In any case, Haqqani's views were so scandalous, according to reports, that the Arabic Study Circle then convened a meeting of community leaders at West Street Masjid in June 1970 to publicly reject Haqqani's views on *bid'a*.[85] Some years later, Durban's *Muslim Digest* even reprinted what purported to be a public "repentance" by Haqqani's family in Gujarat, disavowing his views as "those of the Deobandis and Tablighi Jamaats."[86]

The Haqqani controversy is the immediate context for understanding reactions to a related incident, when in June 1970—the same month in which Haqqani's views had come to a head in Durban—a Barelvi organization, the Sunni Razvi Society, sent its founder and patron, Ibrahim Khushtar of Mauritius, to visit Cape Town and give a series of public lectures at town halls and mosques. Khushtar (d. 2002) was a renowned Indian Barelvi scholar originally from West Bengal. After graduating from the chief Barelvi seminary of India, Miftah al-'Ulum, Khushtar emigrated to Mauritius and established the Sunni Razvi Society in 1965.[87] In the summer of 1970, Khushtar gave a series of lectures in Cape Town on topics such as standing in the presence of the Prophet.[88] At the final lecture, when local Tablighis had gotten word of Khushtar's talks, a melee erupted between Barelvis and Tablighis after an official of the Muslim Judicial Council accused Tablighis of being Wahhabis.[89] Other clashes came in its wake at the end of the decade.[90]

Khushtar was just one of a series of international Barelvi scholars who visited South Africa in the 1970s and '80s. Among the most prominent Barelvi scholars to visit South Africa were Muhammad Shafee Okarvi (d. 1984), who first came to South Africa in 1976 and came again from 1979 to 1980, and his son, Kawkab Noorani Okarvi (b. 1957), who came to South Africa six times between 1987 and 1991, establishing branches of the Maulana Okarvi Academy. In December 1988, Kawkab Okarvi went to the Waterval Islamic Institute to challenge its "Deobandi-Wahaabi-Tableeghi" *'ulama* to a public debate, printing the invitation in a local newspaper. (The invitation was not accepted.)[91] Okarvi's *Truth Wins*, published in South Africa in 1991, was a detailed account of that challenge, very much in the style of the colonial *munazaras* discussed in chapter 3.[92] Okarvi's *Deoband to Bareilly: The Truth*, similarly, became one of the most widely read English-language Barelvi rebuttals of Deobandis.[93]

The Okarvis' visits also prompted the establishment of Barelvi *'ulama* councils, madrasas, and publishing houses, which became the main partisans in their bitter rivalry with Deobandis and Tablighis. The most prominent of these organizations were founded in the 1980s: Cape Town's Ghousia Manzil in 1980,[94] Cape Town's Ahl-e Sunnat wal Jammat in 1984,[95] and the Imam Ahmed Raza Academy—which leveled by far the most attacks against Deobandi *'ulama* and the Tablighi Jama'at—in Durban in 1986.[96] The academy publishes large numbers of pamphlets on standard Barelvi theological positions. One pamphlet printed fatwas—requested by South Africans from a Barelvi scholar, Muhammad Akhtar Raza Khan Azhari (d. 1942), the great-grandson of Ahmad Raza Khan—that forbade praying behind Deobandi imams.[97] The academy also publishes South African translations of works by Ahmad Raza Khan.[98]

The Tablighi Jama'at, meanwhile, continued to make inroads in the very same years. The monumental visit in 1981 of Muhammad Zakariyya Kandhlavi, whose work we have already encountered several times, was an impetus not just to the growth of new Tablighi Jama'at branches, but also to the establishment of two new Deobandi Dar al-'Ulums: the Dar al-'Ulum Azaadville (also known as Madrasa Arabia Islamia), founded in 1981; and the Dar al-'Ulum Zakariyya, founded in 1983.[99] Muhammad Zakariyya Kandhlavi was the nephew of Muhammad Ilyas, and some of his works, especially *Faza'il-i a'mal* (Virtuous deeds), have constituted the unofficial textbooks of the Tablighi Jama'at.[100] In Ramadan 1981, he performed *i'tikaf* (the practice of staying in a mosque for ten days during Ramadan) at a mosque in Stanger, alongside hundreds of South African Muslims. An account of the event minutely reconstructs each day of his visit—the Salat prayers, supererogatory prayers (*tarawih*), meetings, supplications, readings from Jami, readings from Kandhlavi's *Maut ki yad* (Remembrance of death)—without so much as a hint of the political context of South Africa in 1981. The book describes the spiritual effect of his visit, highlighting the wide, mostly middle-class appeal that the Tablighi Jama'at was said to have had:

> [Kandhlavi's] coming to this place of unbelief [*kufr*] and apostasy [*ilhad*] was a blessing, a mercy, and a proof to distinguish truth [*haqq*] from falsehood [*batil*]. His visit changed the entire country and caused a revolution [*inqilab*] in the hearts and actions of the people. Even those who opposed him were moved. All classes of people were astonished at the spectacle.... 'Ulama, students, laborers, traders, Hadith scholars, jurists, mystics ['*arifin*], and Sufis: all present were illuminated with the light of faith and knowledge.[101]

This period was rife with polemics and counterpolemics over *mawlud* and other controversies, most of which transpired via pamphlet wars. These pamphlets in turn were written almost exclusively in English (albeit with transliterated Arabic and Urdu words and phrases) and consisted mostly of cursory summaries of each side's arguments.[102] Here I will briefly examine two of these exchanges.

In 1985, the Deobandi organization Majlisul Ulama of Port Elizabeth— whose polemicist, Ahmed Sadiq Desai, is the focus of the final chapter— published a pamphlet, *Meelaad Celebrations,* which summarily rehearsed earlier Deobandi arguments: that *mawlud* is a *bid'a*, that *bid'a* means "to regard a *mustahab* [commendable] or a permissible act as compulsory," that supporters of the *mawlud* regard it as even more important than Salat, that they stand up (*qiyam*) on behalf of the Prophet, that they believe the Prophet Muhammad to be present (*hazir*), that they organize *qawwali* (Sufi devotional music) performances during the *mawlud,* that they recite verses that "transgress the limits of legitimate praise, thus assigning a position of divinity to our [Prophet]," that they allow the presence of immoral people, permit singing at these functions by young boys and girls, allow intermingling of the sexes, waste resources, imitate the nonbelievers (*tashabbuh bi-l kuffar*), ostracize those who do not participate, and regard the distribution of sweets as essential.[103]

In a response to *Meelaad Celebrations,* Abdun Nabi Hamidi, a Barelvi scholar of Imam Ahmed Raza Masjid in Lenasia, published *Yes, Meelaad Celebration Is Commendable.* Hamidi provided a point-by-point refutation of the Majlisul Ulama's pamphlet. First, he says no Muslim actually believes the *mawlud* to be compulsory, nor has anyone ever claimed standing for the Prophet (*qiyam*) to be obligatory. And of the "hundreds" of *mawluds* Hamidi has attended in South Africa, Hamidi says he has never observed Salat being neglected; even if one misses Salat, it does not follow that one should condemn the entire institution of *mawlud*: "If a person travelling by car from Johannesburg to Cape Town misses a few of his Salaah or misses the Jamaat, will one pass a Fatwa that travelling in a car from Johannesburg to Cape Town is Haraam?"[104] Hamidi adds that he has never observed *qawwalis* in South African *mawluds,* and even if this were the case, it would not a reason to ban the entire celebration. He rejects the notion that any verses of praise in the *mawlud* assign divinity to Muhammad. He argues that one cannot ban *mawlud* because of the presence of immoral individuals any more than one can ban Tablighi gatherings for the same reason, nor can one ban *mawlud* because of the presence of "mature" (*baligha*) youth any more than one can ban Dar al-'Ulums for that reason. If there is intermingling of sexes, he says, one must teach the participants the proper behavior, rather than banning *mawlud* outright. As for accusations of "waste" (*israf*), if feeding the poor at a *mawlud* is a waste, argues Hamidi, then surely the money spent on Tablighis' *ijtima'* tents and organizing those events is even more so.[105]

Other polemical exchanges took place over claiming the mantle of "Sunni" Islam. In 1986 a Majlisul Ulama affiliate, the Young Men's Muslim Association, published *Who Are the People of Sunnah?* This pamphlet implied that Barelvis (frequently called *qabar pujaaris*— "grave worshippers") are opposed to the Sunna:

> The sect of the Qabar Pujaaris have made the Ulama of Deoband and the Tablighi Jamaat their prime targets of attack and vituperation for the single reason that the Ulama of Deoband resolutely declare the falsehood of qabar puja [grave worship] and bid'ah. The Deobandi ulama teach you how to perform Salaat; they do not teach you to make sajdah and ruku' [prostrating and bowing] to the graves. They teach you how to conduct your daily life in conformity with the detailed Sunnah practices of Rasulullah [the Messenger of God].[106]

The notion that Deobandis represent the essence of Sunni Islam—which, as we saw, Qari Muhammad Tayyib lays out in exquisite detail—amounts here to rejecting the very idea of Deoband as a "movement":

> The grave-worshippers seek to convey the impression that the Ulama of Deoband are a new group or a sect which has arisen recently, hence they refer to the Ulama of the Sunnah as the "Deobandi Movement." Deoband is merely the name of a town in India where the famous Darul Uloom is located. If the Deobandi Ulama's beliefs and teachings are unacceptable to the grave-worshippers then in actual fact their dislike is for the beliefs and teachings propagated by the Sahaabah [Companions] since the beliefs and teachings are in fact the Shariah of Islam which was handed to the Ummah by the Sahaabah [Companions] of Rasulullah [the Messenger of God].[107]

The Barelvi organization Sunni Jamiatul Ulama responded with *Confusion or Conclusion: Answer to "Who Are the People of Sunnah?,"* attempting to turn accusations of *bid'a* back upon Deobandis. If celebrating the *mawlud* is an innovation, then surely Tablighi gatherings must be as well. Besides, it submits, Deobandi scholars such as Khalil Ahmad Saharanpuri gave their qualified approval of *mawlud*.[108] The text also reminds the reader that Hajji Imdad Allah testified to participating in *mawluds* often, as we noted in the second chapter.[109] After reporting that Muhammad Qasim Nanautvi himself is said to have visited the Sufi shrine of 'Ala al-Din 'Ali Sabir—originator of the Sabiri Chishti lineage—at Kalyar Sharif, the author asks, "One wonders how this practice of the pagans—Qabar Puja—grave worship was embraced by the very founder of Darul Uloom Deoband."[110]

It is difficult to ascertain who read these pamphlets. They were likely read by staunch partisans to these debates and perhaps ignored by most other Muslims. But as Deobandis and Barelvis issued these diatribes back and forth, a number of far more public confrontations took place in mosques and lecture halls during the same years—encounters that came to define both sides of these debates for those who had little at stake in them. This, in turn, unfolded within a broader Muslim public in South Africa that had become politically charged and increasingly critical of the *'ulama* in general and Deobandis in particular. To understand how the Deobandi brand became so fiercely contested by a wide swath of Muslim activists in this period, it is necessary to turn first to the events that galvanized them.

7

A Tradition Contested

On 16 June 1976, thousands of South African students marched from the township of Soweto toward Johannesburg's Orlando soccer stadium to protest, among other things, mandatory Afrikaans language instruction in public schools. In what is now known as the Soweto Uprising, apartheid security forces fired upon the swelling numbers of protesters, killing nearly two hundred on that day alone, mostly children. Subsequent riots would claim the lives of hundreds more.[1] Soweto was, of course, not the first major event to awaken South Africans, and the world, to the horrors of apartheid. South Africans had already endured decades of institutionalized racism, extrajudicial detentions and killings, and the slaughter of protesters, most notably in the Sharpeville Massacre of 1960.[2]

Still, for a nascent Muslim anti-apartheid movement, the Soweto Uprising was a turning point, as it was for the movement as a whole. In its aftermath, Muslim politicians, community leaders, and organizations condemned the attack vociferously. The front page of the Cape Town-based *Muslim News* deemed it "South Africa's Tragedy," coupled with condemnations from an array of Muslim organizations.[3] In its "Soweto Fatwa," Cape Town's Muslim Judicial Council declared itself to be "part and parcel of the oppressed," and pledged its "full support and solidarity with the youth in their peaceful demonstrations and with all the oppressed in their legitimate aspirations for freedom."[4] In the ensuing years, Muslims joined people of other faiths in opposing the regime, marching by the thousands alongside Christians, Jews, and Hindus in the streets of Johannesburg, Cape Town, Durban, and elsewhere.

The year 1976 was also when the Majlisul Ulama of South Africa, led by Deobandi scholar Ahmed Sadiq Desai, began publishing its controversial periodical, *The Majlis*. Desai went on to spend the next two decades lampooning the very activists who had been roused by events in Soweto. Born in South Africa in 1939, Desai graduated from Miftah al-'Ulum in Jalalabad (Muzaffarnagar), India—the Deobandi madrasa founded by his teacher and Sufi master, Masihullah Khan, who was in turn one of Ashraf 'Ali Thanvi's closest disciples and successors.

This chapter puts Desai and his aversion toward Muslims' political activism in the context of South Africa in the 1970s and '80s and, more broadly, into the trajectory of global Deobandi tradition. It begins, first, with events that mobilized South African Muslims against apartheid, and details how these same Muslims began to connect actively and affectively to the suffering of Muslims globally. It then turns to public confrontations between Tablighis and Barelvis during this period, which were lambasted by activists for their perceived irrelevance to more urgent political concerns. Finally, in the crux of the chapter, it turns to Ahmad Sadiq Desai and his attempts to graft Thanvi's politics onto the local context and the fierce opposition that he met in doing so.

MUSLIM POLITICS UNDER APARTHEID

As conflicts raged between Deobandis and Barelvis in the late 1970s and '80s, as discussed in chapter 6, other South African Muslims looked to new forms of Islamic activism beyond their borders and became increasingly exasperated with the perceived inertia of South Africa's *'ulama*. Even before Soweto, the *'ulama* came under increased scrutiny for their failure to speak out against a spate of detentions and arrests by the apartheid regime, the most noteworthy of which, for Muslims, was the arrest and murder of Imam Abdullah Haron in 1969.[5] *Muslim News,* the most widely read and prominent Muslim newspaper in the Cape, first began to speak out in editorials against the *'ulama* for silence on the issue of detentions in 1974.[6] In 1975 the newspaper issued an impassioned call for South African *'ulama* to become more politically active.[7] The newspaper's editors seemed genuinely surprised that they were not: "Our ulema and representative Muslim bodies have remained strangely quiet about the detention of almost 40 young people by the authorities."[8]

After Soweto, *Muslim News* applauded some local *'ulama* for speaking out, but, pointing to Deobandi institutions in Transvaal (now Gauteng) and Barelvi institutions in Natal, the paper wrote that "the Ulama and Muslim organizations in Transvaal and Natal have remained mute on this most basic issue of justice and freedom for all South Africans."[9] A narrative that regarded South African *'ulama* as broadly "accommodationist" began to grow—one bolstered by the state itself, as when the pro–National Party paper *Die Burger* praised the *'ulama* as "moderates" (*gematigdes*) to distinguish them from Muslim activists.[10]

In this period, public debate about the *'ulama* became entangled with a broader transnational political imaginary that animated many in the burgeoning Muslim anti-apartheid movement. These activists drew attention to the suffering of Muslims globally and called for solidarity locally with fellow victims of apartheid across religious divides. This activist imaginary energized Muslims in the Cape in particular, who came to see the Ummah as "a religious community of transnational suffering."[11] Deobandis and Tablighis were criticized for lacking this identification with the global Ummah as well as for eschewing both inter-religious and *intra*-religious solidarity among Muslims.

Three major Islamic activist movements emerged in the 1970s and '80s, each with its own politics and its own relationship with the *'ulama*. (I will survey these briefly, then return to them again in the context of Ahmed Sadiq Desai and *The Majlis*.) Among the first was the Muslim Youth Movement (MYM). Growing in part out of the earlier Durban-based Arabic Study Circle, the Muslim Youth Movement was established in Durban in 1970. The Durban newspaper *Al-Qalam*, founded in 1971 as the movement's mouthpiece, was vocal in its antipathy toward Deobandi *'ulama* in Natal and Transvaal.[12]

The Muslim Youth Movement deployed a number of tactics. One was imploring lay Muslims to read the Qur'an as a form of political empowerment. In ways reminiscent of Thanvi, South African Deobandis dismissed the Arabic study groups as "modernist" contrivances that attempted to wrest authority of interpretation from the *'ulama*, noting that few if any members of these circles had traditional madrasa training.[13] The MYM also mobilized Muslim students through organizing mass rallies. An MYM "rally manual" from 1983, *Islam for All, Islam Forever*, called on students to resist "anti-Islamic forces" from within and from without, and condemned bickering between Muslims over "trivial matters," seeing such bickering as unwittingly supporting "Jahili systems" that "oppress, exploit and discriminate."[14] The MYM believed that divisive theological disagreements between Deobandis and Barelvis played into the ruling regime's strategy of dominance: "The time has come again for the ulema to emerge from the theological barracks into the field of active politics. . . . The colonialists during the occupation of Muslim countries have made it part of their strategy to divide the ulema on petty theological issues. The ulema soon found themselves dissenting over minor issues of fiqh, while the colonialists were replacing Islamic shariah as a basis of government, with that of their own."[15] MYM appropriated Islamist language from figures such as Sayyid Qutb and Abul A'la Maududi to cast Islam as a comprehensive "system" uniting politics, society, economy, and ethics. The MYM translated and published the works of Maududi, such as his *Islamic Way of Life*.[16]

The second Muslim organization we will discuss here is Qibla, founded in June 1981 by the anti-apartheid activist Achmad Cassiem. Cassiem was arrested in 1964 under the Sabotage Act and sentenced to five years' imprisonment on Robben Island, the notorious island prison off the coast of Cape Town, where his sentence overlapped with Nelson Mandela's. He was repeatedly detained or arrested throughout the 1970s and '80s. Cassiem had long been involved in calling for armed struggle against the government, and sought to align what he saw as Islam's revolutionary spirit with pan-African thought.[17] Qibla issued a manifesto on the occasion of Ramadan 1981—the same Ramadan during which Muhammad Zakariyya Kandhlavi held his massive Tablighi *ijtima'* in Stanger—envisioning the physical and moral discipline of the fast as the ultimate preparation for total personal, social, and political revolution: "Islam has as its main objective the liberation of man and ending the domination of man by man."[18]

As other Muslim activists who typically fall under the rubric of "political Islam" or "Islamism" have argued, Cassiem, too, believed that Islam's principle of divine oneness (*tawhid*) had clear social and political implications. The argument from theological *tawhid* to social and political *tawhid* has often seen the Islamic state as its telos.[19] But Qibla's goal was never an Islamic "state." This would be, at the very least, an improbable goal in a country where Muslims made up less than 2 percent of the population. Instead, Cassiem and Qibla repeatedly called for a "just social order." The political ramifications of *tawhid* were not statehood, but the unity of Muslims against all forms of oppression.[20] "Islam is not only a message, but also a method" was one among several Qibla rallying cries.[21] Qibla's use of politically charged language complicates scholarly assumptions that the telos of "political Islam" is always state-hood—an assumption that Noah Salomon has decisively refuted.[22] Part of Cassiem's campaign for a "just social order" was a critique of South African *'ulama* for not taking the lead on fighting apartheid. Although he recognized that individual *'ulama* have done important work in this regard, "for too long" South Africa's Muslims have "sat apathetically expecting the 'Ulama . . . to do their thinking, their decision–making, and their acting."[23]

The third Muslim organization, the Call of Islam, was founded in June 1984 and aligned itself with the United Democratic Front (UDF). The UDF formed as an umbrella organization for groups opposed to the tricameral parliament proposed by the National Party in 1983. This system, enacted in 1984, gave some parliamentary representation to Indians and Coloureds for the first time, but still excluded Black South Africans. Many saw this as a thinly veiled attempt to foster racial division in the anti-apartheid movement itself, and as a clear affront to the dignity of the majority black population. UDF resistance included major boycotts of white-owned businesses and products.[24] Despite requests for their guidance on whether Muslims should support the tricameral system as a step in the right direction or resist it altogether, *'ulama* councils in Transvaal and Natal remained mum.[25] A letter from a woman in Port Shepstone summarized many Muslims' anger toward these councils: "What guidance have they given us in the recent tricameral elections?" she asked. "The Ulama, leave alone guiding Muslim communities, have accepted the colonial system. In fact they are executing the colonial plan against Islam. By this I mean they tell us that Arabic is too difficult to learn. They have divided the community on minor issues."[26]

The Call of Islam stepped in to fill this apparent leadership vacuum. One of its leaders, Farid Esack, had a seminary education (from a Deobandi institution, no less), and made arguments for supporting UDF boycotts and interfaith marches in Islamic terms.[27] Esack saw Islam as the basis for unifying Muslims above and beyond the racial hierarchies that had been imposed on them by the state: "Apartheid has not helped us to preserve our identity *as Muslims* but as Indians and Malays. It has ignored the fact that there are blacks who share our Islam with us but who are not allowed to share a complete identity with us."[28]

The Call of Islam cast itself as an alternative to the overt militancy of Qibla.[29] Qibla, in turn, looked to the 1979 revolution in Iran as an example of what the *'ulama* could do when properly galvanized against colonialism and imperialism. Meanwhile, Johannesburg-area Tablighis criticized Iran from the pulpit of area mosques, and the Jamiatul Ulama Transvaal denounced the revolution—animated, in part, by Deobandi anti-Shi'a sentiment—and called for a "ban" on Muslims traveling to Iran. Ten South Africans, among them one of Cape Town's foremost anti-apartheid activists, Hassan Solomon, defied the Jamiatul Ulama and flew to Iran to be a part of a "World Ulema Unity Week." Qibla praised the Iranians and the South African delegation to Iran.[30] A group called the Black Students Society slammed the Jamiatul Ulama: "The Jamiatul Ulama did not have the guts to hit out at oppression, racism, Zionism and imperialism the way the Shi'a leaders in Iran are doing."[31] Fatima Meer, whom we encountered earlier for her criticism of the Dar al-'Ulum Deoband fatwa legitimating the collecting of interest, was exasperated:

> In Iran the ulama (theologians) lead the people in the revolution against the tyranny of the Shah. In India, they took the forefront in the resistance against colonial oppression. In South Africa the ulama have a reputation for reaction, narrow orthodoxy, narrow conservatism, and rigidity. They are known for keeping their noses safely buried in ritual and avoiding any controversy that might result in the slightest confrontation with the state.[32]

Muslim News was at the forefront of drawing attention to the evident apathy of the South African *'ulama* toward Muslim suffering at home and abroad. It issued rousing calls to arms in the late 1970s and early 1980s, such as its "Message to the Oppressors and Their Supporters" of September 1979, "Islam's Freedom Charter" of August 1980, and its "Revolutionary Manifesto of the Oppressed People" in August 1983, becoming banned on multiple occasions.[33] In July 1982, the newspaper expressed its vision of transnational solidarity with political movements elsewhere in the Muslim world, in activist language that South African Deobandis found abhorrent:

> We in South Africa must look at ourselves in the context of the brave Mujahideen of Afghanistan who are toiling under the yoke of Soviet Afghanistan. We in South Africa must look at ourselves in the context of our suffering under this ungodly regime. The people of Lebanon and Afghanistan are suffering yet they are actively striving and sacrificing in the face of the assault on their human dignity. Muslims in South Africa suffer the indignity of being reduced to non-people yet we do not fight back. The moment the oppressed people resolve to destroy the system of oppression and actively engage the oppressors then they no longer suffer because they have now resolved to sacrifice. In any struggle, sacrifice is a necessity. Sacrifice towards achieving martyrdom is a fundamental principle of Islam.[34]

TABLIGHI–BARELVI CLASHES IN THE MID-1980S

Amid this widespread and variegated anti-*'ulama* sentiment, clashes between Tablighis and Barelvis in the 1980s brought increased scrutiny on the Deobandi–Barelvi debate in a highly public way that the circulation of polemical pamphlets we discussed in the previous chapter did not. Some of these were tussles at various mosques and *mawlud* functions. In Cape Town, an imam was assaulted for siding with the Tablighi stance on giving salutations (*salam*) to the Prophet Muhammad.[35] In Verulam, a predominantly Indian suburb of Durban, mosque trustees arranged for armed men to block the entrance of some one thousand congregants who had gathered to celebrate *mawlud* on the premises under the aegis of the Barelvi organization Ahl-e Sunnat wal Jammat.[36]

But two events, in 1985 and 1987, exemplified for many South African Muslims the political myopia of the Deobandi–Barelvi rivalry. First, in January 1985, Ebrahim Adam (d. 2013), a graduate of the Dar al-'Ulum Deoband and serving at that time on the Fatwa Committee of the Muslim Judicial Council, gave a lecture on Barelvis in a mosque in the Cape Town neighborhood of Bridgetown.[37] In his lecture, titled "The Barelvi Menace," Adam quoted Ahmad Raza Khan's poetry in an attempt to prove that Ahmad Raza Khan claimed to receive revelation (*wahy*)—a grave charge, and reminiscent of claims by the founder of the Ahmadiyya, Mirza Ghulam Ahmad (d. 1908), despised by both Deobandis and Barelvis.[38] From the Barelvi perspective, the charge implied that Ahmad Raza Khan was outside of the fold of Islam. (An irony of Adam's lecture is that Barelvis have historically accused Deobandis of unbelief [*kufr*] far more than the opposite.)[39] Adam also impugned one of Khan's most prominent disciples, Abdul Aleem Siddiqui, who traveled and taught throughout South Africa in the 1950s,[40] suggesting that Siddiqui regarded Khan to be a prophet.[41] Two Barelvi scholars, Cape Town's Ahmed Mukaddam and Durban's Abdur Rauf Soofie, issued a public challenge to Adam "to prove in public his derogatory statements that . . . the followers of the Qadiri Silsilah," widely associated with the Barelvi movement, "and all the SUNNIS, are KAAFFIR."[42] Editors of Durban's *Muslim Digest* accused Adam of "sowing the seeds of disunity in the Muslim community of the Cape," adding, "[F]or 300 years there was no division in the Muslim Ummah here. They (the Muslims) of the Cape knew little about the Deobandi-Brelvi [*sic*] subject. But since the Deobandi Ulama, the like of Ebrahim Adam, had come to the Cape, the hymns of hate against the so-called Brelvis had begun."[43] In a public forum on the event in Cape Town, Abdur Rauf Soofie dismissed the debate as a reactionary distraction from more pressing matters: "While . . . the world is looking at the [South African Defense Force] shooting innocent people, this man finds time to tell a group of people that there is a very big 'Barelvi menace' in this country."[44]

In the following months, similarly, *Al-Qalam* printed a series of letters from across the country from people who charged that contemporary South African politics left no room for "Indian" theological quibbles. Amid glossy color photos from Palestine and Afghanistan and articles on Malcolm X and Steve Biko, these letters assaulted the Deobandi *'ulama*. The principal of the Dar al-'Ulum Newcastle wrote in defense of the Deobandis: "These ulema and experts of Deen [religion] have acquired their sound and true knowledge of Deen from those ulama of deen who are experts in their field . . . until this line of expert transmitters reached the Holy Prophet."[45] A community leader, Fatih Osman, gave a speech at the Dar al-'Ulum Newcastle imploring the Deobandi *'ulama* directly to "stand up for justice" and entreating them not to let internal squabbles distract them from political causes.[46]

For many South African Muslims, the outrage that met Ebrahim Adam's lecture was minor compared with the second major event. On 7 March 1987, a group of Tablighis stormed into a *mawlud* assembly in the Johannesburg suburb of Azaadville and attacked the congregants. One man was killed, and at least six others were critically injured. A week prior to the attack, madrasa students had issued pamphlets calling for Muslims to "unite against Bid'a" and not attend the upcoming *mawlud* assembly. After the event, police remained on high alert to the continued potential for violence among mosques in the Transvaal. In Lenasia, the Barelvi-affiliated Saabrie Mosque retained a police presence in the weeks following the attack.[47]

The immediate response was fierce. After news of the Azaadville incident, the Muslim Youth Movement stated:

> The latest outbreak of violence between the Sunni [Barelvi] and the Tablighi Jamaats, has done violence to Islam, which stands for peace and tolerance. What can be more damaging to the spread of Islam in this country than the bad example of Muslims killing Muslims? In a country where inter-group violence has become rife, one would expect Muslims, by virtue of their faith which places great stress on brotherhood and unity, to set the example. Can we really afford to quibble while the country is burdened with greater problems which need the energies of the whole country, including Muslims? . . . The dispute between the Tablighi Jamaat and the Sunni Jamaat is more emotional than rational. . . . The theological debate which grips the two groups

has been imported from the Indian subcontinent. It has nothing to do with real Islamic issues and the dynamics of the South African situation. The sooner we export this divisive theological nitpicking back to the Indian subcontinent, the better our chances of getting on with the task of building our country into a land where all the children of Adam will be honoured and their rights upheld.[48]

Other groups used the fiasco to call attention to the broader struggle against apartheid. Ebrahim Rasool spoke on behalf of the Call of Islam, decrying that the attacks came "at a time when the Muslims were able to galvanize themselves into a force to take on even the apartheid state," while a community meeting at the Habibia Masjid in Cape Town ended with a resolution demanding that "Darul Ulooms, organizations and institutions of the Deobandi-Tablighi Movement that are responsible for such aggression must be exposed."[49]

Beyond organizations like the MYM and Call of Islam, Muslim newspapers published scores of angry letters from Muslims around the country. One Muslim in Overport blamed both Deobandis and Barelvis:

> The highly politicized youth see no future in this sectarian and ideologically bankrupt Islam. The process of dawah [proselytization] to non-Muslims has been retarded considerably as nobody is attracted to this "Indian" version of Islam. It is truly amazing that both these groups claim to be practicing the "sunna" and yet none has challenged the illegal "kufr" regime of Botha but each has declared Jihad on fellow Muslims. The Deobandi/Barelvi "schools of thought" have so emasculated Islam that only an impotent shell remains. . . . Ultimately the ulema of both factions are to blame."[50]

The *Muslim Digest* likewise called for a resolution to "differences that have plagued for too long the Muslim community, especially the Deobandi and Bareilly groups."[51] A Sufi organization, the Saberie-Chisty Youth Society of Lenasia, took out a full-page banner in *Muslim Views*. "We condemn the mindless, barbaric atrocities perpetrated against fellow Muslims who were praising Nabi Muhammad (SAW) on 7 March in Azaadville," it read, calling for the administration of mosques in the Transvaal to be transferred to committees tolerant of non-Deobandi viewpoints.[52]

DEVOTIONS OF LIBERATION: THE *MAWLUD* AND THE *ZIKR HALQA*

Finally, throughout the 1980s, the very devotional practices that Deobandis had critiqued became platforms for opposing apartheid locally and engaging struggles of Muslims globally. The decade began with angry reactions to a 1981 fatwa condemning the *mawlud* from the Saudi *'alim* 'Abd al-'Aziz ibn Baz, who later became grand mufti of Saudi Arabia.[53] The Jamiatul Ulama Transvaal allegedly reprinted this fatwa in South Africa, and the Imam Ahmed Raza Academy promptly issued its own rebuttal.[54] In 1982, the *Muslim Digest* censured Ibn Baz's fatwa and called instead for "a united observance by the Muslims of the world of the birth anniversary of the holy Prophet Muhammad."[55] The Barelvi Ahl-e Sunnat wal Jammat responded to the fatwa by organizing the "Meelad-e-Mustapha Conference" at the Soofie Saheb tomb near Durban, which, it claimed, was attended by over ten thousand people.[56]

There were other respects in which the global politics of the *mawlud* intersected with local concerns. In November 1986, just a few months before the Azaadville *mawlud* assault, the Habibia Soofie Saheb Mosque in Cape Town held a *mawlud* calling for global Islamic revolution against oppression in South Africa and abroad, referencing Ayatollah Hussein 'Ali Montazeri's (d. 2009) call to use the Prophet's birthday as an occasion to draw the worldwide Muslim community into a common mission. It beseeched South African Muslims to express solidarity with Muslims in Sudan, Egypt, Lebanon, and Afghanistan; with African-American Muslims in the United States; and with Muslims elsewhere. "Are not those who are languishing in detention without trial in apartheid South Africa, your and my brothers?" it asked of the *mawlud*'s supporters.[57]

The Claremont Main Road Mosque, which had by this point become a major center of anti-apartheid activism in Cape Town, issued a booklet on the political ramifications of the *mawlud* celebration. Under the leadership first of Hassan Solomon (d. 2009), a towering figure in the anti-apartheid movement and the African National Congress (ANC), and later Abdul Rashied Omar of the Muslim Youth Movement, the Claremont Main Road Mosque was the locus of several intersecting strands of Muslim anti-apartheid activism.[58] The booklet introduced the *mawlud* liturgy by rejecting criticism of *mawlud* as an illicit innovation, while acknowledging the effect of Deobandi critiques:

> Despite the attacks on such a customary practice as *bid'a sayyi-a* (evil innovation) by conservative puritanical movements, *mauled* [*sic*] celebrations continue to be a popular activity all over the Muslim world. Our position vis-à-vis the debate has been a pragmatic one. . . . We concur that neither the Prophet Muhammad nor his companions ever celebrated his birthday, and that it was an innovation which was introduced centuries after his demise. . . . It is our considered view that *mauled* celebrations has [*sic*] been and contin-

ues to be a revitalizing institution for our local community, and as such can be classified as a good innovation (*bid'a hasana*). We need to be clear however that it is not an obligation, and that its format is pliable (subject to change and reform).[59]

During the same period in which the *mawlud* took on a political hue, activists called for organizing local *halqas* ("circles") to engage in collective *zikr* ("remembrance"), to support those held in detention by the government, and to discuss and coordinate activist strategies. While these "circles" did not always have explicit Sufi inflections, historically the *halqa* has been closely associated with Sufism.[60] These calls came from a wide array of activists and leaders, even those with very different political perspectives, including Achmad Cassiem of Qibla, Shaykh Nazeem Mohammed of the Muslim Judicial Council, and Ebrahim Moosa, then director of the Muslim Youth Movement.[61] The Muslim Youth Movement also recognized the power of the *halqa* in organizing against apartheid, calling for students to form activist circles (*halaqat*). For the MYM, the *halqa* was both the "epicenter of the Islamic Movement's programme" and "the base for ideological training." Like the Call of Islam, the MYM linked disciplines of the self to personal transformation and, by extension, social transformation: "Effectively the Halqah is the base from which a change in the individual should lead to a change in society and the reconstruction of the entire social order in accordance with the Islamic system of life."[62]

The Call of Islam mobilized Muslims through a similar strategy. The organization's pamphlet *The Struggle* encouraged self-reflection and purification, and the formation of activist *halqas* in the struggle against apartheid. The Call of Islam invoked Sufi concepts of purifying the self (*tazkiyat al-nafs*) to link self and social transformation; what distinguishes its approach from Deobandis' is the entirely different attitude toward political engagement: "We must understand that this participation does not take place in an ideal environment or in a vacuum, but in a situation of conflict; a situation which has been reinforced by division, corruption, selfishness and hunger for power. Challenging this whilst struggling on the road to *tazkiyyah* (self-transformation) will enable us to become subjects in history and not merely objects."[63] They saw the *halqa* as a means of translating individual theological reflection into concrete social action: the "halqah can help individuals to live the values of solidarity, co-operation and brother/sisterhood. . . . The halqah helps each person base his/her choice on the discoveries the group has made in its analysis of reality. As Muslims, we . . . respond to this reality in terms of a total Islam."[64]

INTERLUDE: THANVI'S POLITICS

Amid the chaos of 1970s and '80s South Africa, and against the backdrop of the pamphlet wars and public clashes between Tablighis and Barelvis we have just examined, the Port Elizabeth–based Deobandi scholar Ahmed Sadiq Desai published a periodical, *The Majlis,* vehemently criticizing anti-apartheid activists and other Muslims, and crafting highly polemical arguments with reference to Ashraf 'Ali Thanvi's writings about Sufism, Islamic law, and Muslim politics. Desai approached South Africa in this period in much the same way, and on the same terms, that Thanvi approached India in the 1920s. Indeed, Indian Muslims had asked then the same questions that South Africans were asking. What role or roles should the *'ulama* play in the struggle for independence? Should Muslims mobilize alongside other religious communities toward common political goals? Can they engage in civil disobedience? What forms of resistance does Islamic tradition authorize? Is jihad possible outside of the context of a Muslim polity? We cannot understand Desai's politics without understanding Thanvi's. For this reason, we must briefly return to Thanvi's era to grasp how he formulated his politics at the intersection of Islamic law and Sufi ethics.

In the 1920s and '30s, Thanvi saw an Indian Muslim community in a state of crisis. His works from that era describe it in terms of multiple *"fitnas"*—crises that tested the moral underpinnings of the Muslim community.[65] India's Muslims were, in his view, succumbing to the temptations of mass politics in aligning themselves against the British alongside Hindus. Thanvi was, of course, no fan of the British, but he did not support what he saw as ultimately misguided and even dangerous efforts to overthrow British rule, particularly if they entailed groveling at the feet of the Hindu majority. In his assessment, he singled out the Khilafat Movement of 1919–1924 for particular criticism. As the most influential, though ultimately abortive, attempt to organize Muslims against the British in the wake of the First World War, the Khilafat Movement aimed to prevent the victorious Allied forces from carving up the Ottoman Empire—a symbolically resonant vestige of Muslim political power.[66]

As a number of scholars have noted, several prominent Deobandis supported taking direct action against the British.[67] Two in particular,

Mahmud Hasan and Husain Ahmad Madani, were famously at the forefront of Muslim participation in anticolonial politics. As I mention in the introduction, Madani is the only Deobandi whose status rivals Thanvi's as the most important and influential figure in the history of the movement, known for his political activism rather than, as is the case with Thanvi, his written work, which was comparatively thin. Suffice it to say, the following discussion touches only upon the contours of his thought.

In 1920, soon before his death, Mahmud Hasan issued a fatwa in support of Gandhi's new doctrine of "noncooperation" (tark-i muwalat), drawing on the Qur'an and Hadith to legitimate Muslims withdrawing from government schools, colleges, and employment, and using only Indian goods.[68] Gandhi himself had worked out this new tactic in collaboration with Khilafat Movement leaders in 1919.[69] Madani, who had been Mahmud Hasan's student at Deoband, took up the anticolonial activist mantle after his teacher's death in 1920.[70] In the ensuing years, based on his collaboration with Hindu leaders in the Indian Congress, he would develop a notion of a shared Hindu-Muslim polity, a doctrine he called "composite nationalism" (muttahida qaumiyyat). Madani argued that the British stoked Turkish nationalism in order to undermine the Ottoman Empire, and that Indian Muslims could turn the ideology of nationalism against their colonial overlords precisely by joining non-Muslims in a pragmatic unity.[71]

Thanvi decisively rejected these arguments. The differences of opinion between Thanvi and Madani remain an abiding tension within Deobandi thought, to the extent that other Deobandi scholars have devoted substantial work to mitigating this rift.[72] We must be careful not to overstate these differences. For one, Madani was, in many ways, as fiercely and proudly "Deobandi" as Thanvi. He defended Deobandis from the attacks of Ahmad Raza Khan, for instance, writing a book-length rebuttal of Khan's Husam al-haramayn.[73] But their political differences were not insignificant. Thanvi was deeply critical of Madani's theory of "composite nationalism."[74] Thanvi rejected some prominent Khilafatists' calls for migration (hijrat) to Afghanistan, premised on the notion that India was the "Mecca" to Afghanistan's "Medina"—in other words, a hostile domain that Muslims should leave in order to regroup elsewhere and, ultimately, reclaim. In response to Abdul Kalam Azad's fatwa calling for Muslims to do just this (which some eighteen thousand Muslims took seriously enough to migrate), Thanvi argued there was absolutely no Shari'a basis for doing so, and, in any case, so long as Muslims had freedom to practice their faith openly in India, there was no reason to leave.[75]

But this points at a larger anxiety Thanvi had about the *'ulama* in politics. The fundamental role of the *'ulama* was, for Thanvi, to guide the masses, especially when political movements (*siyasi tahrik*) were such a threat to Islam; instead, as he puts it, they let the masses lead them.[76] But he was also wary of how much Indian politics was dominated by "Hindu" interests. We have already noted how Thanvi insisted on the maintenance of Muslim public distinction as a means of shoring up an Islamic identity under siege, and how he sought to regulate the visual, behavioral, and performative dimensions of Muslim life within a broader Indian public that, he believed, was increasingly dominated by Hinduism.[77] Thanvi was especially vexed by certain *'ulama* attempting to placate Hindus by declaring the slaughter of cows to be forbidden. These scholars found it "permissible to abandon the outward marks of Islam [*shi'ar-i islam*] for the sake of peace." It was especially abhorrent when they invoked the Qur'an in doing so, as when a certain scholar invoked Qur'an 6:108— "Do not insult those they call upon other than God."[78] He was notoriously critical of *'ulama* who collaborated with Gandhi, whom Thanvi called an "idol" (*taghut*), a "Satan" (*shaitan*), a "false messiah/impostor" (*dajjal*), and an "enemy of Islam" (*'adu al-islam*).[79]

The texture of Thanvi's politics was laid bare in an extended conversation in 1932, one worth examining in detail, between Thanvi and an unnamed scholar (*maulvi*) during a gathering of *'ulama* at Thana Bhawan. The *maulvi* sought Islamic legal justification for helping to liberate Kashmir from its Hindu rulers by sending bands of Muslim volunteers to engage in various forms of passive resistance and noncooperation. In Thanvi's era, Kashmir had a sizable Muslim majority, but had been ruled by the Hindu Dogra dynasty since 1846. In the decades prior to the 1930s, Kashmiri Muslims were increasingly marginalized both economically and politically, and tensions hit a boiling point with widespread riots in 1931—most notably, one precipitated by an alleged defamation of the Qur'an by a Hindu constable at Jammu Central Jail.[80] Prominent Muslims, among them Muhammad Iqbal, sought to assist the Muslims of Kashmir by forming the All-India Kashmir Committee in July 1930. But many were deeply disturbed by the appointment of an Ahmadi to the presidency of the committee and put their support behind another new group, the Majlis-i Ahrar-i Islam, spearheaded largely by Deobandi *'ulama*. By October 1931, the Majlis-i Ahrar had adopted the tactic of sending bands of volunteers (*jathas*) to Kashmir from neighboring provinces and from as far away as Delhi. Using a variety of strategies—mass protests, hunger strikes, mass incarceration, tax evasion—the Ahrar movement targeted not just the Hindu Dogra dynasty, but its British supporters and the Ahmadis that were said to be in collusion with them. At the height of their agitation, some thirty-four thousand Ahrar volunteers filled the jails of Jammu and Kashmir as well as the Punjab.[81] While the discussion between Thanvi and the unnamed *maulvi* does not mention the Ahrar by name, it was recorded shortly after the Ahrar began their agitations, and it seems reasonable to infer that the unnamed *maulvi* was a member of this group. Why wouldn't Thanvi have thrown his support behind a movement led by Deobandi *'ulama,* one aligned not with but *against* Hindus, and one focused, among other things, on combatting the Ahmadi presence in Kashmir, a sect that Thanvi was elsewhere always quick to condemn?

The *maulvi* begins the conversation by asking Thanvi a simple question: "Bands of Muslims are going to Kashmir, but not with the intention of fighting. Rather, they are going in order to put pressure on the government. What is the Shari'a status of this?" Thanvi notes, first of all, that the Shari'a legitimates only fighting (*qital*), not other tactics, and even then, only under certain conditions and in specified forms. Moreover, either one has the strength (*qudrat*) to fight or one does not. In the latter case, one must exercise patience (*sabr*). "There is no middle ground between these two choices," Thanvi explains.[82] The *maulvi* counters with an entirely different premise. If we consider the conditions of modern politics, he says, we will see that "the public" (*pablik*) is an entity capable of force and resistance in and of itself, using means that fall outside of the Shari'a-authorized fighting. Thanvi responds by stating that a validation of such resistance would require, at minimum, independent reasoning (*ijtihad*) from the Qur'an and Sunna to substantiate it from clear textual precedents (*nusus*). As Thanvi states, "This [proposed action] is an *ijtihad* in opposition to the textual sources [*nusus*], and it is not our right [*haqq*] to exercise *ijtihad*. The two situations I explained earlier [fighting or exercising restraint] are textually authenticated [*mansus*], whereas your plan and method are not."[83] Thanvi describes himself as a "dyed-in-the-wool *muqallid*," someone who engages in the *taqlid* of Imam Abu Hanifa exclusively—or if he absolutely must, Thanvi states, he will follow Abu Hanifa's students Imam Muhammad and Abu Yusuf. But "nowadays everyone considers himself qualified to do *ijtihad*."[84] The means by which these bands of volunteers are pursuing their goal—hunger strikes, mass protests, and so on—are what he derisively calls *"taqlid* of other nations." In other words, not only is the unnamed *maulvi* failing to remain within the parameters of legal *taqlid,* but he is effectively replacing that *taqlid* with the slavish imitation of non-Muslims. Thanvi adds that these various strategies are not "transmitted from the pious predecessors [*salaf*]."[85]

The *maulvi,* however, sees a potential flaw in Thanvi's reasoning. Is Thanvi not conflating what is *mansus,* textually authenticated, with what is transmitted from the *salaf?* If we wish to model our actions on the first generation of Muslims, the *maulvi* proposes, should we not consider the Battle of the Trench, in which the Prophet took Salman Farsi's advice in adopting the distinctively Persian practice of digging a trench to protect Medina from the Meccan armies? If the Prophet himself would countenance this sort of borrowing from other "nations," then surely we are on firm ground in adapting the "Hindu" practice of passive resistance and noncooperation?[86] Thanvi is quick in his reply: the Prophet Muhammad adopted the Persians' method because, at that time, the very notion of a clear textual proof (*nass*) did not yet exist.[87] Thanvi then asks the *maulvi* how it is, if he wants to invoke the pious predecessors, that neither the Sahaba, nor indeed any Muslims since the advent of Islam, came up with the idea of a hunger strike? "Why, in thirteen hundred years, with similar conditions of oppression, in the whole Ummah, did no one come up with this?" Thanvi pleads.

Thanvi then brings his argument full circle: it is only because they have no strength (*qudrat*) that they must rely on such unsubstantiated methods. He states, "These bands [of Muslims] will be taken to jail and beaten, where they will go on hunger strikes, which is tantamount to suicide. . . . If suicide has some effect on the unbelievers [*kuffar*], will suicide then become permissible?" True *qudrat,* rather, means acting such that one knows there will be "certain harm to one's enemies, and no certain harm to oneself." The Kashmir case was, instead, an inversion of true *qudrat:* these bands of Muslims would certainly be harmed themselves, and would do so with no certainty of harming their antagonists.[88]

The *maulvi* seems to understand he is not going to best Thanvi on the level of legal reasoning. Instead, he proposes a series of arguments based on necessity and utility. "We don't have complete *qudrat,* but how should we use what [power] we do have? We should do *something,*" he urges. But Thanvi shows no interest in an argument from utility. Whether or not hunger strikes and mass protests are "useful" is ultimately irrelevant. At this point, Thanvi raises the oft-abused legal concept of *maslaha*—social good. As the *maulvi* puts it, "If we are successful without fighting, then from a Shari'a perspective, what's the harm?" But here, too, Thanvi states, "Social goods [*masalih*] cannot be given precedence over the Shari'a. This is my natural inclination. I cannot compromise in this." He then goes on to condemn what he calls "*maslaha* worship" (*masalih parasti*).[89] In short, means are as important as ends. A popular struggle, however well intentioned, and however much it invokes the mantle of struggle (*jihad*) authorized by Islamic tradition, can legitimate itself only through textual sources and only within the parameters of legitimate *ijtihad*, and even then, it requires a legally legitimate leader (*amir*) to wage that struggle.[90]

If Islamic law defines the *conditions* for political action for Thanvi, Sufism defines its ethical parameters. Not only must jihad be completely within the scope of legal norms; it depends first and foremost on "purifying" oneself ethically (*tazkiyat al-akhlaq*).[91] It is, in essence, a purification of intention and desire, a means of aligning political means with ethical ends. It is, in turn, predicated on the sincerity of intention or purpose (*ikhlas*). Virtually no one in this age, Thanvi submits, has the sincerity of motives for engagement in the sphere of politics. Muhammad Taqi 'Usmani memorably describes politics as a "briar patch" (*kharzar*), a realm in which one becomes, literally and figuratively, entangled.[92] "It is possible," 'Usmani says, "that when someone engaging in a struggle acts solely through pure ethics and godliness for the exaltation of the true *din* and with the intention of attaining the pleasure of God, and not with the intention of attaining glory for himself, and follows the Shari'a in every aspect, yet even then, politics is such a thicket that the *fitna* of fame and glory emerges step by step."[93]

'Usmani's commentary reiterates two essential points: first, for Thanvi, politics is always a means, and never an end in itself; second, the only legitimate end is the *din*. 'Usmani also stresses the unseen contingencies of politics, particularly mass politics without any grounding in legal normativity. Thanvi ultimately sees the political as a space of dubious motives and insincere intentions, a space where worldliness (*dunya*) prevails over religion (*din*), one where—at least outside of a legitimate Islamic polity—there is little, if any, Shari'a justification for Muslims' involvement in anticolonial politics, let alone that of non-Muslims.

But there remains one important clarification to make before turning back to South Africa. Toward the end of his life, Thanvi tempered the broad rejection of Muslim participation in Indian politics that had defined his earlier thinking. By 1937–1938, Thanvi began to offer cautious support for the Muslim League, which had been courting him. But, as Megan

Robb has recently shown, Thanvi's support for the league was contingent on its implementing certain reforms. The league needed to become more thoroughly pious and observant, insisted Thanvi, and it needed to establish a consultative assembly (*majlis-i shura*) of *'ulama* to advise it going forward. The league claimed victory in winning the support of one of the most important *'ulama* but did little to adopt his recommendations.[94] Still, after Thanvi's death, his disciple Shabbir Ahmad 'Usmani (whom we encountered at the end of chapter 2) gave full-throated support to the league in the lead up to the critical 1945–1946 elections, vouching for its "Islamic" credentials. 'Usmani went on to establish the Jami'at al-'Ulama-yi Islam in 1945, rejecting Madani's "composite nationalism" once and for all.[95]

Would Thanvi have supported Pakistan had he lived to see it? It is impossible to say, though many calling for a Muslim homeland in South Asia certainly claimed his imprimatur. The possibility of a Muslim state and society, governed by Islamic law and with the input of the *'ulama*, would have undoubtedly been tantalizing to him. As Venkat Dhulipala details, in his final years Thanvi remained adamant that the *'ulama* had no place in active politics but also began to endorse a tacit division of labor in which politicians (only pious Muslim politicians, of course) would do the everyday governing of a state while the *'ulama* would advise on the Shari'a permissibility of law and policy.[96]

THE MAJLIS AND ITS DETRACTORS

But South Africa was not, and never would be, a Pakistan. Locating himself directly in Thanvi's lineage, Ahmed Sadiq Desai rearticulated almost all of Thanvi's political perspectives from the 1920s and early '30s in *The Majlis,* a monthly paper that has been published by the Majlisul Ulama of South Africa since 1976. The Majlisul Ulama itself was founded in Port Elizabeth in 1970.[97] Ahmed Sadiq Desai, a Sufi disciple and successor (*khalifa*) of Thanvi's *khalifa* Masihullah Khan, has been the principal writer for *The Majlis* since its inception. The tone of *The Majlis* is as important as its content. Much of this publication rehashes Thanvi's arguments in a highly terse, simplified form, often recapitulating serial lists of Deobandi critiques without the legal reasoning that underpins them, and in a tone that can be best described as acrid.

How Thanvi's views traveled to South Africa by way Masihullah Khan is important. Muhammad Masihullah Khan was born in 1910 at Bariah, near Aligarh, India.[98] Thanvi considered him one of his closest disciples. He became Thanvi's disciple while studying at Deoband. Thanvi introduced Masihullah Khan to Muhammad Ilyas, instigating Khan's involvement in the Tablighi Jama'at. In 1937, Thanvi directed Masihullah to go to Jalalabad and establish a madrasa there, called Miftah al-'Ulum. Thanvi, in fact, laid the foundation stone for the madrasa, acting as its spiritual patron.[99] Masihullah saw his work as merely an elaboration upon Thanvi's; he prescribed a reading list for his own disciples, consisting largely of Thanvi's key works.[100]

Masihullah's connections with South Africa were deep. South African students at the madrasa Miftah al-'Ulum, of whom there were many, were numerous enough to have their own separate dormitory and even collected funds to expand the sitting area where Masihullah would deliver his popular *majalis* (assemblies).[101] Masihullah Khan traveled to South Africa five times over the span of thirteen years, making his first trip in 1970 and his final trip in 1983.[102] His followers have driven Deobandi Sufism's global reach, establishing themselves in South Africa, the United Kingdom, the United States, and elsewhere.[103]

Drawing on Thanvi by way of Masihullah Khan, Ahmed Sadiq Desai has advanced a number of critiques of Sufi devotions and politics. First, and perhaps foremost, Desai sees South Africa as a place where "grave worship" is rampant. The "Qabar Pujaaris [grave worshippers]," says an article in *The Majlis,* "are making frantic efforts to introduce and perpetuate their acts of grave-worship."[104] It goes on to implore South Africa's Muslims to be "on their guard against these semi-Shiah worshippers of graves":

> Their religion of rituals consists of only the clamour of "Hubbe Rasool" [love of the Messenger], the slogan of Takbeer ["*Allahu akbar*"], rituals of grave-worship, merry-making festivals, singing, dancing, qawwali headed by dagga [cannabis] smoking qawwals [singers], feasting and skinning ignorant people of their money in the names of the dead Auliya [saints].[105]

Although *The Majlis* is its main publication, the Majlisul Ulama also makes these critiques in short pamphlets distributed in mosques, such as *Moulood and the Shariah.* In this short pamphlet, Desai asserts a number of standard Deobandi arguments against the *mawlud* that we saw in chapter 2: its participants often believe it to have the same normative status as worship (*'ibadat*); its participants not only regard the practice of standing (*qiyam*) in respect of the Prophet as compulsory, but do not stand in other instances in which his name is mentioned, lending the practice within the context of the *mawlud* a false normativity; the *mawlud* typically includes all manner of other sins and temptations: recitation of poetry that the masses cannot properly understand, intermingling of the sexes, waste of money, *qawwali* performances, and so on.[106] The essence of Desai's criticism of these practices is that they have no basis in the Sunna:

> We see the Sahaabah [Companions] rigidly clinging to the minutest details of Rasulullah's Sunnah—even to such detailed acts which are not imposed on the Ummah by the Shariah. On the contrary we find the loud-mouthed grave-worshippers shunning almost every Sunnat act of Rasulullah. We find clean-shaven fussaaq [sinners]—dagga smoking qawwals—singing the praises of Rasulullah with the accompaniment of haraam musical instruments. Are these fujjaar [libertines] superior in love for Rasulullah than the noble Sahaabah who offered their blessed bodies as shields to protect the mubaraak [holy] body of Nabi-e-Kareem [the Noble Prophet] from the spears and arrows of the kuffaar?[107]

Second, *The Majlis* also advocated the Deobandi approach to Sufi ethics, positioning itself in the space between defending "traditional" Sufism against its Salafi and Wahhabi critics and critiquing the alleged "Sufism" of "grave worshipping" Barelvis, who are concerned only with fleecing the gullible masses:

> Tasawwuf [Sufism] is a misunderstood concept. Its true meaning and significance in the daily life of a Muslim are lost. Commercial "Sufis" (men of guile who exhibit themselves as saints) are trading Tasawwuf as some mysterious cult of "Mysticism" apart from the Shariat and Sunnat of Rasulullah (sallallahu alayhi wasallam). They have reduced Tasawwuf to potions, talismans, incantations, empty rituals, and they have cloaked it with beliefs and theories of kufr and shirk. They have interwoven Tasawwuf with bid'ah and practices of corruption. . . . Muslims who treasure their Imaan [faith] and Islaam have to be aware of such robbers of the Deen who are easily recognized by the high fees which they levy for spiritual initiation (ba'yt) into their "mystical" paths, for their annual renewal fees, for their tabarruk charges and for their many other fees.[108]

The Majlis extends Thanvi's vision of Sufism as an obligatory feature of Islamic piety: Sufism is "Fardh [obligatory] upon every Muslim."[109] As discussed in chapter 4, the very notion of making Sufism "obligatory" depends on its reduction to ethical self-purification; as *The Majlis* puts it, Sufism is "moral training. . . . This is the sum total of Tasawwuf, nothing more and nothing less."[110] This Sufi ethics, in turn, is fully coterminous with the teachings of the Qur'an and Sunna:

> Many people have misunderstood the meaning of Tasawwuf. Tasawwuf is not some mysterious cult apart from the Shariah. Tasawwuf is an integral

part of Islam. Any conception of Tasawwuf which conflicts with the Shariah is a satanic delusion. Tasawwuf is that part of the Shariah which discusses moral purification and spiritual elevation in terms of the Qur'aan and Sunnah. . . . Tasawwuf is not a theoretical branch of study. It is a practical endeavor to purify the nafs from the evil qualities and adorn it with the noble attributes.[111]

Third, for Desai, the true Sufi remains aloof from politics, especially in a Muslim-minority context and when it entails marching alongside non-Muslims, which Desai calls "politics of the kufaar."[112] In this respect, Desai made frequent and explicit comparisons with Thanvi's India.[113] What is especially striking about these comparisons is the way they seem to cut and paste Thanvi's thought with little adaptation to the South African context. *The Majlis* essay "Muslims and Politics," for instance, summarily listed ten criticisms against Muslim participation in "*kufr*" politics, including the charge that Muslim politicians visit Hindu temples to pursue "Hindu" votes.[114] Even if such an accusation had any degree of truth in 1920s or '30s India, it surely made far less sense in 1980s South Africa, where most Hindus and Muslims could not vote in any capacity until 1984, and where many refused to exercise that right as a protest against the fact that the vote was not extended to Blacks.

We can best understand his vitriolic reaction to the Muslim anti-apartheid movement through the tripartite approach that Thanvi himself took: first, that interreligious collaboration diluted Islam's uniqueness; second, that the struggle against apartheid was not a legitimate jihad; and third, that any form of mass politics, let alone jihad, must be premised on Sufi reform of the self. The interfaith protests, marches, and boycotts of the mid and late 1980s were singled out for criticism. In *The Interfaith Trap of Kufr,* written in response to an interfaith seminar in Port Elizabeth, the Majlisul Ulama dismissed the call for interfaith action against apartheid as a satanic ruse:

> Participation in a religious discussion with the kuffaar should be pure *Tableegh* and *Da'wat* [preaching and propagation]. Muslims are not permitted to listen to the propagation of kufr. This is precisely what the inter-faith seminar involves. When a Muslim joins kuffaar preachers who propagate their baatil [false] religions at the same gathering where the Muslim is supposed to propagate, and he sits with them on the same platform listening to their falsehood without having the right to refute it, then he aids and abets in the dissemination of kufr.[115]

The Interfaith Trap of Kufr then attempts to dismantle some of the central tropes of Muslim–Christian dialogue, rejecting the ecumenical interpretation of Qur'an 2:256—"There is no compulsion in religion"—and its suggestion that "religious beliefs of others should be accepted and not decried,"[116] as well as the common citation of Abraham as a "father" of Judaism, Christianity, and Islam.[117]

But it was South African Muslims' use of the language of jihad that Desai castigated above all. Like Thanvi's coreligionists in the 1920s, Muslims began to articulate anti-apartheid sentiments in the language of jihad. For Muslim anti-apartheid activists, jihad "included a multiplicity of struggle techniques, including militancy, *satyagraha* non-violent activism, boycotts, populism, gradualism, and vanguard leadership."[118] Some saw jihad as collective action to translate theological *tawhid* into political praxis. *Muslim News*'s "Islam's Freedom Charter" of 1980 sought to translate *tawhid* into a basis for political action: "To implement Tauhid as a world-view we have to conduct JIHAD in Allah's way, that is, in the way of the people."[119] Achmad Cassiem, the founder of Qibla, also proclaimed that "our struggle in Azania [Africa] is a jihad." Anyone who denied this, in his view, called for "Islam minus Jihad." But "Islam minus Jihad," he wrote, "means Islam minus Islam. . . . Jihad means to enjoin what is good and to forbid what is wrong with all the power at our disposal. Thus, Jihad is standing up with all the power at our disposal against all forms of oppression, exploitation and injustice. It is an effort, an exertion, a striving for truth and justice."[120]

For Desai, this was a haphazard and irresponsible use of the concept of jihad, pressing the idea into the service of "kufaar politics." Like Thanvi, Desai asserted that the call for jihad "devolves on Muslims' rulers and governments, not on leaderless communities and not on Muslim communities which have chosen domicile in non-Muslim lands."[121] In this traditionalist framework, Shari'a governs every conceivable action, and arrogating to oneself the status of *mujahid*—one who engages in jihad—without regard to the Shari'a-mandated rules that stipulate its proper application is both arrogant and dangerous. After the Muslim Youth Movement issued a pamphlet in support of the so-called jihad of Mandela, *The Majlis* declared simply: "'Mandela['s] Jihad' is not Islam's Jihad." Likewise, when the Muslim Youth Movement declared, "There is no need to be afraid of this word revolution," citing the Iranian revolution of 1979 as a model,[122] *The Majlis* deemed these calls for revolution at home "hollow slogans and cries—cries of the communist kufaar—cries of the Shiahs—cries which they subtly present in Islamic hues to hoodwink the Muslim community."[123] The fact that the Muslim Youth Movement found inspiration in Maududi

was reason enough to condemn them. Desai accused the MYM of trying to import into South Africa what he facetiously called the "*mazhab*" (legal school) of Maududi.[124]

In the profound social unrest that pervaded South Africa in the
1980s, Desai saw a society that had become unhinged from any moral
anchor, and even to associate such things with "jihad" was, in his view,
an insult to a noble Islamic institution: "The Command for Jihaad
decreed in the [Qur'an] does not call for the stoning of buses, burning
of human beings, pillaging the homes of innocent persons.... The
Jihaad of Islam is an orderly affair which operates under a host of conditions and stipulations."[125] These new calls for jihad were yet another
"*fitna*" that strained the fabric of the Ummah. Errant political ideologies and the decline of Sufi piety alike conspired, in his view, to test
Muslims' faith and perseverance. In response to a reader's question
about whether Muslims should join the "struggle against oppression,"
Desai replied: "Undoubtedly there does exist oppression in this land
just as there is oppression in all the other lands of the world. But the
way of combating injustice and oppression is not the sowing of *fitnah*
and *fasaad* [corruption]. Muslims are not permitted by the Shariah to
join with anarchical groups of *kufaar* [unbelievers] in any fight against
oppression. Let Muslims first eliminate the oppression which they are
inflicting on their own selves by their gross violations of Allah's Laws,
then Allah Ta'ala will take care of the rest."[126]

But Desai also invoked Thanvi to argue that proper exercise of jihad
must be predicated on the ethical reform of the self. When one South
African Muslim requested a fatwa on the topic, asking, "What do we
do about the oppression in the world and South Africa? The Qur'aan
emphatically speaks that we as Muslims should physically remove it,"
Desai responded that the greater jihad against the *nafs,* the "lower self,"
must come before the lower jihad of struggle against tyranny, and that
South African Muslims have not yet won the war against the lower self.
At the same time, Desai did not deny the importance of jihad in Islam.
He simply denies that any South African Muslim is equipped to wage it
properly:

> Muslim failure on the Jihad front is on account of the abandonment of Islam.
> The Sunnah has been expunged from the life-style of the Ummah.... The
> cause of the failure is ... the moral and spiritual corruption of the Ummah.
> As long as Muslims neglect their moral reformation and as long as they do
> not climb the ladder of spiritual elevation, they are doomed to disgrace and
> defeat in all their campaigns which they proclaim in the name of Jihad.[127]

Following Thanvi, Desai stated that only Sufism can provide such "spiritual elevation." To be sure, casting Sufism as antipathetic toward politics is nothing new. The idea has a rich history throughout Sufism, notably within the Chishtiyya, though the idea was often more a rhetorical trope than it was a social reality.[128] But Desai draws almost exclusively on Thanvi, rather than these older tropes. For the same reasons, Desai rejected any perceived exploitation of Sufi devotion or practice for political ends. Thus, as the popularity of South African *zikr halqas* peaked, as discussed previously, Desai came down strongly against them, labeling them a practice of "Barelvi Bid'atis."[129] In casting Sufism in this light, Desai calls on Muslims to emulate the Sufi saints:

> Those who clamour for Muslim participation in non-Muslim politics are short-sighted. They lack true insight which is a quality of an Imaan [faith] adorned with the higher and beautiful angelic attributes which a Mu'min [believer] gains by companionship with Auliya [Sufi saints]. Those Muslims shouting for Muslim participation in kufr politics are in the majority the followers of lowly desires and despicable motives. . . . They are swayed by mob-rule and mob-opinion.[130]

Many South African Muslims were understandably incensed by Desai. They regarded him as, perhaps, the paramount example of the *'ulama* failing to lead the Muslim community. He proclaimed loudly and sharply, according to this view, what many of the *'ulama* believed silently and implicitly. While this approach is certainly valid, I suggest that it fails to take into account the extent to which Desai participated in a discourse on law and ethics that preceded him. Just as Thanvi opposed Indian Muslims' political alignment with Hindus and calls for jihad during the late colonial period, Desai called for Muslims to resist the temptations of a structureless "jihad," and one enacted, moreover, on behalf of non-Muslims. As much as it was—and remains—easy to malign such a view as retrogressive, it is also worth reiterating that Desai and other Deobandi scholars did not outwardly support apartheid; rather, they saw the realm of the political in general as one of dangerous worldly enchantments, particularly in a space ostensibly unmoored from the Shari'a.

But Desai's critics approached the very concept of the political from a different set of presuppositions and norms. Theirs was a "political Islam," to be sure, but it was an Islamic politics unbound to the pursuit of a state. It was a praxis that saw a revolutionary potential in Islam that could be mobilized toward the very specific, highly local aims of Muslims in Cape Town. Praxis, as a reciprocity of theory and action, is what Desai could not tolerate, for in Desai's (and Thanvi's) view, the entire range of possible actions had already been worked out in the normative order derived from the Qur'an and the Sunna. Yet Muslim anti-apartheid activists were inspired by the Qur'an and Sunna, too, and found in them the basis for a normativity of a different kind. As Farid Esack wrote in 1984, "The idea that paradigms or models of Islamization can be worked out perfectly prior to us being plunged into action is alien to the sirah [biography] of the Holy Prophet Muhammad. They are worked out whilst we are involved. Indeed, they are the synthesis of our action and theological reflection."[131] This is what Matthew Palombo calls a dialogic relationship between a "theology of liberation" and the "liberation of theology."[132] It is a dynamic trinary of text, exegesis, and politics. Whereas Desai forecloses politics prior to, or in absence of, an Islamic state that can govern its application, his opponents see aspirations for statehood as irrelevant to the exercise of an Islamic politics.

It is essential to note, again, that not all Deobandis shared Desai's politics, in South Africa or elsewhere. I do not intend to suggest that all, or even most, South African Deobandis outwardly opposed mass participation in anti-apartheid politics, let alone surmise that there is some inherent aversion to the political in the Deoband movement; there is no such thing. There are, of course, major activist currents in Deobandi thought. We have already noted Mahmud Hasan and Husain Ahmad Madani. Within the orbit of Hasan and Madani, other Deobandis took up the activist cause, most notably 'Ubaidallah Sindhi (d. 1944), a Sikh convert to Islam who entered Dar al-'Ulum Deoband in 1888 where he studied with Mahmud Hasan, who sent him to Kabul in 1915 to foment anticolonial revolution. Over the course of twenty-five years, Sindhi traveled between Afghanistan, the Soviet Union, Turkey, and the Hijaz, being arrested for his work on multiple occasions. At the same time, as Muhammad Qasim Zaman demonstrates, Sindhi's position in the Deoband movement has been a tenuous one; he has been the object of incessant critique from within Deobandi circles. Still, his legacy, though ambivalent, remains very much vital.[133] If Sindhi is the most well-known Deobandi activist after Hasan and Madani, there are still others. The Bengali activist and politician Abdul Hamid Khan Bhashani (d. 1978) studied at Dar al-'Ulum Deoband from 1907–9, was active in the Khilafat Movement and, later, the Muslim League. The crux of his legacy, however, was his political organization of peasants in Bengal and Assam.[134]

In South Africa, too, there were representatives of this activist strain in the Deoband movement. Maulvi Ismail Cachalia (d. 2003) studied at the

Dar al-ʿUlum Deoband from 1925 to 1931, and was active in anti-apartheid politics in the 1950s and ʿ60s, serving as an advisor to Mandela and representing the African National Congress (ANC) at the Bandung Conference of 1955, a landmark event in the formation of Afro-Asian anticolonial alliances.[135] But it is also debatable how much a figure like Cachalia represents the "Deoband movement." As discussed in the introduction, studying at a Deobandi seminary does not necessarily make one a "Deobandi." But it is clear, regardless, that there is nothing inherent in a Deobandi education, let alone in a madrasa education generally, that leads necessarily to political quietism. Farid Esack and Ebrahim Moosa, too, were both products of madrasas. Moosa studied at Dar al-ʿUlum Deoband and Nadwa al-ʿUlama, and Esack at Jamiʿa ʿAlimiyya Islamiyya. Cachalia, Moosa, Esack, and others are reminders that Deobandi madrasas produce ʿulama, first and foremost, only some of whom take up Deobandi critiques or become standard bearers for the Deobandi "brand."

Most South African Deobandis were neither critics, like Desai, nor activists, like the figures I have just discussed. Most simply remained distant from the political fray. To take just one example, Yunus Patel (d. 2011) was a Deobandi Sufi-scholar who taught at a girls' madrasa, Madrasa Sawlehaat, in Durban, where he also led a popular weekly *majlis* for the public and took on scores of Sufi disciples. Patel was inspired to study at Dar al-ʿUlum Deoband after meeting Qari Muhammad Tayyib during his visit to South Africa in 1963. He later became a Sufi successor (*khalifa*) to both Mahmud Hasan Gangohi and Muhammad Hakim Akhtar. Patel devoted his life to teaching Sufi ethics to his students and disciples. He wrote little beyond a handful of short pamphlets exploring Sufi themes, tailored to the needs of his audience. The point that I wish to make here is that Deobandis like Patel engaged with their audiences in a very different way than Desai, one far less "public." Ironically, while he did not involve himself in overt critiques of apartheid, much of the pastoral care that Patel provided centered on improving the lives of Muslims who were apartheid's victims. Violence and drug-use among Muslim youth were frequent themes of his *majalis*.[136]

I want to conclude this chapter by returning to the contested nature of Sufism and politics in the twilight of apartheid. Desai specifically, but to a large extent Deobandis generally, lost popular support in the Cape through their criticism of, and public confrontation with, other Muslims during the heyday of anti-apartheid activism, not just by refusing to mobilize against apartheid, but even by justifying that refusal to mobilize through Sufi vocabularies. At the same time, many Muslims not only mobilized against apartheid, but justified *their* mobilization through Sufi ritual practice. More broadly, these Muslims did not merely reject Deobandis' critique of Sufism, but indeed, they rejected their very authority to lead. At the same time, despite calls by some during the apartheid era for "exporting" debate over *mawlud* and *'urs* back to the Indian subcontinent, these debates clearly remain deeply entrenched in Muslim public discourse in South Africa. If anything, debate over these contentious issues has expanded widely, incorporating new interlocutors and new vocabularies.

The story narrated here also suggests a certain historical irony: the Deobandi *'ulama,* who have been associated in the popular imagination with the jihad of the Taliban, rejected jihad in apartheid South Africa, whereas progressive Muslims, who in other contexts have critiqued jihad, called for jihad against apartheid. Put differently, certain South African Muslims mobilized Islamist language in support of one of the great struggles for human rights and dignity of the late twentieth century, whereas certain South African *'ulama* invoked Sufism to justify their detachment from this struggle and to criticize those who would, in their view, politicize Islam needlessly and irresponsibly.

At the very least, this reminds us of ways in which Sufism is an almost endlessly pliable discourse, used to justify anticolonial rebellion in one context and apolitical quietism in another. Thanvi's, and Desai's, Sufi politics recalls Francis Robinson's ideal types of "otherworldly" and "this-worldly" Islam.[137] In some sense, Thanvi and his spiritual descendants traversed the space between these two polarities. They sought to implement a project of ethical reform among a worldly public, beyond the madrasa and *khanqah,* but it remained a project that reminded Muslims at every step of the ultimate futility of worldly pursuits. In other words, they used "this-worldly" means to achieve otherworldly ends. Of course, as we have seen, not everyone accepted this agenda. And indeed, a sizable number of South Africans, living under apartheid, could not wait until the Day of Judgment for justice to prevail on the earth—or, at the very least, in Cape Town.

Conclusion

What is the fate of Sufism in the twenty-first century? And what might the Deoband movement have to do with it? So far this century has seen a torrent of violence unleashed against Sufis, Sufi shrines, and their devotees. Most recently, militants attacked a Sufi-affiliated mosque in the Sinai Peninsula on 24 November 2017, killing 311 people—the worst terrorist attack in Egyptian history. While no group ever claimed official responsibility, most signs pointed to the Islamic State, or ISIS. The Islamic State did claim responsibility for another attack, one that took place at a Coptic church in Cairo on Sunday, 11 December 2016—a date that, many were quick to note, coincided with celebrations of the Prophet Muhammad's birthday (12 Rabi' al-Awwal) around the city.[1]

The Islamic State is bringing this hatred of Sufism to Pakistan, where recent attacks on Sufis and Sufi shrines bear the hallmarks of an increasingly global anti-Sufi campaign. From November 2016 to February 2017, the Islamic State waged a series of assaults on Sufi shrines across Pakistan, including attacks on the remote shrine known as Shah Noorani, in Balochistan, and the shrine of Lal Shahbaz Qalandar, in Sindh, both killing dozens.[2] In both cases, notably, the bomber targeted the shrine during the Thursday evening *dhamal,* a dance associated with the antinomian Qalandar Sufis of Sindh and Punjab.[3] The Islamic State's perpetration of attacks on Muslim devotional practice, of course, is limited neither to Pakistan, nor to saints' shrines.

But long before the global rise of the Islamic State, the Pakistani Taliban had claimed responsibility for a series of attacks on Sufi shrines, dating at least to March 2009, when the tomb of the Pashtun poet Rehman Baba, outside Peshawar, was bombed during the poet's *'urs*.[4] In July of the following year, a bomb destroyed a sizable portion of the tomb of Lahore's patron saint, Al-Hujwiri, popularly known as Data Ganj Bakhsh.[5] On 7 October 2010, the Tehrik-e-Taliban Pakistan (TTP) claimed responsibility for two explosions that rocked the shrine of 'Abdullah Shah Ghazi in Karachi.[6] The bombers deliberately chose this day, a Thursday, because people gather at shrines on Thursdays at dusk to celebrate the beginning of *jum'a*, the day of congregational prayer. Just a few months later, in April 2011, Taliban affiliates attacked the *'urs* celebration of Sakhi Sarwar in Dera Ghazi Khan. Ehsanullah Ehsan, a spokesperson for the TTP, indicated that it was revenge for a government offensive against the group.[7]

What responsibility does the Deoband movement have for these attacks? According to a 2010 *Time* magazine story, the Taliban attacks Sufis because it "deem[s] Sufism . . . a heresy," which in turn has prompted Sufis, "typically nonviolent and politically quiescent," to begin "preparing for battle."[8] Even in academic studies, we are often simply told that the Taliban is "hostile to Sufism as well as the veneration of shrines and saints."[9] How accurate is this assumption? Let us focus for a moment on the Deobandi roots of the Taliban. If we want to know about these roots, we could do worse than to look closely at the madrasa that nurtured them, the Dar al-'Ulum Haqqaniyya, in Akora Khattak, a small town in northwestern Pakistan. Indeed, Sami' al-Haq, the Dar al-'Ulum Haqqaniyya's director, once boasted that "nearly 90 percent of Taliban leadership graduated from Darul Uloom Haqqaniyya."[10]

The Dar al-'Ulum Haqqaniyya was founded in 1947 by Maulana 'Abd al-Haq (d. 1988), who graduated from the Dar al-'Ulum Deoband in 1933 or '34. Upon 'Abd al-Haq's death in 1988, 'Abd al-Haq's son Sami' al-Haq was appointed chancellor of the Dar al-'Ulum Haqqaniyya, a position he still holds today. The Dar al-'Ulum Haqqaniyya's six-volume collection of fatwas gives us a window onto how its scholars and muftis think about Sufism. In fact, there is very little to distinguish this collection from standard Deobandi positions. Like the Deoband movement as a whole, the *Fatawa-yi Haqqaniyya* regards Sufism as an essential part of Muslim piety. One fatwa substantiates the validity of the four major Sufi orders of the Indian subcontinent (Qadiri, Suhrawardi, Chishti, Naqshbandi).[11] Another makes it clear that all Muslims must discipline the self (*nafs*)—something best done under the tutelage of a Sufi master, one who should be a scholar (*'alim*), pious (*mutaqqi*), and an ascetic (*zahid*) in his sensibilities. One's Sufi master should also be available for companionship (*suhbat*), and he must shun illicit innovations (*bid'at*).[12] Numerous fatwas, too, clarify Sufi meditative practices (*zikr*) and other spiritual techniques. The collection endorses a well-known Chishti *zikr*, known as *zikr haddadi*, with reference to the first Chishti manual on *zikr*.[13] It assuages the doubts of one Muslim who wrote the Dar al-'Ulum Haqqaniyya's muftis to ask about the legal permissibility of the forty-day Sufi meditative retreat known as a *chilla* (Persian, "forty"). The practice is "permissible, without any doubt."[14]

But what about the Sufi saints? Here, too, the responses are standard, almost boilerplate, Deobandi views. The Haqqani muftis believe that saints can and do perform miracles (*karamat*) while alive, and continue to do so after death.[15] It is even possible to form a spiritual connection (*nisbat*) with a deceased saint.[16] It is only in believing that saints have the power to intercede on behalf of their followers independently of God that one begins to tread dangerously close to unbelief (*kufr*).[17] A number of fatwas state clearly that bowing to, or circumambulating, a saint's shrine is impermissible.[18]

Nowhere in these fatwas do the muftis of Dar al-'Ulum Haqqaniyya call for Sufi shrines to be destroyed or for Sufis themselves to be killed. In fact, one of the Dar al-'Ulum Haqqaniyya's muftis was asked whether "un-Islamic" practices at a shrine justified killing the shrine's custodian; he averred that they did not.[19] At the same time, across numerous works by 'Abd al-Haq and Sami' al-Haq, one finds little more than passing references to Sufism. They did not author any works of their own on Sufism, nor are there references to either figure taking on Sufi disciples under their tutelage.[20] Whether, and to what extent, Deobandis' relationship with Sufism has changed in recent years is an open question. Beyond the Haqqani scholars I have just discussed, there is evidence to suggest that Sufism is no longer as central to Deobandi thought as it was for Deobandi scholars from Gangohi to Thanvi and beyond, and even that Deobandi Sufism has become preoccupied with its own "discourse of decline."[21] Sabiri Chishtis in twenty-first century Pakistan, Robert Rozehnal shows, have been critical of contemporary Deobandis for abandoning, in their view, the legacies of Sabiri Chishti masters associated with the Deoband movement, such as Imdad Allah and Gangohi.[22] Yet, narratives of decline have been a fixture of Sufism itself for centuries. This is nothing new.[23] And there is other evidence that contemporary Deobandis, even in

Pakistan, remain devoted to Sufism. To take just one example, Muhammad Rafi' 'Usmani, president of the Dar al-'Ulum Karachi and among the most prominent Deobandis in Pakistan today, has recently reasserted the importance of Sufism generally. Like Thanvi and many others, 'Usmani argues that embodying Sufi ethics is incumbent on all Muslims individually (*farz-i 'ayn*), and that *mastery* of Sufism is a duty of Muslims collectively (*farz-i kifaya*).[24]

It is for all these reasons that reducing the cause of the recent violence to an allegedly primordial hatred of Sufism rooted in the Deoband movement itself, as one recent collection of essays does, is inadequate and deeply misleading.[25] For one, this approach ignores the complexity of attitudes toward Sufism even *within* the Taliban, let alone within the Deoband movement as a whole. But another reason this approach is flawed is that it ignores politics and assumes that "religion" is the sole motivator behind such violence, as scholars such as Elizabeth Shakman Hurd, William Cavanaugh, and others have persuasively argued with respect to the discourse on "religious" violence generally.[26] After the Taliban's destruction of the Buddhas at Bamiyan, scholars called for resisting the easy explanation—that it was simply the expression of a deeply seated, innate iconoclasm within Islam—and urged us to consider a more nuanced one: that it was a context-specific power struggle with precedents throughout the medieval and early modern periods.[27] We should approach the destruction of Sufi shrines in the same light, as A. Afzar Moin has argued.[28] I suggest, then, that we resist the temptation to regard attacks on Sufis and their shrines as simply a "weaponized" version of the Deobandi critique of Sufism. That critique, surely, informs the hostility toward these shrines, but that hostility cannot be reduced to it.

This book has called for renewed attention to Sufism as an ongoing site of contestation in contemporary Islam. Part of this call is taking seriously Deobandis' claims to represent Sufism. By this I do not mean that scholars of Islam must ratify theirs as the "true" Sufism, to the exclusion of other practices and forms of piety (nor should they ratify as "true" the forms of Sufism that align more readily with popular attitudes of what Sufism should be). What I mean is that Deobandis have made a powerful claim on how to define it. Accordingly, this book has called for scholars of Islam to reflect critically on "Sufism" as a category, in all its entanglements—be they "mystical," experiential, ethical, political, institutional, or otherwise. "Sufism" is a diverse, internally contested, constantly debated entity. Rozehnal puts it well when he says Sufism is best approached as "a verb rather than a noun . . . not a static, homogenous 'thing' that can be studied in isolation. Rather, it is a discursive tradition and an embodied practice that is experienced in discrete temporal and cultural locations."[29] And in *locating* Sufism, we must be attuned to subtle shifts in how Muslims debate it, from within and without, in multiple settings, whether in the confines of a *khanqah* or in a political manifesto in Cape Town.

Despite, or perhaps because of, attacks on Sufis and Sufi shrines, mass support for Sufi devotional practices continues unabated. The *'urs* of Mu'in al-Din Chishti regularly attracts numbers of Muslims comparable to the Hajj pilgrimage to Mecca.[30] In Pakistan, devotees of 'Ali Hujwiri and Farid al-Din Ganj-i Shakkar will continue to gather in massive numbers at their shrines, among many others, despite the real, existential risks of doing so. In South Africa, too, support for Sufi devotional practices is unrelenting. If anything, the persistence of rhetorical and physical attacks on Sufis, Sufi shrines, and those who visit them has substantially amplified their power. "In the very act of critique," Michael Taussig observed, the critic "adds to the power of the thing critiqued." The destruction of an object amplifies its sacredness, "magnifying, not destroying, value."[31]

The Deobandi critique originated in texts, but it has since become one debated well beyond texts—in mosques, at Sufi festivals, in lecture halls, on the radio, on the Internet, and elsewhere. And the terms of these debates continue to shift. In Katherine Ewing's view, this means attending to the "everyday arguments" surrounding these debates as much as we attend to the arguments of the *'ulama*.[32] While *'ulama* continue to claim the authority to adjudicate on legal issues, we must also consider extralegal forms of public argumentation. It is important, however, not to see these extralegal perspectives as *antinormative*. Rather, these perspectives represent an alternative form of normativity, perhaps akin to what Shahab Ahmed called "non-legal values as *norms*."[33] If understanding how Deobandis articulate and defend themselves as Sufis is essential, then, so too is understanding how individual Muslims talk back to their critiques. Many of these conversations are located well outside the ambit of *'ulama*-centric discourse. What the *'ulama* argue about a given issue is important; what students, activists, teachers, mothers, and workers say is equally so.

Equally, not more. I submit that we should avoid valorizing the "everyday" Islam of lay Muslims as *more* (or less) authentic, valuable, or legitimate than the Islam of the *'ulama*. In their analysis of the "everyday" as a trope in the anthropology of Muslim societies, Nadia Fadil and Mayanthi Fernando provocatively argue that "[t]he everyday Muslim ...

emerges as a familiar figure," defined by an "ambivalent, critical, and even contestatory relationship to Islamic norms." The everyday, in their view, is "not only an analytical frame but also a normative one."[34] Is the contestation of norms the sole criterion by which we deem a practice "everyday?" Are those who critique legal norms not grounded in other forms of normativity? And are the *'ulama*, too, not part of "everyday" Islam? Furthermore, valorizations of everyday Islam risk reinscribing outmoded notions of the "public sphere" or "civil society" onto debates among contemporary Muslims. These notions, especially in their Habermasian vein, see the public as, intrinsically, a venue for challenging religious authority. Throughout this book, but especially in chapter 3, I have pointed to ways in which the Habermasian model of the public, with its free, rational actors deliberating upon ideas without respect to prior affective commitments, fails to grasp the extent to which colonial publics were already predicated on polemics. I've also pointed to the particular forms of affect that undergird Deobandi ideas of the public and that, in turn, form the very basis for politics, broadly defined. Following in the footsteps of Talal Asad, many scholars of Islam and Religious Studies have made similar interventions in recent years.[35]

To be sure, the Muslim activists we met in chapters 6 and 7 challenged the authority of the Deobandi *'ulama*. Is this not a vindication of the "Muslim public sphere" against "traditional authority?" I think this is a simplistic read, for several reasons. First, many of those engaging in these public critiques were themselves products of seminaries, i.e. *'ulama*. Second, South Africans' critiques of the *'ulama* were by and large not critiques of *'ulama as such*, but of their politics. Third, even those who did critique the *'ulama* as such typically did so by way of modes of argumentation grounded in Islam itself. It is also worth noting, finally, that to the extent these publics were engaged in critiques of authority, the object of their critiques was the apartheid regime; critiques of the *'ulama* were ancillary to this far more fundamental one.

Deobandi critiques and countercritiques are grounded in the exigencies of local politics, as we saw in South Africa, but we must also be attuned to the complex, global peregrinations of these critiques as they travel in and out of specific contexts. We see this in the ways that the Deobandi critique itself morphed over time and across space—as, for instance, in the way that Ahmed Sadiq Desai appropriated Ashraf 'Ali Thanvi's arguments about Sufism and politics even as he reduced Thanvi's textured hermeneutics to a series of shibboleths. In another respect, and with important exceptions, this loss of texture is due to a broad shift across late-twentieth-century Deobandi texts away from invoking the Hanafi legal tradition and toward the sole invocation of Qur'an and Hadith. Ebrahim Moosa argued that this tendency runs deep in the history of the Deoband movement, insofar as Deobandis have had to compete on a discursive terrain with groups like the Ahl-i Hadith, who were already operating on that terrain in their near exclusive use of Qur'an and Hadith.[36] This mode of argument is now common—not just among Salafis, of course, but among Muslims of all views; and not just in books, but on Muslim websites, blogs, chat forums, and the like. In this sense, Deobandi discourse in the late twentieth century and the twenty-first has dovetailed with what we might call a Salafization of public argument. By this I do not mean Deobandis are now Salafis; they are not. Rather, I mean that, broadly speaking, Deobandi argument now overlaps (partly, never completely) with modes of rhetoric associated with (but not limited to) Salafis. These arguments mobilize citations of the Qur'an and Hadith toward a sort of new *sola scriptura* that is more or less foreign to premodern and even most modern ways in which Muslims have engaged with their traditions.[37] As Jonathan A.C. Brown has argued, the rhetoric of Salafism has been premised, in part, on the notion that Islam is "easy" to understand.[38] The Salafization of public argument is enticing: why cite Ibn 'Abidin or Shatibi when you can cite God and his Prophet?

And yet, most Deobandis would regard this as a false choice: even when directed at lay Muslims in public fora, their arguments can, and often do, interweave Hanafi legal authorities with relevant passages from the Qur'an and Hadith. Deobandis have rightly cast themselves as arbiters of a "complex" Islam. As I have argued throughout this book, the perennial challenge for the Deobandis has been how to communicate the complexity of the legal tradition to lay Muslims without diluting it or undermining their authority in the process. In the Indian context, we saw incipient forms of the notion that Islam is easy and accessible in Muhammad Isma'il and his contemporaries, who argued almost solely with reference to Qur'an and Hadith—a scriptural impulse that Deobandis like Thanvi sometimes awkwardly incorporated into their own attempts to render Islam "easy." I would like to suggest, though, that Thanvi succeeded in this endeavor in part by treating Islam's outward simplicity as a mere gateway into its internal complexities. And his work was an invitation to delve into that complexity.

This surely distinguishes him sharply from his acolyte Desai, who not only did not continue in Thanvi's footsteps by producing *new* scholarship in the tradition, but reduced Deobandi thought to a handful of broadsides—whatever could fit in a newsletter or a pamphlet, but little more. In this respect, he was merely following his own teacher (and Thanvi's student) Masihullah Khan, who saw his own work as in essence a commentary on Thanvi's. But if Masihullah Khan's career reminds us that this attitude is not new, it also makes it all the more apparent that there is no Deobandi like Thanvi alive today. Many living Deobandis maintain such deferential awe for Thanvi that the notion that one of them may aspire to be his equal is almost unthinkable—but Thanvi, too, felt this way toward the great Sufis and jurists that came before him.

As we have seen, the rhetoric of decline is built both into the Deoband movement, and even, in a larger sense, into Sufism itself. Perhaps this points to a loss of a certain sensibility at the heart of Deoband, one in which the core aspirations that Deobandis articulated in the first half of the twentieth century—a tradition handed down through the carefully cultivated dynamic between books and bodies, grounded in the intricately theorized interplay between madrasa and *khanqah*, hopeful about the power of print to implement reform but wary of its implications—gave way to a text-driven, superficial, ossified tradition, one whose most salient *public* articulations now take place in chat rooms rather than in the *khanqah*. I do not mean to suggest that complex, nuanced debates about Islam cannot take place on the Internet; they do. What I mean is that the shift of the locus of debate away from spaces defined by human presence and intimacy, and toward spaces defined by distance and disembodiment, has had a palpable effect on the terms and articulations of debate. Along these lines, Humeira Iqtidar has recently theorized Islamic tradition at the nexus of "knowledge production and consumption" and a certain "sensibility" *about* that same knowledge. When the two become uncoupled, when "method is separated markedly from . . . sensibility," she argues, "we can expect a reduction of debate and hence vibrancy within the tradition."[39]

Desai would seem to corroborate this. In some ways, Desai's vituperations represent the very opposite of the "gentleness" (*narmi*) that Thanvi counseled for the 'ulama, and that Gangohi described as an essential part of a Sufi's temperament: "The Sufi regards himself as the lowliest, which is the opposite of pride. The Sufi is kind in dealing with God's creation and patient with people, is gentle with others, shuns wrath and anger, sympathizes with others and lets them take precedence. With abundant compassion, the Sufi . . . is generous, forgiving of faults and mistakes."[40] Perhaps, on occasion, the Sufi's shunning of pride meshes awkwardly with the scholar's sense of certainty.

Despite—or because of—the currents of colonial modernity that merged to make the Dar al-'Ulum Deoband possible, the branch of the Deoband movement emanating from Ashraf 'Ali Thanvi is one we may describe as "modern antimodern"—represented by men whose engagement with tradition, whose very notion of tradition, is a by-product *of* modernity, yet who never felt at home *in* modernity. In this way they are akin to the modern reactionaries recently described by Mark Lilla. "Where others see the river of time flowing as it always has, the reactionary sees the debris of paradise drifting past his eyes. He is time's exile," Lilla writes. Unlike the revolutionary, the reactionary is "the guardian of what actually happened, not the prophet of what might be." His "nostalgia is what makes the reactionary a distinctly modern figure, not a traditional one." The reactionary is the mirror image of the revolutionary: both are products of modernity's self-referentiality, for modernity's "nature is to perpetually modernize itself." Thanvi lived in history but never *dwelled* in it. He was never at home in the passage of time. Whereas the revolutionary places human agency squarely at the center of historical change, the reactionary, says Lilla, sees history "develop slowly and unconsciously . . . with results no one can predict."[41] To be precise, here Lilla is describing the philosophy of Edmund Burke, an icon of European conservative thought. Is it any wonder that Muhammad Taqi 'Usmani compares Thanvi admiringly with Burke?[42]

Accordingly, it is arguably time, more than place, that is the dominant modality through which Deobandis experience and conceptualize tradition. Deobandis' theorization of the normative order is seminally bound up in the experience of time. The near constant recollection of the era of the Prophet and his Companions is part and parcel of the temporal dimension of the normative order. Deobandis have not purported to re-create the era of the Prophet in the modern age; rather, they have seen that era embodied in the very mien of those who are connected to it through their spiritual lineages, through whom they could get a mere glimpse—but a glimpse nonetheless—of the Prophet's own demeanor.

But time informs Deobandi tradition in other ways. *Bid'a* is characterized, in many instances, by a misunderstanding of temporal normativity. Thus, where a Sufi devotee goes is arguably less important than when, how often, and for what purpose. Conversely, the shrine-based Sufism that Deobandis have found unsettling is grounded far more in a sense of *place* than time. The lifeworlds that coalesce around reverence toward the dead are defined by the places where the dead are interred. Saints' bodies, usually, stay put. It is important not to press this argument beyond its usefulness. Shrines, too, are connected to time and the past in complex ways. Saints are saints in part through their sacred genealogies. Conversely, the madrasa is a place, first and foremost. But crucially, its spatiality is not anchored by the body of a saint. Madrasas, like shrines, are nodes in complex spatial itineraries, but these itineraries are markedly different from the networks of pilgrimage that form around shrines.

But ironically, the crux of Deobandis' relationship to time, history, and temporality is borne out by their movements *across space*. As Barbara Metcalf has argued, the Tablighi Jama'at is defined not by the places where its members go but by the "typological" and "non-linear" view of history they adopt when they get there—one configured through "patterns of moral significance."[43] It is the mobility of the Tablighi or the madrasa student *through space* that makes this temporal imaginary all the more salient, for it is "not *space,* the new place where they have chosen to live, but *time,* in which the past and future converge in the present .... Far from being on the periphery, they can make any place a center."[44] We see this typological view of time and history in Tablighis' accounts of their travels. The narrative of Muhammad Zakariyya Kandhlavi's 1981 visit to South Africa, discussed in chapter 6, "contained almost no details of the journey's African locations and instead provided a narrative of praying, blessings, signs of respect, deferential meetings, and moral discussions," Nile Green comments. "Even specific places were presented not as cities but as social networks: Durban, for example, featured in the text solely as a circle of mosques and pious Muslims. In this travelogue, at least, Africa was not so much meaningful in itself but as a crucible of Deobandi piety."[45] While perhaps they *can* make any place a center, as Metcalf notes, the vociferous opposition to the Tablighi Jama'at in South Africa during apartheid suggests that their "spaceless" imaginary intersects, sometimes violently, with other highly localized and spatially grounded ones. Farish Noor makes this point elegantly in arguing that the Tablighi Jama'at is high on "bonding capital" but low on "bridging capital."[46] That is, it offers appealing "patterns of moral significance" that purport to transcend history, but do not easily "bridge" with local contexts because of that very rhetoric of transcendence. This surely informs why the Deobandi critique of Sufism met such fierce resistance in South Africa. South African Muslims contested it not just as a "foreign" matter, a theological rivalry imported from the Indian subcontinent, but, more important, one that never quite planted "roots," that refused to grow organically in the local environment.

But if the Tablighis and the critiques that traveled with them never did plant roots in South Africa, this does not mean the Deoband movement *as a whole* failed to do so. This, finally, brings us full circle to where we started in this book: to the question of the Deoband movement's dynamism and internal complexity. Whether in the case of local madrasas teaching Shafi'i law or South African Deobandi scholars siding against the verdicts of the Dar al-'Ulum Deoband's muftis in the midcentury debate about *riba*, we have seen instances in which the movement did, in fact, adapt to local exigencies. This book, at the very least, has strived to acquaint the reader with some of the major debates that this movement has initiated globally and how those debates were contested locally, in ways that tell us something about global Islam itself: the constantly shifting nexus of people, ideas, texts, and institutions contained within it, and the multiple, sometimes conflicting publics that animate it.

Notes

1. Wilfred Cantwell Smith, *Modern Islam in India* (London: Victor Gollancz, 1946), 295.

2. As Dietrich Reetz has observed, "The longest interaction between the Deoband school and foreign Deobandi networks exists perhaps with its branches in South Africa." See Reetz, "The Deoband Universe: What Makes a Transcultural and Transnational Movement of Islam?," *Comparative Studies of South Asia, Africa and the Middle East* 27, no. 1 (2007): 139–59, at 153. South Africa boasts at least ten Deobandi Dar al-'Ulums, but this number does not include numerous smaller madrasas that are affiliated with the Dar al-'Ulums or staffed by their graduates. Deobandi scholars have also brought their critiques of Sufism to Mozambique as well as Réunion. See Liazzat J.K. Bonnate, "Muslim Religious Leadership in Post-Colonial Mozambique," *South African Historical Journal* 60, no. 4 (2008): 637–54, esp. 640–41; and Marie-France Mourrégot, *L'islam à l'île de la Réunion* (Paris: Harmattan, 2010). Beyond southern Africa, Malaysia and the United Kingdom have comparatively large numbers of Deobandi madrasas. The first Deobandi institution in the United Kingdom was the Dar al-'Ulum Bury, established in 1975 by Yusuf Motala, a disciple of Muhammad Zakariyya Kandhlavi—an important Deobandi discussed in subsequent chapters. See Jonathan Birt and Philip Lewis, "The Pattern of Islamic Reform in Britain: The Deobandis between intra-Muslim Sectarianism and Engagement with Wider Society," in *Producing Islamic Knowledge: Transmission and Dissemination in Western Europe,* ed. Martin van Bruinessen and Stefano Allievi (London and New York: Routledge, 2011), 97.

3. One source states that 199 South Africans graduated from the Dar al-'Ulum Deoband between its founding in 1866 and 1976; this figure represents the largest number of graduates of any country outside of South Asia besides

Malaysia, with 445 students. And the number would be far higher if we were to include South Africans who graduated from Deobandi seminaries in South Asia other than the Dar al-'Ulum Deoband. See Muhammad Faruq, *Afriqah aur khidmat-i Faqih al-Ummat* (Deoband: Maktaba-yi Nashr al-Mahmud, 1990), 144.

4. Carl Schmitt, *The Nomos of the Earth in the International Law of the* Jus Publicum Europaeum, trans. G. L. Ulmen (New York: Telos Press, 2003), 50n1, cited in Dipesh Chakrabarty, *The Calling of History: Sir Jadunath Sarkar and His Empire of Truth* (Chicago and London: University of Chicago Press, 2015), 7.

5. I refer primarily to Barbara Daly Metcalf, *Islamic Revival in British India: Deoband, 1860–1900* (Princeton, NJ: Princeton University Press, 1982); and Muhammad Qasim Zaman, *The Ulama in Contemporary Islam: Custodians of Change* (Princeton, NJ: Princeton University Press, 2002). But both scholars have done other important work on Deoband, to which the book will refer throughout.

6. See, most recently, Arshad Alam, *Inside a Madrasa: Knowledge, Power and Islamic Identity in India* (New Delhi: Routledge, 2011).

7. For the history and politics of this assumption, see Alix Philippon, *Soufisme et politique au Pakistan: Le mouvement barelwi à l'heure de "la guerre contre le terrorisme"* (Paris: Éditions Karthala et Sciences Po Aix, 2011).

8. Usha Sanyal, *Devotional Islam and Politics in British India: Ahmad Riza Khan Barelwi and His Movement, 1870–1920* (Delhi and New York: Oxford University Press, 1996), 82.

9. A notable example would be Izhar al-Hasan Mahmud, *'Ishq-i rasul aur 'ulama-yi Deoband* (Lahore: Maktaba al-Hasan, n.d.). This book consists largely of stories of the passionate love (*'ishq*) of the Deobandi *'ulama* for the Prophet. Rashid Ahmad Gangohi's "extreme passion and love" (*intihai 'ishq o mahabbat*) for the Prophet was such that he owned a tiny piece of the green cloak the Prophet wore during the Hijra from Mecca to Medina and would occasionally display it to his disciples, which they would kiss and place upon their eyes in reverence (111).

10. See, e.g., Yasin Akhtar Misbahi, *Imam Ahmad Raza aur radd-i bid'at wa munkarat* (Karachi: Idara-yi Tahqiqat-i Imam Ahmad Raza, 1985).

11. Marc Gaborieau, *Le Mahdi incompris: Sayyid Ahmad Barelwi (1786–1831) et le millénarisme en Inde* (Paris: CNRS Éditions, 2010), 18–19.

12. Ahmad Raza Khan, *Maqal 'urafa' bi-i'zaz shar' 'ulama, al-ma'ruf shari'at o tariqat* (Karachi: Idara-yi Tasnifat-i Imam Ahmad Raza, 1983), 20–35.

13. On misunderstandings of the madrasa in the context of the global "War on Terror," see Ebrahim Moosa, *What Is a Madrasa?* (Chapel Hill: University of North Carolina Press, 2015).

14. Peter Bergen and Swati Pandey, "The Madrassa Scapegoat," *Washington Quarterly* 29, no. 2 (2006): 117–25.

15. I do not mean to suggest that cosmopolitanism and militancy are mutually exclusive. I refer to arguments like that of Farish Noor and others, who have argued that new restrictions on the transnational movement of madrasa students have threatened a much older "cosmopolitan" flow of people and

ideas. See Farish A. Noor, Yoginder Sikand, and Martin van Bruinessen, "Behind the Walls: Re-Appraising the Role and Importance of Madrasas in the World Today," in *The Madrasa in Asia: Political Activism and Transnational Linkages*, ed. Farish A. Noor, Yoginder Sikand and Martin van Bruinessen (Amsterdam: Amsterdam University Press, 2008), 21.

16. Declan Walsh, "Suicide Bombers Kill Dozens at Pakistan Shrine," *The Guardian*, 2 July 2010, http://www.theguardian.com/world/2010/jul/02/suicide-bombers-kill-dozens-pakistan-shrine. Since its original publication date, the text of this article has been altered and the quote in question has been removed. The original version of the article, including this quote, can be seen here: http://www.wluml.org/node/6476 (last accessed 6 February 2018).

17. 'Abd al-Haq et al., *Fatawa-yi Haqqaniyya*, ed. Mukhtar Allah Haqqani (Akora Khattak: Jami'a Dar al-'Ulum Haqqaniyya, 2002), 1:143.

18. See esp. Carl W. Ernst, *Sufism: An Introduction to the Mystical Tradition of Islam* (Boston: Shambhala, 2011), chap. 1.

19. Zaman, *The Ulama in Contemporary Islam*, 10.

20. Metcalf, *Islamic Revival in British India*, 235. For the most part, the "link" between Deoband and affiliated institutions is informal and unofficial, rendering it difficult even to estimate the number of "Deobandi" madrasas, though in recent decades Deobandi madrasas in India, at least, have attempted to organize into an official body to standardize curricula: Rabita Madaris Arabiyya (Association of Arabic Schools), founded at the Dar al-'Ulum Deoband in 1994. See Dietrich Reetz, "Change and Stagnation in Islamic Education: The Dar ul-'Ulum Deoband after the Split in 1982," in *The Madrasa in Asia*, ed. Farish A. Noor, Yoginder Sikand, and Martin van Bruinessen (Amsterdam: Amsterdam University Press, 2008), 82.

21. Ismail Alie, interview with the author, Qasimul Uloom, Cape Town, September 22, 2009.

22. Sayyid Mahbub Rizvi, *Tarikh-i Dar al-'Ulum Deoband* (Deoband: Idarah-yi Ihtimam-i Dar al-'Ulum Deoband, 1977), 1:24. On the development of the concept of Ahl al-Sunna wa-l Jama'a, see Muhammad Qasim Zaman, *Religion and Politics under the Early Abbasids* (Leiden, New York, and Cologne: E.J. Brill, 1997), 49–61.

23. Thus, a widely circulated anti-Deobandi pamphlet from South Africa is titled *Exposing the Tableeghi-Deobandi-Wahabi Sect* (Durban: Sunni World, n.d.).

24. Muhammad Taqi 'Usmani, foreword to Mufti Muhammad Shafi', *Dil ki dunya* (Karachi: Idara al-Ma'arif, 2013), 7. On 'Usmani, see Kelly Pemberton, "An Islamic Discursive Tradition of Reform as Seen in the Writing of Deoband's Mufti Muhammad Taqi 'Usmani," *Muslim World* 99, no. 3 (2009): 452–77.

25. See Rosemary R. Corbett, *Making Moderate Islam: Sufism, Service, and the "Ground Zero" Mosque Controversy* (Stanford, CA: Stanford University Press, 2016), as well as G.A. Lipton, "Secular Sufism: Neoliberalism, Ethno-Racism, and the Reformation of the Muslim Other," *Muslim World* 101, no. 3 (2011): 427–40.

26. Eleanor Abdella Doumato and Gregory Starrett, "Textbook Islam, Nation Building, and the Question of Violence," in *Teaching Islam: Textbooks*

and Religion in the Middle East, ed. Eleanor Abdella Doumato and Gregory Starrett (Boulder, CO, and London: Lynne Rienner Publishers, 2007), 6.

27. See Elizabeth Shakman Hurd, *Beyond Religious Freedom: The New Global Politics of Religion* (Princeton, NJ: Princeton University Press, 2015).

28. Arthur F. Buehler, *Recognizing Sufism: Contemplation in the Islamic Tradition* (London and New York: I.B. Tauris, 2016), 18–20.

29. Jawid Mojaddedi, "Getting Drunk with Abu Yazid or Staying Sober with Junayd: The Creation of a Popular Typology of Sufism," *Bulletin of SOAS* 66, no. 1 (2003): 1–13.

30. On Muhasibi, see Gavin Picken, *Spiritual Purification in Islam: The Life and Works of al-Muhasibi* (London and New York: Routledge, 2011). On the Qur'anic roots of *tazkiyat al-nafs,* see the same author's "Tazkiyat al-Nafs: The Qur'anic Paradigm," *Journal of Qur'anic Studies* 7, no. 2 (2005): 101–27.

31. Abu Nasr al-Sarraj, *Kitab al-luma' fi al-tasawwuf,* ed. Reynold Nicholson (Leiden: E.J. Brill, 1914), esp. 4–7, 13–15 (Arabic text pagination). See also Ahmet Karamustafa, *Sufism: The Formative Period* (Berkeley: University of California Press, 2007), 67–69.

32. Jawid Mojaddedi, *The Biographical Tradition in Sufism: The Ṭabaqāt Genre from al-Sulamī to Jāmī* (Richmond, Surrey, UK: Curzon Press, 2001), 9–40.

33. See, e.g., Qutb al-Din Dimashqi, *Imdad al-suluk,* ed. Rashid Ahmad Gangohi (Lahore: Idara-yi Islamiyyat, 1984), 155–56. I discuss Dimashqi in chap. 4.

34. Mojaddedi, *The Biographical Tradition in Sufism,* 41–68.

35. On Qushayri, see especially Martin Nyugen, *Sufi Master and Qur'an Scholar: Abu'l-Qasim al-Qushayri and the Lata'if al-Isharat* (Oxford: Oxford University Press, 2012). A single scholarly monograph on Hujwiri remains to be written, but see the discussion in Karamustafa, *Sufism: The Formative Period,* esp. chap. 4.

36. Ashraf 'Ali Thanvi, *Tashil-i qasd al-sabil ma' panj rasa'il* (Karachi: Kutub Khana-yi Mazhari, n.d.), 17. The Urdu translation of al-Ghazali's *Al-Arba'in* (his summary of the *Ihya'*) was commissioned by Thanvi, completed by 'Ashiq Ilahi Mirathi (author of the definitive biography of Rashid Ahmad Gangohi), and published as *Tabligh-i din.* See Thanvi's introduction to Hujjat al-Islam Imam Ghazali, *Tabligh-i din* (Delhi: Naz Publishing House, 1962), 3.

37. Christopher S. Taylor, *In the Vicinity of the Righteous: Ziyara and the Veneration of Muslim Saints in Late Medieval Egypt* (Leiden: E.J. Brill, 1999), 12–14.

38. George Makdisi, "The Hanbali School and Sufism," *Biblos (Coimbra)* 46 (1970): 71–84, at 83.

39. For Ibn Taymiyya's view of Ibn 'Arabi, see Alexander Knysh, *Ibn 'Arabi in the Later Islamic Tradition: The Making of a Polemical Image in Medieval Islam* (Albany: State University of New York Press, 1999), 89–92. For his view on the veneration of saints, see Taylor, *In the Vicinity of the Righteous,* chap. 5.

40. A substantial literature on contestations within, and over, Sufism has emerged in the last two decades. See especially Elizabeth Sirriyeh, *Sufis and Anti-Sufis: The Defense, Rethinking and Rejection of Sufism in the Modern*

World (Richmond, Surrey, UK: Curzon, 1999), as well as the essays collected in *Islamic Mysticism Contested: Thirteen Centuries of Controversies and Polemics,* ed. Frederick de Jong and Bernd Radtke (Leiden: E. J. Brill, 1999).

41. Nile Green, *Sufism: A Global History* (Malden, UK: Wiley Blackwell, 2012), 160.

42. This typology is a heuristic one, of course, and does not mean to suggest watertight distinctions between these labels, or that all who may otherwise be classified as "modernist," "Islamist," or "Salafi" have opposed Sufism, in part or in full.

43. Muhammad Iqbal, *Kulliyat-i Iqbal Urdu* (Aligarh: Educational Book House, 2003), 496–97. For a brief discussion of Iqbal's approach to Sufism, see Sirriyeh, *Sufis and Anti-Sufis,* 124–37. On modernist critiques of Sufism, see Muhammad Qasim Zaman, *Islam in Pakistan: A History* (Princeton, NJ: Princeton University Press, 2018), 196–98.

44. Quoted in Marc Gaborieau, "Criticizing the Sufis: The Debate in Early Nineteenth-Century India," in *Islamic Mysticism Contested,* ed. Frederick de Jong and Bernd Radtke (Leiden: E. J. Brill, 1999), 453. On Maududi and Sufism, see Maulana Shaykh Ahmad, *Maulana Maududi aur tasawwuf* (Deoband: Maktaba-yi Tajalli, 1966).

45. For an overview, see Bernard Haykel, "On the Nature of Salafi Thought and Action," in *Global Salafism: Islam's New Religious Movement,* ed. Roel Meijer (New York: Columbia University Press, 2009), 33–51.

46. Henri Lauzière, *The Making of Salafism: Islamic Reform in the Twentieth Century* (New York: Columbia University Press, 2016), 53. Lauzière suggests that the story, recounted in 1971, may have been embellished by al-Hilali and may reflect the anti-Sufi politics of Salafism in the 1970s more than the 1920s.

47. Seyyed Vali Reza Nasr, *Maududi and the Making of Islamic Revivalism* (Oxford: Oxford University Press, 1996), 128.

48. Rüdiger Seesemann, "Between Sufism and Islamism: The Tijaniyya and Islamist Rule in the Sudan," in *Sufism and Politics,* ed. Paul Heck (Princeton, NJ: Markus Weiner, 2007), 23–57; and Roxanne E. Euben and Muhammad Qasim Zaman, introduction to *Princeton Readings in Islamist Thought,* ed. Roxanne E. Euben and Muhammad Qasim Zaman (Princeton, NJ: Princeton University Press, 2009), 23–27.

49. Mun'im Sirry, "Jamal al-Din al-Qasimi and the Salafi Approach to Sufism," *Die Welt des Islams* 51 (2011): 75–108.

50. I do not intend to suggest, of course, that Islamists are not interested in individual Muslim subjectivities.

51. Nikki Keddie, trans. *An Islamic Response to Imperialism: Political and Religious Writings of Sayyid Jamal al-Din al-Afghani* (Berkeley: University of California Press, 1983), 120.

52. This presumption was most recently called into question by Shahab Ahmed in *What Is Islam? The Importance of Being Islamic* (Princeton, NJ: Princeton University Press, 2016), 528. The presumption itself comes from a variety of sources, most notably Dale F. Eickelman and James Piscatori, *Muslim Politics,* 2nd ed. (Princeton, NJ: Princeton University Press, 2004), 131–35, in

which Eickelman and Piscatori put forth their widely debated argument that the authority of the *'ulama* has been challenged by "new religious intellectuals." James Hoesterey accepts Eickelman and Piscatori's basic premise but usefully challenges the notion that there is a zero-sum competition between the *'ulama* and such "new religious intellectuals," showing how the Indonesian self-help guru Aa Gym meshes Islamic vocabularies with pop psychology while remaining broadly deferential to the legal authority of the *'ulama*. James B. Hoesterey, *Rebranding Islam: Piety, Prosperity, and a Self-Help Guru* (Stanford, CA: Stanford University Press, 2016), 9–15.

53. See Zaman, *Religion and Politics;* and Felicitas Opwis, "Shifting Legal Authority from the Ruler to the *'Ulama*: Rationalizing the Punishment for Drinking Wine during the Saljuq Period," *Der Islam* 86 (2011): 65–92.

54. Fuad Naeem, "Sufism and Revivalism in South Asia: Mawlana Ashraf 'Ali Thanvi of Deoband and Mawlana Ahmad Raza Khan of Bareilly and Their Paradigms of Islamic Revivalism," *Muslim World* 99, no. 3 (2009): 435–51, at 436.

55. Quoted in 'Ashiq Ilahi Mirathi, *Tazkirat al-Khalil* (Saharanpur: Kutub Khana-yi Isha'at al-'Ulum, n.d.), 336.

56. Ashraf 'Ali Thanvi, *Bihishti zewar: Mudallal o mukammal bihishti zewar ma' bihishti gauhar* (Karachi: Altaf and Sons, 2001), 24.

57. Qur'an 11:88.

58. Ashraf 'Ali Thanvi, *Islahi nisab: Tashih-i 'aqa'id o a'mal, tahzib o tamaddun-i Islami* (Lahore: Maktaba-yi Rashidiyya, 1977).

59. Mufti Taqi 'Usmani, *Islahi khutbat*, 16 vols. (Karachi: Meman Islamic Publishers, 1993).

60. A typical example of this tendency would be John O. Voll, "Renewal and Reform in Islamic History: *Tajdid* and *Islah*," in *Voices of Resurgent Islam*, ed. John L. Esposito (New York: Oxford University Press, 1983). Voll's notion of *islah* completely ignores the widespread usage of that term among the *'ulama*, especially in equating *islah* with *ijtihad*. When *islah* in South Asia is discussed, it is likewise discussed in relationship to Islamist and modernist trends. Thus, in the "India/Pakistan" subsection of the *Encyclopaedia of Islam*'s entry on *islah*, Aziz Ahmad mentions none of the traditionalist *'ulama*, concentrating instead on the subcontinent's counterparts to the Middle East's reformist intellectuals—namely, Karamat Ali Jaunpuri, Sayyid Ahmad Khan, Muhammad Iqbal, and similar figures. One senses that the traditionalist *'ulama*, whether of Deobandi or Barelvi inclinations, are simply off the radar because their version of *islah* does not conform to the standard one. P. J. Bearman, Th. Bianquis, C. E. Bosworth, E. J. van Donzel, and W. P. Heinrichs, eds., *Encyclopaedia of Islam*, 2nd ed. (Leiden: E. J. Brill, 2005), s.v. "Islah."

61. Samira Haj, *Reconfiguring Islamic Tradition: Reform, Rationality, Modernity* (Stanford, CA: Stanford University Press, 2008), 35.

62. The Hadith in question is found in the *Sunan* of Abu Dawud: "Truly, God will send to this *umma* at the turn of every century one who will renew religion." Ella Landau-Tasserson, "The 'Cyclical Reform': A Study of the Mujaddid Tradition," *Studia Islamica* 70 (1989): 79–117, at 79. For a brief overview of this Hadith and variant interpretations of it, see Hamid Algar, "The

Centennial Renewer: Bediüzzaman Said Nursi and the Tradition of *Tajdid*," *Journal of Islamic Studies* 12, no. 3 (2001): 291–311.

63. Sajjida Sultana Alvi, *Perspectives on Mughal India: Rulers, Historians, 'Ulamā' and Sufis* (Oxford: Oxford University Press, 2012), 89–115.

64. Nasr, *Maududi*, 57.

65. Ibid., 56–57.

66. Rashid Ahmad Gangohi, *Fatawa-yi Rashidiyya* (Karachi: Educational Press Pakistan, 1985), 176 (emphasis added).

67. Ashraf 'Ali Thanvi, *Imdad al-fatawa*, ed. Muhammad Shafi' (Karachi: Maktaba-yi Dar al-'Ulum Karachi, 2010), 6:168–85. For a fuller discussion of this fatwa, see Altaf Ali Mian, "Surviving Modernity: Ashraf 'Ali Thanvi (1863–1943) and the Making of Muslim Orthodoxy in Colonial India" (PhD diss., Duke University, 2015), 98–100.

68. 'Abd al-Bari Nadvi, *Tajdid-i mu'ashirat, ya'ni tajdid-i din-i kamil* (Lucknow: Majlis-i Tahqiqat o Nashiryat-i Islam, 2010), 45.

69. Ashraf 'Ali Thanvi, *Khutbat-i Hakim al-Ummat* (Multan: Idara-yi Talifat-i Ashrafiyya, 2006), 13:48.

70. The full verse is: "O believers, protect yourselves and your families from the fire whose fuel is people and stones, over which are angels stern and severe who do not disobey God in what he commands of them, but they do what they are commanded."

71. Ashraf 'Ali Thanvi, *Tafsir-i bayan al-Qur'an, mukammal* (Karachi: Dar al-Isha'at, 2015), 2:602.

72. Mufti Muhammad Shafi', *Dil ki dunya* (Karachi: Idara al-Ma'arif, 2013), 49. Shafi' refers to the titles (and themes) of the third and fourth volumes of the *Ihya' 'ulum al-din*, respectively: the *Quarter on That Which Destroys (Rub' al-Muhlikat)*, and the *Quarter on That Which Provides Salvation (Rub' al-Munjiat)*.

73. One could note any number of closely related concepts. In no particular order: *rasm* ("custom"), *'adat* ("habit," "established practice"), *'urf* (also "custom," in Islamic legal terminology), *turath* ("heritage"), *taqlid* ("following past legal precedents").

74. Green, *Sufism: A Global History*, xi.

75. Alasdair MacIntyre, *Whose Justice, Which Rationality?* (South Bend, IN: University of Notre Dame Press, 1989), 12. Scholars such as Talal Asad, Muhammad Qasim Zaman, and Samira Haj, among others, have drawn on MacIntyre for theorizing Islamic tradition in a variety of contexts.

76. See, e.g., Sara Ahmed, "Affective Economies," *Social Text* 22, no. 2 (2004): 117–39.

77. Three recent monographs that take up this theme explicitly are Scott Kugle, *Sufis and Saints' Bodies: Mysticism, Corporeality, and Sacred Power in Islam* (Chapel Hill: University of North Carolina Press, 2007); Shahzad Bashir, *Sufi Bodies: Religion and Society in Medieval Islam* (New York: Columbia University Press, 2011); and Rudolph T. Ware, *The Walking Qur'an: Islamic Education, Embodied Knowledge, and History in West Africa* (Chapel Hill: University of North Carolina Press, 2014).

78. I refer to Talal Asad, "The Idea of an Anthropology of Islam," *Qui Parle* 17, no. 2 (2009): 1–30.

79. Ibid., 20–21.

80. Ware makes a similar point in suggesting that Islam be understood "not only as 'discursive tradition' . . . but also a dense web of fully embodied encounters.'" See Ware, *The Walking Qur'an*, 76.

81. Talal Asad, "Thinking about Tradition, Religion, and Politics in Egypt Today," *Critical Inquiry* 42, no. 1 (2015): 166–214.

82. Basit Iqbal, "Thinking about Method: A Conversation with Talal Asad," *Qui Parle* 26, no. 1 (2017): 195–218, at 199–200.

83. Theodor W. Adorno, "On Tradition," *Telos* 94 (1993/94): 75–82, at 75.

84. Asad, "Thinking about Tradition," 169.

85. I am borrowing and adapting the terms "anthropocentric" and "bibliocentric" from Nile Green, "The Uses of Books in a Late Mughal Takiyya: Persianate Knowledge between Person and Paper," *Modern Asian Studies* 44, no. 2 (2010): 241–65.

86. Ludwik Fleck, *Genesis and Development of a Scientific Fact,* trans. Fred Bradley and Thaddeus J. Trenn (Chicago and London: University of Chicago Press, 1979). I thank Ebrahim Moosa for introducing me to Fleck.

87. Barbara Herrnstein Smith, *Scandalous Knowledge: Science, Truth and the Human* (Durham, NC: Duke University Press, 2005), 67–68.

88. Fleck, *Genesis and Development,* 161.

89. He is variously referred to as Khalil Ahmad Saharanpuri, based on his lifelong affiliation with Mazahir al-'Ulum in Saharanpur, and Khalil Ahmad Ambetwi, based on his place of birth, Ambehta. This book refers to him throughout as Khalil Ahmad Saharanpuri, the more common appellation.

90. The reader may have noted that the main characters are all men. The Deoband movement is an undeniably male-centered tradition, and this book relies overwhelmingly on the texts of its principal architects, all of whom are men. Women are, of course, frequent objects of Deobandi reformist discourse; most famously, Thanvi's *Bihishti zewar* was composed specifically for female readers. This does not mean that women have not had important roles in disseminating (and sometimes contesting) Deobandi tradition. Most of the work on the Deoband movement and women has revolved around the Tablighi Jama'at. See, notably, Barbara Daly Metcalf, "Tablighi Jama'at and Women," in Muhammad Khalid Masud, ed. *Travellers in Faith: Studies of the Tablighi Jama'at as a Transnational Movement for Faith Renewal* (Leiden: E.J., Brill, 2000), 44–58.

1. A MODERN MADRASA

1. Queen Victoria's Proclamation, 1 November 1858, in *The Evolution of India and Pakistan, 1858 to 1947: Select Documents,* ed. C.H. Philips and B.N. Pandey (London: Oxford University Press, 1962), 11.

2. Karuna Mantena, *Alibis of Empire: Henry Maine and the Ends of Liberal Imperialism* (Princeton, NJ: Princeton University Press, 2010), 4. See also Bernard S. Cohn, "Representing Authority in Victorian India," in *The Invention of Tradition,* ed. Eric Hobsbawm and Terence Ranger (Cambridge: Cambridge University Press, 1983), 164–65.

3. Ilyse Morgenstein Fuerst, *Indian Muslim Minorities and the 1857 Rebellion: Religion, Rebels, and Jihad* (London and New York: I. B. Tauris, 2017).

4. Nandini Chatterjee, *The Making of Indian Secularism: Empire, Law and Christianity, 1830–1960* (Basingstoke, UK, and New York: Palgrave Macmillan, 2011), 11.

5. P. F. O'Malley, *Religious Liberty and the Indian Proclamation* (London: W. H. Dalton, 1859), 6 (emphasis added).

6. See, among others, Hussein Ali Agrama, *Questioning Secularism: Islam, Sovereignty, and the Rule of Law in Egypt* (Chicago: University of Chicago Press, 2012); Talal Asad, *Formations of the Secular* (Stanford, CA: Stanford University Press, 2003); Benjamin Berger, *Law's Religion: Religious Difference and the Claims of Constitutionalism* (Toronto, Buffalo, and London: University of Toronto Press, 2015); Mayanthi Fernando, *The Republic Unsettled: Muslim French and the Contradictions of Secularism* (Durham, NC: Duke University Press, 2014); Rebecca Nedostup, *Superstitious Regimes: Religion and the Politics of Chinese Modernity* (Cambridge, MA: Harvard University Press, 2010); and Robert A. Orsi, *History and Presence* (Cambridge, MA: Belknap Press of Harvard University, 2016).

7. Iza Hussin, *The Politics of Islamic Law: Local Elites, Colonial Authority, and the Making of the Muslim State* (Chicago: University of Chicago Press, 2016), 63–64.

8. J. Barton Scott and Brannon D. Ingram, "What Is a Public? Notes from South Asia," *South Asia: Journal of South Asian Studies* 38, no. 3 (2015): 357–70.

9. E.g., Ashwini Tambe and Harald Fischer-Tiné, eds. *The Limits of British Colonial Control in South Asia: Spaces of Disorder in the Indian Ocean Region* (London and New York: Routledge, 2009).

10. Sanjay Subrahmanyam, "Hearing Voices: Vignettes of Early Modernity in South Asia, 1400–1750," *Daedalus* 127, no. 3 (1998): 75–104, at 99–100 (emphasis in original).

11. The passage in question is one in which Rahman contrasts "medieval" Deoband with "modern" Aligarh. See Fazlur Rahman, *Islam and Modernity: Transformation of an Intellectual Tradition* (Chicago and London: University of Chicago Press, 1982), 115. The reference to Qur'anic élan appears on p. 19.

12. I refer to Rahman's influence on contemporary Qur'an scholars such as Amina Wadud, Asma Barlas, and Aysha Hidayatullah, among others.

13. See Frederick Cooper, *Colonialism in Question: Theory, Knowledge, History* (Berkeley: University of California Press, 2005), 117, 142–43. On colonial modernity and Hindu reform movements, see Peter van der Veer, *Imperial Encounters: Religion and Modernity in India and Britain* (Princeton, NJ: Princeton University Press, 2001).

14. Numerous scholars have discussed this aspect of modernity. See, among others, Anthony Giddens, *The Consequences of Modernity* (Stanford, CA: Stanford University Press, 1990); and Reinhart Koselleck, *The Practice of Conceptual History: Timing History, Spacing Concepts* (Stanford, CA: Stanford University Press, 2002).

15. And in this respect, they recall Bruce B. Lawrence's definition of the "fundamentalist": "moderns . . . but not modernists." See his *Defenders of*

God: The Fundamentalist Revolt against the Modern Age (London and New York: I. B. Tauris, 1990), 1.

16. This is an ambivalence comparable to the one that Humeira Iqtidar examines in contemporary Pakistan, where, she argues, Islamist groups like Jama'at-i Islami and Jama'at ad-Da'wa simultaneously reject "secularism" while facilitating discourses of the secular. See Humeira Iqtidar, *Secularizing Islamists? Jama'at-e-Islami and Jama'at-ud-Da'wa in Urban Pakistan* (Chicago: University of Chicago Press, 2011), 38–54.

17. Ashraf 'Ali Thanvi, *Al-Intibahat al-mufida 'an al-ishtibahat al-jadida* (Delhi: Jayyid Barqi Press, 1926). Thanvi indicates that he was inspired, in part, by the Ottoman jurist Husain al-Jisr al-Tarablusi's (d. 1909) influential critique of scientific materialism, *al-Risala al-Hamidiyya* (1888), which had been translated into Urdu in 1897, as Husayn ibn Muhammad Tarabulusi, *Jadid 'ilm-i kalam, ya'ni sains aur Islam* (Delhi: Azad Barqi Press, 1928/29). See Thanvi, *Al-Intibahat al-mufida*, 4. On Husayn al-Jisr, see Marwa Elshakry, *Reading Darwin in Arabic, 1860–1950* (Chicago and London: University of Chicago Press, 2013), 131–59, and, for the date of the Urdu translation, 356n34. Sayyid Ahmad, too, saw modernity "as an intellectual and epistemological, rather than a political, challenge." Muhammad Khalid Masud, "Islam and Modernity in South Asia," in *Being Muslim in South Asia*, ed. Robin Jeffrey and Ronojoy Sen (New Delhi: Oxford University Press, 2014), 2.

18. Christopher Shackle and Javed Majeed, trans., *Hali's Musaddas: The Ebb and Flow of Islam* (Delhi: Oxford University Press, 1997), 142, 166. On the theme of decay, see the translators' introduction, 49–52.

19. See Brannon D. Ingram, "Crises of the Public in Muslim India: Critiquing 'Custom' at Aligarh and Deoband," *South Asia: Journal of South Asian Studies* 38, no. 3 (2015): 403–18, at 411.

20. A *ta'ziya* is a miniature replica of Imam Husayn's mausoleum, used by Indian Shi'a Muslims in public processions during the month of Muharram to commemorate Husayn's martyrdom in 680.

21. 'Ashiq Ilahi Mirathi, *Tazkirat al-Rashid* (Saharanpur: Kutub Khana-yi Isha'at al-'Ulum, 1977), 1:9–10.

22. Sayyid Manazir Ahsan Gilani, *Savanih Qasimi, ya'ni Sirat-i Shams al-Islam* (Lahore: Maktaba-yi Rahmaniyya, n.d.), 1:3.

23. Anvarul Hasan Sherkoti, *Sirat-i Ya'qub o Mamluk* (Karachi: Maktaba-yi Dar al-'Ulum Karachi, 1974), 27–35; M. Ikram Chaghatai, "Dr. Aloys Sprenger and the Delhi College," in *Delhi College: Traditional Elites, the Colonial State, and Education before 1857*, ed. Margrit Pernau (New Delhi: Oxford University Press, 2006), 107.

24. Sayyid Nazar Zaidi, *Hajji Imdad Allah Muhajir Makki: Sirat o savanih* (Gujarat: Maktaba-yi Zafar, 1978), 38–42. This was not Hajji Imdad Allah's only Wali Allahian connection. He was also the Sufi disciple of Nasir al-Din Dihlawi, grandson of Rafi' al-Din Dihlawi, who was a son of Shah Wali Allah. Nasir al-Din, a Sufi successor (*khalifa*) of Sayyid Ahmad Barelvi's, initiated Imdad Allah into the Naqshbandi order. Another *khalifa* of Sayyid Ahmad's, Mianji Nur Muhammad Jhanjhanawi (d. 1845), initiated Imdad Allah into the Chishti Sabiri order.

25. Mirathi, *Tazkirat al-Rashid,* 1:73–74. Some have argued that Imdad Allah had a more active, direct role in waging jihad against the British. Ishtiaq Qureshi, among others, described Imdad Allah as the leader of a jihad campaign against the British in Shamli, which was promptly put down by the British, after which Imdad Allah hastily fled to escape arrest. See Ishtiaq Qureshi, *Ulema in Politics: A Study Relating to the Political Activities of the Ulema in the South-Asian Subcontinent from 1556 to 1947* (Karachi: Ma'aref Ltd., 1972), 200–202. Metcalf cast doubt on these narratives, calling them "nationalist accounts" that appear "only in secondary sources written after about 1920." Metcalf, *Islamic Revival in British India,* 82–83.

26. Rizvi, *Tarikh-i Dar al-'Ulum,* 1:104.

27. Metcalf, *Islamic Revival in British India,* 77–78.

28. Muhammad Qasim Nanautvi, *Intisar-i Islam ma' tashrih o tahsil* (Deoband: Majlis-i Ma'arif al-Qur'an, 1967), and Nanautvi, *Guftagu-yi mazhabi* (Karachi: Dar al-Isha'at, 1977). On his debates with Saraswati, see SherAli Tareen, "The Polemic at Shahjahanpur: Religion, Miracles and History," *Islamic Studies* 51, no. 1 (2012): 49–67. The role of Deoband's founder in interreligious debates is recounted in Muhammad Qasim Nanautvi, *Mubahasah-yi Shahjahanpur* (Karachi: Dar al-Isha'at, 1977).

29. Muhammad Qasim Nanautvi, *Qiblah numa ma' tashrih o tehsil* (Deoband: Majlis-i Ma'arif al-Qur'an, 1969).

30. Muhammad Qasim Nanautvi, *Tasfiyat al-'aqa'id* (Delhi: Matba'-yi Mujtabai, 1934).

31. Muhammad Qasim Nanautvi, *Hadiya al-Shi'a* (Lahore: Nu'mani Kutub Khana, 1977).

32. Gilani, *Savanih Qasimi,* 2:231–32.

33. Ibid., 2:257–59; Sarfraz Khan, *Bani-yi Dar al-'Ulum Deoband* (Gujranwala: Maktaba-yi Safdariyya, 2001), 41. There has been a good deal of confusion about whether the Dar al-'Ulum Deoband was founded in 1866 or 1867. Metcalf's *Islamic Revival in British India* gives 1867 as the year of its founding, but there is some confusion even in Urdu sources: Sarfraz Khan's *Bani-yi Dar al-'Ulum Deoband* provides 15 Muharram 1283 as the *hijri* date but then provides *1867* as the Gregorian date. This is, however, incorrect. All the evidence points to 1866 as the correct date. It seems that most academics have used 1867 based on *Islamic Revival in British India,* but tellingly, Metcalf corrected the date in her *Husain Ahmad Madani: The Jihad for Islam and India's Freedom* (Oxford: Oneworld, 2009), 17.

34. Rizvi, *Tarikh-i Dar al-'Ulum,* 1:187–88.

35. Sayyid Muhammad Miyan, *'Ulama-yi Haqq aur un ke mujahidana karname* (Lahore: Jam'iyat Publications, 2005), 89–90. See also the discussion in Metcalf, *Islamic Revival in British India,* 111–16.

36. Rizvi, *Tarikh-i Dar al-'Ulum,* 1:174–75.

37. Sherkoti, *Sirat-i Ya'qub o Mamluk,* 22–25, 46.

38. Jonathan Berkey, *The Transmission of Knowledge in Medieval Cairo: A Social History of Islamic Education* (Princeton. NJ: Princeton University Press, 1992), 8–9.

39. Michael Chamberlain, *Knowledge and Social Practice in Medieval Damascus, 1190–1350* (Cambridge: Cambridge University Press, 1994), 143, quoted in Jonathan P. Berkey, "Madrasas Medieval and Modern: Politics, Education, and the Problem of Muslim Identity," in *Schooling Islam: The Culture and Politics of Modern Muslim Education,* ed. Robert W. Hefner and Muhammad Qasim Zaman (Princeton, NJ: Princeton University Press, 2007), 47.

40. Berkey, "Madrasas Medieval and Modern," 43.

41. Metcalf, *Islamic Revival in British India,* 94.

42. Gregory C. Kozlowski, *Muslim Endowments and Society in British India* (Cambridge: Cambridge University Press, 1985), 60–78.

43. Rizvi, *Tarikh-i Dar al-'Ulum Deoband,* 1:150–51.

44. Metcalf, *Islamic Revival in British India,* 94.

45. However, it did in time court the support of wealthy patrons, most notably the Nizam of Hyderabad, who became an annual contributor to the institution. See Gail Minault, *Secluded Scholars: Women's Education and Muslim Social Reform in Colonial India* (Oxford: Oxford University Press, 1998), 197. Interestingly, while the end of Hyderabad's princely state in 1948 naturally meant the end of the Nizam's patronage, Nehru intervened personally to continue monthly support for the Dar al-'Ulum Deoband from the central government, insofar as "Deoband has provided quite a good number of nationalist Muslim workers." Deoband was not unique in this regard. Nehru did the same for Aligarh Muslim University, Benares Hindu University, and a number of other institutions that the Nizam had supported. See Taylor C. Sherman, *Muslim Belonging in Secular India: Negotiating Citizenship in Postcolonial Hyderabad* (Cambridge: Cambridge University Press, 2015), 80.

46. Qari Muhammad Tayyib, *Azadi-yi Hindustan ka khamosh rahnuma* (Deoband: Daftar-i Ihtimam-i Dar al-'Ulum Deoband, 1957), 9–11.

47. Muhammad Zakariyya Kandhlavi, *Tarikh-i mazahir* (Saharanpur: Kutub Khana-yi Isha'at al-'Ulum, 1972), 1:5; and Mirathi, *Tazkirat al-Khalil,* 22.

48. Sana Haroon, "Contextualizing the Deobandi Approach to Congregation and Management of Mosques in Colonial North India," *Journal of Islamic Studies* 28, no. 1 (2017): 68–93, at 84–7.

49. Margrit Pernau, *Ashraf into Middle Classes: Muslims in Nineteenth-Century Delhi* (New Delhi: Oxford University Press, 2013), 273.

50. Margrit Pernau, "From a 'Private' Public to a 'Public' Private Sphere: Old Delhi and the North Indian Muslims in Comparative Perspective," in *The Public and the Private: Issues of Democratic Citizenship,* ed. Gurpreet Mahajan (New Delhi: Sage Publications, 2003), 110.

51. Aziz Ahmad, "The Role of Ulema in Indo-Muslim History," *Studia Islamica* 31 (1970): 1–13, at 6.

52. Ali Riaz, "Madrassah Education in Pre-Colonial and Colonial South Asia," *Journal of Asian and African Studies* 46, no. 1 (2010): 69–86, at 71.

53. Francis Robinson, *The Ulama of Farangi Mahall and Islamic Culture in South Asia* (New Delhi: Permanent Black, 2001), 44–46, 53. The *ma'qulat* began to flourish in Mughal India with the arrival of Iranian scholars at Akbar's court, especially the polymath Fath Allah Shirazi (d. 1589). On Shirazi and the adaptation of his ideas in Mughal political ideology, see Ali Anooshahr, "Shirazi

Scholars and the Political Culture of the Sixteenth-Century Indo-Persian World," *Indian Economic and Social History Review* 51, no. 3 (2014): 331–52.

54. S.M. Ikram, *Rud-i kausar: Islami Hind aur Pakistan ki mazhabi aur ruhani tarikh: 'ahd-i mughaliya* (Lahore: Idara-yi Siqafat-i Islamiya, 1975), 606.

55. Zafar al-Islam Islahi makes this point especially well in *Ta'lim 'ahd-i Islami ke Hindustan men* (Azamgarh, India: Shibli Academy, 2007), 29–30. For Sikand's discussion, see Yoginder Sikand, *Bastions of the Believers: Madrasas and Islamic Education in India* (New Delhi: Penguin Books India, 2005), 34.

56. Jamal Malik, "Introduction," *Madrasas in South Asia: Teaching Terror?* ed. Jamal Malik (London and New York: Routledge, 2008), 5–6.

57. Moosa, *What Is a Madrasa?* 110. Moosa argues that the excision of logic and philosophy from these curricula is at least partly responsible for what he sees as an inability of contemporary madrasa students to understand many of the theological texts they read.

58. Islahi, *Ta'lim 'ahd-i Islam ke Hindustan men,* 82.

59. Muhammad Raza Ansari, *Bani-yi dars-i nizami: Ustaz al-Hind Mulla Nizamuddin Muhammad Farangi Mahall* (Aligarh, India: Aligarh Muslim University Publication Division, 1973), 260.

60. Rizvi, *Tarikh-i Dar al-'Ulum Deoband,* 1:171.

61. Mirathi, *Tazkirat al-Rashid,* 1:40–62, 88–96. The Chishti order has two branches: the Nizami branch and the Sabiri branch. The Nizami branch stems from Nizam al-Din Awliya' and the Sabiri branch stems from 'Ala al-Din 'Ali Sabir; both founders were disciples of Farid al-Din Ganj-i Shakkar. The historical record on the Nizami Chishtis is far more profuse than that of the Sabiris. The most important Sabiri Chishti prior to the nineteenth century was 'Abd al-Quddus Gangohi, ancestor of Rashid Ahmad Gangohi. In the nineteenth century, Hajji Imdad Allah al-Makki, the latter Gangohi's master, became the single most influential Sabiri master since 'Abd al-Quddus. See Carl W. Ernst and Bruce B. Lawrence, *Sufi Martyrs of Love: The Chishti Order in South Asia and Beyond* (New York: Palgrave Macmillan, 2002), 118–19.

62. See also Brannon D. Ingram, "Sufis, Scholars and Scapegoats: Rashid Ahmad Gangohi (d. 1905) and the Deobandi Critique of Sufism," *Muslim World* 99, no. 3 (2009): 478–501.

63. It is important to note that Deoband was not the first institution to emphasize *manqulat* over *ma'qulat.* The Madrasa Rahimiyya, founded by Wali Allah's father Shah 'Abd al-Rahim (d. 1719), was perhaps the first, and certainly impacted the Deobandis through the Wali Allahian lineages discussed above. See Harlan O. Pearson, *Islamic Reform and Revival in Nineteenth Century India: The Tariqah-i Muhammadiyah* (New Delhi: Yoda Press, 2008), 9.

64. Mirathi, *Tazkirat al-Khalil,* 61–63.

65. Mirathi, *Tazkirat al-Rashid,* 1:94.

66. Gangohi, *Fatawa-yi Rashidiyya,* 53–55.

67. C.A. Bayly, *Empire and Information: Intelligence Gathering and Social Communication in India, 1780–1870* (Cambridge: Cambridge University Press, 1996), 69–78. On the culture of the Mughal munshi, see Rajeev Kinra, *Writing Self, Writing Empire: Chandar Bhan Brahman and the Cultural World of the Indo-Persian State Secretary* (Oakland: University of California Press, 2015).

68. Thomas R. Metcalf, *Ideologies of the Raj* (Cambridge: Cambridge University Press, 1994), 10.

69. Rosane Rocher, "The creation of Anglo-Hindu law," in Timothy Lubin, Donald R. Davis, and Jayanth K. Krishnan, eds. *Hinduism and Law: An Introduction* (Cambridge: Cambridge University Press, 2010), 79.

70. Quoted in "A Letter to the Chairman of the East India Company on the Danger of interfering in the Religious Opinions of the Natives of India," *Critical Review, or Annals of Literature* 13 (London: J. Mawwan, 1808), 405 (emphasis in original).

71. C. S. Adcock, *The Limits of Tolerance: Indian Secularism and the Politics of Religious Freedom* (Oxford and New York: Oxford University Press, 2013), 25–29.

72. On this debate, see Lynn Zastoupli and Martin Moir, eds., *The Great Indian Education Debate: Documents Relating to the Orientalist-Anglicist Controversy, 1781–1843* (Surrey, UK: Curzon, 1999).

73. Charles Trevelyan, *On the Education of the People of India* (London: Longman, Orme, Brown, Green and Longmans, 1838), 152–53.

74. Carl W. Ernst, "Reconfiguring South Asian Islam: From the 18th to the 19th Century," *Comparative Islamic Studies* 5, no. 2 (2011): 247–72, at 250.

75. Mirathi, *Tazkirat al-Rashid,* 2:290.

76. Kristen Stilt, *Islamic Law in Action: Authority, Discretion, and Everyday Experiences in Mamluk Egypt* (Oxford and New York: Oxford University Press, 2011), 38–42, 73–76.

77. John F. Richards, *The Mughal Empire* (Cambridge: Cambridge University Press, 1995), 175.

78. To resolve legal issues (e.g., marriage disputes) that required a qazi (an Islamic judge), muftis would sometimes advise individuals to go to princely states such as Bhopal that still had them, or later on, to engage in creative borrowing from other legal schools if they provided solutions that the Hanafi school could not provide for a specific issue. See Zaman, *The Ulama in Contemporary Islam,* 27–31. Indeed, with few exceptions (e.g., Bihar's Imarat-i Shari'a, formed in 1921), the absence of qazis was a void that would not be mitigated until after Independence. A Dar al-Qaza would be finally established at Dar al-'Ulum Deoband, e.g., only in 1974. See Rizvi, *Tarikh-i Dar al-'Ulum Deoband,* 1:412. On the Bihar case, see Papiya Ghosh, "*Muttahidah qaumiyat* in *aqalliat* Bihar: The Imarat i Shariah, 1921–1947," *Indian Economic and Social History Review* 34, no. 1 (1997): 1–20.

Qazis were crucial in Mughal administration and in deciding cases of civil and criminal law. There was a supreme qazi (*qazi al-qudat*), as well as provincial qazis posted to towns throughout the empire. See Zameeruddin Siddiqi, "The Institution of the Qazi under the Mughals," in *Medieval India: A Miscellany,* comp. Aligarh Muslim University (London: Asia Publishing House, 1969); and Jadunath Sarkar, *Mughal Administration* (Calcutta: M. C. Sarkar and Sons, 1952), 91–101. Not all administration relied on qazis' decisions; under Aurangzeb, many imperial decisions were made on the basis of his imperial edicts (*zawabit-i Alamgiri*) or customary practice (*qanun-i 'urfi*). See

M.L. Bhatia, *Administrative History of Medieval India* (New Delhi: Radha Publications, 1992).

79. Radhika Singha, *A Despotism of Law: Crime and Justice in Early Colonial India* (New Delhi: Oxford University Press, 1998), 294–96.

80. Jones quoted in Garland Cannon, *The Life and Mind of Oriental Jones: Sir William Jones, the father of modern linguistics* (Cambridge: Cambridge University Press, 1990), 286. See also Muhammad Khalid Masud, "Apostasy and Judicial Separation in British India," in *Islamic Legal Interpretation: Muftis and Their Fatwas*, ed. Muhammad Khalid Masud, Brinkley Messick, and David S. Powers (Cambridge, MA: Harvard University Press, 1996), 197. On the *Fatawa-yi Alamgiri*, see Alan M. Guenther, "Hanafi *Fiqh* in Mughal India: The *Fatawa-i Alamgiri*," in *India's Islamic Traditions: 711–1150*, ed. Richard M. Eaton (New Delhi: Oxford University Press, 2003).

81. Wael Hallaq, *Shari'a: Theory, Practice, Transformations* (Cambridge: Cambridge University Press, 2009), 374–75.

82. Burhan al-Din Abu'l Hasan Marghinani, *Hedaya, a Commentary on the Mussulman Laws*, trans. Charles Hamilton (London: T. Bensley, 1791), xxxi. On Marghinani, see Y. Meron, "Marghinani, His Method and His Legacy," *Islamic Law and Society* 9, no. 3 (2002): 410–16.

83. Scott Alan Kugle, "Framed, Blamed and Renamed: The Recasting of Islamic Jurisprudence in Colonial South Asia," *Modern Asian Studies* 35, no. 2 (2001): 257–313. In a rejoinder to Kugle, John Strawson argues that processes of codification and bureaucratization had already shaped Islamic law long before the colonial period, and that the most critical reshaping of Islamic law took place not in Hamilton's era but in the mid to late nineteenth century, with the "pulling of Islamic law on to the terrain of English law," by which Strawson refers to the development of the full apparatus of English courts, judges, and barristers for adjudicating Islamic law. See John Strawson, "Translating the *Hedaya*: Colonial Foundations of Islamic Law," in *Legal Histories of the British Empire: Laws, Engagements, and Legacies*, ed. Shaunnagh Dorsett and John McLaren (Abingdon, UK: Routledge, 2014), 157–70, at 168.

84. Marghinani, *Hedaya*, iv–v.

85. Jorg Fisch, *Cheap Lives and Dear Limbs: The British Transformation of the Bengal Criminal Law, 1769–1817* (Wiesbaden: Franz Steiner Verlag, 1983), 34, 47.

86. Singha, *A Despotism of Law*, 52–53.

87. Rudolph Peters, *Crime and Punishment in Islamic Law: Theory and Practice from the Sixteenth to the Twenty-First Century* (Cambridge: Cambridge University Press, 2005), 112–16.

88. Hallaq, *Shari'a*, 178.

89. William H. Morley, *The Administration of Justice in British India: its Past History and Present State* (London: Williams and Norgate, 1858), 331.

90. Peters, *Crime and Punishment*, 109–10.

91. Michael R. Anderson, "Classifications and Codifications: Themes in South Asian Legal Studies in the 1980s," *South Asia Research* 10, no. 2 (1990): 158–77, at 166–67.

92. Zaman, *The Ulama in Contemporary Islam*, 29.

93. Hallaq, *Shari'a*, 381.

94. Government of India Legislative Department, *The Unrepealed General Acts of the Governor General in Council*, vol. 3 (Calcutta: Office of the Superintendent of Government Printing, 1898), 330–31, 331n1.

95. Fareeha Khan, "Tafwid al-Talaq: Transferring the Right to Divorce to the Wife," *Muslim World* 99, no. 3 (2009): 502–20, at 503.

96. Masud, "Apostasy and Judicial Separation in British India," 195.

97. Zaman, *The Ulama in Contemporary Islam*, 25. It should be noted that this never completely eclipsed the prestige of individual muftis. Fatwa collections by Gangohi, Ashraf 'Ali Thanvi, Muhammad Kifayat Allah, Mahmud Hasan Gangohi, and other Deobandis drew from their association with Deoband and from their own authority as jurists in equal measure.

98. Rizvi, *Tarikh-i Dar al-'Ulum Deoband*, 1:202.

99. Hussein Ali Agrama, "Ethics, Tradition, Authority: Toward an Anthropology of the Fatwa," *American Ethnologist* 37, no. 1 (2010): 2–18, at 4.

100. Mirathi, *Tazkirat al-Rashid*, 1:112.

101. William Fischer Agnew, *The Law of Trusts in British India* (Calcutta: Thacker, Spink and Co., 1882), 396–407.

102. Nile Green, *Bombay Islam: The Religious Economy of the West Indian Ocean, 1840–1915* (Cambridge: Cambridge University Press, 2011), 11–12.

103. That being said, some prominent British officials continued to argue that the government should have a role in patronizing institutions such as the Calcutta Madrasa, since the scholars trained there "did not show any hostility to the Government during the period of the mutinies," in the words of the Viscount Canning (d. 1862), governor-general during the 1857 uprising. Jamal Malik, *Islamische Gelehrtenkultur in Nordindien: Entwicklungsgeschichte und Tendenzen am Beispiel von Lucknow* (Leiden, New York, Köln: E. J. Brill, 1997), 206.

104. Green, *Bombay Islam*, 7.

105. Rizvi, *Tarikh-i Dar al-'Ulum Deoband*, 1:200.

106. "Letter to Assistant Secretary to the Political Department of Nizam's Government," 14 March 1931, British Library IOR 1/1/2006 (emphasis added).

107. Rivzi, *Tarikh-i Dar al-'Ulum Deoband*, 1:219 (emphasis added).

108. Marghinani, *Hedaya*, ii.

109. "Copy of a Despatch to the Government of India, on the Subject of General Education in India," *House of Commons Sessional Papers* 47 (1854): 155–73.

110. Zastoupli and Moir, *The Great Indian Education Debate*, 116.

111. "Petition of the Muslim Inhabitants of Calcutta to the Government," *Asiatic Journal* 18 (1835): 95–96, reprinted in Zastoupli and Moir, *The Great Indian Education Debate*, 189–93. Citations are on pp. 190 and 192.

112. See Parna Sengupta, *Pedagogy for Religion: Missionary Education and the Fashioning of Hindus and Muslims in Bengal* (Berkeley and Los Angeles: University of California Press, 2011), esp. chap. 6.

113. India Political Department, Mysore, "Monthly Grant-in-Aid of Rs 50 to the Mahomedan Female School in Bangalore," British Library, IOR/L /PS/6/555, coll. 54.

114. Quoted in G. W. Leitner, *History of Indigenous Education in the Panjab since Annexation and in 1882* (New Delhi: Languages Department Punjab, 1971), app. 6, 19–20. See also Zaman, *The Ulama in Contemporary Islam*, 63.

115. Edwin Atkinson, *Statistical, Descriptive and Historical Account of the North-Western Provinces of India* (Allahabad: North-Western Provinces Government Press, 1875), 2:192–93.

116. Sayyid Ahmad Khan Bahadur et al., *Translation of the Report of the Members of the Select Committee for the Better Diffusion and Advancement of Learning among the Muhammadans of India* (Benares: Medical Hall Press, 1872), 8.

117. Ibid., 55 (emphasis added).

118. Sengupta, *Pedagogy for Religion*, 137.

119. Leitner, *History of Indigenous Education*, ii–iii (emphasis in original).

120. Malik, *Islamische Gelehrtenkultur in Nordindien*, 209.

121. Rashid Ahmad Gangohi, *Makatib-i Rashidiyya*, ed. Mahmud Ashraf 'Usmani (Lahore: Idara-yi Islamiyya, 1996), 52.

122. Leitner, *History of Indigenous Education*, 76.

123. Mirathi, *Tazkirat al-Khalil*, 23.

124. Ashraf 'Ali Thanvi, "The Raison d'Être of Madrasah," trans. Muhammad al-Ghazali, *Islamic Studies* 43, no. 4 (2004): 653–75, at 667.

125. S. M. Jaffar, *Education in Muslim India, Being an Inquiry into the State of Education during the Muslim Period of Indian History, 1000–1800* (Delhi: Idarah-i Adabiyat-i Delhi, 1936), 28 (emphasis added).

126. Marmaduke Pickthall, "Muslim Education," *Islamic Culture: The Hyderabad Quarterly Review* 1, no. 1 (1927): 100–108, at 101.

127. Zaman, *The Ulama in Contemporary Islam*, 64.

128. Moosa, *What Is a Madrasa?*, 200.

2. THE NORMATIVE ORDER

1. Robinson uses the phrase to denote new forms of interiority and subjectivity in Indian Muslim thought in the modern period, whereas Metcalf refers mostly to a post-1857 retreat from direct contestations of British rule. See Francis Robinson, *Islam and Muslim History in South Asia* (New Delhi: Oxford University Press, 2000), 9, 117–17; and Metcalf, *Islamic Revival in British India*, 86, 254.

2. See Bearman et al., *Encyclopaedia of Islam*, s.v. "Din."

3. It is thus too simple to define it, as the entry on *bid'a* in the *Encyclopaedia of Islam* does, as "a belief or practice for which there is no precedent in the time of the Prophet." See Bearman et al., *Encyclopaedia of Islam*, s.v. "Bid'a."

4. Jonathan Berkey, "Tradition, Innovation, and the Social Construction of Knowledge in the Medieval Islamic Near East," *Past and Present* 146 (1995): 38–65, at 56.

5. See p. 75–76.

6. Muhammad Khalid Masud long ago noted that the mere existence of entire chapters of Deobandi fatwa collections devoted to *bid'a* was a relative novelty. See Masud, "Trends in the Interpretation of Islamic Law as Reflected

in the Fatawa Literature of the Deoband School" (MA thesis, McGill University, 1969), 17. One might assume that Wahhabism is an obvious example of one such movement similarly focused on *bid'a,* but perusing Muhammad ibn 'Abd al-Wahhab's work suggests that *shirk* is overwhelmingly a far greater concern than *bid'a.*

7. Muhammad Khalid Masud discusses the extent of Shatibi's influence on Deobandi conceptions of *bid'a* in "The Definition of Bid'a in the South Asian *Fatawa* Literature," *Annales Islamologiques* 27 (1993): 55–71, at 61–62.

8. Abu Ishaq Ibrahim ibn Musa al-Shatibi, *Al-I'tisam* (Cairo: Matba' al-Manar, 1913), 30–31. For a fuller analysis of Shatibi's concept of *bid'a,* see Muhammad Khalid Masud, *Shatibi's Philosophy of Islamic Law,* 2nd ed. (New Delhi: Kitab Bhavan, 2009), 218–25. On Shatibi's legal theory more broadly, see Wael Hallaq, *A History of Islamic Legal Theories: An Introduction to Sunni Usul al-Fiqh* (Cambridge: Cambridge University Press, 1997), chap. 5.

9. Thus he dismisses 'Izz al-Din ibn 'Abd al-Salam's (d. 1262) temporal conception of *bid'a* as that which did not exist in the era of the Prophet, and thus his projection, accordingly, of *bid'a* onto to the five Shari'a *ahkam:* obligatory (*wajib*) *bid'a*—e.g., the development of Qur'anic grammar; forbidden (*muharram*) *bid'a*—e.g., various "invented practices opposed to the Shari'a;" recommended (*mandub*) *bid'a*—e.g., the supererogatory prayers prayed during Ramadan (known as *tarawih*); the reprehensible (*makruh*) *bid'a*—e.g., altering the prescribed number of times "praise God" (*subhan Allah*) is uttered during Salat; and permissible (*mubah*) *bid'a*—which would subsume anything that did not fall under the other four. Shatibi regards this typology as conceptually flawed, having what came after the Prophet as the sole criterion of its enumeration, completely misunderstanding the nature of *bid'a* as an *invented* matter *in religion* that *emulates* religion. See Shatibi, *Al-I'tisam,* 246–50. See also Raquel Margalit Ukeles's discussion of Shatibi's critique of 'Izz al-Din in her "Innovation or Deviation: Exploring the Boundaries of Islamic Devotional Law" (PhD diss., Harvard University, 2006), 186–90.

10. Gangohi, *Fatawa-yi Rashidiyya,* 146. See also Khalil Ahmad Saharanpuri's similar discussion of *bid'a hasana* in *Al-Barahin al-qati'a 'ala dhalam al-anwar al-sati'a* (Deoband: Kutub Khana-yi Imdadiyya, n.d.), 35. I discuss this text further in the following chapter.

11. Mufti Muhammad Shafi', *Sunnat o bid'at* (Lahore: Maktaba-yi Khalil, n.d.), 14.

12. Shatibi, *Al-I'tisam,* 31.

13. Ukeles, "Innovation or Deviation," 194.

14. Ashraf 'Ali Thanvi, *Al-Kalam al-hasan,* ed. Mufti Muhammad Hasan (Lahore: Al-Maktaba al-Ashrafiyya, n.d.), 61–62.

15. "Barelvi" signifies Sayyid Ahmad's place of origin—Rai Bareilly—and has no relation at all with the Barelvi movement, Deoband's principal competition in the South Asian context.

16. Some historians have read Sayyid Ahmad's movement in terms of the social history of early-nineteenth-century India, seeing Sayyid Ahmad as a Sunni sayyid responding to the rise of Awadh-based Shi'ism, e.g. Juan Cole, *Roots of*

North Indian Shi'ism in Iran and Iraq: Religion and State in Awadh, 1722–1859 (Berkeley: University of California Press, 1988), 234–40.

17. Muhammad Hedayetullah, *Sayyid Ahmad: A Study of the Religious Reform Movement of Sayyid Ahmad of Ra'e Bareli* (Lahore: Sh. Muhammad Ashraf, 1970), 44, 115–18.

18. Pearson, *Islamic Reform and Revival,* 40.

19. After the defeat at Balakot, some of Sayyid Ahmad's followers regrouped and continued to fight. The movement largely shifted to Patna, where their activities were the basis of emergent British anxieties about so-called Wahhabis in India. See Pearson, *Islamic Reform and Revival,* 42–43; and Julia Stephens, "The Phantom Wahhabi: Liberalism and the Muslim Fanatic in Mid-Victorian India," *Modern Asian Studies* 47, no. 1 (2013): 22–52.

20. Marc Gaborieau, "Late Persian, Early Urdu: The Case of 'Wahhabi' Literature (1818–1857)," in *Confluence of Cultures: French Contributions to Indo-Persian Studies,* ed. Françoise "Nalini" Delvoye (New Delhi: Manohar, 1994), 170–91.

21. Muhammad Isma'il, *Taqwiyyat al-iman ma' tazkir al-ikhwan* (Deoband: Dar al-Kitab Deoband, 1997), 16.

22. As late as 1990, Muhammad 'Ashiq Ilahi's preface to Mahmud Hasan Gangohi's *Hudud-i ikhtilaf,* which will be discussed in subsequent chapters, casts the book as one in "simple and easy language" (*zaban-i salis aur sadah*) that is "beneficial to elite and commoner alike" (*khass o 'amm ke liye mufid*). Mahmud Hasan Gangohi, *Hudud-i ikhtilaf,* ed. Muhammad Faruq Mirathi (Meerut, India: Maktaba-yi Mahmudiyya, 1991), 14.

23. Gaborieau, "Late Persian, Early Urdu," 177.

24. See, e.g., Ashraf 'Ali Thanvi's typology of *shirk* in *Ta'lim al-din:* "associating God with any other entity in knowledge" (*ishrak fi-l 'ilm*), in other words, ascribing certain forms of superhuman knowledge to any entity other than God; "associating God with any other entity in power" (*ishrak fi-l tasarruf*), ascribing certain powers (such as the ability to fulfill a wish) to any entity other than God; "associating God with any other entity in worship" (*ishrak fi-l 'ibadat*), engaging in any normative actions (such as prostrating, circumambulating, or sacrificing) toward or on behalf of any entity other than God; and, finally, "associating God with any other entity in habit or custom" (*ishrak fi-l 'adah*), maintaining customs or habits that acquire such a normativity in and of themselves (such as believing certain dates to be auspicious, or giving children auspicious names, etc.) that they compete with the normativity of the religion. Ashraf 'Ali Thanvi, "Ta'lim al-din," 12–14, an essay compiled in *Islahi nisab: Tashih-i 'aqa'id o a'mal, tahzib o tamaddun-i Islami* (Lahore: Maktaba-yi Rashidiyya, 1977). (Each essay in *Islahi nisab* has its own separate pagination.) Another comparable typology is found in Muhammad Kifayat Allah's *Ta'lim al-Islam,* which includes *shirk* in power (*qudrat*), in knowledge, in "hearing and seeing" (*sama' o basirat*), in sovereignty (*hukm*), and in worship. See Muhammad Kifayat Allah, *Ta'lim al-Islam* (Delhi: Kutub Khana-yi 'Aziziyya, n. d.), 4:20–21.

25. Isma'il, *Taqwiyyat al-iman,* 19.

26. Muhammad Manzur Nu'mani, *Din o shari'at* (Lahore: Idara-yi Islami-yat, 1995), 46–47.

27. Muhammad Isma'il, *Izah al-haqq fi ahkam al-mayyit wa al-darih* (Delhi: Kutub Khana-yi Ashrafiyya, 1937), 6.

28. Ibid., 99 (emphasis added).

29. Ibid., 13–15.

30. The distinction is derived from Qur'an 3:7: "It is He that has sent the Book down to you, which contains clear verses [*muhkamat*], which are the foundation of the Book, and others about which there is doubt [*mutashabi-hat*]." For interpretations of this verse, see Stefan Wild, "The Self-Referentiality of the Qur'an: Sura 3:7 as an Exegetical Challenge," in *With Reverence for the Word: Medieval Scriptural Exegesis in Judaism, Christianity, and Islam*, ed. Jane Dammen McAuliffe, Barry D. Walfish, and Joseph W. Goering (Oxford: Oxford University Press, 2003).

31. Muhammad Zakariyya Kandhlavi, *Shari'at o tariqat ka talazum* (Karachi: Maktaba al-Shaykh, 1993), 9.

32. On Muhammad Isma'il and the Ahl-i Hadith, see Martin Riexinger, "Ibn Taymiyya's Worldview and the Challenge of Modernity: A Conflict among the Ahl-i Hadith in British India," in *Islamic Theology, Philosophy and Law: Debating Ibn Taymiyya and Ibn Qayyim al-Jawziyya*, ed. Birgit Krazietz and Georges Tamer (Berlin and Boston: Walter de Gruyter, 2013), 497–99.

33. Isma'il, *Taqwiyyat al-iman*, 42.

34. Ibid., 43.

35. This will of course remind many readers of Carl Schmitt's famous definition of the sovereign. For an excellent use of Schmitt to analyze Muhammad Isma'il, see SherAli Tareen, "Competing Political Theologies: Intra-Muslim Polemics of the Limits of Prophetic Intercession," *Political Theology* 12, no. 3 (2011): 418–43.

36. Muhammad Qasim Zaman, "The Sovereignty of God in Modern Islamic Thought," *Journal of the Royal Asiatic Society* 25, no. 3 (2015): 389–418, at 391–95.

37. Isma'il, *Taqwiyyat al-iman*, 55; Zaman, "The Sovereignty of God," 391.

38. Isma'il, *Taqwiyyat al-iman*, 40.

39. Ibid., 49. Cf. "O people! Fear this Lord of the Universe [*malik al-mulk*], a King of Kings [*shahanshah*] worthy of honor, whose power [*taqat*] is infinite and immeasurable!" (26).

40. Khurram 'Ali Bilhauri, *Nasihat al-Muslimin* (Lucknow: Dar al-Isha'at Islamiyya, 1964), 11.

41. Gangohi, *Fatawa-yi Rashidiyya*, 83.

42. Ibid., 78.

43. Ibid., 79.

44. Fazl al-Haqq Khairabadi was, like Sayyid Ahmad and Muhammad Isma'il, a disciple of Shah 'Abd al-'Aziz. Khairabadi defended the notion of saintly intercession against Muhammad Isma'il's assertions that believing in intercession was tantamount to *shirk*. He also vilified Muhammad Isma'il for his alleged slandering of the Prophet Muhammad. See Ayesha Jalal, *Partisans of*

Allah: Jihad in South Asia (Cambridge, MA: Harvard University Press, 2008), 80–81; as well as Tareen, "Competing Political Theologies," 433–43.

45. Gangohi, *Fatawa-yi Rashidiyya*, 113.

46. Ibid., 61–62, 100–101, 103.

47. Ibid., 84.

48. Mirathi, *Tazkirat al-Rashid*, 1:122. Gangohi also recommended Khalil Ahmad Saharanpuri's *Al-Barahin al-qati'a*, discussed below.

49. Aviva Schussman, "The Legitimacy and Nature of Mawlud Al-Nabi (Analysis of a Fatwa)," *Islamic Law and Society* 5, no. 2 (1998): 214–34. The Azhar fatwa commended the practice as a natural expression of love for the Prophet Muhammad, provided it remained within a set of legal and performative restraints.

50. On Internet debates about *mawlud*, see Jonas Svensson, "ITZ BIDAH BRO!!!! GT ME??—YouTube Mawlid and Voices of Praise and Blame," in *Muslims and the New Information and Communication Technologies*, ed. Thomas Hoffmann and Göran Larsson (New York: Springer, 2013), 89–111.

51. Kozlowski, *Muslim Endowments and Society*, 74.

52. Shah Wali Allah, *Fuyuz al-haramayn* (Deoband: Kutub Khana-yi Rahimiyya, n.d.), 27.

53. Marion Holmes Katz, *The Birth of the Prophet Muhammad: Devotional Piety in Sunni Islam* (London and New York: Routledge, 2007), 12–15.

54. Ibid., 5.

55. Ibid., 76.

56. Ibid., 130–31.

57. N. J. G. Kaptein, *Muhammad's Birthday Festival: Early History in the Central Muslim Lands and Development in the Muslim West until the 10th/16th Century* (Leiden: E. J. Brill, 1993), 48–67.

58. Katz, *The Birth of the Prophet Muhammad*, 171.

59. Gangohi does not specify the "king" to whom he refers, but it is likely the Fatimid ruler al-Mu'izz li-Din Allah (d. 975), credited with first celebrating the *mawlud*. Kaptein has some doubts about the historicity of this claim, but there is a general scholarly consensus that the Fatimids were the first to institute the *mawlud* as a state-sponsored event. Kaptein, *Muhammad's Birthday Festival*, 20–21.

60. Gangohi, *Fatawa-yi Rashidiyya*, 114.

61. Ibid., 130.

62. Mirathi, *Tazkirat al-Rashid*, 1:127–28.

63. In addition, the Begum's military secretary was one of Khalil Ahmad's disciples. See Siobhan Lambert-Hurley, *Muslim Women, Reform and Princely Patronage: Nawab Sultan Jahan Begam of Bhopal* (London and New York: Routledge, 2007), 56–57. She was also a regular donor to the Dar al-'Ulum Deoband, contributing three thousand rupees annually. Rizvi, *Tarikh-i Dar al-'Ulum Deoband*, 1:207.

64. Qur'an 9:128. The full verse is "Certainly there has come to you a Messenger from among yourselves. Grievous to him is what you suffer. He is concerned for you and is kind and merciful to the believers."

65. This is a reference to Mufti Inayat Ahmad's *Tavarikh-i habib Allah* (Deoband: Maktaba-yi Thanvi, n.d.). Mufti Inayat Ahmad (d. 1863) studied with Shah Muhammad Ishaq in Delhi and was exiled to the Andaman Islands for activities in the 1857 uprising. He established the Madrasa Faiz-i 'Amm in Kanpur, where Ashraf 'Ali Thanvi would later teach. Interestingly, the introduction to Inayat Ahmad's *Bayan-i qadr-i shab-i barat* identifies Inayat Ahmad as a proto-Barelvi. See Mufti Inayat Ahmad, *Bayan-i qadr-i shab-i barat* (Lahore: Markaz Isha'at-i Navadir-i 'Ulama-yi Ahl al-Sunnat, 2012), 3–4. *Tavarikh-i habib Allah* is read in Barelvi madrasas, including Jami'a Ashrafiyya, Mubarakpur, "the leading Ahl-i Sunnat teaching institution in South Asia in the last twenty years," according to Usha Sanyal. See Usha Sanyal, "Ahl-i Sunnat Madrasas: The Madrasa Manzar-i Islam, Bareilly, and Jamiat Ashrafiyya, Mubarakpur," in *Madrasas in South Asia: Teaching Terror?,* ed. Jamal Malik (Abingdon, UK: Routledge, 2008), 39, 42.

66. Quoted in Muhammad Zakariyya Kandhlavi, *Tarikh-i mashaikh-i Chisht* (Karachi: Maktaba al-Shaykh, 1976), 294–95. The same narrative is in Mirathi, *Tazkirat al-Rashid,* 2:284.

67. Khalil Ahmad Saharanpuri, *'Aqa'id-i 'ulama-yi Deoband aur 'ulama-yi haramayn ka fatva* (Delhi: Khwajah Barqi Press, n.d.), 24–25.

68. See Moin Ahmad Nizami, *Reform and Renewal in South Asian Islam: The Chishti-Sabiris in 18th–19th Century North India* (New Delhi: Oxford University Press, 2017), 211–12. *Al-Barahin al-qati'a* relied substantially on Gangohi's thought (and incorporated some of Gangohi's fatwas). Gangohi is therefore sometimes named as coauthor, or even sole author, of *Al-Barahin al-qati'a,* but I have not found any evidence of this. Given how close Gangohi and Saharanpuri were, however, it is entirely likely that he advised his disciple in writing it.

69. Mirathi, *Tazkirat al-Rashid,* 1:32.

70. The sole, deliberately elliptical reference to the 'Illiyun in the Qur'an (83:18–19) is intended as a rhetorical challenge to the Qur'an's audience: "The record of the pious [*abrar*] is preserved in the 'Illiyun. And what can make you know what is the 'Illiyun?" The word is possibly related etymologically to the Hebrew *elyon* ("the highest"). Qur'an commentators took 'Illiyun to denote the seventh and highest level of heaven. See Bearman et al., *Encyclopaedia of Islam,* s.v. "Illiyyun," 3:1132–33.

71. Saharanpuri, *Al-Barahin al-qati'a,* 56. See also SherAli Tareen, "The Limits of Tradition: Competing Logics of Authenticity in South Asian Islam" (PhD Diss. Duke University, 2012), 222–27.

72. Ibid., 54–56. Cf. also Gangohi, *Fatawa-yi Rashidiyya,* 166.

73. Ibid., 197.

74. Ibid., 197–99.

75. Hajji Muhammad Imdad Allah, *Navadir-i Imdadiyya,* ed. Nishar Ahmad Faruqi (Gulbarga, India: Sayyid Muhammad Gesudaraz Tahqiqati Academy, 1996), 100–104. I follow, and slightly alter, Nizami's translation of this letter in *Reform and Renewal,* 213–14.

76. Jamil Ahmad Thanvi, *Sharh-i faisala-yi haft mas'ala* (Lahore: Jami'a-yi Ziya al-'Ulum, 1975), 3. *Faisala-yi haft mas'ala* covers seven "controversies" of

Imdad Allah's day, which he ordered in proportion to the urgency of their need for resolution, with *mawlud* first, followed by the practice of customary *fatiha*, transferring merit to the dead; *'urs* and *sama'*; calling on something or someone other than God; performing a second congregational *salat*; and finally, *imkan-i nazir* and *imkan-i kizb*—whether God can create additional prophets and whether God can tell a lie, respectively.

77. For a summary of the relationship between Imdad Allah and the *'ulama*, see Nizami, *Reform and Renewal*, 197–204.

78. Numerous sources recount this statement—among them Kandhlavi, *Tarikh-i mashaikh-i Chisht*, 259; Rizvi, *Tarikh-i Dar al-'Ulum Deoband*, 1:35; and Ashraf 'Ali Thanvi, *Kamalat-i Imdadiyya: Jis men pir-i tariqat Hajji Imdad Allah Muhajir Makki ke kamalat ko bayan kiya gaya hai* (Lahore: Maktaba al-Furqan, 1976), 10.

79. Ashraf 'Ali Thanvi, *Arvah-i salasa al-ma'ruf bih hikayat-i awliya'* (Karachi: Dar al-Isha'at, 1976), 166.

80. Kandhlavi, *Tarikh-i mashaikh-i Chisht*, 263.

81. Nizami, *Reform and Renewal*, 166–67.

82. Gangohi, *Hudud-i ikhtilaf*, 121.

83. Rashid Ahmad Gangohi, *Irshadat-i Gangohi*, ed. 'Abd al-Rauf Rahimi (Delhi: Farid Book Depot, 2003), 119.

84. Ashraf 'Ali Thanvi, *Al-Ifadat al-yawmiyya min al-ifadat al-qawmiyya* (Multan, Pakistan: Idara-yi Ta'lifat-i Ashrafiyya, 2003), statement no. 366, 1:334.

85. Hajji Muhammad Imdad Allah, *Kulliyat-i Imdadiyya* (Karachi: Dar al-Isha'at, 1977), 72.

86. Annemarie Schimmel, *Mystical Dimensions of Islam* (Chapel Hill: University of North Carolina Press, 1975), 103.

87. Mirathi, *Tazkirat al-Rashid*, 2:184–85.

88. Ibid., 1:122. Here I am using Muhammad Qasim Zaman's translation, in Zaman, *Ashraf Ali Thanawi*, 83.

89. Imdad Allah, *Kulliyat-i Imdadiyya*, 78.

90. Ibid.

91. Ibid.

92. Ibid., 79–80.

93. Ibid. The phrase comes from Rumi's *Masnavi*, book 2, line 872: "Don't burn a new rug for the sake of a flea" (*bahr-i kaiki nau galimi sukhtan*). See Maulana Jalal al-Din Rumi, *Masnavi*, vol. 2 (Tehran: Kitabfurushi-i Zavvar, 1990), 45.

94. Imdad Allah, *Kulliyat-i Imdadiyya*, 80.

95. Mirathi, *Tazkirat al-Rashid*, 1:128.

96. Imdad Allah, *Kulliyat-i Imdadiyya*, 80.

97. 'Aziz al-Hasan, *Ashraf al-savanih* (Multan, Pakistan: Idara-yi Ta'lifat-i Ashrafiyya, n.d.), 1:19–27.

98. Ashraf 'Ali Thanvi, *Majalis-i Hakim al-Ummat*, ed. Muhammad Shafi' (Karachi: Dar al-Isha'at, n.d.), 160.

99. Ibid., 161–62. He makes similar judgments numerous places elsewhere—e.g., in rejecting *mawlud* and *'urs* on the basis that sources of corruption

(*mafasid*) outweigh sources of good (*masalih*), a principle that applies in all circumstances *except* those for which there is a legal necessity for the *masalih*, in which case the *mafasid* must be expurgated rather than the entire practice being abandoned. See Thanvi, *Imdad al-fatawa*, 4:69.

100. Thanvi, *Majalis-i Hakim al-Ummat*, 161 (emphasis added).

101. Ibid., 162 (emphasis added).

102. Ashraf 'Ali Thanvi, *Ashraf al-jawab* (Deoband: Maktaba-yi Thanvi, 1990), 2:116–17.

103. Ibid., 2:117–18.

104. Ashraf 'Ali Thanvi, *Al-Takashshuf 'an muhimmat al-tasawwuf* (Deoband: Matba'-yi Qasimi, 1909), 5:71.

105. Ibid., 5:79.

106. Ashraf 'Ali Thanvi, *Islah al-rusum* (Delhi: Dini Book Depot, 1963), 125.

107. Ibid., 125–26.

108. Ibid., 129.

109. Ibid., 129–30.

110. Ibid., 130–31.

111. Ibid., 131.

112. Ashraf 'Ali Thanvi, *Bid'at ki haqiqat aur us ke ahkam o masa'il*, ed. Muhammad Iqbal Qureshi (Lahore and Karachi: Idara-yi Islamiyya, 2000), 51.

113. Thanvi, *Khutbat-i Hakim al-Ummat*, 5:310–11.

114. Thanvi, *Islah al-rusum*, 132.

115. Ibid., 132. This is a point that Thanvi makes repeatedly—e.g., "If there is concern for a permissible [*mubah*] act corrupting the masses [*fasad-i 'awamm*], it is necessary to abandon this act, especially any permissible act that would invert the religion [*din*]—like supporting a madrasa with the property of a dancing girl." See Ashraf 'Ali Thanvi, *Anfas-i 'Isa, ifadat-i Hakim al-Ummat Hazrat Maulana Ashraf 'Ali Thanvi* (Karachi: H. M. Sa'id Company, 1980), 282. This is a point that Gangohi makes as well in many places—e.g., Mirathi, *Tazkirat al-Rashid*, 1:170.

116. Thanvi, *Islah al-rusum*, 134–35. Cf. Gangohi, *Fatawa-yi Rashidiyya*, 115–16, 132.

117. In some cases, jurists invoked this principle even to override norms established in the Prophet Muhammad's era—e.g., the presence of women in mosques. See Marion Holmes Katz, "The Corruption of the Times and the Mutability of the Shari'a," *Cardozo Law Review* 28, no. 1 (2006): 171–86. On this idea in Hanafi law, see Haim Gerber, *Islamic Law and Culture: 1600–1840* (Leiden, Boston, and Cologne: E. J. Brill, 1999), 124–27.

118. Thanvi, *Islah al-rusum*, 134. For a discussion of *maslaha* within discourses of the *'ulama*, see Muhammad Qasim Zaman, "The 'Ulama of Contemporary Islam and Their Conceptions of the Common Good," in *Public Islam and the Common Good*, ed. Armando Salvatore and Dale F. Eickelman (Leiden: E. J. Brill, 2004). For a more general assessment, with attention to contemporary debates, see Felicitas Opwis, *Maslaha and the Purpose of the Law: Islamic Discourse on Legal Change from the 4th/10th to 8th/14th Century* (Leiden: E. J. Brill, 2010).

119. Thanvi, *Al-Ifadat al-yawmiyya*, statement no. 116, 1:130.

120. Thanvi, *Islah al-rusum,* 136–37.

121. Ashraf ʿAli Thanvi, *Al-Surur bi-zuhur al-nur wa mulaqqab bih irshad al-ʿibad fi ʿeid al-milad* (Sadhaura, India: Bilali Steam Press, 1915), 3.

122. Ibid., 4–6.

123. Ibid., 27–28.

124. Thomas Laqueur, *The Work of the Dead: A Cultural History of Mortal Remains* (Princeton, NJ: Princeton University Press, 2015), 98.

125. Engseng Ho, *The Graves of Tarim: Genealogy and Mobility across the Indian Ocean* (Berkeley: University of California Press, 2006), 25.

126. Nile Green, *Making Space: Sufis and Settlers in Early Modern India* (New Delhi: Oxford University Press, 2012), 44, 48.

127. Ibid., 33, 35.

128. Green, *Sufism: A Global History,* 102.

129. Babur, *The Baburnama: Memoirs of Babur, Prince and Emperor* (New York: Modern Library Classics, 2002), 446.

130. P. M. Currie, *The Shrine and Cult of Muʿin al-Din Chishti of Ajmer* (New York and Delhi: Oxford University Press, 1989), 99–100.

131. Jahanara, *Muʾnis al-arvah* (Karachi: S. M. Hamid Ali, 1991), 120. A passage of this text is translated in Carl W. Ernst, *Teachings of Sufism* (Boston and London: Shambhala, 1999), 196–99.

132. Muhammad Chishti, *Adab al-talibin maʿ rafiq al-tulab wa albab thalatha* (Lahore: Progressive Books, 1984), 61. See also the discussion of Muhammad Chishti in Ernst and Lawrence, *Sufi Martyrs of Love,* 92–93.

133. Carl W. Ernst, "An Indo-Persian Guide to Sufi Shrine Pilgrimage," in *Manifestations of Sainthood in Islam,* ed. Grace Martin Smith and Carl W. Ernst (Istanbul: Isis Press, 1993), 55–56.

134. Ernst, "An Indo-Persian Guide," 60.

135. Dargah Quli Khan, *Muraqqa-yi Dihli: Farsi matan aur Urdu tarjamah,* trans. Khalid Anjum (Delhi: Anjuman-i Taraqqi-yi Urdu, 1993), 120.

136. Imdad Allah, *Kulliyat-i Imdadiyya,* 82.

137. Ibid.

138. Ibid., 82–83.

139. Mirathi, *Tazkirat al-Khalil,* 392–95.

140. Mahmud Hasan Gangohi, *Malfoozat: Statements and Anecdotes of Faqeeh-ul-Ummat,* ed. Mufti Farooq Meeruti (Durban: Madrasah Taleemuddeen, 2010), 279–80.

141. Muhammad Zakariyya Kandhlavi, *Maut ki yad* (Karachi: Idara al-Maʿarif, 2005). Sufi reflections on the spiritual rewards of visiting graves did not begin, of course, with the Deobandis. Al-Ghazali, too, devoted a section of *Ihya' ʿulum al-din* to the subject. See Abu Hamid Muhammad al-Ghazali, *The Remembrance of Death and the Afterlife: Kitab dhikr al-mawt wa-ma baʿdahu* (Cambridge: Islamic Texts Society, 2015), 111–20.

142. On ʿAbd al-Quddus, see Simon Digby, "'Abd al-Quddus Gangohi (1456–1537): The Personality and Attitudes of a Medieval Indian Sufi," *Medieval India: A Miscellany* 3 (1975): 1–66; and Muzaffar Alam, *The Languages of Political Islam: India, 1200–1800* (Chicago: University of Chicago Press, 2004), chap. 3.

143. Quoted in Mirathi, *Tazkirat al-Rashid*, 2:176.

144. Gangohi, *Hudud-i ikhtilaf*, 119.

145. Ibid., 120. This story is also recounted in Thanvi, *Al-Ifadat al-yawmi-yya*, statement no. 4, 1:19–20.

146. Mirathi, *Tazkirat al-Rashid*, 2:9. The same story is related in Kandhlavi, *Tarikh-i mashaikh-i Chisht*, 289.

147. Gangohi, *Fatawa-yi Rashidiyya*, 166.

148. In his response, Gangohi (or Mirathi) accidentally substituted *al-'akifin* ("those who stay there") for *al-qa'imin* ("those who stand there"). The correct phrase in Qur'an 22:26 is: "purify My House for those who walk around it, for those who *stand there* and those who bow and prostrate." It seems he may have been confused by a similar phrase in Qur'an 2:125: "purify My House for those who walk around it, for those who *stay there* and those who bow and prostrate."

149. Mirathi, *Tazkirat al-Rashid*, 1:144–46.

150. In a fatwa of December 1903, Thanvi made the same argument in response to a scholar requesting clarification on the Hadith: "If I were to order anyone to prostrate to another, I would have ordered the wife to prostrate to her husband." Thanvi has some doubts about the reliability of the Hadith, but concludes in any case that the Qur'an and Sunna overwhelmingly forbid any form of prostration from one human to another, and abrogate examples of such prostration before Islam, including even examples of such prostration in the Qur'an, as when others bow before the prophet Joseph in Qur'an 12:4 and 12:100. See Ashraf 'Ali Thanvi, *Bavadir al-navadir* (Lahore: Idara al-Islamiyya, 1985), 134–38; cf. also 400–404.

151. Underscoring how bleakly Thanvi viewed the state of Islam in his day, elsewhere he speculates: "If Muslims were asked the same question today, most would respond, 'Yes, we would prostrate before your grave.'" Thanvi, *Khutbat-i Hakim al-Ummat*, 2:253.

152. Ashraf 'Ali Thanvi, *Hifz al-iman, ma' basat al-banan wa taghayyur al-'unwan* (Deoband: Maktaba-yi Nu'maniyya, 1962), 4–7. See also Thanvi, *Al-Takashshuf*, 5:66, in which he reiterates the distinction between prostration as worship and prostration as reverence, seeing the former as clear *kufr* and *shirk* and the latter as "a grave sin and very close to *kufr*." It is worth noting that this view was not limited to the Deobandis. Ahmad Raza Khan, founder of the Barelvi movement, also condemned "reverential circumambulation" (*tawaf-i ta'zimi*) of anything other than the Ka'aba, as well as "prostrating before anything other than God." Misbahi, *Imam Ahmad Raza*, 521.

153. Thanvi, *Hifz al-iman*, 7–8.

154. Thanvi, *Islah al-rusum*, 140.

155. Thanvi, *Bihishti zewar*, 61.

156. Thanvi, *Islah al-rusum*, 139.

157. Ibid., 139–40.

158. Ibid., 141–42.

159. Ibid., 143.

160. Gangohi, *Fatawa-yi Rashidiyya*, 142.

161. Thanvi, *Islah al-rusum*, 144–45.

162. Ibid., 145.

163. Mufti Muhammad Shafi', *Ma'arif al-Qur'an* (Karachi: Idara al-Ma'arif, 1969), 1:40, 1:43–44.

164. For his education and relation to Thanvi, see Muhammad Sa'd Siddiqi's introduction to Muhammad Idris Kandhlavi, *Ma'arif al-Qur'an* (Shahdapur, Pakistan: Maktaba al-Ma'arif, n.d.), 1:3–4.

165. Ibid., 1:22. Thanvi makes a similar argument in *Bavadir al-navadir,* 82–83.

166. Arthur Buehler, *Sufi Heirs of the Prophet: The Indian Naqshbandiyya and the Rise of the Mediating Sufi Shaykh* (Columbia: University of South Carolina Press, 1998), 12.

167. For more on this history, see Joseph Kostiner, *The Making of Saudi Arabia, 1916–1936: From Chieftaincy to Monarchical State* (Oxford: Oxford University Press, 1993), esp. 100–117.

168. M. Naeem Qureshi, *Pan-Islam in British Indian Politics: A Study of the Khilafat Movement, 1918–1924* (Leiden: E.J. Brill, 1999), 400–401. For a general overview of both the Cairo and Mecca conferences, see Martin Kramer, *Islam Assembled: The Advent of the Muslim Congresses* (New York: Columbia University Press, 1986), 86–122.

169. Muhammad Anwar al-Hasan Anwar Qasimi, *Kamalat-i 'Usmani* (Multan, Pakistan: Idara-yi Ta'lifat-i Ashrafiyya, 2006), 349–50.

170. Shabbir Ahmad 'Usmani, *Anvar-i 'Usmani* (Karachi: Maktaba al-Islamiyya, n.d.), 69.

171. Qasimi, *Kamalat-i 'Usmani,* 355.

172. Quoted in ibid., 354.

173. Zaman makes this point with respect to 'Usmani's visit in *Islam in Pakistan,* 211. On the use of "Wahhabi" in polemical discourses, see Martha K. Hermansen, "Fakirs, Wahhabis and Others: Reciprocal Classifications and the Transformation of Intellectual Categories," in *Perspectives of Mutual Encounters in South Asian History 1760–1860,* ed. Jamal Malik (Leiden: E.J. Brill, 2000); and Alexander Knysh, "A Clear and Present Danger: 'Wahhabism' as a Rhetorical Foil," *Die Welt des Islams* 44, no. 1 (2004): 3–26.

174. Saharanpuri, *'Aqa'id-i 'ulama-yi Deoband,* 7–9.

175. The most prominent example of the latter, written in 1978—a very different historical and political context—is Muhammad Manzur Nu'mani, *Shaykh Muhammad ibn 'Abd al-Wahhab ke khilaf propaganda aur Hindustan ke 'ulama-yi haqq par us ke asarat* (Lucknow: Kutub Khana al-Furqan, 1978).

3. REMAKING THE PUBLIC

1. Thomas R. Metcalf and Barbara D. Metcalf, *A Concise History of Modern India,* 3rd ed. (New York: Cambridge University Press, 2012), 138.

2. Manu Goswami, *Producing India: From Colonial Economy to National Space* (Chicago: University of Chicago Press, 2004); Marian Aguiar, *Tracking Modernity: India's Railway and the Culture of Mobility* (Minneapolis: University of Minnesota Press, 2011).

3. Metcalf and Metcalf, *A Concise History of Modern India,* 95–97.

4. Atkinson, *Statistical, Descriptive and Historical Account*, 2:153.

5. Goswami, *Producing India*, 126. See also Ritika Prasad, "'Time-Sense': Railways and Temporality in Colonial India," *Modern Asian Studies* 47, no. 4 (2013): 1252–82.

6. Sanyal, *Devotional Islam and Politics in British India*, 113–16.

7. Currie, *Shrine and Cult*, 118n7.

8. Nile Green, *Terrains of Exchange: Religious Economies of Global Islam* (Oxford and New York: Oxford University Press, 2013), 188–89.

9. 'Aziz al-Hasan, *Ashraf al-savanih*, 4:355–56.

10. Mirathi, *Tazkirat al-Rashid*, 2:202.

11. Gustave Le Bon, *The Crowd: A Study of the Popular Mind* (Mineola, NY: Dover Publications, 2002), 6. See also William Mazzarella, "Myth of the Multitude, or Who's Afraid of the Crowd?," *Critical Inquiry* 36 (2010): 697–727, at 701–7. Le Bon's *La civilisation des Arabes* (1884) was translated into Urdu in 1896 and published as *Tamaddun-i 'Arab*, trans. Sayyid 'Ali Bilgrami (Sargodha: Zafar Traders, 1975), a work that both reflected and reinforced tropes of Islamic civilizational decline. It does not appear that any of Le Bon's other works were translated into Urdu. *La psychologie des foules* was translated into Arabic, however, as *Ruh al-ijtima'*, trans. Ahmad Fatih Zaghlul (Cairo: Matba'at al-Sha'b, 1909).

12. Thanvi, *Bihishti zewar*, 454.

13. Ernst and Lawrence, *Sufi Martyrs of Love*, 36.

14. Al-Ghazali, in turn, adapted this typology from Junayd.

15. Ashraf 'Ali Thanvi, *Haqq al-sama'* (Karachi: Idara-yi Ashraf al-'Ulum, 1950), 13.

16. Ibid., 15.

17. Thanvi, *Al-Kalam al-hasan*, 22.

18. Thanvi, *Haqq al-sama'*, 23.

19. Gangohi, *Fatawa-yi Rashidiyya*, 107.

20. Thanvi, *Al-Ifadat al-yawmiyya*, statement no. 379, 1:344–45. For Gangohi, too, Hallaj was excused of any wrongdoing, but his words are not meant for public consumption or debate. See Gangohi, *Fatawa-yi Rashidiyya*, 107–8. Although for Gangohi and Thanvi the theological and legal dangers of ecstatic utterances were front and center, Carl Ernst showed how the political context of Hallaj's trial and execution in 922 is more important for understanding reactions to his *shathiyat* than the legal-theological implications. Anxieties about Shi'i resistance to 'Abbasid rule were especially salient; Hallaj was accused of sympathy toward, if not collusion with, the Qarmati sect—a Nizari Isma'ili offshoot that revolted against the 'Abbasids in 899. See Carl W. Ernst, *Words of Ecstasy in Sufism* (Albany: State University of New York Press, 1985), 102–10, esp. 107–8.

21. William Mazzarella, "Affect: What Is It Good For?," in *Enchantments of Modernity: Empire, Nation, Globalization*, ed. Saurabh Dube (London, New York, and New Delhi: Routledge, 2009), 294–95.

22. Redacted versions of such communications were collected, partly under Thanvi's own supervision, and published in Ashraf 'Ali Thanvi, *Tarbiyat al-*

salik (Karachi: Dar al-Isha'at, 1982). Chapter 4 draws on this collection to illustrate points about Deobandi Sufi pedagogy.

23. The collection of Sirhindi's (d. 1624) letters, the *Maktubat-i mujaddid alf-i sani* (Delhi: Matba'-yi Murtazavi, 1873), is probably the best known of many such collections.

24. A seminal source for this dichotomy is Gabriel Tarde's 1898 essay "The Public and the Crowd," in Gabriel Tarde, *On Communication and Social Influence,* ed. Terry N. Clark. (Chicago and London: University of Chicago Press, 1969), 277–94.

25. Immanuel Kant, "An Answer to the Question: What Is Enlightenment?" in *What Is Enlightenment? Eighteenth-Century Answers and Twentieth-Century Questions,* ed. James Schmidt (Berkeley: University of California Press, 1996), 59.

26. Richard Butsch, *The Citizen Audience: Crowds, Publics, Individuals* (New York: Routledge, 2008), 15.

27. Michel Foucault, "What Is Enlightenment?" in *The Foucault Reader,* ed. Paul Rabinow (New York: Pantheon Books, 1984), 36.

28. Armando Salvatore and Dale F. Eickelman, "Muslim Publics," in *Public Islam and the Common Good,* ed. Armando Salvatore and Dale F. Eickelman (Leiden and Boston: E. J. Brill, 2006), 6.

29. On the colonial *munazara,* see Barbara Daly Metcalf, "Imagining Community: Polemical Debates in Colonial India," in *Religious Controversy in British India: Dialogues in South Asian Languages,* ed. Kenneth W. Jones (Albany: State University of New York Press, 1992); Hermansen, "Fakirs, Wahhabis and Others"; and Jamal Malik, "Encounter and Appropriation in the Context of Modern South Asian History," in *Perspectives of Mutual Encounters in South Asian History 1760–1860,* ed. Jamal Malik (Leiden: E. J. Brill, 2000).

30. Avril A. Powell, *Muslims and Missionaries in Pre-Mutiny India* (Richmond, Surrey, UK: Curzon Press, 1993), 226–62.

31. Indeed, sometimes "winning" was hardly the goal; rather, mobilizing one's own supporters was more important than debating a point with an opponent. Metcalf discusses an occasion when the Arya Samaj insisted on carrying out a "debate" with Deobandis in Sanskrit. The fact that the Deobandi *'ulama* could not speak Sanskrit was immaterial, as the Arya Samaj were interested only in firing up their own supporters in the audience. See Metcalf, "Imagining Community," 236.

32. Jesse M. Lander, *Inventing Polemic: Religion, Print and Literary Culture in Early Modern England* (Cambridge: Cambridge University Press, 2006), 11–12.

33. Lander, *Inventing Polemic,* 34. Michael Warner, *Publics and Counterpublics* (New York: Zone Books, 2004), 90–91.

34. See Tareen, "The Polemic at Shahjahanpur."

35. Mirathi, *Tazkirat al-Khalil,* 116–17. To be precise, Saharanpuri never said God did lie, or would lie, but only that he *could* lie, for to deny that possibility, in his view, was to constrain divine sovereignty, as we saw with Muhammad Isma'il.

36. Ibid., 143.

37. See, e.g., Usha Sanyal, *Ahmad Riza Khan Barelwi: In the Path of the Prophet* (Oxford: Oneworld, 2005), 102–9.

38. Ahmad Raza Khan, *Husam al-haramayn 'ala manhar al-kufr wa al-mayn* (Lahore: Maktaba-yi Nabaviyya, 1975), 20–22, 28.

39. Ibid., 32.

40. Ibid., 10.

41. Imdad Allah, *Kulliyat-i Imdadiyya,* 77.

42. Ibid., 85.

43. Thanvi, *Al-Takashshuf 'an muhimmat al-tasawwuf,* 5:43.

44. Quoted in 'Aziz al-Hasan, *Ashraf al-savanih,* 4:355–56.

45. Quoted in Muhammad ibn al-Husain al-Sulami, *Haqa'iq al-tafsir: Tafsir al-Qur'an al-'aziz* (Beirut: Dar al-Kutub al-'Ilmiyya, 2001), 1:22. See also Farhana Mayer, trans., *Spiritual Gems: The Mystical Qur'an Commentary Ascribed to Ja'far al-Sadiq* (Louisville, KY: Fons Vitae, 2011), 1. I have adjusted Mayer's translation very slightly.

46. Pernau, "From a 'Private' Public," 105–6.

47. See Pernau, *Ashraf into Middle Classes.*

48. Gangohi, *Hudud-i ikhtilaf,* 118.

49. See Youshaa Patel, "Muslim Distinction: Imitation and the Anxiety of Jewish, Christian, and Other Influences" (PhD diss., Duke University, 2012). For South Asia specifically, see Muhammad Khalid Masud, "Cosmopolitanism and Authenticity: The Doctrine of *Tashabbuh Bi'l-Kuffar* ('Imitating the Infidel') in Modern South Asian Fatwas," in *Cosmopolitanisms in Muslim Contexts: Perspectives from the Past,* ed. Derryl N. Maclean and Sikeena Karmali Ahmed (Edinburgh: Edinburgh University Press, 2012).

50. Gangohi, *Fatawa-yi Rashidiyya,* 115.

51. Ibid., 82 (emphasis added).

52. Ibid., 142–43.

53. Ibid., 69.

54. Saharanpuri, *Barahin-i qati'a,* 152. Gangohi, *Fatawa-yi Rashidiyya,* 115.

55. 'Abd al-Shakur Mirzapuri, *Tarikh-i milad* (Karachi: Dar al-Isha'at, 1978), 60–64. On Krishna's birth festival, see Denise Cush, Catherine Robinson, and Michael York, eds., *Encyclopedia of Hinduism* (London and New York: Routledge, 2008), s.v. "Janmastami," 386–87.

56. Saharanpuri was asked to clarify this point in *Al-Muhannad 'ala al-mufannad.* See Saharanpuri, *'Aqa'id-i 'ulama-yi Deoband,* 25–26.

57. Mirathi, *Tazkirat al-Rashid,* 1:185.

58. Gangohi, *Fatawa-yi Rashidiyya,* 70.

59. Mirathi, *Tazkirat al-Rashid,* 1:134.

60. Mirzapuri, *Tarikh-i milad,* 61–62.

61. Thanvi, *Anfas-i 'Isa,* 325.

62. Ashraf 'Ali Thanvi, *Hayat al-Muslimin* (Karachi: Idara al-Ma'arif, 2005), 186–87. Cited in Ingram, "Crises of the Public in Muslim India," 416.

63. Thanvi, *Imdad al-fatawa,* 4:268.

64. Thanvi, *Bavadir al-navadir,* 306.

65. Thanvi, *Bihishti zewar,* 24.

66. Ashraf 'Ali Thanvi, *Tuhfat al-'ulama* (Multan: Idara-yi Ta'lifat-i Ashrafi-yya, 1995), 1:480. See also Zaman, *Ashraf Ali Thanawi,* 20.

67. Thanvi, *Bihishti zewar,* 833–34. Quoted in Brannon D. Ingram, "The Portable Madrasa: Print, Publics and the Authority of the Deobandi 'Ulama," *Modern Asian Studies* 48, no. 4 (2014): 845–71, at 859.

68. Thanvi, *Bihishti zewar,* 23. See also Barbara Daly Metcalf, trans., *Perfecting Women: Maulana Ashraf 'Ali Thanvi's "Bihishti Zewar": A Partial Translation with Commentary* (Berkeley: University of California Press, 1990), 48.

69. Mirathi, *Tazkirat al-Rashid,* 1:117–18.

70. Ibid., 1:118.

71. Ibid., 1:120–24.

72. Ibid., 1:124.

73. Zaman suggests Thanvi may have had multiple reasons for the move from Kanpur to Thana Bhawan. In addition to noting the exchange with Gangohi, Zaman points out that Thanvi chafed at pressure from the administration of Faiz-i 'Amm to solicit donations directly, believing it beneath the dignity of the 'ulama to do so. Zaman, *Ashraf Ali Thanawi,* 18–25.

74. Thanvi, *Ta'lim al-din,* 102, in *Islahi nisab.*

75. Franz Rosenthal, *Knowledge Triumphant: The Concept of Knowledge in Medieval Islam* (Leiden and Boston: E. J. Brill, 2007), 30.

76. Thanvi, *Al-Ifadat al-yawmiyya,* statement no. 113, 6:120–1.

77. Abu Hamid Muhammad al-Ghazali, *Kitab al-'Ilm: The Book of Knowledge,* trans. Kenneth Honnerkamp (Louisville, KY: Fons Vitae, 2015), 30–35.

78. Thanvi, *Hayat al-Muslimin,* 18. Quoted in Ingram, "The Portable Madrasa," 860.

79. On print culture in nineteenth-century India generally, see Stuart Blackburn and Vasudha Dalmia, eds., *India's Literary History: Essays on the Nineteenth Century* (Delhi: Permanent Black, 2004); Abhijit Gupta and Swapan Chakravorty, eds., *Print Areas: Book History in India* (Delhi: Permanent Black, 2004); Francesca Orsini, ed., *The History of the Book in South Asia* (Farnham, UK: Ashgate, 2013); and Ulrike Stark, *An Empire of Books: The Naval Kishore Press and the Diffusion of the Printed Word in Colonial India* (Delhi: Permanent Black, 2007).

80. Farina Mir, *The Social Space of Language: Vernacular Culture in British Colonial Punjab* (Berkeley: University of California Press, 2010), 27–32.

81. C. Ryan Perkins, "From the Mehfil to the Printed Word: Public Debate and Discourse in Late Colonial India," *Indian Economic and Social History Review* 50, no. 1 (2013): 47–76, at 52.

82. Sanjay Joshi, *Fractured Modernity: Making of a Middle Class in Colonial North India* (New Delhi: Oxford University Press, 2001), 43–44.

83. Another widely read summary of belief and practice is Mufti Muhammad Kifayat Allah's *Ta'lim al-Islam* (Delhi: Kutub Khana-yi Aziziyya, n.d.). This is used in primary school–level madrasas. Marieke Winkelmann, *From Behind the Curtain: A Study of a Girls' Madrasa in India* (Amsterdam: Amsterdam University Press, 2005), 141.

84. Thanvi, *Bihishti zewar,* 54.

85. Classical sources define the Followers (*ta'biun*) as anyone who saw a Companion (*sahabi*), was a Sunni Muslim, and died a Sunni. The Followers of the Followers (*tabi' al-ta'biyin*), similarly, include anyone who saw one of the Followers, was a Sunni, and died a Sunni. See *Encyclopaedia of Islam*, s.v. "Tabi'un."

86. Kifayat Allah, *Ta'lim al-Islam*, 4:22–23.

87. Thanvi, *Al-Ifadat al-yawmiyya*, statement no. 71, 8:79–81; statement no. 426, 8:311.

88. Thanvi, *Hayat al-Muslimin*, 20–22. Quoted in Ingram, "The Portable Madrasa," 860–61.

· 89. Robinson, *Islam and Muslim History*, 77.

90. Thanvi, *Bavadir al-navadir*, 333–34.

91. See Mohammad Hashim Kamali, *Principles of Islamic Jurisprudence*, 3rd ed. (Cambridge: Islamic Texts Society, 2003), 46–51.

92. A. Kevin Reinhart, "When Women Went to Mosques: Al-Aydini on the Duration of Assessments," in *Islamic Legal Interpretation: Muftis and Their Fatwas*, ed. Brinkley Messick, David S. Powers, and Muhammad Khalid Masud (Cambridge, MA: Harvard University Press, 1996), 120.

93. Ashraf 'Ali Thanvi, *Fiqh-i Hanafi ke usul o zavabit,* ed. Muhammad Zaid Mazahir Nadvi (Karachi: Zam Zam Publishers, 2003), 43–44. We now know, of course, the extent to which *ijtihad* continued in practice long after it was deemed to have ended in theory, most notably through Wael B. Hallaq, "Was the Gate of Ijtihad Closed?," *International Journal of Middle Eastern Studies* 16 (1984): 3–41.

94. Thanvi, *Fiqh-i Hanafi*, 44–45.

95. Ibid., 46, and Thanvi, *Al-Ifadat al-yawmiyya,* statement no. 113, 6:120.

96. Thanvi, *Fiqh-i Hanafi*, 45.

97. Fareeha Khan, "Traditionalist Approaches to *Shari'at* Reform: Mawlana Ashraf 'Ali Thanawi's Fatwa on Women's Right to Divorce" (PhD diss., University of Michigan, 2008), 69–73.

98. Ashraf 'Ali Thanvi, *Al-Masalih al-'aqliyya li-l ahkam al-naqliyya* (Lahore: Kutub Khana-yi Jamili, 1964), 3:14–15.

99. Zaman, *Ashraf 'Ali Thanawi*, 41–42.

100. Thanvi, *Al-Masalih al-'aqliyya*, 3:78.

101. Ibid., 3:18, 3:20.

102. Joel Blecher, *Said the Prophet of God: Hadith Commentary across a Millennium* (Oakland: University of California Press, 2017), 156.

4. REMAKING THE SELF

1. Sara Sviri, "The Self and Its Transformation in Sufism with Special Reference to Early Literature," in *Self and Self-Transformation in the History of Religions*, ed. David Shulman and Guy G. Stromsa (New York: Oxford University Press, 2002), 196.

2. Omnia El Shakry, *The Arabic Freud: Psychoanalysis and Islam in Modern Egypt* (Princeton, NJ: Princeton University Press, 2017), 46–48.

3. Kant, "What Is Enlightenment?," 58.

4. Gerald Dworkin, *The Theory and Practice of Autonomy* (Cambridge: Cambridge University Press, 1998), 12–13.

5. J. Barton Scott, *Spiritual Despots: Modern Hinduism and the Genealogies of Self-Rule* (Chicago and London: University of Chicago Press, 2016), 11–12.

6. Ibid., 16, 20.

7. Michel Foucault, *The History of Sexuality*, vol. 3, *The Care of the Self* (New York: Vintage Books, 1986), 41.

8. Pierre Hadot, *Philosophy as a Way of Life: Spiritual Exercises from Socrates to Foucault* (Oxford: Blackwell, 1995), 82–89.

9. Sajjad H. Rizvi, "Philosophy as a Way of Life in the World of Islam: Applying Hadot to the Study of Mulla Sadra Shirazi (d. 1635)," *Bulletin of SOAS* 75, no. 1 (2012): 33–45, at 39.

10. Barbara Daly Metcalf, " 'Remaking Ourselves': Islamic Self-Fashioning in a Global Movement of Spiritual Renewal," in *Accounting for Fundamentalisms: The Dynamic Character of Movements*, ed. Martin E. Marty and R. Scott Appleby (Chicago and London: University of Chicago Press, 1994), 710–11.

11. Annemarie Schimmel, *Deciphering the Signs of God: A Phenomenological Approach to Islam* (Albany: State University of New York Press, 1994), 90.

12. Paulo G. Pinto, "The Limits of the Public: Sufism and the Religious Debate in Syria," in *Public Islam and the Common Good,* ed. Armando Salvatore and Dale F. Eickelman (Leiden: E. J. Brill, 2004), 186.

13. Zafar Ahmad 'Usmani, *I'la al-sunan* (Dar al-Fikr, 2001), 8827.

14. Dimashqi, *Imdad al-suluk,* 155.

15. This statement is found in multiple texts, including Mirathi, *Tazkirat al-Rashid,* 2:11–12; Muhammad Zakariyya Kandhlavi's introduction to Dimashqi, *Imdad al-Suluk,* 47; and Kandhlavi, *Tarikh-i mashaikh-i Chisht,* 292–93 (emphasis added).

16. Abul Qasim al-Qushayri, *Sufi Book of Spiritual Ascent,* trans. Rabia Harris (Chicago: Kazi Publications, 1997), 280.

17. Ahmed, *What Is Islam?,* 454.

18. Gangohi, *Fatawa-yi Rashidiyya,* 216.

19. Mirathi, *Tazkirat al-Khalil,* 54 (emphasis added).

20. An excellent translation of this text is Ashraf Ali Thanawi, *A Sufi Study of Hadith,* trans. Yusuf Talal Delorenzo (London: Turath Publishing, 2010). Delorenzo notes on p. 19 that the selection of Hadiths follows the order of Hadiths in an earlier compilation, Muhammad al-Shaybani's *Taysir al-wusul ila jami' al-usul.*

21. Thanvi, *Al-Takashshuf,* 5:1–2 (emphasis added).

22. Ghazali, *Tabligh-i din,* 165.

23. Margrit Pernau, "Male Anger and Female Malice: Emotions in Indo-Muslim Advice Literature," *History Compass* 10, no. 2 (2012): 119–28, at 123.

24. Ashraf 'Ali Thanvi, *Ashraf al-tariqat fi-l shari'at wa-l haqiqat, al-ma'ruf bih shari'at aur tariqat,* ed. Muhammad Hasan (Delhi: New Taj Office, 1964), 25.

25. Thanvi, *Al-Ifadat al-yawmiyya,* statement no. 274, 6:247–48.

26. Thanvi, *Ashraf al-tariqat,* 25–26.

27. Thanvi, *Bid'a ki haqiqat,* 38.

28. Dimashqi, *Imdad al-suluk,* 56.

29. Mirathi, *Tazkirat al-Rashid*, 2:84–85.

30. He made a special exception for Masihullah Khan Sherwani, granting him *bai'at* through written correspondence in 1931 while he was still at student at the Dar al-'Ulum Deoband. Masihullah Khan would frequently visit Thana Bhawan to sit with Thanvi during his breaks at the madrasa. Thanvi later considered Masihullah Khan among his closest disciples. See Rashid Ahmad Mewati Miftahi, *Hayat-i Masih al-Ummat* (Faridabad: Idara-yi Ta'lifat-i Masih al-Ummat, 1995), 82–85. Khan was instrumental in the spread of the Deoband movement to South Africa, as we will see in subsequent chapters.

31. Nu'mani, *Din o shari'at*, 226 (emphasis added).

32. Kandhlavi, *Shari'at o tariqat ka talazum*, 101.

33. Mirathi, *Tazkirat al-Khalil*, 72.

34. George Makdisi, *The Rise of Colleges: Institutions of Learning in Islam and the West* (Edinburgh: Edinburgh University Press, 1981), 128–29.

35. Buehler, *Sufi Heirs of the Prophets*, 16–17, 84–85.

36. Gangohi, *Makatib-i Rashidiyya*, 108–9. The letter is undated.

37. Zuhur al-Hasan, introduction to Ashraf 'Ali Thanvi, *Arvah-i salasa al-ma'ruf bih hikayat-i awliya'* (Karachi: Dar al-Isha'at, 1976), 9–11.

38. Buehler, *Sufi Heirs of the Prophet*, 117–18.

39. Rüdiger Seesemann, *The Divine Flood: Ibrahim Niasse and the Roots of a Twentieth-Century Sufi Revival* (Oxford: Oxford University Press, 2011), 42–43. See also Seesemann's excellent discussion of the role of Ahmad al-Tijani (d. 1815) as a conduit of *fayd* for the Tijaniyya (pp. 42–47).

40. Gangohi, *Fatawa-yi Rashidiyya*, 104.

41. Thanvi, *Al-Takashshuf*, 5:30–31.

42. Thanvi, *Al-Ifadat al-yawmiyya*, statement no. 426, 2:285.

43. Thanvi, *Al-Takashshuf*, 5:1–2.

44. Thanvi, *Tashil-i qasd al-sabil*, 13.

45. Thanvi, *Anfas-i 'Isa*, 61–62 (emphasis added).

46. 'Aziz al-Hasan, *Ashraf al-savanih*, 2:245.

47. Thanvi, *Tarbiyat al-salik*, 38.

48. Mirathi, *Tazkirat al-Khalil*, 368.

49. Mirathi, *Tazkirat al-Rashid*, 2:98.

50. Qazi Sanaullah Panipati, *Tuhfat al-salikin, tarjama irshad al-talibin* (Allahabad: Maktaba-yi Jami wa Ikhwanihi, 1954), 17–23.

51. Thanvi, *Tarbiyat al-salik*, 1:45–46.

52. Thanvi, *Bihishti zewar*, 541–53 (emphasis added).

53. Masihullah Khan, *Shari'at o tasawwuf: Fan-i tasawwuf ki mukammal o mudallal-i kitab* (Multan, Pakistan: Idara-yi Ta'lifat-i Ashrafiyya, 1996), 17–18.

54. Thanvi, *Tashil-i qasd al-sabil*, 7–10; Thanvi, *Al-Takashshuf*, 5:61.

55. Thanvi, *Al-Takashshuf*, 5:95.

56. 'Aziz al-Hasan, *Ashraf al-savanih*, 3:154–55.

57. Shafi', *Dil ki dunya*, 59.

58. Thanvi, *Al-Ifadat al-yawmiyya*, statement no. 86, 1:95–96

59. Thanvi, *Tashil-i qasd al-sabil*, 14.

60. Ibid., 17.

61. Ibid., 17–30.

62. Ghazali, *Tabligh-i din,* 75–176.

63. Ibid., 177–266. Curiously, *Tabligh-i din* is not quite a complete Urdu translation of al-Ghazali's *Al-Arba'in fi usul al-din* (Forty principles of the religion): it omits the first section of *Al-Arba'in,* which is primarily about God's knowledge and characteristics.

64. Thanvi, *Tashil-i qasd al-sabil,* 34–35. This is more than a little ironic, given that Rumi is now one of the world's best-selling poets. One can only wonder what Thanvi would have made of his popularity.

65. Thanvi, *Al-Takashshuf,* 5:82.

66. Jamal J. Elias, *The Throne Carrier of God: The Life and Thought of 'Alā' ad-dawla as-Simnānī* (Albany: State University of New York Press, 1995), 104–5.

67. 'Abd al-Haq et al., *Fatawa-yi Haqqaniyya,* 2:255.

68. See Bryan Turner, *Weber and Islam* (London: Routledge and Kegan, 1974), 56–64.

69. Vincent Cornell, *Realm of the Saint: Power and Authority in Moroccan Sufism* (Austin: University of Texas Press, 1998), xxix.

70. Scott Kugle, *Rebel between Spirit and Law: Ahmad Zarruq, Sainthood, and Authority in Islam* (Bloomington and Indianapolis: Indiana University Press, 2006), 27–41.

71. Abu Bakr Muhammad al-Kalabadhi, *Al-Ta'arruf li-madhdhab ahl al-tasawwuf* (Cairo: Maktaba al-Kulliyat al-Azhariyya, 1969), 90–91 (emphasis added). For an English translation, see Abu Bakr Muhammad al-Kalabadhi, *The Doctrine of the Sufis,* trans. A. J. Arberry (Cambridge: Cambridge University Press, 1977).

72. 'Abd al-Rahman Jami, *Nafahat al-uns min hadrat al-quds* (Cairo: Al-Azhar al-Sharif, 1989), 9.

73. Green, *Making Space,* 46.

74. Ahmad Sirhindi, *Maktubat-i Imam Rabbani* (Delhi: Matba'-yi Murtazavi, 1873), 2:101.

75. Arthur F. Buehler, *Revealed Grace: The Juristic Sufism of Ahmad Sirhindi (1564–1625)* (Louisville, KY: Fons Vitae, 2012), 90–93. Cf. Buehler, *Sufi Heirs of the Prophet,* 122–23.

76. Qutb al-Din Dimashqi (d. 1378) was a Sufi about whom we know very little. Gangohi translated select passages of Dimashqi's *Risala* from Arabic to Persian in an unpublished manuscript he called *Imdad al-suluk* (Help along the Sufi path), in honor of his master Hajji Imdad Allah. His biographer, 'Ashiq Ilahi Mirathi, then translated Gangohi's manuscript from Persian to Urdu and published it in 1914. It seems the *Risala* originally made its way to South Asia by way of the Suhrawardi Sufi master Hazrat Jalaluddin Bukhari (d. 1384), popularly known as "Jahangasht" ("World Traveler"), who taught the text to his disciples and claimed to have received a copy directly from Dimashqi. See Amina Steinfels, *Knowledge before Action: Islamic Learning and Sufi Practice in the Life of Sayyid Jalal al-din Bukhari Makhdum-i Jahaniyan* (Columbia: University of South Carolina Press, 2012), 48, 100.

77. Dimashqi, *Imdad al-suluk,* 196–97.

78. Diego R. Sarrio, "Spiritual Anti-Elitism: Ibn Taymiyya's Doctrine of Sainthood (*walaya*)," *Islam and Christian-Muslim Relations* 22, no. 3 (2011): 275–91, at 278.

79. Ahmad ibn Taymiyya, *Amrad al-qulub wa shifa'uha: Yaliha al-tuhfa al-'Iraqiyya fi al-a'mal al-qalbiyya* (Cairo: Al-Matba'at al-Salafiyya wa Makta-batuha, 1966/67), 38. Kandhlavi discusses this passage in *Shari'at o tariqat ka talazum*, 110–11. Cf. a similar discussion from a different text by Ibn Taymiyya in Sarrio, "Spiritual Anti-Elitism," 279.

80. Thanvi, *Ashraf al-tariqat*, 26–27 (emphasis added).

81. Thanvi, *Bihishti zewar*, 53–54.

82. Kifayat Allah, *Ta'lim al-Islam*, 3:17–18.

83. Muhammad Manzur Nu'mani, *Islam kya hai* (Lucknow: Kakori Offset Press, 2008), 11.

84. Hakim Muhammad Akhtar, *Pardes men tazkirah-yi vatan, ya'ni dunya ke pardes men akhirat ke vatan-i asli ka tazkira* (Karachi: Kutub Khana-yi Maz-hari, 2006), 55–56 (emphasis added).

85. Kelly Pemberton, "Islamic and Islamicizing Discourses: Ritual Perform-ance, Didactic Texts, and the Reformist Challenge in the South Asian Sufi Milieu," *Annual of Urdu Studies* 17 (2002): 55–83, at 72.

5. WHAT DOES A TRADITION FEEL LIKE?

1. Schmitt, *The Nomos of the Earth*, 69–71. On various interpretations and applications of this concept, see Stephen Legg, ed., *Spatiality, Sovereignty and Carl Schmitt* (London and New York: Routledge, 2011).

2. Arendt, too, recognized the relationship between the production of space and the production of normativity implicit in the etymology of *nomos*. Hannah Arendt, *The Human Condition*, 2nd ed. (Chicago: University of Chicago Press, 1998), 63n62.

3. Schmitt, *The Nomos of the Earth*, 70–71 (emphasis in original).

4. Thanvi, *Al-Ifadat al-yawmiyya*, statement no. 12, 5:22.

5. See, e.g., Alam, *Inside a Madrasa*, 191–97.

6. Ghulam Nabi Qasimi, *Hayat-i Tayyib* (Deoband: Hujjat al-Islam Acad-emy, 2014), 1:81–83.

7. Ibid., 1:112–13.

8. Ebrahim Moosa, "History and Normativity in Traditional Indian Muslim Thought: Reading Shari'a in the Hermeneutics of Qari Muhammad Tayyab (d. 1983)," in *Rethinking Islamic Studies: From Orientalism to Cosmopolitanism*, ed. Carl W. Ernst and Richard C. Martin (Columbia: University of South Caro-lina Press, 2010), 290–91.

9. See chap. 3, p. 100.

10. *Al-Muhannad 'ala al-mufannad*, which we have encountered already, was subsequently published in Urdu as *'Aqa'id-i 'ulama-yi Deoband* (The beliefs of the Deobandi scholars). The text succinctly summarizes "Deobandi" perspectives on a range of controversial issues: whether the Deobandis believe it commendable to visit the Prophet Muhammad's grave (they do, according to Saharanpuri), whether intercession (*tawassul*) through the Prophet or saints is

permissible (it is, so long as one understands the power to intercede comes from God), whether the Prophet is living in his grave (he is), whether it is permissible to send salutations to the Prophet (it is), whether any part of creation is better than the Prophet (it is not), and whether the Prophet is the seal of the Prophets (he is), among other topics.

11. Tim Winter, introduction to *Cambridge Companion to Classical Islamic Theology*, ed. Tim Winter (Cambridge: Cambridge University Press, 2008), 8–9. To take another example, 'Abd al-Rahman Chishti (d. 1683) taught that the Sufis best represented the "moderation" (*i'tidal*) of the Ahl-i Sunna wa Jama'a. See Muzaffar Alam, "The Debate Within: A Sufi Critique of Religious Law, *Tasawwuf*, and Politics in Mughal India," *South Asian History and Culture* 2, no. 2 (2011): 138–59, at 142.

12. Qari Muhammad Tayyib, *Maslak-i 'ulama-yi Deoband* (Lahore: Aziz Publications, 1975), 15–16.

13. Ibid., 30.

14. Ibid., 29.

15. Ibid., 17.

16. Qari Muhammad Tayyib, *'Ulama-yi Deoband ka dini rukh aur maslaki mizaj* (Deoband: Maktaba-yi Millat, n.d.), 109.

17. See Muhammad Taqi 'Usmani, preface to Tayyib, *'Ulama-yi Deoband*, 11.

18. Tayyib, *'Ulama-yi Deoband*, 18.

19. M.T. 'Usmani, preface to Tayyib, *'Ulama-yi Deoband*, 4–5 (emphasis added).

20. Ibid., 7–9.

21. Thanvi, *Tuhfat al-'ulama*, 1:106.

22. J.M.S. Baljon, *Religion and Thought of Shah Wali Allah, 1703–1762* (Leiden: E.J. Brill, 1986), 4–5. Madrasa Rahimiyya assigned students to read Suhrawardi's (d. 1234) *Awarif al-ma'arif* and multiple works by Jami (d. 1492), including his *Sharh al-ruba'iyyat*, his *Naqd al-nusus* (a commentary on the *Nusus* of Qunawi, one of Ibn 'Arabi's students), and his commentary on the *Lama'at* of Iraqi (d. 1289). See Ghulam Sufi, *Al-Minhaj: Being the Evolution of Curriculum in the Muslim Educational Institutions of India* (Delhi: Idarah-i Adabiyat-i Dihli, 1977), 69–70. In Saiyid Athar Abbas Rizvi's assessment, Mulla Nizam al-Din "intended to keep the *madrasa* (seminary) separate from the *khanqah* (*sufi* monastery)," leaving the *'ulama* "free to choose a worldly career and to obtain training in a *khanqah* later if they so desired." Rizvi, *Shah Wali Allah and His Times* (Canberra: Ma'rifat Publishing House, 1980), 392.

23. Robinson, *The 'Ulama of Farangi Mahall*, 53–54. He also notes that "the lack of books on Sufism certainly did not mean any opposition on the part of Mulla Nizam al-Din and his family to the spiritual dimensions of Islam. . . . [T]hey were, almost without exception, devout Sufis and no student could have sat at their feet without being aware of this."

24. Muhammad Taqi 'Usmani, *Hamara ta'limi nizam* (Deoband: Maktaba-yi Dar al-'Ulum, 1998), 99.

25. Ibid., 94–95.

26. Ibid., 95.

27. Shafi', *Dil ki dunya*, 22.

28. Ibid., 23–24.

29. Muhammad Taqi 'Usmani, *Akabir-i Deoband kya the* (Karachi: Idara al-Ma'arif, 1994), 87.

30. Tayyib, introduction to Rizvi, *Tarikh-i Dar al-'Ulum Deoband,* 1:12.

31. Muhammad Yusuf Ludhianvi, *Ikhtilaf-i ummat aur sirat al-mustaqim* (Karachi: Maktaba-yi Ludhianvi, 1995), 38.

32. Quoted in Anton Blok, "The Narcissism of Minor Differences," *European Journal of Social Theory* 1, no. 1 (1998): 33–56, at 38.

33. Constance Furey, "Body, Society and Subjectivity in Religious Studies," *Journal of the American Academy of Religion* 80, no. 1 (2012): 7–33, at 9.

34. Abu al-Hasan 'Ali Nadvi, *Hazrat Maulana Muhammad Ilyas aur un ki dini da'wat* (Karachi: Majlis-i Nashriyat-i Islam, n.d.), 83.

35. Yoginder Sikand, *The Origins and Development of the Tablighi Jama'at (1920–2000): A Cross-Country Comparative Study* (Hyderabad: Orient Longman, 2002), 124–27.

36. Mirathi, *Tazkirat al-Khalil,* 429.

37. Muhammad 'Ashiq Ilahi, *Che batein* (Karachi: Qadimi Kutub Khana, n.d.), 3–5.

38. Shafiq Ahmad A'zami, *Makatib-i Tayyib* (Deoband: Maktaba-yi Nu'maniyya, 1972), 93.

39. Muhammad Manzur Nu'mani, *Malfuzat-i Hazrat Maulana Muhammad Ilyas* (Lucknow: Kutub Khana al-Furqan, n.d.), 137–38.

40. Ibid., 138.

41. Ibid., 138–39.

42. Ibid., 54.

43. J. Michelle Molina, *To Overcome Oneself: The Jesuit Ethic and Spirit of Global Expansion, 1520–1767* (Berkeley: University of California Press, 2013), 72.

44. Muhammad Faruq, *Hayat-i Mahmud: Savanih Faqih al-Ummat Mufti Mahmud Hasan Gangohi* (Meerut, India: Maktaba-yi Mahmudiyya, 1998), 156–60; S'ad Sanaullah Shuja'abadi, *'Ulama-yi Deoband ke akhiri lamahat* (Delhi: Farid Book Depot, 2006), 281.

45. Faruq, *Afriqah aur khidmat-i Faqih al-Ummat,* 235; Shuja'abadi, *'Ulama-yi Deoband,* 283.

46. Faruq, *Hayat-i Mahmud,* 414–45.

47. Faruq, *Afriqah aur khidmat-i Faqih al-Ummat,* 234–35.

48. Ibid., 252.

49. These have included Ebrahim Saliji of Madrasa Ta'lim al-Din in Isipingo Park, near Durban; Ebrahim Desai of Madrasa In'aamiyya in Camperdown; Fazlur Rahman Azmi of the Dar al-'Ulum Azaadville; and Yunus Patel of Madrasa Sawlehaat in Durban.

50. Fazlur Rahman Azmi, *Hazrat Mufti Mahmud Hasan Sahib Gangohi aur Jama'at-i Tabligh* (Karachi: Zam Publishers, 2003), 16.

51. Ibid., 16. The timing of the speech would suggest that it may be the one subsequently published as *Islah-i nafs aur Tablighi Jama'at,* discussed below in this chapter.

52. Azmi, *Hazrat Mufti Mahmud Hasan Sahib Gangohi,* 31.

53. Ibid., 48.

54. Nu'mani, *Malfuzat-i Hazrat Maulana Muhammad Ilyas,* 55.

55. Quoted in Ilahi, *Che Batein,* 82.

56. Nu'mani, *Malfuzat-i Hazrat Maulana Muhammad Ilyas,* 173.

57. Ibid., 31.

58. Muhammad Ilyas, *A Call to Muslims* (New Delhi: Idara Isha'at-i Diniyat, n.d.), 3.

59. Nu'mani, *Malfuzat-i Hazrat Maulana Muhammad Ilyas,* 57.

60. Miftahi, *Hayat-i Masih al-Ummat,* 67.

61. Muhammad Khalid Masud, introduction to *Travellers in Faith: Studies of the Tablighi Jama'at as a Transnational Movement for Faith Renewal,* ed. Muhammad Khalid Masud (Leiden: E.J. Brill, 2000), liv–lv.

62. Rizvi, *Tarikh-i Dar al-'Ulum Deoband,* 1:225–26.

63. Muhammad Khalid Masud, "Ideology and Legitimacy," in *Travellers in Faith: Studies of the Tablighi Jama'at as a Transnational Movement for Faith Renewal,* ed. Muhammad Khalid Masud (Leiden: E.J. Brill, 2000), 100.

64. Masud, "Ideology and Legitimacy," 100.

65. 'Aziz al-Hasan, *Ashraf al-savanih,* 3:233.

66. Thanvi, *Khutbat-i Hakim al-Ummat,* 13:162–63.

67. Ibid., 138.

68. Ibid., 164.

69. Ibid., 47–48.

70. Ibid., 16, 24–26.

71. Ibid., 47–50.

72. Thanvi, *Ashraf al-tariqat,* 98–102.

73. Jonathan P. Berkey, *Popular Preaching and Religious Authority in the Medieval Islamic Near East* (Seattle and London: University of Washington Press, 2001), 76–77.

74. Gangohi, *Hudud-i ikhtilaf,* 211.

75. The publication does not provide the date of the speech, but Tayyib refers to the Tablighi Jama'at being active for forty years at the time of the speech. The publication also does not supply the place where the speech was given or any other context; however, the timing would suggest it was a speech at a Tablighi gathering (*ijtima'*) in Saharanpur at which Tayyib had been invited to speak by Mahmud Hasan Gangohi.

76. Qari Muhammad Tayyib, *Islah-i nafs aur Tablighi Jama'at* (Lahore: 'Umar Publications, n.d.), 12–13.

77. Ibid., 12–20.

78. Ibid., 21.

79. Ibid., 24–25.

80. Ibid., 25.

6. HOW A TRADITION TRAVELS

1. See the discussion in chap. 5, p. 157.

2. Kerry Ward, *Networks of Empire: Forced Migration in the Dutch East India Company* (Cambridge: Cambridge University Press, 2009), esp. 127–78.

3. Ebrahim Moosa, "Islam in South Africa," in *Living Faiths in South Africa,* ed. Martin Prozesky and John de Gruchy (New York: St. Martin's Press, 1995), 130.

4. Suleman Dangor, *A Critical Biography of Shaykh Yusuf* (Durban: Centre for Research in Islamic Studies, 1983). Shaykh Yusuf's gravesite at Faure, near Cape Town, is the most important grave on the Cape *kramat* (Sufi shrine) circuit, built in its present form by a Cape Muslim philanthropist, Hajji Suleiman Shah Mohammed, in 1927. See Achmat Davids, *The Mosques of the Bo-Kaap: A Social History of Islam at the Cape* (Cape Town: South African Institute of Arabic and Islamic Research, 1980), 144.

5. Robert C. Shell, "Madrasahs and Moravians: Muslim Educational Institutions in the Cape Colony, 1792–1910," *New Contree* 51 (2006): 101–13.

6. Martin Legassick and Robert Ross, "From Slave Economy to Settler Capitalism: The Cape Colony and Its Extensions, 1800–1854," in *The Cambridge History of South Africa,* vol. 1, ed. Carolyn Hamilton, Bernard K. Mbenga, and Robert Ross (Cambridge: Cambridge University Press, 2010), 262.

7. Achmat Davids, *The History of the Tana Baru* (Cape Town: Committee for the Preservation of the Tana Baru, 1985).

8. Ebrahim Mahida, *History of Muslims in South Africa: A Chronology* (Durban: Arabic Study Circle, 1993), 18.

9. John Edwin Mason, "'A Faith for Ourselves': Slavery, Sufism, and Conversion to Islam at the Cape," *South African Historical Journal* 46 (2002): 3–24. See also Robert C. Shell, "Rites and Rebellion: Islamic Conversion at the Cape, 1808 to 1915," *Studies in the History of Cape Town* 5 (1984): 1–46.

10. Achmat Davids, "Practice of Moulood Has Deep Roots in the Cape," *Muslim Views,* June 1998, 10.

11. These clubs have distinctive names (e.g., the Red Crescents, Ubuntu, Summer Roses, White Water Lillies) and are usually based in individual neighborhoods. "Moulood Jamaahs 2002," *Boorhaanul Islam,* March–June 2002, 64–69. See also Yusuf da Costa and Achmat Davids, *Pages from Cape Muslim History* (Cape Town: Naqshbandi-Muhammadi South Africa, 1994), 140.

12. Davids, *The Mosques of the Bo-Kaap,* 25.

13. K. M. Jeffreys, "The Malay Tombs of the Holy Circle," *Cape Naturalist,* 5 June 1938.

14. "Faure Karamat Hosts Successful Easter Festival," *Al-Qalam,* May 2001, 5.

15. "Committee to Care for 'Kramats,'" *Muslim News,* 3 September 1982, 11. The society was established after the retirement of Shaikh Kaderi of Kensington, Cape Town, who had personally cared for the shrines of 'Abd al-Rahman Matura on Robben Island.

16. This remains a contested term. See Shamil Jeppie, "Reclassifications: Coloured, Malay, Muslim," in *Coloured by History, Shaped by Place: New Perspectives on Coloured identities in Cape Town,* ed. Zimitri Erasmus (Colorado Springs: International Academic Publishers, 2001), as well as his *I. D. du Plessis and the "Re-Invention" of the "Malay," c. 1935–1952* (Cape Town: Centre for African Studies, 1988).

17. On British efforts to recruit Indians to work in Natal, see Thomas R. Metcalf, *Imperial Connections: India in the Indian Ocean Arena, 1860–1920* (Berkeley: University of California Press, 2007), chap. 5.

18. On Muslims in modern Indian Ocean history, see James L. Gelvin and Nile Green, eds., *Global Muslims in the Age of Steam and Print* (Berkeley and Los Angeles: University of California Press, 2014); Edward Simpson and Kai Kresse, "Cosmopolitanism Contested: Anthropology and History in the Western Indian Ocean," in *Struggling with History: Islam and Cosmopolitanism in the Western Indian Ocean*, eds. Edward Simpson and Kai Kresse (New York: Columbia University Press, 2008); and Scott S. Reese, *Imperial Muslims: Islam, Community and Authority in the Indian Ocean, 1839–1937* (Edinburgh: Edinburgh University Press, 2018).

19. T.R. Metcalf, *Imperial Connections*, 1.

20. Surendra Bhana and Joy B. Brain, *Setting Down Roots: Indian Migrants in South Africa, 1860–1911* (Johannesburg: Witwaterstrand University Press, 1990), 11–15.

21. Goolam H. Vahed, "A Sufi Saint's Day in South Africa: The Legend of Badsha Peer," *South African Historical Journal* 49 (2003): 96–122, at 98–99.

22. Ibid., 100–101. See also Nile Green, "Islam for the Indentured Servant: A Muslim Missionary in Colonial South Africa," *Bulletin of the School of Oriental and African Studies* 71, no. 3 (2008): 529–53.

23. Abdulkader Tayob, *Islamic Resurgence in South Africa: The Muslim Youth Movement* (Cape Town: University of Cape Town Press, 1995), 55.

24. Goolam H. Vahed, "Mosques, Mawlanas and Muharram: Indian Islam in Colonial Natal, 1860–1910," in *Journal of Religion in Africa*, 31, no. 3 (2002): 305–35, at 314.

25. Tayob, *Islamic Resurgence in South Africa*, 58.

26. See Vahed, "Mosques, Mawlanas and Muharram," 316; and Goolam H. Vahed, "An 'Imagined Community' in Diaspora: Gujaratis in South Africa," *South Asian History and Culture* 1, no. 4 (October 2010): 615–29.

27. Vahed, "Mosques, Mawlanas and Muharram," 317.

28. Quoted in ibid.

29. Abdulkader Tayob, "Race, Ideology and Islam in Contemporary South Africa," in *Islam in World Cultures: Comparative Perspectives*, ed. R. Michael Feener (Santa Barbara, CA: ABC-CLIO, 2004), 258–59.

30. See Surendra Bhana and Goolam H. Vahed, *The Making of a Political Reformer: Gandhi in South Africa, 1893–1914* (New Delhi: Manohar, 2005).

31. Rehana Ebr.-Vally, *Kala Pani: Caste and Colour in South Africa* (Colorado Springs: International Academic Publishers, 2001), 83.

32. Tayob, *Islamic Resurgence in South Africa*, 57. Tayob does not indicate whether this mosque was Surti, Memon, neither, or a combination thereof. I have been unable to find this information elsewhere.

33. Ibid., 57–58.

34. For a portrait of several Muslim scholars' movements through these networks, focusing on movement between Ottoman and British domains, see

Seema Alavi, *Muslim Cosmopolitanism in the Age of Empire* (Cambridge, MA: Harvard University Press, 2015).

35. These would have been relatively small, local schools providing basic Islamic education to local populations rather than training *'ulama*. There were no Dar al-'Ulums in South Africa at this point. Students who wanted to become *'ulama* had to pursue this abroad.

36. *Al-Qasim* 2, no. 4 (1911): 32.

37. Tayob, *Islamic Resurgence in South Africa*, 65.

38. Charl Le Roux, "Die Hanafitiese Ulama: Hulle Rol in Suid-Afrikaanse Konteks" (MA thesis, Rand Afrikaans University, 1978), 61–62.

39. Rizvi, *Tarikh-i Dar al-'Ulum Deoband*, 2:152–53.

40. Faruq, *Afriqah aur khidmat-i Faqih al-Ummat*, 258.

41. Anzar Shah Ma'sudi, *Naqsh-i davam* (Deoband: Shah Book Depot, n.d.), 42–47.

42. Zaman, *The Ulama in Contemporary Islam*, 52–53.

43. Especially Kandhlavi's work anthologized in the enormously influential *Faza'il-i a'mal*, among the most central texts for the Tablighi Jama'at. Also occasionally called the *Tablighi nisab*, this collection features Kandhlavi's reflections on pious and edifying tales from the Companions of the Prophet as well as "virtues" (*faza'il*) of the Qur'an, prayer, *zikr*, *tabligh*, and fasting during Ramadan. The collection also features Ihtisham al-Hasan Kandhlavi's essay "Muslim Degeneration and Its Only Remedy" and 'Ashiq Ilahi's "Six Points." The Waterval Islamic Institute's version is now in its seventh printing, testifying to its popularity in South Africa: *Faza'il-e-A'maal* (Johannesburg: Waterval Islamic Institute, 2000).

44. These madrasas are not Dar al-'Ulums, meaning they were not equipped to train students to become *'ulama*. Until 1973, with the opening of the Dar al-'Ulum Newcastle, South Africans had to go abroad to become *'ulama*. Charl Le Roux's 1978 study of South African *'ulama* lists sixty-three of these smaller madrasas that affiliated with the Jamiatul Ulama in the Transvaal region. See Le Roux, "Die Hanafitiese Ulama," app. 2.

45. A handwritten letter from the Jamiatul Ulama, dated 20 January 1976, discusses the introduction of the *Tablighi nisab* into its affiliated madrasas. Le Roux, "Die Hanafitiese Ulama," app. 3. On the *Tablighi nisab*, see note oo above.

46. "Death of Prominent Moulana," *Muslim News*, 3 May 1963.

47. Moulana I. E. Akoo, *Biography of the Founder of Darul Uloom Newcastle: Moulana Cassim Mohamed Sema Saheb* (Newcastle: Darul Uloom Newcastle, 2007), 24.

48. The Jamiatul Ulama Natal is now known as the Jamiatul Ulama KwaZulu Natal (KZN). See www.jamiat.org.za.

49. Akoo, *Darul Uloom Newcastle*, 42.

50. Green, "Islam for the Indentured Indian," 543.

51. Ebrahim Moosa, "Worlds 'Apart': The Tablighi Jama'at under Apartheid: 1963–1993," in *Travellers in Faith: Studies of the Tablighi Jama'at as a Transnational Movement for Faith Renewal*, ed. Muhammad Khalid Masud (Leiden: E. J. Brill, 2000), 209.

52. Qasimul Uloom, "Tabligh Work in the Cape," *1st Annual Bukhari Khatam Jalsa*, 7 December 2003, 28–31.

53. "Tablighi Jamaat Invades Slums," *Muslim News*, 16 June 1967, 9.

54. "Programme of Natal Tabligh Jamaats," *Muslim News*, 25 August 1967.

55. "Tablighi Jamaat Discouraging?" *Muslim News*, 25 April 1969, 12; "Tabligh Methods Too Rigid" and "Tabligh Defended," *Muslim News*, 4 July 1969.

56. Marc Gaborieau, "The Transformation of the Tablighi Jama'at into a Transnational Movement," in *Travellers in Faith: Studies of the Tablighi Jama'at as a Transnational Islamic Movement for Faith Renewal*, ed. Muhammad Khalid Masud (Leiden: E. J. Brill, 2000), 126, 129.

57. Including Dar al-'Ulum Zakariyya in Lenasia; Madrasa In'aamiyya in Camperdown; Madrasa Arabia Islamia in Azaadville; Dar al-'Ulum Newcastle; Dar al-'Ulum Abu Bakr in Port Elizabeth; Dar al-'Ulum al-Arabiyya al-Islamiyya in Strand; Qasim al-'Ulum in Mitchell's Plain, outside of Cape Town; Madrasa Ta'lim al-Din in Isipingo Beach; Jami'a Mahmudiyya in Springs; and Ashraf al-'Ulum in De Deur.

58. On this, see Zaman, *The Ulama in Contemporary Islam*, chap. 2.

59. Ismail Akoo, interview with author, Dar al-'Ulum Newcastle, 23 March 2010.

60. Muhammad Khalid Sayed, "South African Madrasahs Move into the Twenty-First Century," in *Muslim Schools and Education in Europe and South Africa*, ed. Abdulkader Tayob, Inga Niehaus, and Wolfram Weissem (Münster: Waxmann, 2011), 76.

61. Munier Adams, interview with author, Qasim al-'Ulum, 22 September 2009.

62. Ismail Alie, interview with author, Qasim al-'Ulum, 22 September 2009. Alie was the director of Qasim al-'Ulum at the time of the interview.

63. Qasimul Uloom, "Friendship and Tolerance," *3rd Annual Graduation of Ulama Jalsah*, 11 December 2005, 9–15.

64. Mufti Raza al-Haq, *Fatawa-yi Dar al-'Ulum Zakariyya*, ed. Shabbir Ahmad Saluji (Karachi: Zam Zam Publishers, 2015), 1:32.

65. Ibid., 1:644–66.

66. Ibid., 2:270-2. It is difficult to discern which fatwas are requested from South Africans. Like many fatwa collections, details about the *mustafti* (the one requesting the fatwa) have been removed. Questions and answers are written exclusively in Urdu (often with Arabic citations), suggesting either that the requests came from Urdu-speaking *mustaftis* in South Africa and abroad, or that requests in other languages (e.g., English, Afrikaans) were translated into Urdu for the purposes of publication. (Most Shafi'is in South Africa will not speak Urdu as a first language.)

67. Ibid., 1:29.

69. Universal Truth Movement, "Universal Truth Movement General Report" (n.p., Universal Truth Movement, 1964).

70. "Mayor Welcomes Moulana," *Muslim News*, 28 June 1963, 4. See also Rizvi, *Tarikh-i Dar al-'Ulum Deoband*, 1:378–79. Rizvi says that Tayyib cleared

up some "misunderstandings about the Dar al-'Ulum Deoband" in South Africa, but does not specify what those misunderstandings were.

71. The Muslim Judicial Council had been founded in 1945 as a body of *'ulama* to give advice to the Cape Muslim community and issue *halal* certification licenses, among other tasks. See Gerrie Lubbe, "The Muslim Judicial Council: Custodian or Catalyst?" *Journal for Islamic Studies,* 14 (1994): 34–62.

72. "Tumultuous Welcome for Moulana by Cape Muslims," *Muslim News,* 9 August 1963, 1. According to the reports, he lectured on the theme of "remembering" (*dhikr*) in the Qur'an, as well as other assorted topics.

73. "Moulana's Farewell Message: Praise for Cape Muslims," *Muslim News,* 23 August 1963, 1.

74. The Irony of the Doeband [*sic*] Fatwa," *Muslim News,* 8 April 1966, 26. Mohammed Makki, "Deoband Ulamas Declare South Africa a Darul Harb," *Muslim Digest,* February 1966, 2–12; Ismail Abed, "A Refutation of the Deobandi Fatwa on Interest and Usury," *Muslim Digest,* February 1966, 13–19; "Deoband Fatwa Rejected," *Muslim News,* 11 March 1966; the April issue contained a large collection of furious letters grouped under the banner "THE DOEBAND [*sic*] BLUNDER."

75. Ebrahim Moosa, "Ethical Landscape: Laws, Norms and Morality," in *Islam in the Modern World,* ed. Jeffrey T. Kenney and Ebrahim Moosa (Abingdon, UK: Routledge, 2012), 44. The fatwa from Deoband was ironic in other ways. Ashraf 'Ali Thanvi had received a similar request in 1928 from a *mufti* in Hyderabad. The *mufti,* hoping for Thanvi to sign off on his fatwa, argued that the Qur'anic ban on *riba* applied only to commercial loans and that noncommercial loans were exempt. Thanvi delegated the task of responding to Zafar Ahmad 'Usmani, who issued a blistering point-by-point rebuttal. See Zaman, *Ashraf Ali Thanawi,* 70–72.

76. Fatima Meer, "Interest and Dar-ul-Harb in Islam: A Preliminary Analysis of the Fatwa on Riba of the Muftees of Dar-ul-Uloom, Deoband," supp., *Views and News,* 10 February 1966, 2.

77. Ibid., 10.

78. Ibid., 2.

79. See Shamil Jeppie, *Language, Identity, Modernity: The Arabic Study Circle of Durban* (Cape Town: Human Sciences Research Council Press, 2007).

80. Moosa, "Worlds 'Apart,'" 220.

81. Muhammad Palan Haqqani, *Shari'at ya jahalat* (Karachi: Qadimi Kutub Khana, 1975), 16–17.

82. Ibid., 26.

83. With the exception of a short section on Hanafi views on "knowledge of the unseen" (*'ilm-i ghayb*). Ibid., 278–80.

84. Ibid., 531–39 (on *munazara*), 619–22 (on *'urs*), 689–732 (on various issues pertaining to the *mawlud*).

85. *Views and News,* June 1970. See also Goolam H. Vahed, "Contesting 'Orthodoxy': The Tablighi–Sunni Conflict among South African Muslims in the 1970s and 1980s," *Journal of Muslim Minority Affairs* 23, no. 2 (2003): 313–34, at 318–19; as well as Jeppie, *Language, Identity, Modernity,* 71.

86. *Muslim Digest,* August 1975, 19.

87. See www.sunnirazvisociety.com (last accessed 18 June 2018).

88. "Cape Town Tablighi Jamaa Declares Itself Wahabi," *Muslim News,* 17 July 1970, 1.

89. *Muslim News,* 17 July 1970, 12.

90. On 27 April 1979, Imam Nazir Ahmed of Mooi River in Natal gave a Friday sermon (*khutbah*) in the mosque, siding with the Tablighi view that one should not read *salaami* (devotional praises of the Prophet Muhammad) inside the mosque. He was accosted by a group of angry congregants and then beaten. *Cape Herald,* 28 April 1979, 4. Another confrontation took place at the Grey Street Masjid in Durban on 22 September 1981. Three Muslim men were charged with assaulting seven others in a Tablighi–Barelvi dispute, but unfortunately the article does not report which side committed the assault. *Natal Witness,* 23 September 1981.

91. *Muslim Digest,* December 1988/January 1989, 4.

92. Kaukab Noorani Okarvi, *Truth Wins: The Full Account of a Historic Challenge to Establish Truth as the Truth and Falsehood as the Falsehood* (Durban: Maulana Okarvi Academy, 1991).

93. See Kaukab Noorani Okarvi, *Deoband to Bareilly: The Truth* (Lahore: Zia ul-Quraan Publications, 1996), as well as the same author's *White and Black: Deobandi-ism Caught Up in Its Own Web* (Durban: Maulana Okarvi Academy, 1991).

94. *Muslim News,* 21 March 1980, 2. The Ghousia Manzil was established as a Sufi lodge for Qadiri Sufis, the *silsila* that Hazrat Sayed Zainul Abedien established in Cape Town during his visit in 1961. Many, if not most, Barelvi-oriented Sufis in South Africa are Qadiris, though many Chishtis and Naqshbandis are strong ideological allies. Speaking on behalf of the *khanqah* during its opening, Shaikh M.S. Dien vaunted the implicit political power of Sufism: "People in South Africa have the wrong idea of Tasawwuf and its power in propagation. Not only does the khanqah serve as a retreat but it is a centre where social and political activity is generated."

95. *Muslim News,* 25 January 1985. Barelvi Sufi leaders in the community met at Ghousia Manzil *khanqah* in November 1984 to establish the Ahl-e Sunnat wal-Jammat, with Maulana Ahmed Mukkadam in charge.

96. Mahida, *A History of Muslims in South Africa,* 132.

97. Mohammad Akhtar Raza Khan Azhari, *Azharul Fatawa* (Bareilly, India: Idara Sunni Dunya, n.d.). This text is distributed in South Africa by Habibi Darul Ifta.

98. E.g., Ahmed Raza Khan, *The Validity of Saying "Ya Rasoolallah,"* trans. Durwesh Abu Muhammad Abdul Hadi al-Qadiri (Durban: Imam Ahmed Raza Academy, n.d.).

99. Ebrahim Muhammad, *A Guide to Madrasah Arabia Islamia* (Azaadville, South Africa: Madrasa Arabia Islamia, 2000), 6–7. For an overview of both institutions, see Dietrich Reetz, "The Tablighi Madrassas in Lenasia and Azaadville: Local Players in the Global 'Islamic Field,'" in *Muslim Schools and Education in Europe and Africa,* ed. Abdulkader Tayob, Inga Niehaus, and Wolfram Weissem (Münster: Waxmann, 2011), 84–104.

100. See n. 43 above on the role of the Waterval Islamic Institute in translating many of these into English.

101. Mufti Muhammad Shahid, *Qutb al-Aqtab Imam al-'Arifin Shaykh al-Mashaikh Hazrat Aqdas Shaykh al-Hadith al-Hajj al-Hafiz Maulana Muhammad Zakariyya Muhajir Madani ka safarnama-yi Afriqah o England: Ramadan al-Mubarak 1401/1981* (Karachi: Al-Maktaba al-Islamiyya, 1982), 40–41. On the middle-class appeal of the Tablighi Jama'at in South Africa specifically, see Vahed, "Contesting 'Orthodoxy,'" 317.

102. There are scores of these. Barelvi pamphlets in support of *mawlud* include, e.g., Mufti Akbar Hazarvi's *Meelaad-un-Nabie Celebration in the Light of Shariah* (Laudium, South Africa: Soutul Islam Publications, 1999), published by (and read by students at) Darul Uloom Pretoria, a Barelvi Dar al-'Ulum. Deobandi polemics against *mawlud* include, e.g., Majlisul Ulama's, *The Spreading of Confusion and Falsehood about the Tablighi Jamaat / What Is Meelaad?* (Benoni, South Africa: Young Men's Muslim Association, 1988).

103. Majlisul Ulama of South Africa, *Meelaad Celebrations* (Benoni, South Africa: Young Men's Muslim Association, 1985), 9–16.

104. Abdun Nabi Hamidi, *Yes, Meelaad Celebration Is Commendable* (Azaadville, South Africa: Sunni Ulema Council, n.d.), 1–9. Hamidi has also responded to Deobandis' critiques of loud *zikr*. See his *Permissibility of Loud Zikr in the Masjid and Elsewhere* (Johannesburg: Sarwari Qaaderi Publications, 2000). This is specifically a reply to Mufti A.H. Elias' tract *Impermissibility of Loud Zikr in the Masjid*.

105. Hamidi, *Yes, Meelaad Celebration Is Commendable*, 12–13.

106. Young Men's Muslim Association, *Who Are the People of Sunnah?* (Benoni, South Africa: Young Men's Muslim Association, 1987), 3.

107. Ibid., 4.

108. Sunni Jamiatul Ulama, *Confusion or Conclusion: Answer to "Who Are the People of Sunnah?"* (Durban: Sunni Jamiatul Ulama, n.d.), 2–3. Saharanpuri, to clarify, listed a number of Deobandi complaints about the *mawlud* and said, "If the *mawlud* assembly were free of such things, how could we say that recalling the noble birth is impermissible and an innovation [*bid'a*]?" See chap. 2, p. 67.

109. Sunni Jamiatul Ulama, *Confusion or Conclusion*, 3.

110. Ibid., 15.

7. A TRADITION CONTESTED

1. For this event in the context of anti-apartheid activism, see Anthony W. Marx, *Lessons of Struggle: South African Internal Opposition, 1960–1990* (New York: Oxford University Press, 1992).

2. The literature on apartheid history is, of course, substantial. For an overview that places apartheid governance in its wider colonial context, see Deborah Posel, "The Apartheid Project, 1948–1970," in *The Cambridge History of South Africa*, vol. 2, ed. Robert Ross, Anne Kelk Mager, and Bill Nasson (Cambridge: Cambridge University Press, 2011).

3. *Muslim News*, 25 June 1976, 1–2.

4. Gerrie Lubbe, "The Soweto Fatwa: A Muslim Response to a Watershed Event in South Africa," *Journal of Muslim Minority Affairs* 17, no. 2 (1997): 335–43, at 342.

5. See Ursula Günther, "The Memory of Imam Haron in Consolidating Muslim Resistance in the Apartheid Struggle," in *Religion and the Political Imagination in a Changing South Africa*, ed. Gordon Mitchell and Eve Mullen (New York and Münster: Waxmann, 2002); as well as Shamil Jeppie, "Amandla and Allahu Akbar: Muslims and Resistance in South Africa, c. 1970–1987," *Journal for the Study of Religion* 4, no. 1 (1991): 3–19.

6. See Muhammed Haron, "*Muslim News* (1973–1986): Its Contribution towards an Alternative Press at the Cape," *Muslim World* 85, nos. 3/4 (1995): 317–32.

7. "Our Ulema and Injustice," *Muslim News,* 14 March 1975, 2.

8. "Do We Not Protest?" *Muslim News,* 20 December 1974, 2.

9. *Muslim News,* 24 September 1976, 3.

10. Ebrahim Moosa, "Muslim Conservatism in South Africa," *Journal of Theology for Southern Africa* 69 (1989): 73–81, at 75.

11. Sindre Bangstad, *Global Flows, Local Appropriations: Facets of Secularization and Re-Islamization among Contemporary Cape Muslims* (Amsterdam: Amsterdam University Press, 2007), 55.

12. Muhammed Haron and Imraan Buccus, "*Al-Qalam*: An Alternative Muslim Voice in the South African Press," *South African Historical Journal,* 61, no. 1 (2009): 121–37.

13. Tayob, *Islamic Resurgence in South Africa,* 127–28.

14. Muslim Youth Movement of South Africa, *Islam for All, Islam Forever: Rally Manual* (Durban: Muslim Youth Movement of South Africa, 1983). "Jahili" (lit., "ignorance") refers to the period prior to the revelation of the Prophet Muhammad. The word became prominent within twentieth-century Islamist rhetoric.

15. "The Ulema Should Lead," *Al-Qalam,* December 1982, 2.

16. Abul A'la Maududi, *Islamic Way of Life,* trans. Khurshid Ahmad (Durban: Muslim Youth Movement of South Africa, n.d.). Khurshid Ahmad (d. 1932) is a politician, economist, and major figure within the leadership of the Jama'at-i Islami, the political party founded by Maududi in 1941. See John L. Esposito and John O. Voll, "Khurshid Ahmad: Muslim Activist-Economist," *The Muslim World,* 80, no. 1 (1990): 24–36.

17. See Qibla, *One Solution, Islamic Revolution* (Athlone, Cape Town: Qibla, n.d.); and Qibla, *Eid Message: The Intellectual Roots of the Oppressed and Islam's Triumph over Apartheid* (Athlone, Cape Town: Qibla, 1992).

18. "Eid-ul-Fitr: Islam's Triumph over Apartheid," *Muslim News,* 24 July 1984, 17–22.

19. One example, among many, would be Hasan al-Turabi's essay "The Islamic State:" "The ideological foundation of an Islamic state lies in the doctrine of tawhid—the unity of God and of human life—as a comprehensive and exclusive program of worship." See Euben and Zaman, *Princeton Readings in Islamist Thought,* 213.

20. Qibla, *Dimensions of the Kalimah* (Athlone, Cape Town: Qibla, n.d.); and Achmad Cassiem, *Quest for Unity* (Cape Town: Silk Road Publishers, 1992), esp. 30–34.

21. *Muslim News,* 24 July 1981, 4.

22. Noah Salomon, *For Love of the Prophet: An Ethnography of Sudan's Islamic State* (Princeton, NJ: Princeton University Press, 2016).

23. Cassiem, *Quest for Unity,* 81.

24. Jeremy Seekings, *The UDF: A History of the United Democratic Front in South Africa, 1983–1991* (Athens: Ohio University Press, 2000), 29–48. To be sure, the tricameral parliament was the catalyst for forming the UDF, but the collaborations on which the UDF was based had been taking shape at least since 1976, as Seekings shows.

25. Moosa, "Muslim Conservatism in South Africa," 75–77.

26. *Al-Qalam,* March 1985, 9.

27. From 1974 to 1978, Esack studied at the Jami'a al-'Ulum al-Islamiyya, established by Deobandi scholar Yusuf Binnori in Karachi in 1953, and then transferred to Jami'a 'Alimiyya Islamiyya, also in Karachi, where he completed his Dars-i Nizami degree in 1980, followed by Qur'anic Studies at Jami'a Abi Bakr, also in Karachi (Farid Esack, email correspondence with author, 6 February 2018). I return below to the fact that Esack, one of the Deobandis' major critics, was educated in a Deobandi institution and what this tells us about the movement more broadly.

28. Farid Esack, *But Musa Went to Fir-aun! A Compilation of Questions and Answers about the Role of Muslims in the South African Struggle for Liberation* (Maitland, Cape Town: Clyson Printers, 1989), 2–5. On the history of Call of Islam with particular attention to its efforts to organize Muslims across racial divides, see Jill E. Kelly, "'It Is *Because* of Our Islam That We Are There': The Call of Islam in the United Democratic Front Era," *African Historical Review* 41, no. 1 (2009): 118–39.

29. Adli Jacobs, *Punching above Its Weight: The Story of the Call of Islam* (Bloomington, IN: AuthorHouse, 2014), 31–33.

30. "Muslims Defy Ban," *Cape Herald,* 8 January 1983.

31. "Islamic Iran: Local Ulema Sow Dissension," *Muslim News,* 3 September 1982, 1, 4.

32. Fatima Meer, preface to *But Musa Went to Fir-aun! A Compilation of Questions and Answers about the Role of Muslims in the South African Struggle for Liberation,* by Farid Esack (Maitland, Cape Town: Clyson Printers, 1989).

33. "Message to the Oppressors and Their Supporters," *Muslim News,* 21 September 1979; "Islam's Freedom Charter," *Muslim News,* 8 August 1980; "Revolutionary Manifesto of the Oppressed People," *Muslim News,* 12 August 1983. On *Muslim News*'s role in the anti-apartheid movement, see Haron, "*Muslim News* (1973–1986)," 317–32.

34. "Where Do We Stand?," *Muslim News,* 16 July 1982, 40.

35. *Cape Herald,* 28 April 1979, 4. The article reports, "The controversy is a long standing one which has split the Muslim community right down the middle, resulting in a series of violent incidents over the last few years."

36. *Natal Daily News,* 23 February 1983.

37. Ebrahim Adam studied in India from 1959 to 1971, and at the Dar al-'Ulum Deoband from 1964 to 1969, becoming a Sufi initiate of Muhammad Zakariyya Kandhlavi. When Kandhlavi and Mahmud Hasan Gangohi visited the Cape, Ebrahim Adam hosted them in Stellenbosch. Ebrahim Adam, interview with author, Pelican Park, Cape Town, 29 April 2010.

38. I have never been able to find a transcript or recording of the lecture. I corroborated the content of the lecture in my interview with Adam. On Mirza Ghulam Ahmad and revelation (*wahy*), see Yohanan Friedmann, *Prophecy Continuous: Aspects of Ahmadi Religious Thought and Its Medieval Background* (Berkeley: University of California Press, 1989).

39. See the discussion of Ahmad Raza Khan's *Husam al-haramayn* in chap. 3.

40. Siddiqui's arrival was covered in *Muslim Digest* in 1952: "Our Patron Arrives in South Africa," "Durban's Great Welcome to his Eminence," and "30,000 Cheer His Eminence in Cape Town." *Muslim Digest,* August 1952, 5–22.

41. Adam commented on a statement of Siddiqui's: "When I went to Arabia and envisioned it in scope and magnitude, I realized without a doubt that [Ahmed Raza Khan] was the Qibla of the non-Arab peoples." Adam repeated the statement in his lecture and gave the following gloss on its meaning: "[The Barelvis] say Rasulullah is a Prophet unto the Arabs and Ahmed Reza Khan is a Prophet unto the non-Arabs." *Muslim Digest,* March/April 1985, 19–20. These quotes, it is important to note, come from an article that was critical of Adam, and they cannot be otherwise verified.

42. *Muslim Digest,* March/April 1985, 7–8.

43. Ibid., 16.

44. *Muslim News,* March 1985, 8b.

45. *Al-Qalam,* March 1985, 9.

46. Ibid., August 1986, 3.

47. *The Star,* 19 March 1987. The paper described the reasons behind the clash as follows: "The Deobandi Tabligh group disagreed with the Barelvi group which sought to spread the religion by singing praises to Mohammed. On Saturday, the Barelvi group went through the streets of Lenasia singing and advertising their gathering." See also the discussion in Jacobus A. Naude, "A Historical Survey of Opposition to Sufism in South Africa," in *Islamic Mysticism Contested: Thirteen Centuries of Conflicts and Polemics,* ed. Frederick de Jong and Bernd Radtke (Leiden: E. J. Brill, 1999), 398.

48. *Al-Qalam,* March 1987, 1.

49. *Muslim Views,* March 1987, 2.

50. *Al-Qalam,* 4 April 1987, 6.

51. *Muslim Digest,* November 1986/February 1987, 2–3.

52. *Muslim Views,* March 1987, 8.

53. See Katz, *The Birth of the Prophet Muhammad,* 186–87, for a discussion of Baz's fatwa.

54. I say "allegedly" since I was not able to find a reprint of the fatwa myself. This claim comes from Sunni World, *An Attack on Our Sunni Beliefs by the*

Wahabi/Deobandi/Tablighi Sect and Our Reply (Durban: Sunni World, n.d.), 7. For the academy's response, see Imam Ahmed Raza Academy, "The Permissibility of Celebrating the Meelad-Un Nabi (saw): In Refutation of the Fatwa of Sheikh Abdul Aziz Bin Baaz of Saudi Arabia," accessed 4 February 2018, www.sunnah.org/publication/salafi/mawlid_refute.htm.

55. "Mecca Ulema Should Reconsider Fatwa against Meelad-un-Nabie," *Muslim Digest*, July/August 1982, 193.

56. "'Meelad-e-Mustapha Conference' in Durban," *Muslim Digest*, January/February 1983.

57. "International Islamic Unity Week: Commemorating the Birth of the Greatest Benefactor to Mankind-Nabi Muhammad (S.A.W.)" (unpublished flyer, 16 November 1986), Islamic ephemera collection, African Studies Library, University of Cape Town.

58. The Claremont Main Road Mosque dates to 1854 and holds an immense, if often controversial, stature among Muslims at the Cape. It became especially noteworthy when, in August 1994, the female African-American Qur'an scholar Amina Wadud gave a pre-*khutbah* talk on women's rights in this mosque before a mixed-gender audience. See Abdulkader Tayob, *Islam in South Africa: Mosques, Imams, and Sermons* (Gainesville: University Press of Florida, 1999), 56–58.

59. Claremont Main Road Mosque, "Mawlud an-Nabi: Poetry in Honor of the Prophet's Birth" (n.p., n.d.), Islamic ephemera collection, African Studies Library, University of Cape Town.

60. This is especially true in the Indian Sufi context. For a discussion of the *halqa-i zikr* among Sabiri Chishtis, see Robert Rozehnal, *Islamic Sufism Unbound: Politics and Piety in Twenty-First Century Pakistan* (New York: Palgrave Macmillan, 2007), 194–96.

61. "Call for Dhikr to Show Solidarity," *Muslim Views*, March 1988, 3. For Moosa's biography, see his *What Is a Madrasa?*, 15–30.

62. Muslim Youth Movement of South Africa, *From Where Shall We Begin?* (Durban: Muslim Youth Movement of South Africa, n.d.), 13.

63. Call of Islam, *The Struggle* (Cape Town: Call of Islam, 1988), 14.

64. Farid Esack, "Review of Faith" (n.p., 1984), 23. I thank Matthew Palombo for sharing this document with me.

65. E.g., Thanvi, *Al-Ifadat al-yawmiyya*, statement no. 188, 5:186–91.

66. On the Khilafat Movement, see esp. Gail Minault, *The Khilafat Movement: Religious Symbolism and Political Mobilization in India* (New York: Columbia University Press, 1982); and Qureshi, *Pan-Islam in British Indian Politics*.

67. The first monograph on this subject was in fact the first in English on any aspect of Deobandi history: Zia ul-Hasan Faruqi, *The Deoband School and the Demand for Pakistan* (New York: Asia Publishing House, 1963). More recently, Metcalf's *Husain Ahmad Madani*, Zaman's *Ashraf Ali Thanawi* (esp. pp. 35–56), and Qureshi's *Pan-Islam in British Indian Politics* (esp. pp. 233–316) have all explored Deobandi politics, with attention to the disagreement between Thanvi and Madani.

68. Qureshi, *Pan-Islam in British Indian Politics*, 249.

69. Francis Robinson, *Separatism among Indian Muslims: The Politics of the United Provinces' Muslims, 1860–1923* (Cambridge: Cambridge University Press, 1974), 296–301.

70. Metcalf, *Husain Ahmad Madani*, 78–79.

71. Husain Ahmad Madani, *Muttahida qawmiyyat aur Islam*, ed. Amjad 'Ali Shakir (Lahore: Jami'at Publications, 2006), 136–37, 147–48.

72. E.g., Muhammad Zakariyya Kandhlavi, *Al-I'tidal fi maratib al-rijal, ya'ni Islami siyasat* (Deoband: Ittihad Book Depot, n.d.); and Gangohi, *Hudud-i ikhtilaf*.

73. Husain Ahmad Madani, *Al-Shihab al-saqib 'ala al-mustariq al-kazib* (Lahore, 1979).

74. Venkat Dhulipala, *Creating a New Medina: State Power, Islam, and the Quest for Pakistan in Late Colonial North India* (New Delhi: Cambridge University Press, 2015), 106–10.

75. Ahmad Sa'id, *Maulana Ashraf 'Ali Sahib Thanvi aur tahrik-i azadi* (Rawalpindi, Pakistan: Khalid Nadim Publications, 1972), 69–71. For the text of Azad's fatwa, see Qureshi, *Pan-Islam in British Indian Politics*, 188–89.

76. Thanvi, *Al-Ifadat al-yawmiyya*, statement no. 34, 1:60–61; statement no. 12, 5:22.

77. See pp. 103–4 above and the discussion in Zaman, *Ashraf Ali Thanawi*, 39–44.

78. Thanvi, *Al-Ifadat al-yawmiyya*, statement no. 10, 1:35–36.

79. Sa'id, *Maulana Ashraf 'Ali Sahib Thanvi*, 52–57, esp. 53.

80. Chitralekha Zutshi, *Languages of Belonging: Islam, Regional Identity, and the Making of Kashmir* (New York: Oxford University Press, 2004), 211.

81. Ayesha Jalal, *Self and Sovereignty: Individual and Community in South Asian Islam since 1850* (London: Routledge, 2000), 356; David Gilmartin, *Empire and Islam: Punjab and the Making of Pakistan* (London: I.B. Tauris, 1988), 96–99.

82. Thanvi, *Al-Ifadat al-yawmiyya*, statement no. 116, 1:120.

83. Ibid.

84. Ibid., 1:122, 1:127.

85. Ibid., 1:120.

86. Ibid., 1:121.

87. Interestingly, Yusuf al-Qaradawi disagrees. Citing the same point about the Persian origins of the practice of digging trenches in warfare, Qaradawi argues that "[t]here is no Islamic legal impediment to acquiring an idea or a practical solution from non-Muslims." Zaman and Euben, *Princeton Readings in Islamist Thought*, 237.

88. Thanvi, *Al-Ifadat al-yawmiyya*, 1:124, 1:122.

89. Ibid., 1:130.

90. Ibid., 1:133.

91. Thanvi, *Ashraf al-tariqat*, 85–90.

92. Muhammad Taqi 'Usmani, *Hakim al-Ummat ke siyasi afkar* (Karachi: Idara al-Ma'arif, 2000), 44.

93. Ibid., 44–45.

94. Megan Eaton Robb, "Advising the Army of Allah: Ashraf Ali Thanawi's Critique of the Muslim League," in *Muslims against the Muslim League: Critiques of the Idea of Pakistan,* ed. Ali Usman Qasmi and Megan Eaton Robb (Cambridge: Cambridge University Press, 2017), 152–55.

95. Dhulipala, *Creating a New Medina,* 21.

96. Ibid., 110–14.

97. Its original members consisted of Ismail Moosagie, who acted as president; Muhammad Hanif Ismail Moosagie; and Ahmed Sadiq Desai, who became the public face and principal writer of the group's literature. All three studied at Miftah al-'Ulum in Jalalabad, India, with Masihullah Khan. "Port Elizabeth gets second Ulema body," *Muslim News,* 27 February 1970.

98. Miftahi, *Hayat-i Masih al-Ummat,* 56.

99. Muhammad Faruq, *Zikr-i Masih al-Ummat* (Brixton, South Africa: Maktaba Noor, 1998), 8.

100. Ibid., 67. These works include *Bayan al-Qur'an, Imdad al-fatawa, Bihishti zewar, Tarbiyat al-salik, Islahi nisab,* and *Ashraf al-sawanih.*

101. Faruq, *Zikr-i Masih al-Ummat,* 54–55.

102. Ibid., 17.

103. Ibid., 47–48. His *khalifas* in South Africa numbered at least ten out of approximately sixty in total. They include Maulana Munshi Moosa Yaqub of Verulam, Maulana Ismail Kathrada of Natal, Maulana Ahmed Sadiq Desai of Port Elizabeth, Dr. Abdul Qadir Hansa of Ladysmith, Maulana Abdul Haq Omarjee of Durban, Dr. Ismail Mangera of Johannesburg, Haji Yusuf Kathrada of Verulam, Mufti Rashid Mia of Waterval, Maulana Muhammad Hashim Boda of Lenasia, Maulana Qasim Dawood of Parlock, and Yusuf Navlakhi of Lenasia.

104. *Puja* is of course a Hindu ritual term, one chosen deliberately.

105. "The Curse of Grave Worship," *The Majlis* 7, no. 9, p. 1. Issues of *The Majlis* are undated; they do not provide the month or year of publication. They provide only the volume and issue number. Some of the articles are titled, and some are not. Page numbers are usually provided, but some of the *Majlis* citations below are from issues without page numbers. The citations below provide all the information available for a given issue.

106. Young Men's Muslim Association, *Moulood and the Shariah* (Benoni, South Africa: Young Men's Muslim Association, n.d.), 11–21.

107. Ibid., 34.

108. *The Majlis* 4, no. 12, p. 7.

109. Ibid.

110. "Tasawwuf Misunderstood," *The Majlis* 14, no. 6, p. 6.

111. "What Is Tasawwuf?," *The Majlis* 11, no. 6, p. 9.

112. *The Majlis* 6, no. 6, p. 1. Also see *The Majlis* 7, no. 2, p. 8.

113. *The Majlis* 6, no. 6, p. 1; *The Majlis* 7, no. 2, p. 8.

114. *The Majlis* 6, no. 7, p. 5.

115. Majlisul Ulama of South Africa, *The Interfaith Trap of Kufr* (Benoni, South Africa: Young Men's Muslim Association, n.d.), 17.

116. Ibid., 40.

117. Ibid., 42.

118. Matthew Palombo, "The Emergence of Islamic Liberation Theology in South Africa," *Journal of Religion in Africa* 44 (2014): 28–61, at 44.

119. *Muslim News*, 8 August 1980, 32.

120. Cassiem, *Quest for Unity*, 66.

121. *The Majlis* 8, no. 9, p. 9.

122. *Al-Qalam* 10, no. 2 (1985): 8.

123. *The Majlis* 8, no. 5. p. 1.

124. "Maududi-ism," *The Majlis* 2, no. 7, p. 4.

125. *The Majlis* 7, no. 3, p. 7.

126. *The Majlis* 8, no. 7, p. 5.

127. *The Majlis* 11, no. 4, p. 11.

128. In the Chishti context, this usually took the form of refusing the largesse or patronage of rulers. On this, see esp. Tanvir Anjum, *Chishti Sufis in the Sultanate of Delhi, 1190–1400: From Restrained Indifference to Calculated Defiance* (Oxford: Oxford University Press, 2011).

129. "The Bid'ah of Halqah Thikr in the Musaajid," *The Majlis* 14, no. 3, p. 8.

130. *The Majlis* 6, no. 7, p. 2.

131. Esack, "Review of Faith," 25–26, quoted in Palombo, "Islamic Liberation Theology in South Africa," 47. Esack elaborates on his understanding of praxis in *Quran, Liberation & Pluralism: An Islamic Perspective on Interreligious Solidarity against Oppression* (Oxford: Oneworld, 1997), 107–8.

132. Palombo, "Emergence of Islamic Liberation Theology," 50.

133. Muhammad Qasim Zaman, *Modern Islamic Thought in a Radical Age: Religious Authority and Internal Criticism* (Cambridge: Cambridge University Press, 2012), introduction, chaps. 2 and 5. See also SherAli Tareen, "Revolutionary Hermeneutics: Translating the Qur'an as a Manifesto for Revolution," *Journal of Religious and Political Practice* 3, nos. 1–2 (2017): 1–24.

134. Peter Custers, "Maulana Bhashani and the Transition to Secular Politics in East Bengal," *The Indian Economic and Social History Review* 47, no. 2 (2010): 231–59.

135. Yousuf Dadoo, "Maulvi Cachalia: The Contributions of a Thinker Activist in the Political Liberation of South Africa," *Journal of Muslim Minority Affairs* 16, no. 1 (1996): 129–33.

136. Yunus Patel, interview with author, Madrasa Sawlehaat, Durban, 12 November 2009. More information on Patel's life and work is available on his website, www.yunuspatel.co.za (last accessed 23 June 2018).

137. Francis Robinson, "Other-Worldly and This-Worldly Islam and the Islamic Revival: A Memorial Lecture for Wilfred Cantwell Smith," *Journal of the Royal Asiatic Society*, ser. 3, vol. 14, no. 1 (2004): 47–58.

CONCLUSION

1. Declan Walsh and Nour Youssef, "Attack on Coptic Cathedral in Cairo Kills Dozens," *New York Times*, 11 December 2016.

2. "Attack on Shah Noorani Shrine in Pakistan kills dozens," *Al-Jazeera*, 12 November 2016; "Blast Hits Pakistan's Lal Shahbaz Qalandar Sufi Shrine," *Al-Jazeera*, 16 February 2017.

3. On the *dhamal*, focusing on the shrine of Lal Shahbaz Qalandar, see Jürgen Wasim Frembgen, "*Dhamal* and the Performing Body: Trance Dance in the Devotional Sufi Practice of Pakistan," *Journal of Sufi Studies* 1, no. 1 (2012): 77–113. On the Qalandars in Islamic history, see Ahmet T. Karamustafa, *God's Unruly Friends: Dervish Groups in the Later Islamic Middle Period, 1200–1550* (Oxford: Oneworld, 2006).

4. Sher Alam Shinwari, "Footprints: Rahman Baba's Devotees in Grip of Fear," *Dawn,* 5 April 2015. On the rise of the Pakistani Taliban, see Hassan Abbas, *The Taliban Revival: Violence and Extremism on the Pakistan–Afghanistan Border* (New Haven, CT: Yale University Press, 2014), 141–67.

5. Declan Walsh, "Suicide Bombers Kill Dozens at Pakistan Shrine," *The Guardian,* 2 July 2010.

6. Huma Imtiaz, "Sufi Shrine in Pakistan Is Hit by a Lethal Double Bombing," *New York Times,* 7 October 2010.

7. Ashraf Buzdar, "Suicide Hits at Sakhi Sarwar Shrine Kill 41," *The Nation* (Pakistan), 4 April 2011.

8. Rania Abouzeid, "Taliban Targets, Pakistan's Sufis Fight Back," *Time,* 10 November 2010. The author interviews Sayyid Safdar Shah Gilani, head of a Barelvi organization, the Sunni Ittehad Council, who has proposed among other things a ban on "incendiary Deobandi literature," according to Abouzeid.

9. Thomas Barfield, *Afghanistan: A Cultural and Political History* (Princeton, NJ: Princeton University Press, 2010), 261.

10. Sami' al-Haq, *Afghan Taliban: War of Ideology, Struggle for Peace* (Islamabad: Emel Publications, 2015), xvii.

11. M. A. Haqqani et al., *Fatawa-yi Haqqaniyya,* 2:261.

12. Ibid., 2:245–47.

13. Ibid., 2:249. The manual is Nizam al-Din Awrangabadi's *Nizam al-qulub.* On *Nizam al-qulub* and its centrality for the Chishti-Sabiri lineage, see Kugle, *Sufis and Saints' Bodies,* 232. Hajji Imdad Allah outlines the *zikr haddadi* in his manual on *zikr,* "Ziya al-Qulub," in Imdad Allah, *Kulliyat-i Imdadiyya,* 21–22.

14. M. A. Haqqani et al., *Fatawa-yi Haqqaniyya,* 2:254. On the role of the *chilla* in Chishti piety, see Ernst and Lawrence, *Sufi Martyrs of Love,* 96. Ernst and Lawrence also note (on p. 122) that Thanvi likewise supported the *chilla* as long as it was done "to cure some moral defect" (their words, not Thanvi's).

15. M. A. Haqqani et al., *Fatawa-yi Haqqaniyya,* 2:267.

16. Ibid., 2:256–57.

17. Ibid., 1:189.

18. Ibid., 1:182–86.

19. Zaman, *Islam in Pakistan,* 343n174.

20. One of Sami' al-Haq's works, a detailed treatise on Qur'anic ethics, draws on much of the standard language of Deobandi works on Sufism, including ethical reform (*islah-i ahklaq*) of the self (*nafs*), and targeting love of wealth (*hubb-i mal*) and lust (*shavat*) as particularly harmful "negative ethical traits" (*raza'il-i akhlaq*). These are the negative attributes that nearly all Deobandi Sufi texts also single out. But there is no mention of Sufism in the entire text; indeed, the Qur'an alone, along with the core ritual commandments of Islam, are single-

handedly equipped to effect this ethical reform of the self. The Hajj, for instance, is a "system [*nisab*] for purifying the self [*tahzib-i akhlaq*] and ethical training." See Sami' al-Haq, *Qur'an aur ta'mir-i akhlaq* (Akora Khattak, Pakistan: Maktaba al-Haq, 1984), 46.

21. Ron Geaves, "The Contested Milieu of Deoband: 'Salafis' or 'Sufis'?," in *Sufis and Salafis in the Contemporary Age*, ed. Lloyd Ridgeon (London and New York: Bloomsbury Academic, 2015), 191–216.

22. Rozehnal, *Islamic Sufism Unbound*, 36.

23. Ernst and Lawrence, *Sufi Martyrs of Love*, 11–13.

24. Muhammad Rafi' 'Usmani, *Fiqh aur tasawwuf: Ek ta'arruf* (Karachi: Idara al-Ma'arif, 2004), 37.

25. The collection I have in mind is Jawad Syed, Edwina Pio, Tahir Kamran, and Abbas Zaidi, eds. *Faith-Based Violence and Deobandi Militancy in Pakistan* (London: Palgrave Macmillan, 2016). To be clear, the collection is not entirely without merit. A few of the essays are well argued and well sourced, though the collection relies predominantly on news reports and policy papers rather than primary source materials. But on the whole, the essays do exactly what the title suggests: argue that "Deobandi militancy" is (exclusively) "faith-based." I submit that this may be one among many approaches to understanding militancy, but the meaning of "faith-based" must be clarified (the collection assumes throughout that the meaning is self-evident), and it cannot be the only approach.

26. See Elizabeth Shakman Hurd, *Beyond Religious Freedom*, and William T. Cavanaugh, *The Myth of Religious Freedom: Secular Ideology and the Roots of Modern Conflict* (Oxford, New York: Oxford University Press, 2009).

27. See Finbarr Barry Flood, "Between Cult and Culture: Bamiyan, Islamic Iconoclasm, and the Museum," *Art Bulletin* 84, no. 4 (2002): 641–59; and Jamal Elias, "Un/Making Idolatry: From Mecca to Bamiyan," *Future Anterior: Journal of Historic Preservation* 4, no. 2 (2007): 2–29.

28. A. Afzar Moin, *The Millennial Sovereign: Sacred Kingship and Sainthood in Islam* (New York: Columbia University Press, 2012), 271n121.

29. Rozehnal, *Islamic Sufism Unbound*, 14.

30. Usha Sanyal, "Tourists, Pilgrims and Saints: The Shrine of Mu'in al-Din Chisti of Ajmer," in *Raj Rhapsodies: Tourism, Heritage and the Seduction of History*, ed. Carol E. Henderson and Maxine Weisgrau (Hampshire, UK: Ashland, 2007), 183.

31. Michael T. Taussig, *Defacement: Public Secrecy and the Labor of the Negative* (Stanford, CA: Stanford University Press, 1999), 43, 54.

32. Katherine Ewing, *Arguing Sainthood: Modernity, Psychoanalysis, and Sainthood* (Durham, NC: Duke University Press, 1997), 93–127.

33. Ahmed, *What Is Islam?*, 95.

34. Nadia Fadil and Mayanthi Fernando, "Rediscovering the 'Everyday' Muslim: Notes on an Anthropological Divide," *Hau: Journal of Ethnographic Theory* 5, no. 2 (2015): 59–88, at 74. See also the responses to Fadil and Fernando from Lara Deeb and Samuli Schielke in the same issue.

35. I am thinking especially of Salomon, *For Love of the Prophet*, and Irfan Ahmad, *Religion as Critique: Islamic Critical Thinking from Mecca to the Marketplace* (Chapel Hill: University of North Carolina Press, 2017).

36. Ebrahim Moosa, "Introduction," *Muslim World* 99, no. 3 (2009): 427–34, at 429–30.

37. It is essential not to oversimplify Salafi thought here; in recent years, numerous scholars have complicated the common perception of Salafis as uniformly anti-Sufi and/or anti-*madhhab*, and have stressed local iterations of regional or transnational Salafi currents. Much of this pioneering work has been carried about by Africanists. See, for instance, Terje Østebø, *Localising Salafism: Religious Change among Oromo Muslims in Bale, Ethiopia* (Leiden: Brill, 2012); and Alexander Thurston, *Salafism in Nigeria: Islam, Preaching, and Politics* (Cambridge: Cambridge University Press, 2016).

38. Jonathan A. C. Brown, "Is Islam Easy to Understand or Not? Salafis, the Democratization of Interpretation and the Need for the Ulema," *Journal of Islamic Studies* 26, no. 2 (2015): 117–44.

39. Humeira Iqtidar, "Redefining 'Tradition' in Political Thought," *European Journal of Political Theory* 15, no. 4 (2016): 424–44, at 425.

40. See p. 120.

41. Mark Lilla, *The Shipwrecked Mind: On Political Reaction* (New York: New York Review of Books, 2016), xii–xiii.

42. M. T. 'Usmani, *Hakim al-Ummat ke siyasi afkar,* 22.

43. Barbara Daly Metcalf, "New Medinas: The Tablighi Jama'at in America and Europe," in *Making Muslim Space in North America and Europe,* ed. Barbara Daly Metcalf (Berkeley: University of California Press, 1996), 119.

44. Ibid., 123 (emphasis added).

45. Nile Green, "Urdu as an African Language: A Survey of a Source Literature," *Islamic Africa* 3, no. 2 (2012): 173–99, at 190–91.

46. Farish A. Noor, "Pathans to the East! The Tablighi Jama'at Movement in Northern Malaysia and Southern Thailand," *Comparative Studies of South Asia, Africa and the Middle East* 27, no. 1 (2007): 7–25, at 24.

Bibliography

Abbas, Hassan. *The Taliban Revival: Violence and Extremism on the Pakistan–Afghanistan Border.* New Haven, CT: Yale University Press, 2014.

Adcock, C.S. *The Limits of Tolerance: Indian Secularism and the Politics of Religious Freedom.* Oxford and New York: Oxford University Press, 2013.

Adorno, Theodor W. "On Tradition." *Telos* 94 (1993/94): 75–82.

Agnew, William Fischer. *The Law of Trusts in British India.* Calcutta: Thacker, Spink and Co., 1882.

Agrama, Hussein Ali. "Ethics, Tradition, Authority: Toward an Anthropology of the Fatwa." *American Ethnologist* 37, no. 1 (2010): 2–18.

———. *Questioning Secularism: Islam, Sovereignty, and the Rule of Law in Egypt.* Chicago: University of Chicago Press, 2012.

Aguiar, Marian. *Tracking Modernity: India's Railway and the Culture of Mobility.* Minneapolis: University of Minnesota Press, 2011.

Ahmad, Aziz. "The Role of Ulema in Indo-Muslim History." *Studia Islamica* 31 (1970): 1–13.

Ahmad, Irfan. *Religion as Critique: Islamic Critical Thinking from Mecca to the Marketplace.* Chapel Hill: University of North Carolina Press, 2017.

Ahmad, Maulana Shaykh. *Maulana Maududi aur tasawwuf.* Deoband: Maktaba-yi Tajalli, 1966.

Ahmad, Mufti Inayat. *Bayan-i qadr-i shab-i barat.* Lahore: Markaz Isha'at-i Navadir-i 'Ulama-yi Ahl al-Sunnat, 2012.

———. *Tavarikh-i habib Allah.* Deoband: Maktaba-yi Thanvi, n.d.

Ahmed, Sara. "Affective Economies." *Social Text* 22, no. 2 (2004): 117–39.

Ahmed, Shahab. *What Is Islam? The Importance of Being Islamic.* Princeton, NJ: Princeton University Press, 2016.

Akhtar, Hakim Muhammad. *Pardes men tazkira-yi vatan, ya'ni dunya ke pardes men akhirat ke vatan-i asli ka tazkira.* Karachi: Kutub Khana-yi Mazhari, 2006.

Akoo, Moulana I. E. *Biography of the Founder of Dar al-'Ulum Newcastle: Moulana Cassim Mohamed Sema Saheb.* Newcastle, South Africa: Darul Uloom Newcastle, 2007.

Alam, Arshad. *Inside a Madrasa: Knowledge, Power and Islamic Identity in India.* New Delhi: Routledge, 2011.

Alam, Muzaffar. "The Debate Within: A Sufi Critique of Religious Law, *Tasawwuf,* and Politics in Mughal India." *South Asian History and Culture* 2, no. 2 (2011): 138–59.

———. *The Languages of Political Islam: India, 1200–1800.* Chicago: University of Chicago Press, 2004.

Alavi, Seema. *Muslim Cosmopolitanism in the Age of Empire.* Cambridge, MA: Harvard University Press, 2015.

Algar, Hamid. "The Centennial Renewer: Bediüzzaman Said Nursi and the Tradition of *Tajdid.*" *Journal of Islamic Studies* 12, no. 3 (2001): 291–311.

Alvi, Sajida Sultana. *Perspectives on Mughal India: Rulers, Historians, 'Ulamā' and Sufis.* Karachi: Oxford University Press, 2012.

Anderson, Michael R. "Classifications and Codifications: Themes in South Asian Legal Studies in the 1980s." *South Asia Research* 10, no. 2 (1990): 158–77.

Anjum, Tanvir. *Chishti Sufis in the Sultanate of Delhi, 1190–1400: From Restrained Indifference to Calculated Defiance.* Oxford: Oxford University Press, 2011.

Anooshahr, Ali. "Shirazi Scholars and the Political Culture of the Sixteenth-Century Indo-Persian World." *Indian Economic and Social History Review* 51, no. 3 (2014): 331–52.

Ansari, Muhammad Raza. *Bani-yi dars-i nizami: Ustaz al-Hind Mulla Nizamuddin Muhammad Farangi Mahall.* Aligarh, India: Aligarh Muslim University Publication Division, 1973.

Arendt, Hannah. *The Human Condition.* 2nd ed. Chicago: University of Chicago Press, 1998.

Asad, Talal. *Formations of the Secular: Christianity, Islam, Modernity.* Stanford, CA: Stanford University Press, 2003.

———. "The Idea of an Anthropology of Islam." *Qui Parle* 17, no. 2 (2009): 1–30.

———. "Thinking about Tradition, Religion, and Politics in Egypt Today." *Critical Inquiry* 42, no. 1 (2015): 166–214.

Atkinson, Edwin. *Statistical, Descriptive and Historical Account of the North-Western Provinces of India.* 14 vols. Allahabad: North-Western Provinces Government Press, 1875.

A'zami, Shafiq Ahmad. *Makatib-i Tayyib.* Deoband: Maktaba-yi Nu'maniyya, 1972.

Azhari, Mohammad Akhtar Raza Khan. *Azharul fatawa.* Bareilly, India: Idara Sunni Dunya, n.d.

Azmi, Fazlur Rahman. *Hazrat Mufti Mahmud Hasan Sahib Gangohi aur Jama'at-i Tabligh*. Karachi: Zam Publishers, 2003.

Babur, *The Baburnama: Memoirs of Babur, Prince and Emperor*. New York: Modern Library Classics, 2002.

Bahadur, Sayyid Ahmad Khan, et al. *Translation of the Report of the Members of the Select Committee for the Better Diffusion and Advancement of Learning among the Muhammadans of India*. Benares: Medical Hall Press, 1872.

Baljon, J. M. S. *Religion and Thought of Shah Wali Allah, 1703–1762*. Leiden: E. J. Brill, 1986.

Bangstad, Sindre. *Global Flows, Local Appropriations: Facets of Secularization and Re-Islamization among Contemporary Cape Muslims*. Amsterdam: Amsterdam University Press, 2007.

Barfield, Thomas. *Afghanistan: A Cultural and Political History*. Princeton, NJ: Princeton University Press, 2010.

Bashir, Shahzad. *Sufi Bodies: Religion and Society in Medieval Islam*. New York: Columbia University Press, 2011.

Bayly, C. A. *Empire and Information: Intelligence Gathering and Social Communication in India, 1780–1870*. Cambridge: Cambridge University Press, 1996.

Bearman, P. J., Th. Bianquis, C. E. Bosworth, E. J. van Donzel, and W. P. Heinrichs, eds. *Encyclopaedia of Islam*. 2nd ed. Leiden: E. J. Brill, 1960–2005.

Bergen, Peter, and Swati Pandey. "The Madrassa Scapegoat." *Washington Quarterly* 29, no. 2 (2006): 117–25.

Berger, Benjamin. *Law's Religion: Religious Difference and the Claims of Constitutionalism*. Toronto, Buffalo, and London: University of Toronto Press, 2015.

Berkey, Jonathan P. "Madrasas Medieval and Modern: Politics, Education, and the Problem of Muslim Identity." In *Schooling Islam: The Culture and Politics of Modern Muslim Education*, edited by Robert W. Hefner and Muhammad Qasim Zaman. Princeton, NJ: Princeton University Press, 2007.

———. *Popular Preaching and Religious Authority in the Medieval Islamic Near East*. Seattle and London: University of Washington Press, 2001.

———. "Tradition, Innovation, and the Social Construction of Knowledge in the Medieval Islamic Near East." *Past and Present* 146 (1995): 38–65.

———. *The Transmission of Knowledge in Medieval Cairo: A Social History of Islamic Education*. Princeton Studies on the Near East. Princeton, NJ: Princeton University Press, 1992.

Bhana, Surendra, and Goolam H. Vahed. *The Making of a Political Reformer: Gandhi in South Africa, 1893–1914*. New Delhi: Manohar, 2005.

Bhana, Surendra, and Joy Brain. *Setting Down Roots: Indian Migrants in South Africa, 1860–1911*. Johannesburg: Witwatersrand University Press, 1990.

Bhatia, M. L. *Administrative History of Medieval India*. New Delhi: Radha Publications, 1992.

Bilhauri, Khurram 'Ali. *Nasihat al-Muslimin*. Lucknow: Dar al-Isha'at Islamiyya, 1964.

Birt, Jonathan, and Philip Lewis. "The Pattern of Islamic Reform in Britain: The Deobandis between Intra-Muslim Sectarianism and Engagement with Wider

Society." In *Producing Islamic Knowledge: Transmission and Dissemination in Western Europe,* edited by Martin van Bruinessen and Stefano Allievi. London and New York: Routledge, 2011.

Blecher, Joel. *Said the Prophet of God: Hadith Commentary across a Millennium.* Oakland: University of California Press, 2017.

Blok, Anton. "The Narcissism of Minor Differences." *European Journal of Social Theory* 1, no. 1 (1998): 33–56.

Bonnate, Liazzat J.K. "Muslim Religious Leadership in Post-Colonial Mozambique." *South African Historical Journal* 60, no. 4 (2008): 637–54.

Brown, Jonathan A.C. "Is Islam Easy to Understand or Not? Salafis, the Democratization of Interpretation and the Need for the Ulema." *Journal of Islamic Studies* 26, no. 2 (2015): 117–44.

Buehler, Arthur F. *Recognizing Sufism: Contemplation in the Islamic Tradition.* London and New York: I.B. Tauris, 2016.

———. *Revealed Grace: The Juristic Sufism of Ahmad Sirhindi (1564–1625).* Louisville, KY: Fons Vitae, 2012.

———. *Sufi Heirs of the Prophet: The Indian Naqshbandiyya and the Rise of the Mediating Sufi Shaykh.* Columbia: University of South Carolina Press, 1998.

Butsch, Richard. *The Citizen Audience: Crowds, Publics, Individuals.* New York: Routledge, 2008.

Call of Islam. *The Struggle.* Cape Town: Call of Islam, 1988.

Cannon, Garland. *The Life and Mind of Oriental Jones: Sir William Jones, the Father of Modern Linguistics.* Cambridge: Cambridge University Press, 1990.

Cassiem, Achmad. *Quest for Unity.* Cape Town: Silk Road Publishers, 1992.

Cavanaugh, William T. *The Myth of Religious Freedom: Secular Ideology and the Roots of Modern Conflict.* Oxford and New York: Oxford University Press, 2009.

Chaghatai, M. Ikram. "Dr. Aloys Sprenger and the Delhi College." In *Delhi College: Traditional Elites, the Colonial State, and Education before 1857,* edited by Margrit Pernau. New Delhi: Oxford University Press, 2006.

Chakrabarty, Dipesh. *The Calling of History: Sir Jadunath Sarkar and His Empire of Truth.* Chicago and London: University of Chicago Press, 2015.

Chamberlain, Michael. *Knowledge and Social Practice in Medieval Damascus, 1190–1350.* Cambridge: Cambridge University Press, 1994.

Chatterjee, Nandini. *The Making of Indian Secularism: Empire, Law and Christianity, 1830–1960.* Basingstoke, UK, and New York: Palgrave Macmillan, 2011.

Chishti, Muhammad. *Adab al-talibin ma' rafiq al-tulab wa albab thalatha.* Lahore: Progressive Books, 1984.

Cohn, Bernard S. "Representing Authority in Victorian India." In *The Invention of Tradition,* edited by Eric Hobsbawm and Terence Ranger. Cambridge: Cambridge University Press, 1983.

Cole, Juan. *Roots of North Indian Shi'ism in Iran and Iraq: Religion and State in Awadh, 1722–1859.* Berkeley: University of California Press, 1988.

Cooper, Frederick. *Colonialism in Question: Theory, Knowledge, History.* Berkeley: University of California Press, 2005.

Corbett, Rosemary R. *Making Moderate Islam: Sufism, Service, and the "Ground Zero" Mosque Controversy.* Stanford, CA: Stanford University Press, 2016.

Cornell, Vincent J. *Realm of the Saint: Power and Authority in Moroccan Sufism.* Austin: University of Texas Press, 1998.

Costa, Yusuf da, and Achmat Davids. *Pages from Cape Muslim History.* Cape Town: Naqshbandi-Muhammadi South Africa, 1994.

Currie, P. M. *The Shrine and Cult of Mu'in al-Din Chishti of Ajmer.* New York and Delhi: Oxford University Press, 1989.

Cush, Denise, Catherine Robinson, and Michael York, eds. *Encyclopedia of Hinduism.* London and New York: Routledge, 2008.

Custers, Peter. "Maulana Bhashani and the Transition to Secular Politics in East Bengal." *Indian Economic and Social History Review* 47, no. 2 (2010): 231–59.

Dadoo, Yousuf. "Maulvi Cachalia: The Contributions of a Thinker Activist in the Political Liberation of South Africa." *Journal of Muslim Minority Affairs* 16, no. 1 (1996): 129–33.

Dangor, Suleman Essop. *A Critical Biography of Shaykh Yusuf.* Durban: Centre for Research in Islamic Studies, 1983.

Davids, Achmat. *The History of the Tana Baru.* Cape Town: Committee for the Preservation of the Tana Baru, 1985.

———. *The Mosques of the Bo-Kaap: A Social History of Islam at the Cape.* Cape Town: South African Institute of Arabic and Islamic Research, 1980.

De Jong, Frederick, and Bernd Radtke, eds. *Islamic Mysticism Contested: Thirteen Centuries of Controversies and Polemics.* Leiden: E. J. Brill, 1999.

Dhulipala, Venkat. *Creating a New Medina: State Power, Islam, and the Quest for Pakistan in Late Colonial North India.* New Delhi: Cambridge University Press, 2015.

Digby, Simon. "'Abd al-Quddus Gangohi (1456–1537): The Personality and Attitudes of a Medieval Indian Sufi." *Medieval India: A Miscellany* 3 (1975): 1–66.

Dimashqi, Qutb al-Din. *Imdad al-suluk.* Edited by Rashid Ahmad Gangohi. Lahore: Idara-yi Islamiyya, 1984.

Doumato, Eleanor Abdella, and Gregory Starrett. "Textbook Islam, Nation Building, and the Question of Violence." In *Teaching Islam: Textbooks and Religion in the Middle East,* edited by Eleanor Abdella Doumato and Gregory Starrett. Boulder, CO, and London: Lynne Rienner Publishers, 2007.

Dworkin, Gerald. *The Theory and Practice of Autonomy.* Cambridge: Cambridge University Press, 1998.

Ebr.-Vally, Rehana. *Kala Pani: Caste and Colour in South Africa.* Colorado Springs: International Academic Publishers, 2001.

Eickelman, Dale F., and James Piscatori. *Muslim Politics.* 2nd ed. Princeton, NJ: Princeton University Press, 2004.

Elias, Jamal J. *The Throne Carrier of God: The Life and Thought of 'Alā' ad-dawla as-Simnānī.* Albany: State University of New York Press, 1995.

———. "Un/Making Idolatry: From Mecca to Bamiyan." *Future Anterior: Journal of Historic Preservation* 4, no. 2 (2007): 2–29.

Elshakry, Marwa. *Reading Darwin in Arabic, 1860–1950.* Chicago and London: University of Chicago Press, 2013.

Ernst, Carl W. "An Indo-Persian Guide to Sufi Shrine Pilgrimage." In *Manifestations of Sainthood in Islam,* edited by Grace Martin Smith and Carl W. Ernst. Istanbul: Isis Press, 1993.

——. "Reconfiguring South Asian Islam: From the 18th to the 19th Century." *Comparative Islamic Studies* 5, no. 2 (2011): 247–72.

——. *Sufism: An Introduction to the Mystical Tradition of Islam.* Boston: Shambhala, 2011.

——. *Teachings of Sufism.* Boston and London: Shambhala, 1999.

——. *Words of Ecstasy in Sufism.* Albany: State University of New York Press, 1985.

Ernst, Carl W., and Bruce B. Lawrence. *Sufi Martyrs of Love: The Chishti Order in South Asia and Beyond.* New York: Palgrave Macmillan, 2002.

Esack, Farid. *But Musa Went to Fir-aun! A Compilation of Questions and Answers about the Role of Muslims in the South African Struggle for Liberation.* Maitland, Cape Town: Clyson Printers, 1989.

——. *Quran, Liberation & Pluralism: An Islamic Perspective on Interreligious Solidarity against Oppression.* Oxford: Oneworld, 1997.

——. "Review of Faith." Unpublished manuscript, 1984.

Euben, Roxanne E., and Muhammad Qasim Zaman. Introduction to *Princeton Readings in Islamist Thought,* edited by Roxanne E. Euben and Muhammad Qasim Zaman. Princeton, NJ: Princeton University Press, 2009.

Ewing, Katherine. *Arguing Sainthood: Modernity, Psychoanalysis, and Sainthood.* Durham, NC: Duke University Press, 1997.

Fadil, Nadia, and Mayanthi Fernando. "Rediscovering the 'Everyday' Muslim: Notes on an Anthropological Divide." *Hau: Journal of Ethnographic Theory* 5, no. 2 (2015): 59–88.

Faruq, Muhammad. *Afriqah aur khidmat-i Faqih al-Ummat.* Deoband: Maktaba-yi Nashr al-Mahmud, 1990.

——. *Hayat-i Mahmud: Savanih Faqih al-Ummat Mufti Mahmud Hasan Gangohi.* Meerut, India: Maktaba-yi Mahmudiyya, 1998.

——. *Zikr-i Masih al-Ummat.* Brixton, South Africa: Maktaba Noor, 1998.

Faruqi, Zia ul-Hasan. *The Deoband School and the Demand for Pakistan.* New York: Asia Publishing House, 1963.

Fernando, Mayanthi. *The Republic Unsettled: Muslim French and the Contradictions of Secularism.* Durham, NC: Duke University Press, 2014.

Fisch, Jorg. *Cheap Lives and Dear Limbs: The British Transformation of the Bengal Criminal Law, 1769–1817.* Wiesbaden: Franz Steiner Verlag, 1983.

Fleck, Ludwik. *Genesis and Development of a Scientific Fact.* Translated by Fred Bradley and Thaddeus J. Trenn. Chicago and London: University of Chicago Press, 1979.

Flood, Finbarr Barry. "Between Cult and Culture: Bamiyan, Islamic Iconoclasm, and the Museum." *Art Bulletin* 84, no. 4 (2002): 641–59.

Frembgen, Jürgen Wasim. "*Dhamal* and the Performing Body: Trance Dance in the Devotional Sufi Practice of Pakistan." *Journal of Sufi Studies* 1, no. 1 (2012): 77–113.

Friedmann, Yohanan. *Prophecy Continuous: Aspects of Ahmadi Religious Thought and Its Medieval Background.* Berkeley: University of California Press, 1989.

Foucault, Michel. *The History of Sexuality.* Vol. 3, *The Care of the Self.* New York: Vintage Books, 1986.

———. "What Is Enlightenment?" In *The Foucault Reader,* edited by Paul Rabinow. New York: Pantheon Books, 1984.

Fuerst, Ilyse Morgenstein. *Indian Muslim Minorities and the 1857 Rebellion: Religion, Rebels, and Jihad.* London and New York: I. B. Tauris, 2017.

Furey, Constance. "Body, Society and Subjectivity in Religious Studies." *Journal of the American Academy of Religion* 80, no. 1 (2012): 7–33.

Gaborieau, Marc. "Criticizing the Sufis: The Debate in Early-Nineteenth Century India." In *Islamic Mysticism Contested: Thirteen Centuries of Controversies and Polemics,* edited by Frederick de Jong and Bernd Radtke. Leiden: E. J. Brill, 1999.

———. "Late Persian, Early Urdu: The Case of 'Wahhabi' Literature (1818–1857)." In *Confluence of Cultures: French Contributions to Indo-Persian Studies,* edited by Françoise "Nalini" Delvoye. New Delhi: Manohar, 1994.

———. *Le Mahdi incompris: Sayyid Ahmad Barelwi (1786–1831) et le millénarisme en Inde.* Paris: CNRS Éditions, 2010.

———. "The Transformation of the Tablighi Jama'at into a Transnational Movement." In *Travellers in Faith: Studies of the Tablighi Jama'at as a Transnational Islamic Movement for Faith Renewal,* edited by Muhammad Khalid Masud. Leiden: E. J. Brill, 2000.

Gangohi, Mahmud Hasan. *Hudud-i ikhtilaf.* Edited by Muhammad Faruq Mirathi. Meerut, India: Maktaba-yi Mahmudiyya, 1990.

———. *Malfoozat: Statements and Anecdotes of Faqeeh-ul-Ummat.* Edited by Mufti Farooq Meeruti. Durban: Madrasah Taleemuddeen, 2010.

Gangohi, Rashid Ahmad. *Fatawa-yi Rashidiyya.* Karachi: Educational Press Pakistan, 1985.

———. *Irshadat-i Gangohi.* Edited by 'Abd al-Rauf Rahimi. Delhi: Farid Book Depot, 2003.

———. *Makatib-i Rashidiyya.* Edited by Mahmud Ashraf 'Usmani. Lahore: Idara-yi Islamiyya, 1996.

Geaves, Ron. "The Contested Milieu of Deoband: 'Salafis' or 'Sufis'?" In *Sufis and Salafis in the Contemporary Age,* edited by Lloyd Ridgeon. London and New York: Bloomsbury Academic, 2015.

Gelvin, James L., and Nile Green, eds., *Global Muslims in the Age of Steam and Print.* Berkeley and Los Angeles: University of California Press, 2014.

Gerber, Haim. *Islamic Law and Culture: 1600–1840.* Leiden, Boston, and Cologne: E. J. Brill, 1999.

Ghazali, Abu Hamid Muhammad al-. *Kitab al-'Ilm: The Book of Knowledge.* Translated by Kenneth Honnerkamp. Louisville, KY: Fons Vitae, 2015.

———. *The Remembrance of Death and the Afterlife: Kitab dhikr al-mawt wa-ma ba'dahu.* Cambridge: Islamic Texts Society, 2015.

Ghosh, Papiya. "*Muttahidah qaumiyat* in *aqalliat* Bihar: The Imarat i Shariah, 1921–1947." *Indian Economic and Social History Review* 34, no. 1 (1997): 1–20.

Giddens, Anthony. *The Consequences of Modernity.* Stanford, CA: Stanford University Press, 1990.

Gilani, Sayyid Manazir Ahsan. *Savanih Qasimi, ya'ni sirat-i shams al-Islam.* 3 vols. Lahore: Maktaba-yi Rahmaniyya, n.d.

Gilmartin, David. *Empire and Islam: Punjab and the Making of Pakistan.* London: I. B. Tauris, 1988.

Goswami, Manu. *Producing India: From Colonial Economy to National Space.* Chicago: University of Chicago Press, 2004.

Government of India. Legislative Department. *The Unrepealed General Acts of the Governor General in Council.* Calcutta: Office of the Superintendent of Government Printing, 1898.

Green, Nile. *Bombay Islam: The Religious Economy of the West Indian Ocean, 1840–1915.* Cambridge: Cambridge University Press, 2011.

———. "Islam for the Indentured Servant: A Muslim Missionary in Colonial South Africa." *Bulletin of the School of Oriental and African Studies* 71, no. 3 (2008): 529–53.

———. *Making Space: Sufis and Settlers in Early Modern India.* New Delhi: Oxford University Press, 2012.

———. *Sufism: A Global History.* Malden, UK: Wiley Blackwell, 2012.

———. *Terrains of Exchange: Religious Economies of Global Islam.* Oxford and New York: Oxford University Press, 2013.

———. "Urdu as an African Language: A Survey of a Source Literature." *Islamic Africa* 3, no. 2 (2012): 173–99.

———. "The Uses of Books in a Late Mughal Takiyya: Persianate Knowledge between Person and Paper." *Modern Asian Studies* 44, no. 2 (2010): 241–65.

Guenther, Alan M. "Hanafi *Fiqh* in Mughal India: The *Fatawa-i Alamgiri*." In *India's Islamic Traditions: 711–1150*, edited by Richard M. Eaton. New Delhi: Oxford University Press, 2003.

Günther, Ursula. "The Memory of Imam Haron in Consolidating Muslim Resistance in the Apartheid Struggle." In *Religion and the Political Imagination in a Changing South Africa*, edited by Gordon Mitchell and Eve Mullen. New York and Münster: Waxmann Verlag, 2002.

Hadot, Pierre. *Philosophy as a Way of Life: Spiritual Exercises from Socrates to Foucault.* Oxford: Blackwell, 1995.

Haj, Samira. *Reconfiguring Islamic Tradition: Reform, Rationality, Modernity.* Stanford, CA: Stanford University Press, 2008.

Hallaq, Wael. *A History of Islamic Legal Theories: An Introduction to Sunni Usul al-Fiqh.* Cambridge: Cambridge University Press, 1997.

———. *Shari'a: Theory, Practice, Transformations.* Cambridge: Cambridge University Press, 2009.

———. "Was the Gate of Ijtihad Closed?" *International Journal of Middle Eastern Studies* 16 (1984): 3–41.

Hamidi, Abdun Nabi. *Permissibility of Loud Zikr in the Masjid and Elsewhere.* Johannesburg: Sarwari Qaaderi Publications, 2000.

———. *Yes, Meelaad Celebration Is Commendable.* Azaadville, South Africa: Sunni Ulema Council, n.d.

Haq, ʿAbd al-., et al. *Fatawa-yi Haqqaniyya.* Edited by Mukhtar Allah Haqqani. 6 vols. Akora Khattak, Pakistan: Jamiʿa Dar al-ʿUlum Haqqaniyya, 2002.

Haq, Mufti Raza al-. *Fatawa-yi Dar al-ʿUlum Zakariyya.* 7 vols. Edited by Shabbir Ahmad Saluji. Karachi: Zam Zam Publishers, 2015.

Haq, Samiʿ al-. *Afghan Taliban: War of Ideology, Struggle for Peace.* Islamabad: Emel Publications, 2015.

———. *Qur'an aur taʿmir-i akhlaq.* Akora Khattak, Pakistan: Maktaba al-Haq, 1984.

Haqqani, Muhammad Palan. *Shariʿat ya jahalat.* Karachi: Qadimi Kutub Khana, 1975.

Haron, Muhammed. "*Muslim News* (1973–1986): Its Contribution towards the Establishment of an Alternative Press at the Cape." *Muslim World* 85, nos. 3/4 (1995): 317–32.

Haron, Muhammed, and Imraan Buccus. "*Al-Qalam*: An Alternative Muslim Voice in the South African Press." *South African Historical Journal* 61, no. 1 (2009): 121–37.

Haroon, Sana. "Contextualizing the Deobandi Approach to Congregation and Management of Mosques in Colonial North India." *Journal of Islamic Studies* 28, no. 1 (2017): 68–93.

Hasan, ʿAziz al-. *Ashraf al-savanih.* 4. vols. Multan, Pakistan: Idara-yi Taʾlifat-i Ashrafiyya, n.d.

Haykel, Bernard. "On the Nature of Salafi Thought and Action." In *Global Salafism: Islam's New Religious Movement,* edited by Roel Meijer. New York: Columbia University Press, 2009.

Hazarvi, Mufti Akbar. *Meelaad-Un-Nabie Celebration in the Light of Shariah.* Laudium, South Africa: Soutul Islam Publications, 1999.

Hedayetullah, Muhammad. *Sayyid Ahmad: A Study of the Religious Reform Movement of Sayyid Ahmad of Rae Bareli.* Lahore: Sh. Muhammad Ashraf, 1970.

Hermansen, Marcia K. "Fakirs, Wahhabis and Others: Reciprocal Classifications and the Transformation of Intellectual Categories." In *Perspectives of Mutual Encounters in South Asian History 1760–1860,* edited by Jamal Malik. Leiden: E. J. Brill, 2000.

Ho, Engseng. *The Graves of Tarim: Genealogy and Mobility across the Indian Ocean.* Berkeley: University of California Press, 2006.

Hoesterey, James B. *Rebranding Islam: Piety, Prosperity, and a Self-Help Guru.* Stanford, CA: Stanford University Press, 2016.

Hujjat al-Islam Imam Ghazali. *Tabligh-i din.* Delhi: Naz Publishing House, 1962.

———. See also: Ghazali, Abu Hamid Muhammad al-.

Hurd, Elizabeth Shakman. *Beyond Religious Freedom: The New Global Politics of Religion.* Princeton, NJ: Princeton University Press, 2015.

Hussin, Iza. *The Politics of Islamic Law: Local Elites, Colonial Authority, and the Making of the Muslim State.* Chicago: University of Chicago Press, 2016.

Ibn Taymiyya, Ahmad. *Amrad al-qulub wa shifa'uha: Yaliha al-tuhfa al-'Iraqiyya fi al-a'mal al-qalbiyya*. Cairo: Al-Matba'at al-Salafiyya wa Maktabatuha, 1966/67.

Ikram, S. M. *Rud-i kausar: Islami Hind aur Pakistan ki mazhabi aur ruhani tarikh; 'ahd-i mughaliya*. Lahore: Idara-yi Siqafat-i Islamiya, 1975.

Ilahi, Muhammad 'Ashiq. *Che Batein*. Karachi: Qadimi Kutub Khana, n.d.

Ilyas, Muhammad. *A Call to Muslims*. New Delhi: Idara Isha'at-i Diniyat, n.d.

Imdad Allah, Hajji Muhammad. *Kulliyat-i Imdadiyya*. Karachi: Dar al-Isha'at, 1977.

———. *Navadir-i Imdadiyya*. Edited by Nishar Ahmad Faruqi. Gulbarga, India: Sayyid Muhammad Gesudaraz Tahqiqati Academy, 1996.

Ingram, Brannon D. "Crises of the Public in Muslim India: Critiquing 'Custom' at Aligarh and Deoband." *South Asia: Journal of South Asian Studies* 38, no. 3 (2015): 403–18.

———. "The Portable Madrasa: Print, Publics and the Authority of the Deobandi 'Ulama." *Modern Asian Studies* 48, no. 4 (2014): 845–71.

———. "Sufis, Scholars and Scapegoats: Rashid Ahmad Gangohi (d. 1905) and the Deobandi Critique of Sufism." *Muslim World* 99, no. 3 (2009): 478–501.

Iqbal, Basit. "Thinking about Method: A Conversation with Talal Asad." *Qui Parle* 26, no. 1 (2017): 195–218.

Iqbal, Muhammad. *Kulliyat-i Iqbal Urdu*. Aligarh: Educational Book House, 2003.

Iqtidar, Humeira. "Redefining 'Tradition' in Political Thought," *European Journal of Political Theory* 15, no. 4 (2016): 424–44.

———. *Secularizing Islamists? Jama'at-e-Islami and Jama'at-ud-Da'wa in Urban Pakistan*. Chicago: University of Chicago Press, 2011.

Islahi, Zafar al-Islam. *Ta'lim 'ahd-i Islami ke Hindustan men*. Azamgarh, India: Shibli Academy, 2007.

Isma'il, Muhammad. *Izah al-haqq fi ahkam al-mayyit wa al-darih*. Delhi: Kutub Khana-yi Ashrafiyya, 1937.

———. *Taqwiyyat al-iman ma' tazkir al-ikhwan*. Deoband: Dar al-Kitab Deoband, 1997.

Jacobs, Adli. *Punching above Its Weight: The Story of the Call of Islam*. Bloomington, IN: AuthorHouse, 2014.

Jaffar, S. M. *Education in Muslim India, Being an Inquiry into the State of Education during the Muslim Period of Indian History, 1000–1800*. Delhi: Idarah-i Adabiyat-i Delhi, 1972.

Jahanara. *Mu'nis al-arvah*. Karachi: S. M. Hamid Ali, 1991.

Jalal, Ayesha. *Partisans of Allah: Jihad in South Asia*. Cambridge, MA: Harvard University Press, 2008.

———. *Self and Sovereignty: Individual and Community in South Asian Islam since 1850*. London: Routledge, 2000.

Jami, 'Abd al-Rahman. *Nafahat al-uns min hadrat al-quds*. Cairo: Al-Azhar al-Sharif, 1989.

Jeppie, Shamil. "Amandla and Allahu Akbar: Muslims and Resistance in South Africa, c. 1970–1987." *Journal for the Study of Religion* 4, no. 1 (1991): 3–19.

———. *I. D. Du Plessis and the "Re-Invention" of the "Malay," c. 1935–1952.* Cape Town: Centre for African Studies, 1988.

———. *Language, Identity, Modernity: The Arabic Study Circle of Durban.* Cape Town: Human Sciences Research Council Press, 2007.

———. "Reclassifications: Coloured, Malay, Muslim." In *Coloured by History, Shaped by Place: New Perspectives on Coloured Identities in Cape Town,* edited by Zimitri Erasmus. Colorado Springs: International Academic Publishers, 2001.

Joshi, Sanjay. *Fractured Modernity: Making of a Middle Class in Colonial North India.* New Delhi: Oxford University Press, 2001.

Kalabadhi, Abu Bakr Muhammad al-. *Al-Ta'arruf li-madhdhab ahl al-tasawwuf.* Cairo: Maktaba al-Kulliyat al-Azhariyya, 1969.

Kamali, Mohammad Hashim. *Principles of Islamic Jurisprudence.* 3rd ed. Cambridge: Islamic Texts Society, 2003.

Kandhlavi, Muhammad Idris. *Ma'arif al-Qur'an.* 8 vols. Shahdapur, Pakistan: Maktaba al-Ma'arif, n.d.

Kandhlavi, Muhammad Zakariyya. *Al-I'tidal fi maratib al-rijal, ya'ni Islami siyasat.* Deoband: Ittihad Book Depot, n.d.

———. *Maut ki yad.* Karachi: Idara al-Ma'arif, 2005.

———. *Shari'at o tariqat ka talazum.* Karachi: Maktaba al-Shaykh, 1993.

———. *Tarikh-i mashaikh-i Chisht.* Karachi: Maktaba al-Shaykh, 1976.

———. *Tarikh-i mazahir.* 2 vols. Saharanpur: Kutub Khana-yi Isha'at al-'Ulum, 1972.

Kant, Immanuel. "An Answer to the Question: What Is Enlightenment?" In *What Is Enlightenment? Eighteenth-Century Answers and Twentieth-Century Questions,* edited by James Schmidt. Berkeley: University of California Press, 1996.

Kaptein, N. J. G. *Muhammad's Birthday Festival: Early History in the Central Muslim Lands and Development in the Muslim West until the 10th/16th Century.* Leiden: E. J. Brill, 1993.

Karamustafa, Ahmet T. *Sufism: The Formative Period.* Berkeley: University of California Press, 2007.

Katz, Marion Holmes. *The Birth of the Prophet Muhammad: Devotional Piety in Sunni Islam.* London and New York: Routledge, 2007.

———. "The Corruption of the Times and the Mutability of the Shari'a." *Cardozo Law Review* 28, no. 1 (2006): 171–86.

Keddie, Nikki, trans. *An Islamic Response to Imperialism: Political and Religious Writings of Sayyid Jamal al-Din al-Afghani.* Berkeley: University of California Press, 1983.

Kelly, Jill E. "'It Is *Because* of Our Islam That We Are There': The Call of Islam in the United Democratic Front Era." *African Historical Review* 41, no. 1 (2009): 118–39.

Khan, Ahmad Raza. *Husam al-haramayn 'ala manhar al-kufr wa al-mayn.* Lahore: Maktabah-yi Nabawiyya, 1975.

———. *Maqal 'urafa' bi-i'zaz shar' 'ulama, al-ma'ruf shari'at o tariqat.* Karachi: Idara-yi Tasnifat-i Imam Ahmad Raza, 1983.

———. *The Validity of Saying "Ya Rasoolallah."* Translated by Durwesh Abu Muhammad Abdul Hadi al-Qadiri. Durban: Imam Ahmed Raza Academy, n.d.

Khan, Dargah Quli. *Muraqqa-yi Dihli: Farsi matn aur̤ Urdu tarjamah.* Translated by Khalid Anjum. Delhi: Anjuman-i Taraqqi-yi Urdu, 1993.

Khan, Fareeha. "Tafwid al-Talaq: Transferring the Right to Divorce to the Wife." *Muslim World* 99, no. 3 (2009): 502–20.

———. "Traditionalist Approaches to *Shari'at* Reform: Mawlana Ashraf 'Ali Thanawi's Fatwa on Women's Right to Divorce." PhD diss., University of Michigan, 2008.

Khan, Masihullah. *Shari'at o tasawwuf: Fan-i tasawwuf ki mukammal o mudallal-i kitab.* Multan, Pakistan: Idara-yi Ta'lifat-i Ashrafiyya, 1996.

Khan, Sarfraz. *Bani-yi Dar al-'Ulum Deoband.* Gujranwala: Maktaba-yi Safdariyya, 2001.

Kifayat Allah, Muhammad. *Ta'lim al-Islam.* 4 vols. Delhi: Kutub Khana-yi 'Aziziyya, n.d.

Kinra, Rajeev. *Writing Self, Writing Empire: Chandar Bhan Brahman and the Cultural World of the Indo-Persian State Secretary.* Oakland: University of California Press, 2015.

Knysh, Alexander D. "A Clear and Present Danger: 'Wahhabism' as a Rhetorical Foil." *Die Welt des Islams* 44, no. 1 (2004): 3–26.

———. *Ibn 'Arabi in the Later Islamic Tradition: The Making of a Polemical Image in Medieval Islam.* Albany: State University of New York Press, 1999.

Koselleck, Reinhart. *The Practice of Conceptual History: Timing History, Spacing Concepts.* Stanford, CA: Stanford University Press, 2002.

Kostiner, Joseph. *The Making of Saudi Arabia, 1916–1936: From Chieftaincy to Monarchical State.* Oxford: Oxford University Press, 1993.

Kozlowski, Gregory C. *Muslim Endowments and Society in British India.* Cambridge: Cambridge University Press, 1985.

Kramer, Martin. *Islam Assembled: The Advent of the Muslim Congresses.* New York: Columbia University Press, 1986.

Kugle, Scott Alan. "Framed, Blamed and Renamed: The Recasting of Islamic Jurisprudence in Colonial South Asia." *Modern Asian Studies* 35, no. 2 (2001): 257–313.

———. *Rebel between Spirit and Law: Ahmad Zarruq, Sainthood, and Authority in Islam.* Bloomington and Indianapolis: Indiana University Press, 2006.

———. *Sufis and Saints' Bodies: Mysticism, Corporeality, and Sacred Power in Islam.* Chapel Hill: University of North Carolina Press, 2007.

Lambert-Hurley, Siobhan. *Muslim Women, Reform and Princely Patronage: Nawab Sultan Jahan Begam of Bhopal.* London and New York: Routledge, 2007.

Landau-Tasserson, Ella. "The 'Cyclical Reform': A Study of the Mujaddid Tradition." *Studia Islamica* 70 (1989): 79–117.

Lander, Jesse M. *Inventing Polemic: Religion, Print and Literary Culture in Early Modern England.* Cambridge: Cambridge University Press, 2006.

Laqueur, Thomas. *The Work of the Dead: A Cultural History of Mortal Remains.* Princeton, NJ: Princeton University Press, 2015.

Lauzière, Henri. *The Making of Salafism: Islamic Reform in the Twentieth Century*. New York: Columbia University Press, 2016.

Lawrence, Bruce B. *Defenders of God: The Fundamentalist Revolt against the Modern Age*. London and New York: I. B. Tauris, 1990.

Le Bon, Gustave. *The Crowd: A Study of the Popular Mind*. Mineola, NY: Dover Publications, 2002.

Legassick, Martin, and Robert Ross. "From Slave Economy to Settler Capitalism: The Cape Colony and Its Extensions, 1800–1854." In *The Cambridge History of South Africa*, vol. 1, edited by Carolyn Hamilton, Bernard K. Mbenga, and Robert Ross. Cambridge: Cambridge University Press, 2010.

Leitner, G. W. *History of Indigenous Education in the Panjab since Annexation and in 1882*. New Delhi: Languages Department Punjab, 1971.

Lilla, Mark. *The Shipwrecked Mind: On Political Reaction*. New York: New York Review of Books, 2016.

Lipton, G. A. "Secular Sufism: Neoliberalism, Ethno-Racism, and the Reformation of the Muslim Other." *Muslim World* 101, no. 3 (2011): 427–40.

Lubbe, Gerrie. "The Muslim Judicial Council: Custodian or Catalyst?" *Journal for Islamic Studies* 14 (1994): 34–62.

———. "The Soweto Fatwa: A Muslim Response to a Watershed Event in South Africa." *Journal of Muslim Minority Affairs* 17, no. 2 (1997): 335–43.

Ludhianvi, Muhammad Yusuf. *Ikhtilaf-i ummat aur sirat al-mustaqim*. Karachi: Maktaba Ludhianvi, 1995.

MacIntyre, Alasdair. *Whose Justice, Which Rationality?* South Bend, IN: University of Notre Dame Press, 1989.

Madani, Husain Ahmad. *Al-Shihab al-saqib 'ala al-mustariq al-kazib*. Lahore, 1979.

———. *Muttahida qawmiyyat aur Islam*. Edited by Amjad 'Ali Shakir. Lahore: Jami'at Publications, 2006.

Mahida, Ebrahim Mahomed. *History of Muslims in South Africa: A Chronology*. Durban: Arabic Study Circle, 1993.

Mahmud, Izhar al-Hasan. *'Ishq-i rasul aur 'ulama-yi Deoband*. Lahore: Maktaba al-Hasan, n.d.

Majlisul Ulama of South Africa. *The Interfaith Trap of Kufr*. Benoni, South Africa: Young Men's Muslim Association, n.d.

———. *Meelaad Celebrations*. Benoni, South Africa: Young Men's Muslim Association, 1985.

———. *Moulood and the Shariah*. Benoni, South Africa: Young Men's Muslim Association, n.d.

———. *The Spreading of Confusion and Falsehood about the Tablighi Jamaat / What Is Meelaad?* Benoni, South Africa: Young Men's Muslim Association, 1988.

———. *Who Are the People of Sunnah?* Benoni, South Africa: Young Men's Muslim Association, n.d.

Makdisi, George. "The Hanbali School and Sufism." *Biblos (Coimbra)* 46 (1970): 71–84.

———. *The Rise of Colleges: Institutions of Learning in Islam and the West*. Edinburgh: Edinburgh University Press, 1981.

Malik, Jamal. "Encounter and Appropriation in the Context of Modern South Asian History." In *Perspectives of Mutual Encounters in South Asian History 1760–1860,* edited by Jamal Malik. Leiden: E. J. Brill, 2000.

———. Introduction to *Madrasas in South Asia: Teaching Terror?,* edited by Jamal Malik. London and New York: Routledge, 2008.

———. *Islamische Gelehrtenkultur in Nordindien: Entwicklungsgeschichte und Tendenzen am Beispiel von Lucknow.* Leiden, New York, and Cologne: E. J. Brill, 1997.

Mantena, Karuna. *Alibis of Empire: Henry Maine and the Ends of Liberal Imperialism.* Princeton, NJ: Princeton University Press, 2010.

Marghinani, Burhan al-Din Abu'l Hasan. *Hedaya, a Commentary on the Mussulman Laws.* Translated by Charles Hamilton. London: T. Bensley, 1791.

Marx, Anthony W. *Lessons of Struggle: South African Internal Opposition, 1960–1990.* New York: Oxford University Press, 1992.

Mason, John Edwin. "'A Faith for Ourselves': Slavery, Sufism, and Conversion to Islam at the Cape." *South African Historical Journal* 46 (2002): 3–24.

Masud, Muhammad Khalid. "Apostasy and Judicial Separation in British India." In *Islamic Legal Interpretation: Muftis and Their Fatwas,* edited by Muhammad Khalid Masud, Brinkley Messick, and David S. Powers. Cambridge, MA: Harvard University Press, 1996.

———. "Cosmopolitanism and Authenticity: The Doctrine of *Tashabbuh Bi'l-Kuffar* ('Imitating the Infidel') in Modern South Asian Fatwas." In *Cosmopolitanisms in Muslim Contexts: Perspectives from the Past,* edited by Derryl N. Maclean and Sikeena Karmali Ahmed. Edinburgh: Edinburgh University Press, 2012.

———. "The Definition of Bid'a in the South Asian *Fatawa* Literature." *Annales Islamologiques* 27 (1993): 55–71.

———. "Ideology and Legitimacy." In *Travellers in Faith: Studies of the Tablighi Jama'at as a Transnational Movement for Faith Renewal,* edited by Muhammad Khalid Masud. Leiden: E. J. Brill, 2000.

———. Introduction to *Travellers in Faith: Studies of the Tablighi Jama'at as a Transnational Movement for Faith Renewal,* edited by Muhammad Khalid Masud. Leiden: E. J. Brill, 2000.

———. "Islam and Modernity in South Asia." In *Being Muslim in South Asia,* edited by Robin Jeffrey and Ronojoy Sen. New Delhi: Oxford University Press, 2014.

———. *Shatibi's Philosophy of Islamic Law.* 2nd ed. New Delhi: Kitab Bhavan, 2009.

———. "Trends in the Interpretation of Islamic Law as Reflected in the Fatawa Literature of the Deoband School," MA thesis, McGill University, 1969.

Ma'sudi, Anzar Shah. *Naqsh-i davam.* Deoband: Shah Book Depot, n.d.

Maududi, Abul A'la. *Islamic Way of Life.* Translated by Khurshid Ahmad. Durban: Muslim Youth Movement of South Africa, n.d.

Mayer, Farhana, trans. *Spiritual Gems: The Mystical Qur'an Commentary Ascribed to Ja'far al-Sadiq.* Louisville, KY: Fons Vitae, 2011.

Mazzarella, William. "Affect: What Is It Good For?" In *Enchantments of Modernity: Empire, Nation, Globalization,* edited by Saurabh Dube. London, New York, and New Delhi: Routledge, 2009.

———. "Myth of the Multitude, or Who's Afraid of the Crowd?" *Critical Inquiry* 36 (2010): 697–727.

Meer, Fatima. "Interest and Dar ul-Harb in Islam: A Preliminary Analysis of the Fatwa on Riba of the Muftees of Dar-ul-Uloom, Deoband." Supp., *Views and News,* 10 February 1966.

Meron, Y. "Marghinani, His Method and His Legacy." *Islamic Law and Society* 9, no. 3 (2002): 410–16.

Metcalf, Barbara Daly. *Husain Ahmad Madani: The Jihad for Islam and India's Freedom.* Oxford: Oneworld, 2009.

———. "Imagining Community: Polemical Debates in Colonial India." In *Religious Controversy in British India: Dialogues in South Asian Languages,* edited by Kenneth W. Jones. Albany: State University of New York Press, 1992.

———. *Islamic Revival in British India: Deoband, 1860–1900.* Princeton, NJ: Princeton University Press, 1982.

———. "New Medinas: The Tablighi Jama'at in America and Europe." In *Making Muslim Space in North America and Europe,* edited by Barbara Daly Metcalf. Berkeley: University of California Press, 1996.

———, trans. *Perfecting Women: Maulana Ashraf 'Ali Thanvi's "Bihishti Zewar": A Partial Translation with Commentary.* Berkeley: University of California Press, 1990.

———. "'Remaking Ourselves': Islamic Self-Fashioning in a Global Movement of Spiritual Renewal." In *Accounting for Fundamentalisms: The Dynamic Character of Movements,* edited by Martin E. Marty and R. Scott Appleby. Chicago: University of Chicago Press, 1994.

———. "Tablighi Jama'at and Women." In *Travellers in Faith: Studies of the Tablighi Jama'at as a Transnational Movement for Faith Renewal,* edited by Muhammad Khalid Masud. Leiden: E. J., Brill, 2000.

Metcalf, Thomas R. *Ideologies of the Raj.* Cambridge: Cambridge University Press, 1994.

———. *Imperial Connections: India in the Indian Ocean Arena, 1860–1920.* Berkeley: University of California Press, 2007.

Metcalf, Thomas R., and Barbara D. Metcalf. *A Concise History of Modern India.* 3rd ed. New York: Cambridge University Press, 2012.

Mian, Ali Altaf. "Surviving Modernity: Ashraf 'Ali Thanvi (1863–1943) and the Making of Muslim Orthodoxy in Colonial India." PhD diss., Duke University, 2015.

Miftahi, Rashid Ahmad Mewati. *Hayat-i Masih al-Ummat.* Faridabad: Idara-yi Ta'lifat-i Masih al-Ummat, 1995.

Minault, Gail. *The Khilafat Movement: Religious Symbolism and Political Mobilization in India.* New York: Columbia University Press, 1982.

———. *Secluded Scholars: Women's Education and Muslim Social Reform in Colonial India.* Oxford: Oxford University Press, 1998.

Mir, Farina. *The Social Space of Language: Vernacular Culture in British Colonial Punjab.* Berkeley: University of California Press, 2010.

Mirathi, Muhammad 'Ashiq Ilahi. *Tazkirat al-Khalil.* Saharanpur: Kutub Khana-yi Isha'at al-'Ulum, n.d.

———. *Tazkirat al-Rashid.* 2 vols. Saharanpur: Kutub Khana-yi Isha'at al-'Ulum, 1977.

Mirzapuri, 'Abd al-Shakur. *Tarikh-i milad.* Karachi: Dar al-Isha'at, 1978.

Misbahi, Yasin Akhtar. *Imam Ahmad Raza aur radd-i bid'at wa munkarat.* Karachi: Idara-yi Tahqiqat-i Imam Ahmad Raza, 1985.

Miyan, Sayyid Muhammad. *'Ulama-yi haqq aur un ke mujahidana karname.* Lahore: Jam'iyat Publications, 2005.

Moin, A. Afzar. *The Millennial Sovereign: Sacred Kingship and Sainthood in Islam.* New York: Columbia University Press, 2012.

Mojaddedi, Jawid. *The Biographical Tradition in Sufism: The Ṭabaqāt Genre from al-Sulamī to Jāmī.* Richmond, Surrey, UK: Curzon Press, 2001.

———. "Getting Drunk with Abu Yazid or Staying Sober with Junayd: The Creation of a Popular Typology of Sufism." *Bulletin of SOAS* 66, no. 1 (2003): 1–13.

Molina, J. Michelle. *To Overcome Oneself: The Jesuit Ethic and Spirit of Global Expansion, 1520–1767.* Berkeley: University of California Press, 2013.

Moosa, Ebrahim. "Ethical Landscape: Laws, Norms and Morality." In *Islam in the Modern World,* edited by Jeffrey T. Kenney and Ebrahim Moosa. Abingdon, UK: Routledge, 2012.

———. "History and Normativity in Traditional Indian Muslim Thought: Reading Shari'a in the Hermeneutics of Qari Muhammad Tayyab (d. 1983)." In *Rethinking Islamic Studies: From Orientalism to Cosmopolitanism,* edited by Carl W. Ernst and Richard C. Martin. Columbia: University of South Carolina Press, 2010.

———. "Introduction," *Muslim World* 99, no. 3 (2009): 427–34.

———. "Islam in South Africa." In *Living Faiths in South Africa,* edited by Martin Prozesky and John de Gruchy. New York: St. Martin's Press, 1995.

———. "Muslim Conservatism in South Africa." *Journal of Theology for Southern Africa* 69 (1989): 73–81.

———. *What Is a Madrasa?* Chapel Hill: University of North Carolina Press, 2015.

———. "Worlds 'Apart': The Tablighi Jama'at under Apartheid, 1963–1993." In *Travellers in Faith: Studies of the Tablighi Jama'at as a Transnational Movement for Faith Renewal,* edited by Muhammad Khalid Masud. Leiden: E.J. Brill, 2000.

Morley, William H. *The Administration of Justice in British India: Its Past History and Present State.* London: Williams and Norgate, 1858.

Mourrégot, Marie-France. *L'islam à l'île de la Réunion.* Paris: Harmattan, 2010.

Muhammad, Ebrahim. *A Guide to Madrasa Arabia Islamia.* Azaadville, South Africa: Madrasa Arabia Islamia, 2000.

Muslim Youth Movement of South Africa. *From Where Shall We Begin?* Durban: Muslim Youth Movement of South Africa, n.d.

———. *Islam for All, Islam Forever: Rally Manual.* Durban: Muslim Youth Movement of South Africa, 1983.

Nadvi, 'Abd al-Bari. *Tajdid-i mu'ashirat, ya'ni tajdid-i din-i kamil.* Lucknow: Majlis-i Tahqiqat o Nashiryat-i Islam, 2010.

Nadvi, Abu al-Hasan 'Ali. *Hazrat Maulana Muhammad Ilyas aur un ki dini da'wat.* Karachi: Majlis-i Nashriyat-i Islam, n.d.

Naeem, Fuad. "Sufism and Revivalism in South Asia: Maulana Ashraf 'Ali Thanvi of Deoband and Maulana Ahmad Raza Khan of Bareilly and Their Paradigms of Islamic Revivalism." *Muslim World* 99, no. 3 (2009): 435–51.

Nanautvi, Muhammad Qasim. *Guftagu-yi mazhabi.* Karachi: Dar al-Isha'at, 1977.

———. *Hadiya al-Shi'a.* Lahore: Nu'mani Kutub Khana, 1977.

———. *Intisar-i Islam ma' tashrih o tahsil.* Deoband: Majlis-i Ma'arif al-Qur'an, 1967.

———. *Mubahasah-yi Shahjahanpur.* Karachi: Dar al-Isha'at, 1977.

———. *Qiblah numa ma' tashrih o tehsil.* Deoband: Majlis-i Ma'arif al-Qur'an, 1969.

———. *Tasfiyat al-'aqa'id.* Delhi: Matba'-yi Mujtabai, 1934.

Nasr, Seyyed Vali Reza. *Maududi and the Making of Islamic Revivalism.* New York: Oxford University Press, 1996.

Naude, Jacobus A. "A Historical Survey of Opposition to Sufism in South Africa." In *Islamic Mysticism Contested: Thirteen Centuries of Conflicts and Polemics,* edited by Frederick de Jong and Bernd Radtke. Leiden: E. J. Brill, 1999.

Nedostup, Rebecca. *Superstitious Regimes: Religion and the Politics of Chinese Modernity.* Cambridge, MA: Harvard University Press, 2010.

Nizami, Moin Ahmad. *Reform and Renewal in South Asian Islam: The Chishti-Sabiris in 18th–19th Century North India.* New Delhi: Oxford University Press, 2017.

Noor, Farish A. "Pathans to the East! The Tablighi Jama'at Movement in Northern Malaysia and Southern Thailand." *Comparative Studies of South Asia, Africa and the Middle East* 27, no. 1 (2007): 7–25.

Noor, Farish A., Yoginder Sikand, and Martin van Bruinessen. "Behind the Walls: Re-Appraising the Role and Importance of Madrasas in the World Today." In *The Madrasa in Asia: Political Activism and Transnational Linkages,* edited by Farish A. Noor, Yoginder Sikand, and Martin van Bruinessen. Amsterdam: Amsterdam University Press, 2008.

Nu'mani, Muhammad Manzur. *Din o shari'at.* Lahore: Idara-yi Islamiyat, 1995.

———. *Islam kya hai.* Lucknow: Kakori Offset Press, 2008.

———. *Malfuzat-i Hazrat Maulana Muhammad Ilyas.* Lucknow: Kutub Khana al-Furqan, n.d.

———. *Shaykh Muhammad ibn 'Abd al-Wahhab ke khilaf propaganda aur Hindustan ke 'ulama-yi haqq par us ke asarat.* Lucknow: Kutub Khana al-Furqan, 1978.

Nyugen, Martin. *Sufi Master and Qur'an Scholar: Abu'l-Qasim al-Qushayri and the Lata'if al-Isharat.* Oxford: Oxford University Press, 2012.

Okarvi, Kaukab Noorani. *Deoband to Bareilly: The Truth.* Lahore: Zia-ul-Quraan Publications, 1996.

————. *Truth Wins: The Full Account of a Historic Challenge to Establish Truth as the Truth and Falsehood as the Falsehood.* Durban: Maulana Okarvi Academy, 1991.

————. *White and Black: Deobandi-ism Caught Up in Its Own Web.* Durban: Maulana Okarvi Academy, 1991.

O'Malley, P. F. *Religious Liberty and the Indian Proclamation.* London: W. H. Dalton, 1859.

Opwis, Felicitas. *Maslaha and the Purpose of the Law: Islamic Discourse on Legal Change from the 4th/10th to 8th/14th Century.* Leiden: E. J. Brill, 2010.

————. "Shifting Legal Authority from the Ruler to the 'Ulama: Rationalizing the Punishment for Drinking Wine during the Saljuq Period." *Der Islam* 86 (2011): 65–92.

Orsi, Robert A. *History and Presence.* Cambridge, MA: Belknap Press of Harvard University, 2016.

Palombo, Matthew. "The Emergence of Islamic Liberation Theology in South Africa." *Journal of Religion in Africa* 44 (2014): 28–61.

Panipati, Qazi Sanaullah. *Tuhfat al-salikin, tarjuma irshad al-talibin.* Allahabad: Maktaba-yi Jami wa Ikhwanihi, 1954.

Patel, Youshaa. "Muslim Distinction: Imitation and the Anxiety of Jewish, Christian, and Other Influences." PhD diss., Duke University, 2012.

Pearson, Harlon O. *Islamic Reform and Revival in Nineteenth-Century India: The Tariqah-i Muhammadiyah.* New Delhi: Yoda Press, 2008.

Pemberton, Kelly. "Islamic and Islamicizing Discourses: Ritual Performance, Didactic Texts, and the Reformist Challenge in the South Asian Sufi Milieu." *Annual of Urdu Studies* 17 (2002): 55–83.

————. "An Islamic Discursive Tradition of Reform as Seen in the Writing of Deoband's Mufti Muhammad Taqi 'Usmani." *Muslim World* 99, no. 3 (2009): 452–77.

Perkins, C. Ryan. "From the Mehfil to the Printed Word: Public Debate and Discourse in Late Colonial India." *Indian Economic and Social History Review* 50, no. 1 (2013): 47–76.

Pernau, Margrit. *Ashraf into Middle Classes: Muslims in Nineteenth-Century Delhi.* New Delhi: Oxford University Press, 2013.

————. "From a 'Private' Public to a 'Public' Private Sphere: Old Delhi and the North Indian Muslims in Comparative Perspective." In *The Public and the Private: Issues of Democratic Citizenship,* edited by Gurpreet Mahajan. New Delhi: Sage Publications, 2003.

————. "Male Anger and Female Malice: Emotions in Indo-Muslim Advice Literature." *History Compass* 10, no. 2 (2012): 119–28.

Peters, Rudolph. *Crime and Punishment in Islamic Law: Theory and Practice from the Sixteenth to the Twenty-First Century.* Cambridge: Cambridge University Press, 2005.

Philippon, Alix. *Soufisme et politique au Pakistan: Le mouvement barelwi à l'heure de "la guerre contre le terrorisme."* Paris: Éditions Karthala et Sciences Po Aix, 2011.

Philips, C. H., and B. N. Pandey, eds. *The Evolution of India and Pakistan, 1858 to 1947: Select Documents.* London: Oxford University Press, 1962.

Picken, Gavin. *Spiritual Purification in Islam: The Life and Works of al-Muhasibi.* London and New York: Routledge, 2011.

———. "Tazkiyat al-Nafs: The Qur'anic Paradigm." *Journal of Qur'anic Studies* 7, no. 2 (2005): 101–27.

Pickthall, Marmaduke. "Muslim Education." *Islamic Culture: The Hyderabad Quarterly Review* 1, no. 1 (1927): 100–108.

Pinto, Paulo G. "The Limits of the Public: Sufism and the Religious Debate in Syria." In *Public Islam and the Common Good,* edited by Armando Salvatore and Dale F. Eickelman. Leiden: E.J. Brill, 2004.

Posel, Deborah. "The Apartheid Project, 1948–1970." In *The Cambridge History of South Africa,* vol. 2, *1885–1994,* edited by Robert Ross, Anne Kelk Mager, and Bill Nasson. Cambridge: Cambridge University Press, 2011.

Powell, Avril A. *Muslims and Missionaries in Pre-Mutiny India.* Richmond, Surrey, UK: Curzon Press, 1993.

Prasad, Ritika. "'Time-Sense': Railways and Temporality in Colonial India." *Modern Asian Studies* 47, no. 4 (2013): 1252–82.

Qasimi, Ghulam Nabi. *Hayat-i Tayyib.* 2 vols. Deoband: Hujjat al-Islam Academy, 2014.

Qasimi, Muhammad Anwar al-Hasan Anwar. *Kamalat-i 'Usmani.* Multan, Pakistan: Idara-yi Ta'lifat-i Ashrafiyya, 2006.

Qibla. *Dimensions of the Kalimah.* Athlone, Cape Town: Qibla, n.d.

———. *Eid Message: The Intellectual Roots of the Oppressed and Islam's Triumph over Apartheid.* Athlone, Cape Town: Qibla, 1992.

———. *One Solution, Islamic Revolution.* Athlone, Cape Town: Qibla, n.d.

Qureshi, Ishtiaq. *Ulema in Politics: A Study Relating to the Political Activities of the Ulema in the South-Asian Subcontinent from 1556 to 1947.* Karachi: Ma'aref Ltd., 1972.

Qureshi, M. Naeem. *Pan-Islam in British Indian Politics: A Study of the Khilafat Movement, 1918–1924.* Leiden: E.J. Brill, 1999.

Qushayri, Abul Qasim al-. *Sufi Book of Spiritual Ascent.* Translated by Rabia Harris. Chicago: Kazi Publications, 1997.

Rahman, Fazlur. *Islam and Modernity: Transformation of an Intellectual Tradition.* Chicago and London: University of Chicago Press, 1982.

Reese, Scott S. *Imperial Muslims: Islam, Community and Authority in the Indian Ocean, 1839–1937.* Edinburgh: Edinburgh University Press, 2018.

Reetz, Dietrich. "Change and Stagnation in Islamic Education: The Dar ul-'Ulum Deoband after the Split in 1982." In *The Madrasa in Asia,* edited by Farish A. Noor, Yoginder Sikand, and Martin van Bruinessen. Amsterdam: Amsterdam University Press, 2008.

———. "The Deoband Universe: What Makes a Transcultural and Transnational Educational Movement of Islam?" *Comparative Studies of South Asia, Africa and the Middle East* 27, no. 1 (2007): 139–59.

———. "The Tablighi Madrassas in Lenasia and Azaadville: Local Players in the Global 'Islamic Field.'" In *Muslim Schools and Education in Europe and Africa,* edited by Abdulkader Tayob, Inga Niehaus, and Wolfram Weissem. Münster: Waxmann, 2011.

Reinhart, A. Kevin. "When Women Went to Mosques: Al-Aydini on the Duration of Assessments." In *Islamic Legal Interpretation: Muftis and Their Fatwas,* edited by Brinkley Messick, David S. Powers, and Muhammad Khalid Masud. Cambridge, MA: Harvard University Press, 1996.

Riaz, Ali. "Madrassah Education in Pre-Colonial and Colonial South Asia." *Journal of Asian and African Studies* 46, no. 1 (2010): 69–86.

Richards, John F. *The Mughal Empire.* Cambridge: Cambridge University Press, 1995.

Riexinger, Martin. "Ibn Taymiyya's Worldview and the Challenge of Modernity: A Conflict among the Ahl-i Hadith in British India." In *Islamic Theology, Philosophy and Law: Debating Ibn Taymiyya and Ibn Qayyim al-Jawziyya,* edited by Birgit Krazietz and Georges Tamer. Berlin and Boston: Walter de Gruyter, 2013.

Rizvi, Saiyid Athar Abbas. *Shah Wali Allah and His Times.* Canberra: Ma'rifat Publishing House, 1980.

Rizvi, Sajjad H. "Philosophy as a Way of Life in the World of Islam: Applying Hadot to the Study of Mulla Sadra Shirazi (d. 1635)." *Bulletin of SOAS* 75, no. 1 (2012): 33–45.

Rizvi, Sayyid Mahbub. *Tarikh-i Dar al-'Ulum Deoband.* 2 vols. Deoband: Idarah-yi Ihtimam-i Dar al-'Ulum Deoband, 1977.

Robb, Megan Eaton. "Advising the Army of Allah: Ashraf Ali Thanawi's Critique of the Muslim League." In *Muslims against the Muslim League: Critiques of the Idea of Pakistan,* edited by Ali Usman Qasmi and Megan Eaton Robb. Cambridge: Cambridge University Press, 2017.

Robinson, Francis. *Islam and Muslim History in South Asia.* New Delhi: Oxford University Press, 2000.

———. "Other-Worldly and This-Worldly Islam and the Islamic Revival: A Memorial Lecture for Wilfred Cantwell Smith." *Journal of the Royal Asiatic Society,* ser. 3, vol. 14, no. 1 (2004): 47–58.

———. *Separatism among Indian Muslims: The Politics of the United Provinces' Muslims, 1860–1923.* Cambridge: Cambridge University Press, 1974.

———. *The Ulama of Farangi Mahall and Islamic Culture in South Asia.* New Delhi: Permanent Black, 2001.

Rocher, Rosane. "The Creation of Anglo-Hindu Law." In *Hinduism and Law: An Introduction,* edited by Timothy Lubin, Donald R. Davis, and Jayanth K. Krishnan. Cambridge: Cambridge University Press, 2010.

Rosenthal, Franz. *Knowledge Triumphant: The Concept of Knowledge in Medieval Islam.* Leiden and Boston: E. J. Brill, 2007.

Roux, Charl du Plessis le. "Die Hanafitiese Ulama: Hulle Rol in Suid-Afrikaanse Konteks." MA thesis, Rand Afrikaans University, 1978.

Rozehnal, Robert Thomas. *Islamic Sufism Unbound: Politics and Piety in Twenty-First Century Pakistan.* New York: Palgrave Macmillan, 2007.

Rumi, Maulana Jalal al-Din. *Masnavi.* Tehran: Kitabfurushi-i Zavvar, 1990.

Saharanpuri, Khalil Ahmad. *Al-Barahin al-qati'a 'ala dhalam al-anwar al-sati'a.* Deoband: Kutub Khana-yi Imdadiyya, n.d.

———. *'Aqa'id-i 'ulama-yi Deoband aur 'ulama-yi haramayn ka fatva.* Delhi: Khwajah Barqi Press, n.d.

Sa'id, Ahmad. *Maulana Ashraf 'Ali Sahib Thanvi aur tahrik-i azadi*. Rawalpindi, Pakistan: Khalid Nadim Publications, 1972.

Salomon, Noah. *For Love of the Prophet: An Ethnography of Sudan's Islamic State*. Princeton, NJ: Princeton University Press, 2016.

Salvatore, Armando, and Dale F. Eickelman. "Muslim Publics." In *Public Islam and the Common Good*, edited by Armando Salvatore and Dale F. Eickelman. Leiden and Boston: E. J. Brill, 2006.

Sanyal, Usha. "Ahl-i Sunnat Madrasas: The Madrasa Manzar-i Islam, Bareilly, and Jamiat Ashrafiyya, Mubarakpur." In *Madrasas in South Asia: Teaching Terror?*, edited by Jamal Malik. Abingdon, UK: Routledge, 2008.

———. *Ahmad Riza Khan Barelwi: In the Path of the Prophet*. Oxford: Oneworld, 2005.

———. *Devotional Islam and Politics in British India: Ahmad Riza Khan Barelwi and His Movement, 1870–1920*. Delhi and New York: Oxford University Press, 1996.

———. "Tourists, Pilgrims and Saints: The Shrine of Mu'in al-Din Chisti of Ajmer." In *Raj Rhapsodies: Tourism, Heritage and the Seduction of History*, edited by Carol E. Henderson and Maxine Weisgrau. Hampshire, UK: Ashland, 2007.

Sarkar, Jadunath. *Mughal Administration*. Calcutta: M. C. Sarkar and Sons, 1952.

Sarraj, Abu Nasr al-. *Kitab al-luma' fi al-tasawwuf*. Edited by Reinhold Nicholson. Leiden: E. J. Brill, 1914.

Sarrio, Diego R. "Spiritual Anti-Elitism: Ibn Taymiyya's Doctrine of Sainthood (*walaya*)." *Islam and Christian-Muslim Relations* 22, no. 3 (2011): 275–91.

Sayed, Muhammad Khalid. "South African Madrasahs Move into the Twenty-First Century." In *Muslim Schools and Education in Europe and South Africa*, edited by Abdulkader Tayob, Inga Niehaus, and Wolfram Weissem. Münster: Waxmann, 2011.

Schimmel, Annemarie. *Deciphering the Signs of God: A Phenomenological Approach to Islam*. Albany: State University of New York Press, 1994.

———. *Mystical Dimensions of Islam*. Chapel Hill: University of North Carolina Press, 1975.

Schmitt, Carl. *The Nomos of the Earth in the International Law of the Jus Publicum Europaeum*. Translated by G. L. Ulmen. New York: Telos Press, 2003.

Schussman, Aviva. "The Legitimacy and Nature of Mawlud al-Nabi (Analysis of a Fatwa)." *Islamic Law and Society* 5, no. 2 (1998): 214–34.

Scott, J. Barton. *Spiritual Despots: Modern Hinduism and the Genealogies of Self-Rule*. Chicago and London: University of Chicago Press, 2016.

Scott, J. Barton, and Brannon D. Ingram, "What Is a Public? Notes from South Asia." *South Asia: Journal of South Asian Studies* 38, no. 3 (2015): 357–70.

Seekings, Jeremy. *The UDF: A History of the United Democratic Front in South Africa, 1983–1991*. Athens: Ohio University Press, 2000.

Seesemann, Rüdiger. "Between Sufism and Islamism: The Tijaniyya and Islamist Rule in the Sudan." In *Sufism and Politics*, edited by Paul Heck. Princeton, NJ: Markus Weiner, 2007.

———. *The Divine Flood: Ibrahim Niasse and the Roots of a Twentieth-Century Sufi Revival.* Oxford: Oxford University Press, 2011.

Sengupta, Parna. *Pedagogy for Religion: Missionary Education and the Fashioning of Hindus and Muslims in Bengal.* Berkeley and Los Angeles: University of California Press, 2011.

Shackle, Christopher, and Javed Majeed, trans. *Hali's Musaddas: The Ebb and Flow of Islam.* Delhi: Oxford University Press, 1997.

Shafi', Mufti Muhammad. *Dil ki dunya.* Karachi: Idara al-Ma'arif, 2013.

———. *Ma'arif al-Qur'an.* 8 vols. Karachi: Idara al-Ma'arif, 1969.

———. *Sunnat o bid'at.* Lahore: Maktaba-yi Khalil, n.d.

Shahid, Mufti Muhammad. *Qutb al-Aqtab Imam al-'Arifin Shaykh al-Mashaikh Hazrat Aqdas Shaykh al-Hadith al-Hajj al-Hafiz Maulana Muhammad Zakariyya Muhajir Madani ka safarnama-yi Afriqah o England: Ramadan al-Mubarak 1401/1981.* Karachi: Al-Maktaba al-Islamiyya, 1982.

Shakry, Omnia El. *The Arabic Freud: Psychoanalysis and Islam in Modern Egypt.* Princeton, NJ: Princeton University Press, 2017.

Shatibi, Abu Ishaq Ibrahim ibn Musa al-. *Al-I'tisam.* Cairo: Matba' al-Manar, 1913.

Shell, Robert C. "Madrasahs and Moravians: Muslim Educational Institutions in the Cape Colony, 1792–1910." *New Contree* 51 (2006): 101–13.

———. "Rites and Rebellion: Islamic Conversion at the Cape, 1808 to 1915." *Studies in the History of Cape Town* 5 (1984): 1–46.

Sherkoti, Anvarul Hasan. *Sirat-i Ya'qub o Mamluk.* Karachi: Maktaba-yi Dar al-'Ulum Karachi, 1974.

Sherman, Taylor C. *Muslim Belonging in Secular India: Negotiating Citizenship in Postcolonial Hyderabad.* Cambridge: Cambridge University Press, 2015.

Shuja'abadi, S'ad Sanaullah. *'Ulama-yi Deoband ke akhiri lamahat.* Delhi: Farid Book Depot, 2006.

Siddiqi, Zameeruddin. "The Institution of the Qazi under the Mughals." In *Medieval India: A Miscellany,* comp. Aligarh Muslim University. London: Asia Publishing House, 1969.

Sikand, Yoginder. *Bastions of the Believers: Madrasas and Islamic Education in India.* New Delhi: Penguin Books India, 2005.

———. *The Origins and Development of the Tablighi Jama'at (1920–2000): A Cross-Country Comparative Study.* Hyderabad: Orient Longman, 2002.

Simpson, Edward, and Kai Kresse. "Cosmopolitanism Contested: Anthropology and History in the Western Indian Ocean." In *Struggling with History: Islam and Cosmopolitanism in the Western Indian Ocean,* edited by Edward Simpson and Kai Kresse. New York: Columbia University Press, 2008.

Singha, Radhika. *A Despotism of Law: Crime and Justice in Early Colonial India.* New Delhi: Oxford University Press, 1998.

Sirhindi, Ahmad. *Maktubat-i Imam Rabbani.* 3 vols. Delhi: Matba'-yi Murtazavi, 1873.

Sirriyeh, Elizabeth. *Sufis and Anti-Sufis: The Defense, Rethinking and Rejection of Sufism in the Modern World.* Curzon Sufi Series. Richmond, Surrey, UK: Curzon, 1999.

Sirry, Mun'im. "Jamal al-Din al-Qasimi and the Salafi Approach to Sufism." *Die Welt des Islams* 51 (2011): 75–108.

Smith, Barbara Herrnstein. *Scandalous Knowledge: Science, Truth and the Human.* Durham, NC: Duke University Press, 2005.

Smith, Wilfred Cantwell. *Modern Islam in India.* London: Victor Gollancz, 1946.

Steinfels, Amina. *Knowledge before Action: Islamic Learning and Sufi Practice in the Life of Sayyid Jalal al-din Bukhari Makhdum-i Jahaniyan.* Columbia: University of South Carolina Press, 2012.

Stephens, Julia. "The Phantom Wahhabi: Liberalism and the Muslim Fanatic in Mid-Victorian India." *Modern Asian Studies* 47, no. 1 (2013): 22–52.

Stilt, Kristen. *Islamic Law in Action: Authority, Discretion, and Everyday Experiences in Mamluk Egypt.* Oxford and New York: Oxford University Press, 2011.

Strawson, John. "Translating the *Hedaya*: Colonial Foundations of Islamic Law." In *Legal Histories of the British Empire: Laws, Engagements, and Legacies,* edited by Shaunnagh Dorsett and John McLaren. Abingdon, UK: Routledge, 2014.

Subrahmanyam, Sanjay. "Hearing Voices: Vignettes of Early Modernity in South Asia, 1400–1750." *Daedalus* 127, no. 3 (1998): 75–104.

Sufi, Ghulam. *Al-Minhaj: Being the Evolution of Curriculum in the Muslim Educational Institutions of India.* Delhi: Idarah-i Adabiyat-i Dihli, 1977.

Sulami, Muhammad ibn al-Husain al-. *Haqa'iq al-tafsir: Tafsir al-Qur'an al-'aziz.* 2 vols. Beirut: Dar al-Kutub al-'Ilmiyya, 2001.

Sunni Jamiatul Ulama. *Confusion or Conclusion: Answer to "Who Are the People of the Sunnah?"* Durban: Sunni Jamiatul Ulama, n.d.

Sunni World. *An Attack on Our Sunni Beliefs by the Wahabi/Deobandi/Tablighi Sect and Our Reply.* Durban: Sunni World, n.d.

———. *Exposing the Tableeghi-Deobandi-Wahabi Sect.* Durban: Sunni World, n.d.

Svensson, Jonas. "ITZ BIDAH BRO!!!! GT ME??—YouTube Mawlid and Voices of Praise and Blame." In *Muslims and the New Information and Communication Technologies,* edited by Thomas Hoffmann and Göran Larsson. New York: Springer, 2013.

Sviri, Sara. "The Self and Its Transformation in Sufism with Special Reference to Early Literature." In *Self and Self-Transformation in the History of Religions,* edited by David Shulman and Guy G. Stromsa. New York: Oxford University Press, 2002.

Syed, Jawad, Edwina Pio, Tahir Kamran, and Abbas Zaidi, eds. *Faith-Based Violence and Deobandi Militancy in Pakistan.* London: Palgrave Macmillan, 2016.

Tambe, Ashwini, and Harald Fischer-Tiné, eds. *The Limits of British Colonial Control in South Asia: Spaces of Disorder in the Indian Ocean Region.* London and New York: Routledge, 2009.

Tarabulusi, Husayn ibn Muhammad. *Jadid 'ilm-i kalam, ya'ni sains aur Islam.* Delhi: Azad Barqi Press, 1928/29.

Tarde, Gabriel. *On Communication and Social Influence*. Edited by Terry N. Clark. Chicago and London: University of Chicago Press, 1969.

Tareen, SherAli. "Competing Political Theologies: Intra-Muslim Polemics of the Limits of Prophetic Intercession." *Political Theology* 12, no. 3 (2011): 418–43.

———. "The Limits of Tradition: Competing Logics of Authenticity in South Asian Islam." PhD Diss. Duke University, 2012.

———. "The Polemic at Shahjahanpur: Religion, Miracles and History." *Islamic Studies* 51, no. 1 (2012): 49–67.

———. "Revolutionary Hermeneutics: Translating the Qur'an as a Manifesto for Revolution." *Journal of Religious and Political Practice* 3, no. 1–2 (2017): 1–24.

Taussig, Michael T. *Defacement: Public Secrecy and the Labor of the Negative*. Stanford, CA: Stanford University Press, 1999.

Taylor, Christopher S. *In the Vicinity of the Righteous: Ziyara and the Veneration of Muslim Saints in Late Medieval Egypt*. Leiden: E. J. Brill, 1999.

Tayob, Abdulkader. *Islam in South Africa: Mosques, Imams, and Sermons*. Gainesville: University Press of Florida, 1999.

———. *Islamic Resurgence in South Africa: The Muslim Youth Movement*. Cape Town: University of Cape Town Press, 1995.

———. "Race, Ideology and Islam in Contemporary South Africa." In *Islam in World Cultures: Comparative Perspectives*, edited by R. Michael Feener. Santa Barbara, CA: ABC-CLIO, 2004.

Tayyib, Qari Muhammad. *Azadi-yi Hindustan ka khamosh rahnuma*. Deoband: Daftar-i Ihtimam-i Dar al-'Ulum Deoband, 1957.

———. *Islah-i nafs aur Tablighi Jama'at*. Lahore: 'Umar Publications, n.d.

———. *Maslak-i 'ulama-yi Deoband*. Lahore: Aziz Publications, 1975.

———. *'Ulama-yi Deoband ka dini rukh aur maslaki mizaj*. Deoband: Maktaba-yi Millat, n.d.

Thanawi, Ashraf Ali. *A Sufi Study of Hadith*. Translated by Yusuf Talal Delorenzo. London: Turath Publishing, 2010.

———. See also: Thanvi, Ashraf 'Ali.

Thanvi, Ashraf 'Ali. *Al-Ifadat al-yawmiyya min al-ifadat al-qawmiyya*. 10 vols. Multan, Pakistan: Idara-yi Ta'lifat-i Ashrafiyya, 2003.

———. *Al-Intibahat al-mufida 'an al-ishtibahat al-jadida*. Delhi: Jayyid Barqi Press, 1926.

———. *Al-Kalam al-hasan*. Edited by Mufti Muhammad Hasan. Lahore: Al-Maktaba al-Ashrafiyya, n.d.

———. *Al-Masalih al-'aqliyya lil-ahkam al-naqliyya*. 3 vols. Lahore: Kutub Khana-yi Jamili, 1964.

———. *Al-Surur bi-zuhur al-nur wa mulaqqab bih irshad al-'ibad fi 'eid al-milad*. Sadhaura, India: Bilali Steam Press, 1915.

———. *Al-Takashshuf 'an muhimmat al-tasawwuf*. 5 vols. Deoband: Matba'-yi Qasimi, 1909.

———. *Anfas-i 'Isa, ifadat-i Hakim al-Ummat Hazrat Maulana Ashraf 'Ali Thanvi*. Karachi: H. M. Sa'id Company, 1980.

———. *Arvah-i salasa al-ma'ruf bih hikayat-i awliya'*. Karachi: Dar al-Isha'at, 1976.

———. *Ashraf al-jawab*. Deoband: Maktaba-yi Thanvi, 1990.

———. *Ashraf al-tariqat fi-l shari'at wa-l haqiqat, al-ma'ruf bih shari'at aur tariqat*. Edited by Muhammad Hasan. Delhi: New Taj Office, 1964.

———. *Bavadir al-navadir*. Lahore: Idara al-Islamiyya, 1985.

———. *Bid'a ki haqiqat aur us ke ahkam o masa'il*. Edited by Muhammad Iqbal Qureshi. Lahore and Karachi: Idara-yi Islamiyya, 2000.

———. *Bihishti zewar: Mudallal o mukammal bihishti zewar ma' bihishti gauhar*. Karachi: Altaf and Sons, 2001.

———. *Fiqh-i Hanafi ke usul o zavabit*. Edited by Muhammad Zaid Mazahiri Nadvi. Karachi: Zam Zam Publishers, 2003.

———. *Haqq al-sama'*. Karachi: Idara-yi Ashraf al-'Ulum, 1950.

———. *Hayat al-Muslimin*. Karachi: Idara al-Ma'arif, 2005.

———. *Hifz al-iman, ma' basat al-banan wa taghayyur al-'unwan*. Deoband: Maktaba-yi Nu'maniyya, 1962.

———. *Imdad al-fatawa*. Edited by Muhammad Shafi'. 6 vols. Karachi: Maktaba-yi Dar al-'Ulum Karachi, 2010.

———. *Islah al-rusum*. Delhi: Dini Book Depot, 1963.

———. *Islahi nisab: Tashih-i 'aqa'id o a'mal, tahzib o tamaddun-i Islami*. Lahore: Maktaba-yi Rashidiyya, 1977.

———. *Kamalat-i Imdadiyya: Jis men pir-i tariqat Hajji Imdad Allah Muhajir Makki ke kamalat ko bayan kiya gaya hai*. Lahore: Maktaba al-Furqan, 1976.

———. *Khutbat-i Hakim al-Ummat*. 32 vols. Multan, Pakistan: Idara-yi Ta'lifat-i Ashrafiyya, 2006.

———. *Majalis-i Hakim al-Ummat*. Edited by Muhammad Shafi'. Karachi: Dar al-Isha'at, n.d.

———. "The Raison d'Être of Madrasah." Translated by Muhammad al-Ghazali. *Islamic Studies* 43, no. 4 (2004): 653–75.

———. *Tafsir-i bayan al-Qur'an, mukammal*. 3 vols. Karachi: Dar al-Isha'at, 2015.

———. *Tarbiyat al-salik*. 2 vols. Karachi: Dar al-Isha'at, 1982.

———. *Tashil-i qasd al-sabil ma' panj rasa'il*. Karachi: Kutub Khana-yi Mazhari, n.d.

———. *Tuhfat al-'ulama*. 2 vols. Multan, Pakistan: Idara-yi Ta'lifat-i Ashrafiyya, 1995.

Thanvi, Jamil Ahmad. *Sharh-i faisala-yi haft mas'ala*. Lahore: Jami'a-yi Ziya al-'Ulum, 1975.

Trevelyan, Charles. *On the Education of the People of India*. London: Longman, Orme, Brown, Green and Longmans, 1838.

Turner, Bryan. *Weber and Islam*. London: Routledge and Kegan, 1974.

Ukeles, Raquel Margalit. "Innovation or Deviation: Exploring the Boundaries of Islamic Devotional Law." PhD diss., Harvard University, 2006.

Universal Truth Movement. "Universal Truth Movement General Report." N.p.: Universal Truth Movement, 1964.

'Usmani, Muhammad Rafi'. *Fiqh aur tasawwuf: Ek ta'arruf*. Karachi: Idara al-Ma'arif, 2004.

'Usmani, Muhammad Taqi. *Akabir-i Deoband kya the*. Karachi: Idara al-Ma'arif, 1994.

―――. Foreword to Mufti Muhammad Shafi', *Dil ki dunya*. Karachi: Idara al-Ma'arif, 2013.

―――. *Hakim al-Ummat ke siyasi afkar*. Karachi: Idara al-Ma'arif, 2000.

―――. *Hamara ta'limi nizam*. Deoband: Maktaba-yi Dar al-'Ulum, 1998.

―――. *Islahi khutbat*. 16 vols. Karachi: Meman Islamic Publishers, 1993.

'Usmani, Shabbir Ahmad. *Anvar-i 'Usmani*. Karachi: Maktaba al-Islamiyya, n.d.

'Usmani, Zafar Ahmad. *I'la al-sunan*. Dar al-Fikr, 2001.

Vahed, Goolam H. "Contesting 'Orthodoxy': The Tablighi-Sunni Conflict among South African Muslims in the 1970s and 1980s." *Journal of Muslim Minority Affairs* 23, no. 2 (2003): 313–34.

―――. "An 'Imagined Community' in Diaspora: Gujaratis in South Africa." *South Asian History and Culture* 1, no. 4 (October 2010): 615–29.

―――. "Mosques, Mawlanas and Muharram: Indian Islam in Colonial Natal, 1860–1910." *Journal of Religion in Africa* 31, no. 3 (2001): 305–35.

―――. "A Sufi Saint's Day in South Africa: The Legend of Badsha Peer." *South African Historical Journal* 49 (2003): 96–122.

van der Veer, Peter. *Imperial Encounters: Religion and Modernity in India and Britain*. Princeton, NJ: Princeton University Press, 2001.

Voll, John O. "Renewal and Reform in Islamic History: Tajdid and Islah." In *Voices of Resurgent Islam*, edited by John L. Esposito. New York: Oxford University Press, 1983.

Wali Allah, Shah. *Fuyuz al-haramayn*. Deoband: Kutub Khana-yi Rahimiyya, n.d.

Ward, Kerry. *Networks of Empire: Forced Migration in the Dutch East India Company*. Cambridge: Cambridge University Press, 2008.

Ware, Rudolph T. *The Walking Qur'an: Islamic Education, Embodied Knowledge, and History in West Africa*. Chapel Hill: University of North Carolina Press, 2014.

Warner, Michael. *Publics and Counterpublics*. New York: Zone Books, 2004.

Wilson, Ronald K. *Anglo-Muhammadan Law: A Digest*. London: W. Thacker and Co., 1903.

Winkelmann, Marieke. *From Behind the Curtain: A Study of a Girls' Madrasa in India*. Amsterdam: Amsterdam University Press, 2005.

Winter, Tim. Introduction to *Cambridge Companion to Classical Islamic Theology*, edited by Tim Winter. Cambridge: Cambridge University Press, 2008.

Zaidi, Sayyid Nazar. *Hajji Imdad Allah Muhajir Makki: Sirat o savanih*. Gujarat: Maktaba-yi Zafar, 1978.

Zaman, Muhammad Qasim. *Ashraf Ali Thanawi: Islam in Modern South Asia*. Oxford: Oneworld, 2008.

―――. *Islam in Pakistan: A History*. Princeton, NJ: Princeton University Press, 2018.

―――. *Modern Islamic Thought in a Radical Age: Religious Authority and Internal Criticism*. Cambridge: Cambridge University Press, 2012.

———. *Religion and Politics under the Early Abbasids.* Leiden, New York, and Cologne: E. J. Brill, 1997.

———. "The Sovereignty of God in Modern Islamic Thought." *Journal of the Royal Asiatic Society* 25, no. 3 (2015): 389–418.

———. *The Ulama in Contemporary Islam: Custodians of Change.* Princeton, NJ: Princeton University Press, 2002.

———. "The 'Ulama of Contemporary Islam and Their Conceptions of the Common Good." In *Public Islam and the Common Good,* edited by Armando Salvatore and Dale F. Eickelman. Leiden: E. J. Brill, 2004.

Zastoupli, Lynn, and Martin Moir, eds. *The Great Indian Education Debate: Documents Relating to the Orientalist-Anglicist Controversy, 1781–1843.* Surrey, UK: Curzon, 1999.

Zutshi, Chitralekha. *Languages of Belonging: Islam, Regional Identity, and the Making of Kashmir.* New York: Oxford University Press, 2004.

Index

'Abd al-'Aziz, Shah, 36, 58
'Abd al-Ghani, Shah, 42, 58, 67–68
'Abd al-Haq, Maulana, 208, 209
'Abd al-Rahim, Shah, 231n63
'Abd al-Rahman Matura shrine, 258n15
'Abd al-Salam, 'Izz al-Din ibn, 236n9
'Abdullah Shah Ghazi, 208
Abedien, Hazrat Sayed Zainul, 263n94
'Abid Husain, Muhammad, 37, 39
Adam, Ebrahim, 185–86
Adorno, Theodor W., 22
Afrikaans language, 179, 261n66
Ahl-e Sunnat wal-Jamaat (Barelvi
    organization), 175, 185, 188, 263n95
Ahl-i Hadith, 62, 141–42, 169, 213
Ahl al-Sunna wal-Jama'a (Sunni concept),
    10, 142–44, 221n22, 255n11
Ahmad, Mufti Inayat, 240n65
Ahmad ibn Hanbal, 13
Ahmed, Imam Nazir, 263n90
Ahmed, Shahab, 120, 211, 223n52
Ahrar movement, 192–95
Akhtar, Hakim Muhammad, 136–37
Akora Khattak, 208
Al-Azhar, 2, 65
Al-Qalam (periodical), 181, 186
analogy, in Islamic law. *See qiyas*
Anglicist position (in British debate about
    Muslim education), 43–44, 45, 49–50.
    See also Orientalist position
Anglo-Muhammadan law, 34–35, 46

anthropocentrism, 22, 23, 116, 145,
    226n85. *See also* bibliocentrism
anti-apartheid politics: jihad and, 187, 200,
    205; *The Majlis* (periodical), 190,
    196–204; *mawlud* and *zikr halqa*
    devotions, 187–90; Muslims' role in,
    180–84; overview, 28–29, 179–80;
    Tablighi-Barelvi clashes, 185–87; Thanvi
    and, 190–96. *See also* Barelvi move-
    ment; Desai, Ahmed Sadiq; Islamic
    activism; Tablighi Jama'at
anticolonial politics, 25, 29, 49, 191, 195,
    203–4
Arabic language, 20, 44, 60, 100, 104–5,
    108, 111, 142, 162, 176, 183, 246n11,
    253n76, 261n66
Arabic Study Circle, 173, 174, 181
Arendt, Hannah, 254n2
Arya Samaj revivalist movement, 37, 156,
    247n31
Asad, Talal, 21–22, 212, 225n75
asceticism, in Sufism. *See zuhd*
Ash'ari theology, 7, 148
astronomy, 17, 37, 41, 42, 52
attacks: Azaadville *mawlud* assault, 186–88;
    Cairo Coptic church attack 2016, 207;
    Deoband movement and, 9, 91, 208; in
    Dera Ghazi Khan, 208; by ISIS, 207–8;
    Lal Shahbaz Qalandar shrine attack,
    208; by Pakistani Taliban, 91, 211; Shah
    Noorani terrorist attack, 208; shrine

attacks *(continued)*
attacks in Pakistan, 9, 208; Sinai
Peninsula militant attack, 207; in South
Africa, 179, 186–88; on Sufis, 210–11;
on Sufi saints' shrines, 9, 207–8,
210–11
Aurangzeb, Emperor of the Mughal Empire,
40–41, 45
authority: maintenance of, 23; Maududi on,
63; M. Isma'il on sources of, 60–62;
rejection of *'ulama* by *'awamm* (lay
Muslims), 23; *'ulama* claims of, 16–17,
211
autonomy, 27, 98, 117
'awamm (lay Muslims): authority and, 6,
23; *bid'at* (illicit innovations) and, 56,
76; corruption of beliefs of, 78, 83, 96;
as everyday Muslims, 211–12; Gangohi
and, 48; lay/elite hierarchy, 101–5; legal
issues and, 47; *maslak* and, 23; Qur'an
and, 111; support for Dar al-'Ulum
Deoband by, 39–40; understanding of,
23, 69, 92, 131; Urdu language and, 59
Ayatollah Khomeini, 15
Azad, Abdul Kalam, 191
Azhari, Muhammad Akhtar Raza Khan, 175
Azmi, Fazlur Rahman, 256n49

Babur, Emperor of the Mughal Empire, 81
Bahadur Shah Zafar, Emperor of the
Mughal Empire, 3, 34
bai'at (pledge, from Sufi disciple to Sufi
master), 123, 127–28, 129, 150, 252n30
Bakhsh, Data Ganj, 208
Bakhsh, Maulvi Rahim, 50
Bamiyan Buddhas destruction, 210
*Al-Barahin al-qati'a 'ala dhalam al-anwar
al-sati'a* (Definitive proofs on the
darkness of *al-Anwar al-Sati'a*)
(Saharanpuri), 67–69, 240n68
barakat (blessings), 12, 39, 71, 74, 76
Barani, Zia al-Din, 40
Barelvi movement: Deobandi-Barelvi
polemics, 27, 148, 161, 165, 173–78,
264n102, 267n47, 272n8; Deobandi-
Barelvi rivalry, 11, 100, 143, 161, 182,
187; Habibia Mosque, 172; Inayat
Ahmad and, 240n65; *The Majlis*
(periodical) and, 198; *maslak* of, 141,
148; *munazara* and, 99; in Natal, 181;
overview, 7–8; Qadiri order and, 263n94;
Shah Barkatullah of Marahra and, 94;
Tablighi-Barelvi clashes and, 159, 180,
185–87, 263n90; UTM and, 171. *See*

also Ahl-e Sunnat wal-Jamaat (Barelvi
organization); Khan, Ahmad Raza
Barelvi, Sayyid Ahmad, 24, 37, 58, 102,
228n24, 236nn15–16, 237n19, 238n44
Bengal, 1–2, 43, 144
Bengal Regulation XIX of 1810, 48
Berkey, Jonathan P., 157
Bhashani, Abdul Hamid Khan, 203
bibliocentrism, 22–23, 116, 125, 144–45,
160, 226n85. *See also* anthropocentrism
bid'at (illicit innovations); defined, 56, 57;
Deobandi-Barelvi polemics over, 161,
173, 176; in Deobandi texts, 109;
devotional practices and, 138; discourse
of, 26; Gangohi on, 57, 64, 72, 83, 103;
Ibn Sa'ud on, 90; Imdad Allah on, 72;
A. R. Khan on, 8; *mawlud* and, 65–68,
72, 73–80; M. P. Haqqani on, 174; M.
Isma'il on, 60; normative order and,
55–64, 92, 95, 215; *qiyam* as, 66, 68;
Shatibi on, 57, 60; Thanvi and, 73–80,
106
Bihishti zewar (Heavenly ornaments)
(Thanvi), 87, 105, 107, 109, 129,
136
Bilhauri, Khurram 'Ali, 63
Binnori, Yusuf, 167–68, 266n27
Black Students Society, 184
Blecher, Joel, 114
blessings. *See barakat*
British empire in India: Anglo-Muhammadan law, 34, 46; anticolonial politics,
49; decline of Muslim political
hegemony and, 17; East India Company,
31, 43, 45; effects of, 34; governance
and religion in, 31, 43; Indian
secularism and, 32, 33; Islamic criminal
law and, 46–47; Islamic learning under,
43–45, 50; judicial administration, 34;
Kazis Act of 1880, 47; limits of power,
33; patronage networks, 43, 44, 45, 50,
234n103; secularization of colonial
India, 48–54; Victorian discourse on
religion, 31–32, 34. *See also* Anglicist
position, Orientalist position
Brown, Jonathan A. C., 213
Buehler, Arthur F., 12, 89
Burke, Edmund, 215

Cachalia, Maulvi Ismail, 203–4
Cairo Coptic church attack 2016, 207
Calcutta Madrasa, 43, 50, 234n103
Call of Islam, 183, 187, 189–90
Cape Mazaar Society, 163

Cape Muslims (Cape "Malays"), 162–63, 262n71
Cassiem, Achmad, 182–83, 189, 200
Cavanaugh, William T., 210
center/periphery, 23–24, 216
Chamberlain, Michael, 38
Chatta Masjid, 37, 39
chilla (forty-day Sufi meditative retreat), 209, 272n14
Chishti, 'Abd al-Rahman, 255n11
Chishti, Muhammad, 81
Chishti, Mu'in al-Din, 165, 211
Chishti order: bai'at (pledge), 127–28; Barelvi-oriented Sufis in, 263n94; chilla (forty-day Sufi meditative retreat), 209, 272n14; Deobandi-Barelvi polemics and, 148, Deobandis and, 4, 209; fatwas (legal opinions) on, 208–9; habs-i dam (holding the breath), 103; Imdad Allah and, 69, 228n24; Maududi and, 15; Mu'in al-Din Chishti shrine, 81, 82–84, 94, 165, 211; Nizami and Sabiri branches of, 231n61; patronage and, 271n128; sama' and, 95; Sufi masters of, 42; zikr halqa, 209; ziyarat (visiting saints' graves) and, 80
Christianity, 6, 31, 32, 42, 98, 99, 102, 163, 199–200
circumambulation. See tawaf
colonial modernity, 32–34, 40, 215
companionship, in Sufism. See suhbat
Companions of the Prophet, 16, 66, 74, 79–80, 109, 124–25, 142, 155, 156, 158, 178, 188, 198, 215, 260n43
consensus, in Islamic law. See ijma'
Cooper, Frederick, 34
Cornell, Vincent J., 132
corporeality, 22
counterpolemics, 14, 99, 176
Cover, Robert, 32
customs. See rusum

damnation, 6, 42, 123
Dar al-Ifta', 47, 170, 172
Dar al-'Ulum Azaadville, 175–76, 256n49, 261n57
Dar al-'Ulum Bury, 219n2
Dar al-'Ulum Deoband; 1872 survey and, 51; overview, 25–26, 31–35; 'Abd al-Haq and, 208; E. Adam and, 267n37; bibliocentrism and, 22; colonial modernity and, 33–34, 215; conceptualizing "religious" knowledge, 40–45; Dar al-Ifta' and, 47; defined, 10; Deobandi (term) and, 9–10; founding of, 32, 35–38; innovations of, 38–40; Islamic law and, 45–48; making religious experts, 40–45; as a "modern" madrasa, 38–40; name of, 1, 37; Nanautvi's vision and, 36; Tayyib and, 139; "useful" secular knowledge, 48–54; "useless" religious knowledge, 48–54
Dar al-'Ulum Haqqaniyya: chancellor of, 208; on chilla (forty-day Sufi meditative retreat), 209; fatwas (legal opinions) of, 208; founding of, 208; views of Sufism, 208–9; violence against Sufis and, 209; Taliban and, 208
Dar al-'Ulum Karachi, 210
Dar al-'Ulum Newcastle, 169, 186, 260n44
Dar al-'Ulum Zakariyya, 170–71, 176; fatwa collection, 170
Dars-i Nizamiyya (Nizami curriculum), 40–42, 145, 266n27
decline narratives, 35–38, 58, 209, 214
Deobandi (term), 9–10
Deobandi-Barelvi polemics, 26, 99–100, 173–78
Deobandi brand, 28, 171–73
Deoband to Bareilly (Okarvi), 175
Desai, Ahmed Sadiq: Deobandi thought and, 213–14; loss of support, 204; The Majlis (periodical), 181, 190, 196–203; Majlisul Ulama and, 176, 180, 270n97; M. Khan and, 25, 270n103; Sufi politics and, 205; Thanvi's politics in South Africa and, 29, 180, 196–97, 212
Desai, Ebrahim, 170, 256n49
dhamal, terrorist attacks during, 208
dhikr (Sufi meditative practices). See zikr
Dhulipala, Venkat, 196
dialectical theology (kalam), 37, 41
Dien, Shaikh M.S., 263n94
Dimashqi, Qutb al-Din, 134–35, 253n76
divine sovereignty, 59, 62–63, 64, 80
Doumato, Eleanor Abdella, 12

East India Company, 31, 43, 45. See also British empire in India
ecstasy, in Sufism. See wajd
Education Despatch of 1854, 50
Ehsan, Ehsanullah, 208
Eickelman, Dale F, 223n52
elites. See khawass
endowments: charitable endowments (awqaf), 38, 39; Religious Endowments Act (Act XX) of 1863, 48–49

Ernst, Carl W., 44, 246n20
Esack, Farid, 183, 203, 204, 266n27
evils. See munkarat
Ewing, Katherine, 211

Fadil, Nadia, 211–12
Faisala-yi haft mas'ala (A decision on seven controversies) (Imdad Allah), 69, 71, 100–101
faiz (spiritual energy), 21, 97, 125–27, 137, 145
farz-i 'ayn (obligation upon Muslims, individually), 137, 210
farz-i kifaya (obligation upon Muslims, collectively), 137, 210
Fatawa-yi Alamgiri, 45
Fatawa-yi Haqqaniyya, 208
fatwas (legal opinions): of Ahmad Raza Khan, 8; in British India, 47–48; Fatawa-yi Haqqaniyya, 208; Gangohi's, 42, 48, 66, 103; Imdad Allah and, 70; issued by madrasas, 47; published collections of, 47–48; requested by lay Muslims, 48; requested by South Africans, 261n66; of Thanvi, 73, 244n150; as tool of mass moral reform, 48; violence against Sufis and, 209; zikr (Sufi meditative practices) and, 209
faza'il (virtues), 3, 13, 20, 27, 48, 65, 66, 71, 76, 121, 260n43. See also suhbat (companionship, in Sufism)
Faza'il-i a'mal (Virtuous deeds) (M. Z. Kandhlavi), 176, 260n43
Fernando, Mayanthi, 211–12
Fleck, Ludwik, 23
Foucault, Michel, 118
Fuerst, Ilyse Morgenstein, 31
Furey, Constance, 148

Gaborieau, Marc, 8, 169
Gandhi, Mohandas, 49, 118, 165, 191–92
Gangohi, 'Abd al-Quddus, 83–84, 231n61
Gangohi, Mahmud Hasan, 25, 153–54, 158, 161, 204, 267n37
Gangohi, Rashid Ahmad: overview, 26; Al-Barahin al-qati'a 'ala dhalam al-anwar al-sati'a (Defnitive proofs on the darkness of al-Anwar al-Sati'a) (Saharanpuri) and, 240n68; on the centennial renewer (mujaddid), 18–19; as co-founder of Deoband movement, 13, 24, 41; critique of bid'a and shirk, 57, 64, 72; critiques of mawlud and 'urs, 66, 67, 72, 83–85; death of, 149; decline narrative of, 35,

209; Dimashqi translation, 134; disciples of in South Africa, 161; fatwas (legal opinions) of, 42, 48, 66, 103; Ilyas and, 10–11, 149; Imdad Allah and, 69, 70–73; on intercession, 87–88; on knowledge, 41–42; Mamluk 'Ali and, 36, 37–38; M. Isma'il and, 58, 64; Nanautvi and, 36; patronage networks and, 44; on philosophy, 52; on Qur'an, 244n148; on rational sciences (ma'qulat), 41–42; Saharanpuri and, 25, 67; as spiritual patron (sarparast), 41–42; Sufi bai'at (pledge) and, 128; Sufism and, 209, 214; Thanvi and, 26–27, 64, 72; on transmitted knowledge (manqulat), 41–42
al-Ghazali, Abu Hamid Muhammad, 12, 14, 20, 95, 108, 121, 131, 146, 159, 222n36, 243n141, 246n14, 253n63
Ghousia Manzil, 175, 263nn94–95
Gilani, Sayyid Manazir Ahsan, 36
Gilani, Sayyid Safdar Shah, 272n8
globalization: overview, 4, 28, 160–62; Deobandi-Barelvi polemics, 173–78; Deobandi brand, 171–73; Deobandi scholars in South Africa, 166–68; Deobandi tradition and, 23; Islam(s) in South Africa, 162–63; madrasas and, 8; Muslim migrations in the Indian Ocean, 164–66; South African tabligh and, 168–71
Goswami, Manu, 93
"grave worship," 177–78, 197–98
Green, Nile, 14, 20, 49, 81, 216, 226n85

habs-i dam (holding the breath), 103
Hadith: commentaries, 7; defined, 4; Deobandi texts shifting toward, 213; ethics and, 121; Hadith jurisprudence, 8; Mishkat al-masabih, 41; M. Isma'il citing of, 60; M. Isma'il on authority of, 61–62; M. Ya'qub and, 38; on mujaddid (renewer), 18; references, 213; Shafi' and, 57; Thanvi on, 244n150
Hadot, Pierre, 118
Haj, Samira, 225n75
Hajj. See pilgrimage
Hali, Altaf Hussain, 35
Hallaq, Wael, 47, 250n93
Hamidi, Abdun Nabi, 177, 264n104
Hamilton, Charles, 46, 50, 233n83
Hanafi legal tradition, 7, 42, 45–46, 66, 73–75, 112, 114, 133, 144–45, 148, 169–73, 213

al-Haq, Mufti Raza, 171
al-Haq, Sami', 208, 209, 272n20
Haqqani, Muhammad Palan, 174
Haron, Imam Abdullah, 180
Hasan, Mahmud, 146–47, 191, 203
al-Hasan, Ihtisham, 151, 260n43
Hastings, Warren, 43, 46
Hazarvi, Mufti Akbar, 264n102
Hidaya (Marghinani), 45–46, 50
al-Hilali, Taqi al-Din, 15
Hindus: debates over nature of God, 99; devotional practices of, 102–3; Judicial Plan of 1772 and, 43; noninterference policy, 32; political alignment with, 180, 190, 199, 202; at Sufi shrines, 82, 94; Thanvi and, 190, 192–93
Hujjat Allah al-baligha (The conclusive argument from God) (Wali Allah), 114
al-Hujwiri (aka Data Ganj Bakhsh), 'Ali, 13, 208, 211, 222n35
Hurd, Elizabeth Shakman, 210
Husn al-maqsad fi 'amal al-mawlid (The good intention of celebrating the mawlid) (Suyuti), 66
Hussin, Iza, 32

Ibn 'Abidin, 42, 86, 170, 213
Ibn 'Arabi, 12, 14, 16, 255n22
Ibn Khaldun, 41
Ibn Sa'ud, 'Abd al-'Aziz, 89–90
Ibn Taymiyya, Ahmad, 14, 16, 135
Ihya' 'ulum al-din (al-Ghazali), 14, 95, 131, 146, 222n36, 225n32, 243n141
ijaza (permission to transmit a text in Islamic education), 22, 38
ijma' (consensus, in Islamic law), 57, 75, 100, 111
ijtihad (independent reasoning), 18, 112, 141–42, 193, 195, 224n60, 250n93
illicit innovations (*bid'at*). See bid'at (illicit innovations)
'ilm (knowledge), 19, 21, 27, 53, 59, 102, 120, 121, 130, 141, 150, 152; knowledge consumption, 214; knowledge production, 214; knowledge transmission, 23; religious/secular binary and, 26; secular knowledge, 48–54
'ilm-i ghayb (knowledge of the unseen), 7, 64, 72
Ilyas, Muhammad, 10–11, 25, 115, 139–40, 149–56, 158, 168, 176, 197. See also Tablighi Jama'at
Imam Ahmed Raza Academy, 175, 188

Imdad Allah al-Makki, Hajji: overview, 26; disciples of, 67, 70; *Faisala-yi haft mas'ala* (A decision on seven controversies), 69, 71, 100–101; Gangohi and, 26, 36, 70–73, 84, 253n76; Hadith and, 75; Indian Uprising of 1857 and, 36–37; influence of, 24, 26, 231n61; jihad and, 229n25; *mawlud* and, 69–74, 77, 84, 178; Nanautvi and, 36, 69–70, 71; Rampuri and, 67; Sabiri Chishtis on, 209; Saharanpuri and, 69; Thanvi and, 24, 26, 70–71, 73–74, 107; *'urs* and, 82; views of *mawlud* and *bid'a*, 71–72; Wali Allahian connections, 228n24; Ya'qub and, 37–38; on *zikr haddadi*, 272n13
imkan-i kizb (possibility of God telling a lie), 7, 64, 99, 100, 161, 241n76
imkan-i nazir (possibility of God creating another Prophet equal to Muhammad), 7, 62, 64, 161, 241n76
independent reasoning. See ijtihad
India: British response to Indian Uprising of 1857, 3; decline narratives, 35, 58; Deoband (city), 1, 9, 37; Indian independence, 2; Indian Penal Code of 1860, 47; Indian Uprising of 1857, 31; judicial administration of, 34; Mazahir al-'Ulum Deoband, 39; *mujaddid* (renewer) in, 18; revival of Islam in, 35–36; Saharanpur, 37. See also British empire in India; Dar al-'Ulum Deoband
Indian Education Commission of 1882, 51–52
Indian Ocean, Muslim migrations in, 164–66
Indian Penal Code of 1860, 47
Indian Uprising of 1857, 3, 25, 31, 34, 36
Iqbal, Muhammad, 15, 192, 224n60
Iqtidar, Humeira, 214, 228n16
Iran, 29, 183–84
al-Isfahani, Abu Nu'aym, 13
Ishaq, Muhammad, 36, 84, 240n65
ISIS (Islamic State in Iraq and Syria), 207, 208
islah (reform), 4, 17, 18–19, 107, 126, 128, 152, 154,
islah-i nafs (self-reform), 18, 138, 158
islah-i qalb (reform of the heart), 18, 143
Islah al-rusum (The reformation of customs) (Thanvi), 76, 107
Islamic activism: overview of, 29, 179–80; *Al-Qalam* (periodical), 181; Call of Islam, 183, 187, 189–90; Cassiem and, 182–83; Desai and, 196–202; Jamiatul

Islamic activism *(continued)*
Ulama Transvaal, 184; *The Majlis* (periodical) and, 196–202; *Muslim News* (periodical), 184; Muslim Youth Movement (MYM), 181–82; Qibla, 182–83, 200; UDF, 183. *See also* anti-apartheid politics; Tablighi Jama'at

Islamic law: administration of, 45–48; British reformulation of, 46–47; Deobandi madrasas and, 8; Hanafi *Fiqh al-akbar,* 42; Imdad Allah on, 72; legal precedent (*stare decisis*), 47; legal proofs (*dala'il*), 75; legal scholars (*fuqaha'*), 13; legal-theological issues (*masa'il*), 23, 27, 47–48, 70, 99, 111–12, 115, 123, 130, 139, 157–58; M. T. 'Usmani on, 145; Pickthall on, 53; sources of, 111; Sufi initiations and, 146; Sufism through, 34; Thanvi on Sufism and, 122–23. *See also ijtihad* (independent reasoning), *qazis,* Shari'a

Islamic State in Iraq and Syria (ISIS), 207, 208

Islamic tradition(s): affect and, 21; debating of, 20–24; Deobandi claims to revive, 32; discursivity of, 21; as nexus of knowledge production and sensibility, 214; transmission of, 21–22; valorization of, 32–33

Islam kya hai (*What is Islam?*) (Nu'mani), 136

Isma'il, Muhammad: accessibility of Islam, 213; Barelvi rebuke of, 102; critique of *bid'a* and *shirk,* 60–61, 63–64; debates and, 7–8; on divine sovereignty, 62–64; early life, 58; Gangohi and, 64; influence of, 24; *Izah al-haqq fi ahkam al-mayyit wa al-darih* (Elucidating the truth about the rules concerning the dead and tombs) (M. Isma'il), 60, 64; normative order and, 58; populist hermeneutics of, 26, 114; on Qur'anic accessibility, 110, 213; Shah 'Abd al-'Aziz and, 238n44; Shah 'Abd al-Ghani and, 67; *Taqwiyyat al-iman* (Strengthening the faith), 59–64, 174; *'urs* and, 85; writings of, 58–65, 67

Izah al-haqq fi ahkam al-mayyit wa al-darih (Elucidating the truth about the rules concerning the dead and tombs) (M. Isma'il), 60, 64

jadid (modern), 34
Jahanara, 81
Jama'at ad-Da'wa, 228n16

Jama'at-i Islami, 15, 228n16, 265n16
Jami, 'Abd al-Rahman, 133–34, 176, 255n22, 266n27
Jami'a Abi Bakr, 266n27
Jami'a 'Alimiyya Islamiyya, 204, 266n27
Jami'a al-'Ulum al-Islamiyya, 266n27
Jami'a Ashrafiyya, 240n65
Jami'a Islamiyya Dabhel, 167
Jami'at 'Ulama-yi Hind, 10
Jami'at 'Ulama-yi Islam, 10, 196
Jamiatul Ulama Natal, 168, 260n48
Jamiatul Ulama Transvaal, 166–68, 172, 184, 188, 260n44
Jaunpuri, Karamat Ali, 224n60
Jaunpuri, Mulla Mahmud, 37
jihad, 58, 90, 190, 195, 199–202, 205, 229n25
Jilani, 'Abd al-Qadir, 125, 163, 165
Jones, William, 45
judges. *See qazis*
Judicial Plan of 1772, 43
jum'a (the day of congregational prayer), 208
Junayd Baghdadi, 13

Ka'aba, 37, 62, 74, 85, 87, 244n152
al-Kalabadhi, Abu Bakr Muhammad, 133–35
Kamran, Tahir, 273n25
Kandhlavi, Muhammad Idris, 88–89
Kandhlavi, Muhammad Ilyas. *See* Ilyas, Muhammad
Kandhlavi, Muhammad Zakariyya, 158, 170; E. Adam and, 267n37; autobiography of, 146; *Faza'il-i a'mal* (Virtuous deeds), 176, 260n43; Haqqani and, 174; *Maut ki yad* (Remembrance of death), 83, 176; M. H. Gangohi and, 153; Motala and, 219n2; on Qur'an, 62; on sainthood, 134–35; endorsement of *Shari'at ya jahalat* (Shari'a or ignorance) (M. P. Haqqani), 174; in South Africa, 161, 175–76, 182, 216, 267n37; Tablighi Jama'at and, 25; translations of, 167; on *'ulama* authority, 158
Kant, Immanuel, 98, 117, 118, 119
Kaptein, N.J.G., 239n59
Karaan, Yusuf, 172
karamat (miracles), 35, 81, 89, 130, 136, 163, 209
Kazis Act of 1880, 47
Khairabadi, Fazl al-Haqq, 64, 238n44
Khan, Ahmad Raza, 8, 99–100, 142, 175, 185, 191, 244n152, 267n41

Khan, Dargah Quli, 81
Khan, Fareeha, 112
Khan, Masihullah: Desai and, 25, 196–97, 214, 270n97; Ilyas and, 197; Miftah al-'Ulum and, 180, 197, 270n97; M. Ilyas and, 197; in South Africa, 161, 197; on Sufism, 129; Tablighi Jama'at and, 197; Thanvi and, 25, 29, 129, 180, 196–97, 214, 252n30
Khan, Sarfraz, 229n33
Khan, Sayyid Ahmad, 34, 35, 37, 51, 224n60, 228n17, 228n24, 236nn15–16
khanqah (Sufi lodge): ecstasy (*wajd*) and, 96; Ghousia Manzil, 263nn94–95; of Imdad Allah in Thana Bhawan (Khanqah Imdadiyya), 70, 73, 107; madrasa and, 214; in medieval Islamic society, 38; Mulla Nizam al-Din on, 255n22; reform (*islah*) and, 27, 205, 211; Soofie Saheb and, 164; spiritual training and, 118, 127, 140, 146–47; Tablighi Jama'at and, 152–54, 160; Thanvi and, 94, 127
Khanqah Imdadiyya, 70, 73
khawass (elites), 48, 59, 76, 78, 83, 92–93, 101–2, 104, 111, 131
Khilafat Movement, 190–91, 203
Khushtar, Ibrahim, 174–75
Kifayat Allah, Muhammad, 109, 136, 234n97, 237n24, 249n83
knowledge. See *'ilm*
kufr (unbelief), 42–43, 72, 86, 95, 100, 109, 123, 126, 128, 134, 150, 176, 185, 187, 198, 199, 202, 209, 244n152
Kugle, Scott Alan, 132, 233n83

Laqueur, Thomas, 80
Lawrence, Bruce B., vii
lay Muslims. See *'awamm*
Le Bon, Gustave, 94, 246n11
Leitner, G.W., 52
Le Roux, Charl, 260n44
Lilla, Mark, 215
logic, 37, 41, 42, 52
Ludhianvi, Muhammad Yusuf, 148

MacIntyre, Alasdair, 20–21, 225n75
Madani, Husain Ahmad, 25, 49–50, 141, 153, 191, 196, 203
Madras Regulation VII of 1817, 48
Madrasa Arabia Islamia, 175–76, 256n49, 261n57
Madrasa Faiz-i 'Amm, 73, 240n65
Madrasa In'aamiyya, 256n49, 261n57

Madrasa Rahimiyya, 145, 231n63, 255n22
madrasas: Calcutta Madrasa, 43, 50; as charitable endowments (*awqaf*), 38; under Delhi sultans, 40; Deobandi identity and, 32; early history of, 38; government funding and, 51; Nizam and, 255n22; oral mode of learning in, 38; overview of role, 26; as pious institutions, 8; as private (nongovernmental) space, 40; reimagining of, 34; religious/secular binary and, 53–54; spatiality of, 216; students' movement through space, 8, 216; Tablighi Jama'at and, 10–11; teaching Shaf'i law, 217; text memorization, 38. See also Dar al-'Ulum Deoband; Dar al-'Ulum Haqqaniyya; Dar al-'Ulum Karachi; *specific madrasas*
Madrasa Sawlehaat, 204, 256n49
Madrasa Ta'lim al-Din, 256n49, 261n57
Mahmud, Izhar al-Hasan, 11, 220n6
Mahomedan Female School, 51
The Majlis (periodical), 180–81, 190, 196–204
Majlisul Ulama of South Africa, 10, 176–77, 180, 196–99
maktabs (Muslim primary schools), 51, 52, 53
Malik, Jamal, 41
Mamluk 'Ali, 36, 38
manqulat (transmitted/revealed knowledge), 33, 41–42
Mantena, Karuna, 31
ma'qulat (rational knowledge), 33, 40–41, 52
Marghinani, Burhan al-Din Abu'l Hasan, 45–46
market inspector (*muhtasib*), 44–45
Masjid, Ahmed Raza, 177
maslak concept, 10, 22–23, 24, 28
Masnavi (Rumi), 72, 74, 131
Masud, Muhammad Khalid, 235n6, 236n7
mathematics, 42, 52
Matura, 'Abd al-Rahman, 258n15
Maturidi theology, 7, 148
Maududi, Sayyid Abul A'la: on authority, 63; influence of, 15; on Islamic system of law, 18; Muslim Youth Movement and, 200–201; works of, 182
Maulana Okarvi Academy, 175
Maut ki yad (Remembrance of death) (Kandhlavi), 83, 176
mawlid. See mawlud

mawlud (celebration of the Prophet Muhammad's birthday): anti-apartheid politics and, 187–90; as a *bid'a,* 67; counterpolemics over, 28; debate and critique of, 65–80, 205; Deobandi-Barelvi rivalry and, 11; as devotional piety, 26; devotional practices and, 29; Gangohi and, 66, 69–73; Imdad Allah on, 69–72; legal proofs (*dala'il*) against, 75; *qiyam* during, 66; Saharanpuri and, 66–67, 264n108; Thanvi on, 73–74; typical festivities of, 65; al-Wahhab and, 66

Mazahir al-'Ulum Saharanpur, 39, 51, 67, 149, 152, 153

medieval, 17, 33, 38, 63

Meer, Fatima, 173, 184

Metcalf, Barbara Daly, 6, 10, 39, 55, 216

Metcalf, Thomas, 43

Mia, Muhammad bin Musa bin Isma'il, 167–68, 172

Miftah al-'Ulum, 174, 180, 197, 270n97

milad. See mawlud

Mill, James, 50

"Minute on Indian Education" (Macaulay), 44

miracles. *See karamat*

Mirathi, Muhammad 'Ashiq Ilahi, 222n36, 237n22, 244n148, 253n76

Mir zahid (al-Taftazani), 37

Mishkat al-masabih, 41

modernity, 17, 32–34, 40, 53, 97, 215

Moin, A. Afzar, 210

Molina, J. Michelle, 153

Moosa, Ebrahim, 41, 53, 173, 189, 204, 213, 231n57

moral self-formation: overview, 116–19; *suhbat* (companionship, in Sufism) and, 58, 123–28; ethical sainthood and, 131–37; obligatory nature of, 128–31; Sufi ethics of life, 119–23

Morley, William H., 47

mosques: assaults at, 263n90; attacks on, 207; Claremont Main Road Mosque, 188, 268n58; congregational mosque funding, 39–40; on Dar al-'Ulum Deoband campus, 147; debates in, 211; Deobandi-Barelvi polemics in, 161, 178, 184; Habibia Mosque, 170; Hanafis/ Shafi'is and, 170; knowledge transmission and, 22, 38, 110; madrasas and, 37; Muir Street Mosque, 168; non-Deobandi viewpoints and, 187; pamphlet distribution in, 197; Quawatul Islam Mosque, 166; Religious Endowments Act (Act XX) of 1863, 48; Saabrie Mosque, 186; secular education and, 51, 53; Sinai Peninsula militant attack, 207; Soofie Saheb Mosque, 168, 188; in South Africa, 162–66, 167, 168, 170, 185–88, 268n58; Tablighi-Barelvi clashes in, 185–86; Tablighi Jama'at and, 149–50

Motala, Yusuf, 219n2

Mughal Empire: Aurangzeb, 40–41, 45; Babur, Emperor, 81; Bahadur Shah Zafar, Emperor, 3; communication during, 97; Dars-i Nizamiyya (Nizami curriculum), 40–41; decline of, 34, 43; Islamic learning under, 26; Jahanara, 81; Naqshbandi Sufi texts and, 134; patronage networks, 40, 49; Shah Jahan, Emperor, 81; theological hierarchy during, 101

Muhammad: birthday of, 3, 11, 26, 65–80, 207; *'ilm-i ghayb* (knowledge of the unseen), 7, 59, 64, 72, 77; *imkan-i nazir* (possibility of God creating another Prophet equal to Muhammad), 7, 62, 64, 161, 241n76; as model of human behavior, 5; Pledge of the Tree, 74; Taqi al-Din al-Hilali dream of, 15; Thanvi reference to, 19. *See also mawlud*

al-Muhasibi, Harith, 13

muhtasib (market inspector), 44–45

Mu'in al-Din Chishti shrine, 81, 82–84, 94, 165, 211

mujaddid (renewer), 18–19

Mukkadam, Ahmed, 263n95

munkarat (evils), 74, 90, 157

Musaddas (Hali), 35

Muslim Judicial Council, 172, 175, 179, 185, 189, 262n71

Muslim League, 195, 203

Muslim News (periodical), 172, 179, 180–81, 184, 200

Muslim public(s): common (*'amm*)/elite (*khass*) hierarchies of, 101–5; crowd dynamics and, 93–97; debate over *mawlud* and *'urs,* 205; polemics and, 97–101; print and, 105–11; reform (*islah*) and, 17; knowledge (*'ilm*) and, 105–15; *'ulama* and, 16–20

Muslim Youth Movement (MYM), 181–82, 186, 188–89, 200

mustahabb (praiseworthy), 68, 72, 74, 78

Nadvi, 'Abd al-Bari, 19

Nadvi, Abu al-Hasan 'Ali, 149

Nadwa al-'Ulama, 204

Naeem, Fuad, 17

Nafahat al-uns (Breaths of intimacy) (Jami), 133–34

nafs (lower self), 120–21, 130, 133, 134, 189, 199, 201, 209, 272n20. *See also* asceticism (*zuhd*)

Nanautvi, Muhammad Qasim: critiques by, 37; early life, 36; Imdad Allah and, 69–70, 71; individual donor model, 39; innovation of, 37; on knowledge, 41; studies, 37; studies of, 38; vision of, 36

Naqshbandi order, 4, 42, 45, 134, 148, 150, 208, 263n94

Nasr, Seyyed Vali Reza, 18

Nizam al-Din, Mulla, 40–41, 145, 255nn22–23

Nizam al-Din Awliya', 81, 149, 231n61

Nizami Chishtis, 231n61

Nizami curriculum. *See* Dars-i Nizamiyya

Nizam of Hyderabad, 49, 230n45

Noor, Farish A., 216

normative order: overview, 55–56; *bid'a* and *shirk* as threats to, 56–64; death anniversary celebrations (*'urs*) and, 80–91; *mawlud* and, 65–80; M. Isma'il and, 58; time and, 215; visiting saints' graves (*ziyarat*), 80–91

Nu'mani, Muhammad Manzur, 60, 136

Okarvi, Kaukab Noorani, 175

O'Malley, P.F., 32

omnipotence of God, 37, 59, 62, 63, 100

Orientalist position (in British debate about Muslim education), 43–45. *See also* Anglicist position

Osman, Fatih, 186

Osmania University, 19

Pakistan: 'Ali Hujwiri and Farid al-Din Ganj-i Shakkar shrines, 211; Dar al-'Ulum Haqqaniyya in Akora Khattak, 208; Dar al-'Ulum Karachi in, 210; ISIS attacks on/hatred of Sufism in, 207; Jama'at-i Islami, 15; Lal Shahbaz Qalandar (Sindh), 208; M.R.'Usmani and, 210; Pakistani Taliban, 208; M. Shafi', 20; Shah Noorani (Balochistan), 208; shrine attacks in, 9; Taliban emergence from Deobandi seminaries in NW, 2

Palombo, Matthew, 203

Panipati, Qazi Sanaullah, 128

Patel, Yunus, 204, 256n49

patron (*sarparast*), 24, 41, 49

patronage networks, 34, 39, 40, 44

Pemberton, Kelly, 137

Pernau, Margrit, 40

Persian language, 20, 43, 44, 51, 58, 253n76, 261n66

philosophy, 37, 41, 42, 52

Pickthall, Marmaduke, 53

pilgrimage: to Mecca (Hajj and *'umrah*), 37, 58, 65, 70, 73, 74, 85, 94, 128, 157, 211, 273n20; to Sufi saints' shrines. *See ziyarat*

Pio, Edwina, 273n25

Piscatori, James, 223n52

pledge, from Sufi disciple to Sufi master. *See bai'at*

Pledge of the Tree, 74

polemics: Barelvi movement and, 27, 148, 161, 165, 173–78, 264n102, 267n47, 272n8; *bid'at* (illicit innovations) and, 161, 173, 176; brief survey of, 28; counterpolemics, 14, 28, 99, 176; globalization and, 173–78; in mosques, 161, 178, 184; Muslim public(s) and, 97–101; in South Africa, 173–78; in support of *mawlud*, 66; Urdu language and, 176

politics: affect and, 3, 212; apartheid and, 180–84; contested nature of, 204; of Deobandi scholars, 49; A.S. Desai and, 196–203, 212; *islah* (reform) and, 18; "religious" violence and, 210; Sufism and, 187–89, 195, 199

populist hermeneutics, 26, 59, 61, 64

praiseworthy. *See mustahabb*

print: Deobandi reform and, 105, 108; fatwas and, 47–48; hermeneutic risks of, 93, 110; and Muslim publics, 107–8

prostration (*sajda*), 8, 83, 85–86, 89, 90, 143, 177, 237n24, 244nn148–150, 244n152

La psychologie des foules (The psychology of crowds) (Le Bon), 94

Qadiri order, 4, 103, 128, 148, 150, 163, 185, 208, 263n94

Qalandars, 207, 272n3

al-Qari, 'Ali, 42

Qasim al-'Ulum: Hanafi law at, 170; Shafi'i law at, 169–70

Qasimi, Jamal al-Din, 15–16

qazis (judges), 26, 35, 45, 47, 48

Qibla, 182–84, 200

qiyam (standing in reverence of the Prophet), 66–69, 72, 78, 176–77, 197 *qiyas* (analogy, in Islamic law), 57, 75, 111

Qur'an; commentaries on, 7; Deobandi texts and, 213; ethics and, 121; exegesis (*tafsir*), 41; fatwas (legal opinions) and, 48; Judicial Plan of 1772 and, 43; M. Isma'il on authority of, 61–62; M.Z. Kandhlavi on, 62; normative order and, 56; Qur'anic ethics, 13; Qur'anic hermeneutics, 33; recitation of, 74; references, 19, 61, 63, 68, 69, 70, 74, 75, 81, 85, 88, 90, 111, 119, 126, 133–35, 157, 192, 200, 213; self-referentiality of, 238n30; values of, 17; *wali* (ally/friend/protector) concept in, 27, 133–35

Qureshi, Ishtiaq, 229n25

al-Qushayri, Abul Qasim, 13–14, 120

Qutb, Sayyid, 15, 182

Rahman, Fazlur, 33, 227nn11–12

Rampuri, 'Abd al-Sami', 67–68, 99

raza'il (vices), 20

Reetz, Dietrich, 219n2

reform. *See islah*

Rehman Baba, 208

Reinhart, A. Kevin, 111–12

religion: British governance and, 31, 43, 48–54; Victorian discourse on, 31–32, 34; violence and, 210

Religious Endowments Act (Act XX) of 1863, 48–49

religious knowledge/secular knowledge distinction, 26

renewal. *See tajdid*

Rizvi, Saiyid Athar Abbas, 255n22

Rizvi, Sajjad H., 118

Rizvi, Sayyid Mahbub, 261n70

Robb, Megan Eaton, 195–96

Robinson, Francis, 55, 110, 145, 205, 235n1

Rocher, Rosane, 43

Rosenthal, Franz, 107

Le Roux, Charl du Plessis, 260n44

Rozehnal, Robert Thomas, 209, 210–11

Rumi, Maulana Jalal al-Din, 12, 69, 72, 74, 81, 131

rusum (customs): constraints of, 27, 117; critiques and reformation of, 18, 76, 107; crowd dynamics and, 35, 94–95; Isma'il on, 61; maintenance of, 237n24; Sufism as, 147

Saabrie Mosque, 186

Sabir, 'Ala al-Din 'Ali, 82, 178, 231n61

Sabiri Chishtis, 69, 209, 231n61

Saharanpur, 37, 42, 51, 94, 97, 149, 152, 153

Saharanpuri, Khalil Ahmad, 11, 17, 25, 42, 52–53, 66–69, 68, 264n108

sainthood, Sufi (*walayat*), 27, 132, 134–35. *See also* saints, Sufi

saints, Sufi: Ahmad Raza Khan and, 8; Catholicism comparison, 132; death anniversary celebrations ('*urs*), 2, 11, 26; ethical sainthood, 131–37; Haqqani *muftis* on, 209; lay Muslims as, 131–37; miracles (*karamat*) and, 209; as moral exemplars, 27; sacred genealogies of, 216; *shirk* and, 56–57, 87–89; spiritual connections (*nisbat*) with, 71, 125, 209. *See also* shrines, Sufi saints'

Sakhi Sarwar, 208

Salafi movement, 18, 62, 213, 223n46

Salat prayer, 68, 77, 170, 176–77, 236n9

Saliji, Ebrahim, 256n49

Salomon, Noah, 183

salvation, 6, 11, 19, 20, 42, 45, 53–54, 58, 86, 107–8, 111, 116, 123, 138, 155

Sanskrit language, 43, 44

Sanyal, Usha, 240m65

Saraswati, Dayananda, 37

al-Sarraj, Abu Nasr, 13

Sayyid Ahmad Barelvi. *See* Barelvi, Sayyid Ahmad

Schimmel, Annemarie, 119

Schmitt, Carl, 5, 140

Scott, J. Barton, 117–18

secularity: in colonial India, 32–34, 48–54; defined, 32; "secular" knowledge, 41, 48–54

Seekings, Jeremy, 266n24

selfhood: fatwas (legal opinions) and, 48; Iqbal on, 15; liberated from base qualities (*akhlaq-i razila*), 27, 120; in Sufi ethics, 118–23. *See also nafs* (lower self)

Sema, Qasim, 168–71

seminary. *See* madrasas

Shafi', Mufti Muhammad, 11, 20, 57, 73, 88, 147, 225n72

Shafi'i law: Dar al-'Ulum Newcastle and, 169; Dar al-'Ulum Zakariyya and, 170–71; at local madrasas, 166, 217; Qasim al-'Ulum and, 169–70

Shah Jahan, Emperor of the Mughal Empire, 81

Shah Noorani terrorist attack, 208

Shakkar, Farid al-Din Ganj-i, 211, 231n61

Shams-i bazigha (Mulla Mahmud Jaunpuri), 37

Shari'a: Ahrar movement and, 192–95; Barelvis/Deobandis comparison on, 8; *bid'a* and, 56–58, 60, 109; ethics and, 120–21; Hanafi law and, 74–76; intentionality and, 78; jihad and, 200–201; knowledge of, 85, 110; lay Muslims' understandings of, 111–14; Muslim distinction under, 104; public good (*maslaha*) under, 78–79; rationale for mandates of, 113; *Shari'at ya jahalat* (Shari'a or ignorance) (M. P. Haqqani), 174; standing in reverence of the Prophet (*qiyam*), 72; *shirk* and, 59–61; Sufism and, 11, 27, 122–23, 143; Tablighi Jama'at and, 154; Thanvi on, 74; Uprising of 1857 and, 36; *'urs* and, 85–88. *See also* Islamic law

Shari'at ya jahalat (Shari'a or ignorance) (M. P. Haqqani), 174

Sharpeville Massacre of 1960, 179

Shatibi, Abu Ishaq Ibrahim ibn Musa, 57, 58, 60, 74, 213

Shi'a: commemorations of 'Ashura, 103; Dawoodi Bohra sect, 164; Deobandi anti-Shi'a sentiment, 103, 184; Ja'far al-Sadiq, 101; leaders in Iran, 184; Nanautvi as critic of, 37; *ta'ziya*, 228n20

shirk (beliefs or practices that compromise integrity of God's oneness): Bilhauri on, 63–64; defined, 56–57; discourse of, 26; M. Isma'il on, 59, 60–61, 63; Nu'mani on, 60; prostration towards persons as, 86, 244n152; *ta'ziya*, 35, 87, 228n20; *qiyam* and, 69; as threat to normative order, 55

shrines, Sufi saints': approach to destruction of, 210; attacks on, 9, 211; devotions at, 56–64; sense of place and, 215–16; sense of time and, 215

Shuayb (prophet), 17

Sikand, Yoginder, 41

Sikhs, 58, 203

al-Simnani, 'Ala ad-Dawla, 131–32

Sinai Peninsula militant attack, 207

Sindhi, 'Ubaidallah, 203

Sirhindi, Ahmad, 18, 126, 134, 144, 247n23

Six Points (*che batein*) program, 150, 152, 260n43

Smith, Barbara Herrnstein, 23

Smith, Wilfred Cantwell, 2

"sobriety" (*sahw*), 13

sola scriptura, 213

Solomon, Hassan, 184

Soofie, Abdur Rauf, 186

Soweto Uprising of 1976, 179–80, 181

spatiality, 140, 216

spiritual connection (*nisbat*), 125, 209

spiritual energy. *See faiz*

standing in reverence of the Prophet. *See qiyam*

stare decisis principle, 47

Starrett, Gregory, 12

Stilt, Kristen, 44–45

Strawson, John, 233n83

Subrahmanyam, Sanjay, 33

Sudan, 15, 188

Sufi devotional practices: critiques of, 65–91, 207–11; ISIS attacks on, 208; *kramats,* 163; normative disorder and, 55–56; support for in South Africa, 187–90, 211; violence and, 211. *See also mawlud*

Sufism: apolitical quietism and, 205; classical, 13–14; contested nature of, 2–3, 5–6, 14–16, 210; Dar al-'Ulum Haqqaniyya (Akora Khattak, Pakistan) scholars' thoughts on, 208–9; defining, 7–8, 12–13; Deobandis' alleged hatred of, 9, 208; Deobandis' conception of, 2–3, 9, 27, 116–37; ethics and, 20, 27, 29, 34, 119–23; in the modern world, 11–16; politics of defining, 12; rhetoric of decline, 214; Shari'a and, 27, 119–23; Sufi ethics as obligatory in Deobandi thought, 128–31; Taliban and, 208, 210; as "tradition," 20. *See also khanqah* (Sufi lodge), Sufi devotional practices, *suhbat* (companionship, in Sufism)

"Sufism" (poem) (Iqbal), 15

suhbat (companionship, in Sufism), 22, 27, 28, 116, 123–28, 139, 209

Suhrawardi, Abu Hafs Umar, 146, 255n22

Suhrawardi order, 4, 128, 148, 150, 208

Sultan Jahan Begam, Nawab of Bhopal, 66–67

Sunna: *bid'a* (illicit innovation) as opposite of, 56–57, 60, 80; Deobandis and, 22, 24; embodiment of, 117–18, 123–28; Gangohi on, 18, 57; normative order and, 56–57, 60, 80, 85; revivification of, 5, 18, 25, 27; Sunni legal sources, 57, 75, 111; Thanvi on, 19, 112–13; as tradition, 5, 20

Sunni Ittehad Council, 272n8
Sunni Jamiatul Ulama, 178
Sunni Razvi Society, 174–75
Suyuti, Jalal al-Din, 66
Sviri, Sara, 116–17
Syed, Jawad, 273n25

Tablighi Jama'at: in 1950s and 60s, 168–69;
Dar al-'Ulums in South Africa and,
168–71; *Faza'il-i a'mal* (Virtuous deeds)
(M.Z. Kandhlavi), 176; M.H. Gangohi
and, 153–54; as global reformist
movement, 10–11, 149–59; Ilyas and,
10–11, 25, 115, 139, 140, 149–56, 197;
M.Z. Kandhlavi and, 25, 168–69, 176;
in South Africa, 168–69, 176, 185–87,
216–17; Tablighi-Barelvi clashes, 159,
174–75, 180, 185–87, 263n90; view of
time and history, 216. *See also* Ilyas,
Muhammad
tajdid (renewal): *islah* (reform) and, 18,
19, 224n60; *mujaddid* (renewer)
and, 18; Thanvi and, 19; *'ulama,* role
of in, 19
Taliban: attitudes toward Sufism within,
210; Bamiyan Buddhas destruction, 210;
Deobandi roots of, 2, 10, 208; Pakistani
Taliban attacks on Sufi shrines, 208
Ta'lim al-Islam (Instruction in Islam)
(Kifayat Allah), 109
Taqwiyyat al-iman (Strengthening the faith)
(M. Isma'il), 59–64, 174
Tarabulusi, Husayn ibn Muhammad, 228n17
Tarde, Gabriel, 247n24
Taussig, Michael T., 211
tawaf (circumambulation), 8, 81, 83,
85–87, 102, 143, 209, 237n24,
244n152
tawhid (unity of God), 57, 59–60, 71, 87,
92, 182, 200, 265n19
Taylor, Charles, 118
Tayob, Abdulkader, 166–67, 259n32
Tayyib, Qari Muhammad, 28, 139–40,
141–49, 151, 153, 158–59, 160–61,
171–73, 178, 204, 257n75, 261n70
Tehrik-e-Taliban Pakistan (TTP), 208
texts: dangers for lay Muslims, 93, 104–5,
110–15; *ijaza* (permission to transmit a
text in Islamic education), 22; knowledge transmission and, 22–24, 38;
orality and, 38; publics and, 97–100,
105–15; print culture and, 107–10
Thanvi, Ashraf 'Ali: overview, 24, 73;
appointment of *qazis* and, 47; on *chilla*

(Sufi retreat), 272n14; critiques of
mawlud, 73–80; Desai, appropriation of
arguments of by, 196–202; early life, 73;
Gangohi and, 26, 64, 72, 73, 75; on
gentleness (*narmi*), 157; Imdad Allah
and, 70–71, 73–74; importance and
influence of, 14, 24, 25; *Islahi nisab*
(The reformist program), 17; at
Madrasa Faiz-i 'Amm, 240n65; M.M.
Khan and, 25, 180; on modernity, 34;
modernity and, 215; obligatory/
non-obligatory aspects of fasting, 56;
Pledge of the Tree, 74; politics of, 24,
190–96; on prostration, 86, 244n152;
public reform project of, 105–8; as
reactionary, 215; religious/secular
binary and, 53; as renewer (*mujaddid*),
19; on salvation, 19; S.A. 'Usmani and,
196; *'ulama,* importance of, 17, 104–5,
110–14
thought collective (*Denkkollektiv*), 23
transnational solidarity, 29, 184
Trevelyan, Charles, 44
Truth Wins (Okarvi), 175
Turner, Bryan, 132
Twining, Thomas, 43

Ukeles, Raquel Margalit, 58
unbelief. *See kufr*
unbeliever (*kafir*), 42, 64, 90, 100
United Democratic Front (UDF), 183,
266n24
unity of God. *See tawhid*
Urdu language: *'awamm* (lay Muslims) and,
6, 14, 24, 55; Deobandi-Barelvi
polemics and, 176; Deobandi works
and, 20, 58–59; Thanvi and, 19, 24, 28,
222n36; translations into, 222n36,
228n17, 246n11, 253n63, 253n76,
254n10, 261n66
'urs (saint's death anniversary): attacks
during, 208; Cape Mazaar Society and,
163; Deobandi-Barelvi polemics and,
161, 174; Deobandi critiques of, 2, 26,
64, 67, 80–89, 109, 174; of Mu'in
al-Din Chishti, 81, 94, 165, 211; Thanvi
on, 87; visibility of, 12
'Usmani, Muhammad Rafi', 210
'Usmani, Muhammad Taqi, 11, 17–18, 137,
144–49, 195, 215
'Usmani, Shabbir Ahmad, 89–90, 167,
196
'Usmani, Zafar Ahmad, 119, 262n75
'Uthman ibn 'Affan, 74–75

'ulama: authority of, 5, 29, 211; colonial modernity and, 32; contempt for, 35; custodial view of, 8, 9, 26, 27, 34, 40, 44; defined, 5; Deoband identity and, 11, 13, 32; fatwas (legal opinions) and, 48; indispensability of, 22–23, 27; as medieval relics, 17; in Muslim public life, 6, 16–20, 35; Orientalists' view of, 9; overview of role, 26; patronage networks, 40–41, 43; privatization of, 34, 40; public critiques and, 212; public polemics and, 12; reform and, 19, 26–27; as religious experts, 40–45, 49–50; in renewal (*tajdid*), 19. *See also suhbat* (companionship, in Sufism); *specific 'ulama*

virtues. *See faza'il*
Voll, John O., 224n60

al-Wahhab, Muhammad ibn 'Abd, 9, 66, 89, 236n6
Wahhabism, 9, 66, 89, 90–91
wajd (ecstasy, in Sufism), 35, 95, 96
walayat (Sufi sainthood), 27, 132, 134–35. *See also* saints, Sufi
wali (ally/friend/protector) concept, in Qur'an, 27, 133–35

Wali Allah, Shah, 7, 18, 36, 37, 41, 58, 65, 67, 84, 114, 144, 145, 147–48, 228n24, 231n63
Ware, Rudolph T., 226n80
Warner, Michael, 98
War on Terror, 2, 12
Waterval Islamic Institute, 175, 260n43
What is Islam? (Ahmed), 223n52
World Ulema Unity Week, 184

Ya'qub, Muhammad, 37–38
Young Men's Muslim Association, 177

Zaidi, Abbas, 273n25
Zaman, Muhammad Qasim, 6, 53, 63, 113, 203, 225n75, 241n88, 245n173, 249n73
zehni varzish (mental exercise), 41
zikr (Sufi meditative practices): fatwas (legal opinions) and, 209; Hamidi on, 264n104; Ilyas on, 150, 152; in *Tablighi nisab*, 260n43; Thanvi on, 130–31; *zikr haddadi*, 209, 272n13; *zikr halqa*, 187–90, 202
ziyarat (visiting saints' graves), 14, 80–89
zuhd (Sufi asceticism), 21, 120, 121, 131